Proven Success with QRPD®

> *"QRPD played a major role in keeping a project on schedule that gained us $150,000 per week. These results, and the enthusiasm, fun, and excitement felt by the team about how QRPD helped them, prompted us to incorporate QRPD into our product life cycle for all of our projects, company-wide."*
>
> *Larsh Johnson, Co-Founder, Vice President and CTO,*
> *CellNet Data Systems, a wireless networking company*

"The project was completed in 9 months vs. 18 months…We satisfied a major customer, Intel,…with a novel award-winning product in record time…We could easily do this again and again.…"

Gordon Simmons
Project Leader, Plantronics, the world's leading supplier of communication headsets

"We are delivering projects in months instead of years and at costs far less than even a year ago."

Jon Hockenberry
Project Manager, Shell Services

"Following QRPD allowed us to ship our latest voice mail system in 10 months, and in half the time of the previous, comparable system."

Pedro Rump
Director of Engineering, Rolm Systems, a Siemens Company

"A 60% improvement in product development time was achieved (18-20 months vs. 42 months)."

Abbott Critical Care Systems

"Ori may be a visionary for what new product development will be like in the next century."

David Andersen
Instructor on Design For Manufacturability, University of California Berkeley

"From the time we convened and said, "Let's make an Intellipad," to the time we shipped was seven months. If we had done it the old way, it would have taken a year and a half."

Frank Stern
Vice President Sales, Niles Audio, a leading entertainment manufacturer

© 1998 Global Brain, Inc.

Before my organization took QRPD training, we were trying to do too much at one time. Of all the QRPD teachings, "do less sooner" had the greatest impact. Saying the words helped, but the regular, consistent coaching by the Global Brain team enabled us to live the words and walk the talk. Now there is no one in my organization who does not know what project they are working on or what the goals of the organization and project are. As a result, I work less hard today but get more done than before.

Rick Gottscho
General Manager, PCVD Division, Lam Research

"QRPD provides an *excellent* framework for effective management of *any* difficult project, and emphasizes the elements essential to reducing product development times to meet the demands of today's business environment. Today, the principles apply to an advanced development laboratory as well as to a product development and manufacturing operation."

Dr. James Boyden
Interval Research Corporation, former Hewlett-Packard Laboratory Director,
HP LaserJet and InkJet technologies developer

"QRPD's vision process uncovered major disagreements and disconnects on business and technology issues early in our Billing Project that would have caused serious design problems and delays later."

Carol Cain
Senior Vice President, VISA

"We completed the latest Molecular Beam Epitaxy machine, for depositing gallium arsenide on wafers, in eight months instead of the usual year and a half. Eighty percent of the stuff we tried from the methodology worked on this first implementation attempt, and as we learn more we'll do even better."

Dave Atchley
Engineering Manager, Intevac

"QRPD supplied the glue…to pull our TQM, MOB, RPD training together and finally get an ROI…The 'impossible' can be done with QRPD."

Laurie Hewitt
Project Manager, Runzheimer International, a software services and products company

"QRPD put into place many of the techniques which we have applied, tried to apply, or should have applied on our projects."

Cindy Hendershot
Program Manager, HTI-Link Space Station Simulation and Training Facility

"Does QRPD work? Damn right it does!"

Robert J. Russell
Senior Manager of International Engineering Projects, VeriFone

© 1998 Global Brain, Inc.

"Q*R*PD identified the common success factors that maximize the probability of a successful product introduction. Today, the elements of Q*R*PD assist project teams to do the right things... With the new philosophy of empowering project teams, Q*R*PD is changing the way we do business... We saw an improvement not only in the timeliness of new product development but also in the excitement and pride the participants in the process felt. Today the entire team takes ownership of the project objectives and makes it happen... When they see something that should be done, they make sure it gets done!"

Tina Ohlhaver
R&D Productivity Manager, Avantek, a subsidiary of Hewlett-Packard

"He's a lively speaker and has a lot of anecdotal experience to draw from and share. He exemplifies many of the themes of the course: professionalism, quality, rapid results."

*Q*R*PD Student*
University of California Berkeley Extension

"Although the material in *Q*R*PD: The Guidebook* appears at first glance to be targeted at manufacturers, I've personally found the concepts quite applicable to service organizations too. In addition, the Q*R*PD methodology is very useful to those responsible for technology assessment, particularly the areas of risk analysis and management."

Neil K. Jablon
Manager for Wireless Development, AirTouch Communications

"Everybody has to go through this course. With the synergy it creates 10 people who take it could do the work of 20 people. We met our demanding schedule and successfully deployed a complex satellite transceiver system in Brazil right on time. This experience, and if everyone on the team takes the course, will make the next project go even faster!"

Jim Barbera
Project Leader, Vitacom Corporation

"This would be a great course for ANYONE who's company does product development and wants to improve the efficiency of the process."

*Q*R*PD Student*
University of California Berkeley Extension

"I found it [*Q*R*PD: The Guidebook*] to be a very interesting distillation of a ton of management wisdom, much of which is applicable outside the product development function."

Pat McMahon
Quality Improvement Manager, Acuson

"Great stuff, thorough, well presented and really useful NOW."

*Q*R*PD Student*
University of California Berkeley Extension

© 1998 Global Brain, Inc.

"This course is timely and relevant. It fills a gap between Engineering and Business courses. The instructor is articulate and keeps the subject matter interesting."

QRPD Student
University of California Berkeley Extension

"The 10 Commandments and checklist of techniques contain a wealth of tips, tricks, and traps to avoid."

QRPD Student
University of California Berkeley Extension

"Excellent course. I learned of several important new techniques to add to our existing Rapid Product Development Program."

Participant
IEEE Engineering Management Society Workshop on QRPD

"This course has had an immediate impact on my life (and not just making me late for dinner). I now have a clear picture of project management, and a powerful methodology for making things happen."

Participant
IEEE Engineering Management Society Workshop on QRPD

"Very good detailed oriented type of workshop—real things I can use in the future—not only theory."

Jose Ysaguirre
Project Leader, Raytek

"This course is a real jewel! I've recommended it to numerous colleagues."

QRPD Student
University of California Berkeley Extension

"Thanks for teaching this inspiring course. I can use ALL of the things in many situations in life!"

Paul Tang
Technical Support Engineer, Verifone

© 1998 Global Brain, Inc.

Projects at Warp-Speed With QRPD®...

The Definitive Guidebook to Quality *Rapid* Product Development

Orion Moshe Kopelman
and **Cinda Voegtli** with **Adam Josephs**

Contributing Authors:
Jon Hockenberry, Konrad Knell, W. Bradley Stewart, and Gilbert Wai

---

In this increasingly interconnected and synergistic world....
Global Brain®, Inc.'s mission is to accelerate the development of appropriate technological products and services and personal evolution. We provide management products and services to individuals and corporations that promote *lasting* success and prosperity, including QRPD (Quality *Rapid* Product Development), consulting, and consciousness-raising publications.

Global Brain®, Inc.
Palo Alto, California, USA
Warp-Speed Development of
Technology, Individuals, & Organizations

© 1998 Global Brain, Inc.

Published By:
Global Brain®, Inc.
Warp-Speed Development of Technology, Individuals, & Organizations
555 Bryant St. #369
Palo Alto, California, USA 94301-1704
Tel#: (650) 327-2012
Fax#: (650) 327-2028
Tel: 800 UGO GLOBAL (800 846-4562)
E-Mail: missioncontrol@globalbrain.com
Web url: http://www.qrpd.com

All rights reserved. No part of this book may be reproduced or transmitted in any form or by any means, electronic or mechanical, including photocopying, recording or by any information storage and retrieval system without written permission from the author, except for the inclusion of brief quotations in a review.

Copyright © 1991, 1994, 1998 by Orion Moshe Kopelman.
First Edition 1991
Second Edition 1992, completely revised
Third Edition 1992, revised
Fourth Edition 1992, revised
Fifth Edition 1992, completely revised
Sixth Edition 1992, revised
Seventh Edition, First Printing 1994, completely revised
Seventh Edition, Second Printing 1995, revised
Seventh Edition, Third Printing 1996
Seventh Edition, Fourth Printing 1997, revised
Eighth Edition, First Printing 1998, completely revised
Eighth Edition, Second Printing 1998, revised
Eighth Edition, Third Printing 1998, revised
Eighth Edition, Fourth Printing 1998, revised
Printed in the United States of America

Contributing Authors: Jon Hockenberry, Konrad Knell, W. Bradley Stewart, Gilbert Wai
Copy editing: Patricia Gall, Troy Lapsys, Elizabeth Park
Cover design: Lightbourne Images, Ashland, Oregon

Publishers Cataloging-in-Publication
(Provided by Quality Books, Inc.)
Kopelman, Orion Moshe.
    Projects at warp-speed with QRPD-- the definitive guidebook to quality rapid product development /
    Orion Moshe Kopelman and Cinda Voegtli with Adam Josephs. -- 8th ed., rev.
    p. cm.
    Includes bibliographical references.
    ISBN: 1-885261-16-0
    1. New products. 2. Product Management. I. Voegtli, Cinda. II. Title.

    TS170.KSS 1998   658.575
                                  QBI98-173

© 1998 Global Brain, Inc.

Table of Contents

Overview

Introduction	1
Part I. Blitzkrieg	67
Part II. Techniques: The Q*R*PD Toolkit	91
Part III. Project Leader and Team	215
Part IV. Flow	263
Part V. DIRFT	387
Appendices	455

Full Table of Contents

INTRODUCTION
Proven Success with Q*R*PD®	1
About the Instructors	15
Reading: Why Q*R*PD and What Is It?	19
Objectives of the Q*R*PD Workshop	39
Reading: Executive Overview of Q*R*PD Principles and Practices	43

PART I. BLITZKRIEG — 67
Blitzkrieg ("Lightning-Fast-War") Product Development	69
The Four Product Development Objectives: PTCC	70
Simple Benefit-Cost Trade-Off Analysis	71
Benefit-Cost Trade-off Case Study: "Emebo" Cost Reduction	72
Benefit-Cost Trade-off: "Fax-it" Board Cost Reduction	73
When To Emphasize Development Speed	74
Project LCPW and ROI Calculation	75
The New Product Development Funnel	76
Q*R*PD 4 Phases and Functions of Concurrent Development	77
3 Secrets To Successful Blitzkriegs: Just-In-Time Product Development (JITPD)	78
How Q*R*PD Teams Get *LUCKy*	79
Article: *Warp*-Speed Product Development with Q*R*PD	81

© 1998 Global Brain, Inc.

Full Table of Contents (continued)

PART II. TECHNIQUES: The QRPD Toolkit — 91

10 Commandments and 150 Techniques: The Toolkit of QRPD 93
- #1. Focus on a Clear, Limited, and On-Target Vision 94
  - Figure 1A Incremental Innovation 94
- #2. Assemble the Right Team and Leader(s) 96
  - Figure 2O. Resource Profiles 97
- #3. Initiate Early Cross-Functional Cooperation 98
  - Figure 3A. The Skyrocketing Cost of Development Changes 98
- #4: Create a Synergistic, Mission-oriented, Productive Environment. 100
  - Figure 4C. Communication vs. Distance 100
  - Figure 4M. The Fuzzy Front End 100
- #5. Reward all Participants Commensurably 102
- #6. Use Innovative, Parallel, Iterative Design Strategies 103
  - Figure 6D. Concentrating Technical Risk 104
- #7. Invest Money to Buy Time and Tools, and to Minimize Risks 105
- #8. Prototype and Test Key Design Concepts Early 106
  - What is a Chicken Test? 107
- #9. Follow a Flow Process to Meet Milestones, Manage Risk, and Ensure Quality .. 108
- #10. Get Early Feedback and Nail Defects Quickly 110
- #11. Learn From and Improve the Above Process 111

Exercises: Techniques and Case Studies 113
- Exercises Using Techniques 115
- A Less Successful Blitzkrieg: "BlownBalloon" Case Study 116
- A Successful Blitzkrieg "Verichina" Case Study: 118

Reading: QRPD Techniques Detailed Explanations and Examples 121

Part III. Project Leader and Team — 215

Project Leader Selection Criteria I: Personality Traits 217
Project Leader Traits and Behaviors 218
Project Leader Traits and Behaviors (continued) 219
Project Leader Selection Criteria II: Experience 220
- Ways to Gain Experience: Ability to Deliver Results 221
- Ways to Gain Experience: Cross-functional Understanding 222
- Ways to Gain Experience: Understanding of Organization, People, Processes 223
Project Leader Responsibilities 224
Project Leader Success Wisdoms 225
Listening Effectively 226
Dealing with People: Personality Types 227
Myers-Briggs Type Indicator® (MBTI) 227
Impact of Team Member Personality Types 228
A Time Management Matrix for Effective Teams 229
The 4 Stages of Team Development: *"Form, Storm, Norm, Perform"* 230
Building and Motivating Technical Teams 231

© 1998 Global Brain, Inc.

Full Table of Contents (continued)

Part III. Project Leader and Team (continued)
The Cross-Functional Team And the Power of Asking Questions 232
Project Leader Survival/Sanity Wisdoms 233
Zigzagging From Point A To Point B 233
Typical QRPD Team Players 234
Typical QRPD Team Players for IT and Software Projects 235
Virtual Team Checklist 236
Process and Forms for Project-based Performance Appraisal Input 237
    Project Leader Performance Appraisal Input Form 238
    Team Member Performance Appraisal Input Form 239
A Special Team Role: The Product Engineer's Responsibilities During Product
    Life Cycle 240
    Product Engineering Advantages 241
    Product Engineer Candidates 242
    Product Engineering Sample Charter 243
Article: Using Virtual Teams and QRPD to Do Projects at *Warp*-Speed 245
Reading: Using QRPD to Manage a Strategic Partnership 255

PART IV. FLOW   263
QRPD 4 Phases and 13 Steps of Product Development Flow 265
Description of Each QRPD Flow Step 266
How Quality is "Built In" to QRPD Flow 267

Phase I
Objectives for Phase I: Kickoff 268
Phase I Flow Steps and Deliverables 269
Flow Step 1: New Product/Project Proposal 270
    New Product/Project Proposal (NPP) Form 270
Flow Step 2: New Project Evaluation Request 271
    New Project Evaluation Request (NPER) Form 271
Flow Step 3: Select Project Leader, Core Team 272
    Typical Core Team Members Assigned at Beginning of Phase I 272
    Team Roles List and Responsibility Matrix 273
    Sample Team Roles List 274
    Sample PSI Responsibility Matrix 275
Tools for Managing Phase I and the Project 276
    Example Phase I Timeline 276
    Action Item Matrix 277
    Key Decisions List 277
    Critical Issues and Dependencies List 278
    Example Critical Issues and Dependencies List Entries 278
Preparing for Effective Project Meetings 279
    Meeting Guidelines and Schedule Document 279
    QRPD Meetings Overview 280
    Meetings Throughout Flow 281

Full Table of Contents (continued)

Part IV. Flow (continued)

    Meeting Guidelines: Process and Mechanics 282
        Meeting Agenda Contents 283
        Example Agenda, Team Meeting 283
        Meeting Guidelines: Agenda 284
        Meeting Guidelines: Roles 285
        Meeting Guidelines: Behavioral Tips 286
        Meeting Guidelines: 7 Steps to Brainstorming 286

Flow Step 4: Product Vision and See-Saw Specifications And Schedules
        (SSSS) Process 287
    Concurrent SSSS Activities to Create the Vision 288
    Iterative See-Saw Specifications and Scheduling 288
    Deliverables Evolution, Phase I SSSS Iterations 289
    Guidelines for the Vision and SSSS Process 290
    Quality: How the Vision Process Ensures Customer-Perceived Value
        (Satisfaction) 291
    The Product Vision
        Product Vision Contents 292
        Niles Audio Intellipad Product Vision 293
        PC Software Product Vision 294
    High-level Design and Risk Assessment
        High Level Design Iterations in Phase I SSSS 295
        Typical High-Level Design Deliverables 296
        Technological Risk Assessment 296
         Product Innovations Risk List 297
         Chicken Test Definition Document 297
        Risk Assessment and Management 297
    Assessing Other PTCC Elements 299
        <u>Typical</u> Timeline for a Q*R*PD Project 299
        Preliminary Test Plans and Testing Timelines 300
        Product Costs 300
        Project Costs (Budget) 300
        Late Cost Per Week (LCPW) 301
        ROI Analysis and 5-Year Road Map 301
        PTCC Trade-off Table 302
        Sample PTCC Trade-off Table 303
        Preliminary Design Reviews (PDR) 304
        Preliminary Design Review (PDR) Checklist 305
    A Summary of the See-Saw Process and How to Get Started Correctly 306
    Typical Phase I Calendar: The Vision and See-Saw Process 307
    Exercises: Sample Product Visions from Flow Step 4,
            See-Saw Specifications and Schedules 309
        Macintosh/PC Exchange 311
        Chip-placer2 312

© 1998 Global Brain, Inc.

Full Table of Contents (continued)

Part IV. Flow (continued)
    SunShield 314
    RAPIDSOFT Statement of Purpose and Direction 315
    QUAKESENSE 316
    BioComf 317
    Internet-Based Contracting Service 318
    Electronic Mail Software 319
    Article: Powerful Product Visions for Developing Products
        in Half the Time 321
  Evolving the Phase I SSSS Deliverables 335
    "*SMART*" Scheduling..335
    Scheduling Process and Tips...336
    Guidelines for Milestones List 337
    Sample Milestone Chart..337
    List of Tools and Equipment...338
    New Product Introduction Checklist 340
  Flow Step 5. New Project Kickoff Announcement to Exit Phase I.......................339
    Checklist of 19 Deliverables To Exit Phase I 339
    New Project Kickoff Announcement Form 342

Phase II
  Objectives for Phase II: Development 343
  Phase II Flow Steps and Deliverables 343
  Phase II Activities 344
  Q*R*PD Design Review Meetings...345
    Design Review Meetings 346
    Who Should Attend Design Reviews...346
    Key Factors for Successful Design Reviews..347
  Flow Step 6. Detailed Design Review (DDR) Checklist 348
  Flow Step 6. Critical Design Review (CDR) Checklist 349
    CDR Signoff Form (System Chicken Test Passed) 350
  Flow Step 7. Final Design Review (FDR) Checklist 351
  Flow Step 8. Development Pre-Releases..352
    Typical Development Pre-Release Deliverables....................................352
    Change Control after Development Pre-Releases 352
  Change Control and Development Releases 353
    Development Release (DR) Meetings..354
    Who Should Attend Release Meetings 354
    Key Factors for Successful Release Meetings 354
    Typical Revision Control Levels for Releases (Hardware Product) 355
    Typical Revision Control Levels for Releases (Software)..............................356

© 1998 Global Brain, Inc.

Full Table of Contents (continued)

Part IV. Flow (continued)

Phase III
- Objectives for Phase III: Approval 357
- Phase III Flow Steps and Deliverables 357
- **Flow Step 9.** Internal Testing (Alpha) 358
  - Alpha Test Plan Contents 359
  - Alpha Test Results Reviews 359
  - Change Control during Alpha Testing 359
- **Flow Step 10.** Development Release to Pilot 360
  - Typical Deliverables at Release to Pilot 360
  - Change Control after Release to Pilot 360
- **Flow Step 11.** External Testing (Beta, Regulatory) 361
  - External Test Plan Contents 361
  - Beta and Regulatory Test Results Reviews 362
  - Change Control during External Testing 362

Phase IV
- Objectives for Phase IV: Delivery 363
- Phase IV Flow Steps and Deliverables 363
- **Flow Step 12.** Pilot Builds/Deliveries 364
  - First Customer Ship (FCS) Approval Form 365
- **Flow Step 13.** Release to Production/Delivery 366
  - Final Release Meeting for Flow Step 13 367
  - Change Control after Final Release 367

Article: QRPD — A New Way to Quickly Deliver Enabling IT Solutions 369
Reading: QRPD Phase I Project Evaluation and Project Portfolio Management 379

PART V. DIRFT — 387

- 5 Keys to DIRFT: Doing It Right The First Time 389
- Quality Definitions 390
- DIRFT #1: How NOT to Write a Specification 391
- DIRFT #2: Management By Objectives (MBO) 392
- DIRFT #4: QRPD Testing 393
  - Testing Ideas 394
- Using DIRFT Daily 395
- The 7 Deadly Sins that Prevent Quality *Rapid* Product Development, ... 397
- Salvaging A Project In Trouble (Didn't DIRFT) 398
- Case Studies
  - "Emebo Opportunity #2:" An Enhanced Benefit-Cost Trade-Off Case Study 399
  - "Solar444:" A Complete QRPD Case Study 400
  - "SysTD:" A Complete QRPD Case Study 402

© 1998 Global Brain, Inc.

Full Table of Contents (continued)

Part V. DIRFT (continued)

Implementing QRPD Into An Organization 404
   Time to Adopt QRPD...405
   Characterization of Adopters 406
   Changes Required for QRPD Absorption 406

Article: Do It Right the First Time and Develop Products in Half the Time!
         The 5 Keys to DIRFT..407
Article: The Seven Sins that Prevent Quality *Rapid* Product Development,
         and Their Remedies 419
Article: Rescuing and Revitalizing the Off-Course Project......................................429
Article: Overcoming Obstacles to Rapid Product Development:
         Implementing QRPD..443

APPENDICES   455

Appendix A. Exercise Solutions 457
   Simple Benefit-Cost Solution 457
   EMEBO Solution..458
   FAXIT Solution 459
   Verichina Solution..460
   Product Vision Solutions 461
   Emebo Opportunity #2 Solution 462
   Solar444 Solution..463

Appendix B. Recommended Reading for QRPD..464
   QRPD: Quality *Rapid* Product Development Most Recommended Reading List...464
   QRPD: Quality *Rapid* Product Development Further Reading List.........................466

Appendix C. Recommended Reading for Personal Development 468
   Personal Development, The Global Brain, and Evolution of Consciousness
       Most Recommended Reading List 468
   Personal Development, The Global Brain, and Evolution of Consciousness
       Further Recommended Reading List...470

Appendix D. Glossary..472

ORDER FORM 479

© 1998 Global Brain, Inc.

About the Instructors

Orion ("Ori") Kopelman, author of this guidebook, is President of Global Brain, Inc., the founder of Q*R*PD, and one of America's leading product development experts. He has helped many technology-driven companies world-wide to significantly accelerate their projects and deliver products in record time. Previously, Ori was Vice-President of Engineering and division co-founder at Mountain Computer, a company which grew from 50 to 500 people between 1984-1990, with 32 consecutively profitable quarters.

An inventor and experienced project leader, Kopelman's enthusiasm for quality and solid command of the product development cycle have made him a much sought after lecturer. He served for three years as Chairman of IEEE's Engineering Management Society in Silicon Valley, and teaches Q*R*PD at UC Berkeley Extension and at project management conferences throughout the United States. He earned his BSEE with distinction from Stanford University.

He has been honored as an Outstanding Young Man of America, Who's Who in America, and has published numerous papers and articles on rapid product development. In 1997 he won a Small Press Book Award for *The 2nd Ten Commandments: Your Guide to Success In the Consciousness Age,* a book on how to live a happier, healthier, less stressful, and more balanced life in this highly technological age.

Ori was 1980 Michigan high school tennis doubles state champion, and had a brief stint in college as a stand-up comedian. He loves personal growth, scuba diving, skiing, and travel; speaks Hebrew, German, and some French; and makes his home in Maui, Hawaii and Palo Alto, California.

© 1998 Global Brain, Inc.

About the Instructors

Cinda Voegtli, BSEE/CS, is a consulting partner with Global Brain, Inc. and co-author of this guidebook. She has over 15 years experience in hardware and software development, engineering and project management, and product development process improvement. Her experience spans a wide variety of industries such as data and telecommunications systems, medical devices, robotics and computer systems, software and information systems, and virtual reality and game products.

Cinda has held director-level positions at high-technology companies in Dallas, Los Angeles, and Silicon Valley. She has managed projects in start-up, high-growth, and established large corporate environments. Since 1992 she has provided clients with product development expertise focused on rapid time-to-market, led related workshops at companies across the country, and taught QRPD at UC Berkeley Extension. She is a frequent speaker at project and engineering management conferences.

She currently serves as President of the worldwide Institute of Electrical and Electronics Engineers' Engineering Management Society. Previously she served for two years as Chairman of the Silicon Valley EMS chapter, as well as coordinator of EMS' 40 worldwide chapters. She was guest editor of the winter '96 issue of *IEEE Engineering Management Review* on project management.

Cinda makes her home in Los Altos, California.

About the Instructors

Adam Josephs is a partner at Global Brain, Inc. and a contributing author of this guidebook. He has 10 years experience in high-tech product development. At both Microsoft and Apple, he was a senior program manager with extensive experience in managing complex hardware and software product development. His specialty included multi-platform object oriented technologies and joint venture partnerships.

Adam has held director-level management positions at Internet and electronic commerce companies in Silicon Valley and New York City. He has managed projects and product development organizations in start-up and large corporate environments.

He has consulted extensively with companies in the computer, pharmaceutical, consumer electronics, semiconductor manufacturing equipment, automotive and communications industries on product development strategy and process improvement. He has taught these topics at the UC Berkeley Extension and at companies around the world.

He is an active member of the American Society for Training and Development and the Project Management Institute. He earned his BA in Decision Analysis from Stanford University.

Adam makes his home in both New York City and San Francisco where he also continues to lecture on wine and Shakespeare.

© 1998 Global Brain, Inc.

About the Instructors

Richard Piehl is a partner at Global Brain, Inc. He has over 20 years experience in product development, operations, document control, product validation, and technical support disciplines. His experience spans a variety of industries such as computer systems and peripherals, semiconductor equipment, power equipment, and instrumentation.

Dick has held vice president-level positions at high-technology companies in Silicon Valley. He has managed and coached projects in start-up, medium size, and large companies, and has been responsible for engineering, production, and technical support departments. He has extensive experience with reengineering organizations, ISO 9001, and network design.

He is an active member of the Computer and Engineering Management Societies of the Institute of Electrical and Electronics Engineering and the Project Management Institute. He received a BS and MS in Electrical Engineering and Computer Science from the University of California, Berkeley and an MBA from Santa Clara University. He has also been awarded three patents.

Dick makes his home in San Ramon, California.

Reading: Why Q*R*PD® and What Is It?

© 1998 Global Brain, Inc.

Why Q*R*PD and What Is It?

Table of Contents

Q*R*PD is Just-in-Time Product Development (JITPD) 21
    The Power of Q*R*PD 22
    The Globally Spiraling Acceleration of Technology 23
    Needed: A Practical, Mission-Oriented Methodology 26
    Avoiding the Cost of Change 26
Q*R*PD: A Mission-Oriented Methodology for Product Development 27
    Q*R*PD's History 27
    The Significance of the Q*R*PD Name 31
    Quality 31
    Benefits of Q*R*PD 34
    Elements of the Q*R*PD Methodology 36
    Cornerstones of Q*R*PD 37
    The Q*R*PD Workshop 39
Patience for Speed 39

© 1998 Global Brain, Inc.

Q*R*PD is Just-in-Time Product Development

Not long ago, Xerox used 600 engineers to design a 50 page/minute $150,000 color printer in only three years, while the previous black-and-white took them over six years to complete. Why can some companies consistently practice accelerated product development and reduce time-to-market, and not others? Which new practices and management methodologies allow companies like Xerox to drastically reduce development times and costs? Do they work for all size companies?

Business Week (August 16, 1993) reports that 46% of all R&D (Research and Development) money spent in the U.S. goes to what eventually becomes a product flop! This means that almost half of our well-intentioned, hard-working efforts result in much ado about nothing. What a shame. What a poor utilization of our greatest national resource for global economic competition in the next millennium—our technological industrial base.

The *Business Week* cover story article, "FLOPS: Too many new products fail. Here's why —and How to Do Better" focused on numerous reasons, including marketing strategy. Nonetheless, they concluded that the single greatest factor in these failures remains the ineffectiveness of the new product development process—particularly, choosing the right product to develop and getting it to the market in the shortest cycle time possible.

So our companies' financial health increasingly depend on executing Just In Time (JIT) Product Development, or *JITPD*. Lagging the market by taking too long to develop and release a product can prove disastrous, while proper execution of JITPD results in tremendous rewards. Typical Late Costs per Week (LCPW) range from $5000 to $250,000, numbers no company can afford to ignore. (See p. 75 for more on LCPW.)

JITPD is a critical concept for all industries and types of projects. Every project can be seen as a product development effort, requiring an investment in time, money, and people to satisfy customer needs, and resulting in some sort of product. Every project must incorporate the disciplines of planning, risk and resource management, and team accountability to ensure success.

This guidebook provides the tools and techniques for accelerating product development times by up to 50 percent. It explains how to practice Quality *Rapid* Product Development (Q*R*PD), a management methodology for developing products in half the time. With broad definitions of "product" and "customer," Q*R*PD pertains to

- the creation of tangible widgets such as the latest computer, composite material, or software program;
- services such as consulting, training;
- combined offerings such as cellular phone service;
- and the development or re-engineering of business processes and systems for corporate information systems support, customer order taking, and so forth.

Quality *Rapid* Product Development (Q*R*PD):

A methodology of global best-practices for developing technology-related products, processes, and services quickly, at low cost, with high quality, while achieving maximum return-on-investment (ROI) for the company.

© 1998 Global Brain, Inc.

The Power of Q*R*PD

Companies who use Q*R*PD-like practices can complete their projects in half the time and at half the cost of their previous efforts, resulting in substantial gains in competitiveness, productivity, and overall profitability (See figure 1).

- GM's Buick division rolled out its "Park Avenue" in 36 months compared to 60 for a previous comparable model,

- HP developed a printer in 24 months versus 50.

- A small audio electronics company completed a next-generation product using Q*R*PD in 7 months instead of the 18 months their previous comparable product required, winning a prestigious award and selling twice their forecasted volume in the first year.

- The IT applications development department of a major oil company completed a sales force automation project in an unprecedented 9 months, then adopted Q*R*PD for all its development projects to stay competitive with the outside vendors also bidding for the IT work.

- The IT data warehousing department of another major oil company rescued a project in trouble and delivered a major new warehouse subject area to their business analysts using Q*R*PD within 3 weeks of the original schedule.

- A medical device manufacturer delivered a major new instrument in 18 months using Q*R*PD instead of the previous 48, including FDA approval.

These companies all found a new and better way to accomplish their product development. Given the acceleration of technological change and the intensity of the competition they faced, they realized that they would have to "thwart the laws of physics"—bend the product development rules of yesteryear—to thrust forward at warp-speed.

Figure 1. Is Moving Faster Than Light Really Possible?

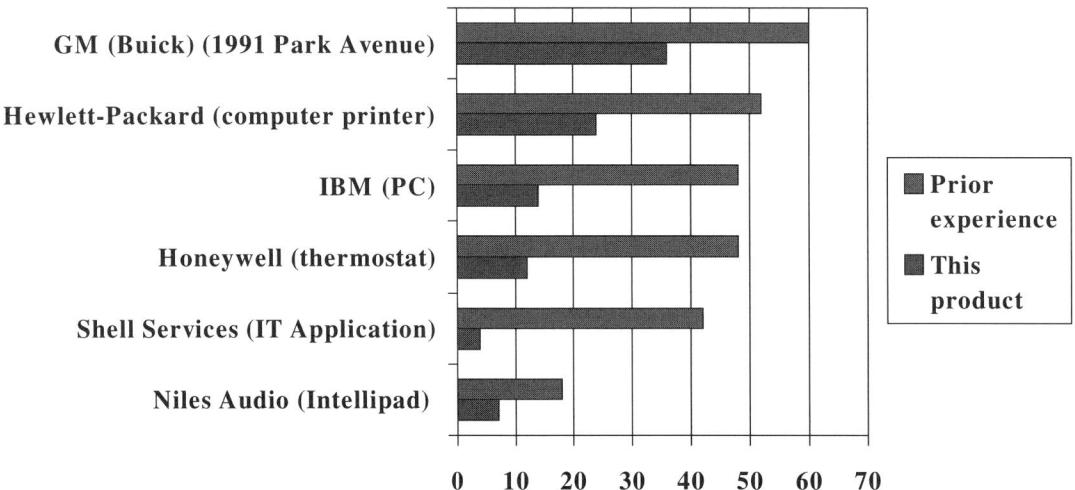

The Globally Spiraling Acceleration of Technology

> "Time seems to be speeding up. New ideas and technologies have accelerated our culture into an almost unrecognizable reality... this renaissance has been interpreted by many as an evolutionary leap for humanity into another dimension. Whether or not this is true, those who can comprehend the nature of this shift will be better prepared to survive in the twenty-first century."
>
> ~ Douglas Rushkoff, *Cyberia: Life In the Trenches of Hyperspace* [1]

Did you know that collective human scientific knowledge is doubling every eighteen months? Several years ago, researchers decided to quantify the growth of this knowledge. Starting with 0 A.D. they normalized the data and called the knowledge at that point "1 unit," meaning that all technological and scientific know-how in humanity's hands at that time was considered to be 1 unit of knowledge. The team proceeded to chart the growth up to the present time through 1992. Table 1 shows the results.

The "doubling time" column illustrates the acceleration Douglas Rushkoff refers to above. Notice that the first doubling of scientific knowledge took 1500 years to occur. Think of the awakenings in science and technology during this time, including the invention of the printing press. Only 4 centuries later, the doubling time for knowledge was down to only 10 years, as the 1950s and 1960s brought us the introduction and advancement of computer technology and electronics.

Regardless of the exact manner of measuring unit of knowledge, the trend in table 1 is clear: we have seen the growth of technological change accelerate incredibly in our lifetimes. The affects of this exponential growth are most clearly evident in the technology industry, where many products are obsolete before they even get to market. In the 1980s project schedules routinely ran 3 to 5 years in length. No more. In today's Silicon Valley, 80% of projects run on a schedule of 1 year or less.

Most technology developers are familiar with a proven rule called Moore's Law, which says that microprocessor power doubles every 18 months for the same cost. Intel Corporation now believes that it happens in even less time. In Intel's industry, as materials science advances, and faster and more powerful integrated circuits are produced, product developers race to create the latest best offering using the new technology, in ever-shorter "cycle times."

Figure 2 graphs the data in Table 1. Following the trend, the doubling time appears to be continuing to accelerate, and is rapidly approaching 0. Indeed, one recent estimate says that by 2020, our knowledge base will double every 75 days [2]. In the next decade we'll see typical schedules of 6 months or less.

This acceleration is being played out again and again across all our industries. Can you imagine how the Internet will contribute to the growth of knowledge and speed of product development, as it enables real-time scientific and technological collaboration around the globe? No wonder our schedules are now less than a year and a half and getting shorter!

© 1998 Global Brain, Inc.

Just for fun, a Taylor's series can be used to calculate when this doubling time would theoretically asymptotically approach 0. The result is December 22, 2012. (See figure 3.) Interestingly enough, this is the last date on the ancient Mayan calendar.

The implications for our projects are clear, and we see the impacts every day in the urgency of our product development efforts. The global technology race is on and superior quality is merely the price of admission. To stay in the game you need to stay ahead. We must find a way to keep up with the accelerating pace of scientific knowledge and continually translate it into technologies and quality products that meet the needs of our customers, while making profits for our companies. So it's critical that we approach product development with a precise and effective strategy that not only ensures team commitment and innovation but rapid, just-in-time development. Q*R*PD provides us with the tools.

Table 1. Growth of Collective Human Scientific Knowledge

Year	Units of knowledge	Doubling Time (years)	Tenfold Time (years)
0 AD	1	50,000	50,000
1500	2	1500	
1750	4	250	
1900	8	150	1900
1950	16	50	1200
1960	**32**	10	335
1967	64	7	142
1973	128	6	48
1978	256	5	23
1982	512	4	17
1985	1024	3.5	12
1988	2048	2.5	10
1990	4096	2	9
1992	8192	1.5	6
1994	16384	**1.?**	5?
1996	100,000	?	4?
1999	**1,000,000**	?	3?

Normalized to 1 in the year 0 AD. Meaning assume that all technological and scientific know-how in humanity's hands at that time was 1 unit of knowledge.

Sources: Georges Anderla, Organization for Economic Cooperation and Development, 1973; from Peter Russell's *The White Hole In Time: Our Future Evolution and the Meaning of Now*, Harper San Francisco, 1992, p. 28, quoted in Prometheus Rising and elsewhere by Robert Anton Wilson. Also French astrophysicist Dr. Jacques Vallee, and mathematical extrapolation.

Figure 2. Graph of Collective Human Scientific Knowledge

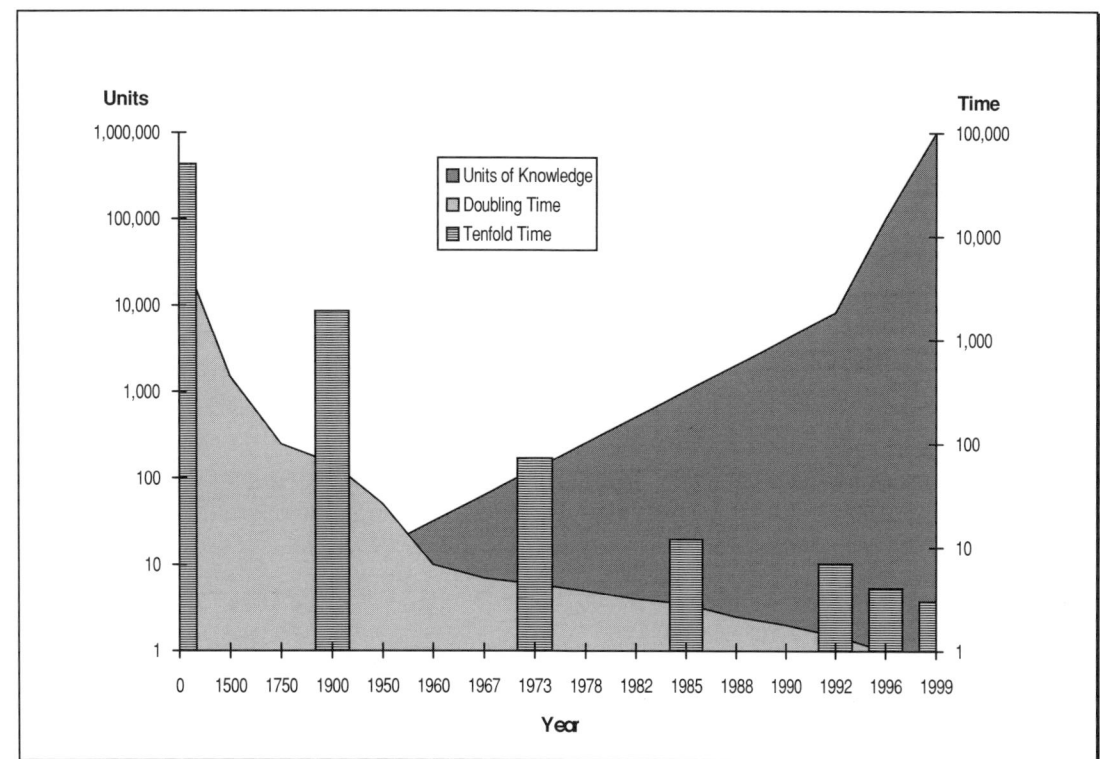

Figure 3. Technology Acceleration Spiral (ends on December 22, 2012)

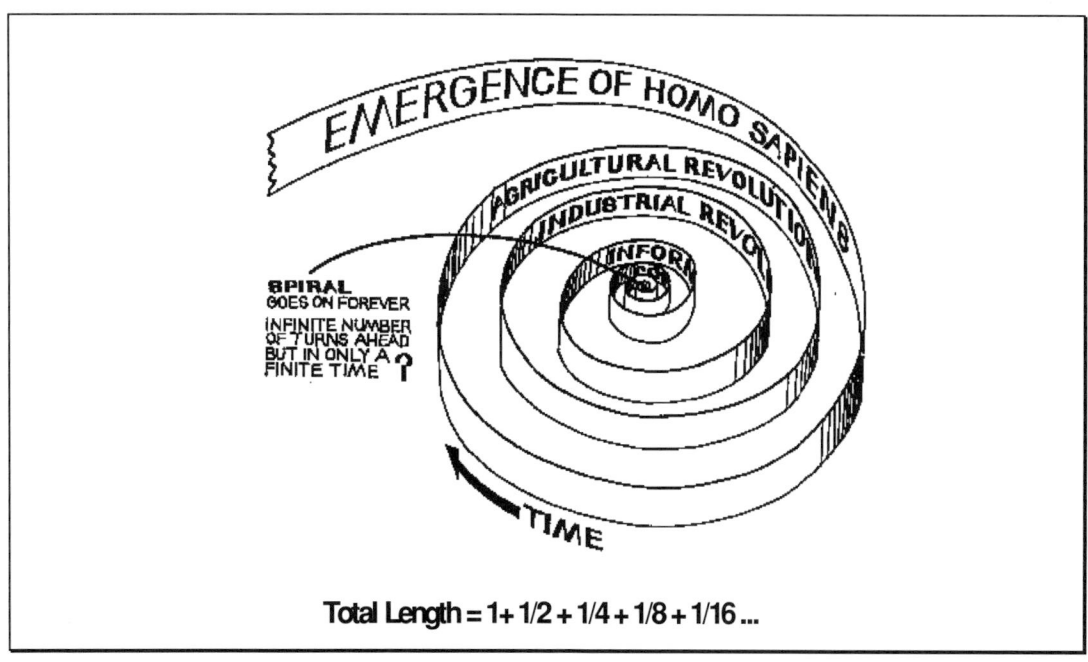

© 1998 Global Brain, Inc.

Needed: A Practical, Mission-Oriented Methodology

The faster your pace of innovation, the stronger and yet more flexible your project structure needs to be to achieve JITPD. QRPD synthesizes the best management practices of the last two decades with a new paradigm for product development. The QRPD methodology ensures JITPD by providing the tools for accelerating new product development times by as much as 50%.

Fundamentally, it's a mission-oriented methodology that combines both quality and speed to ensure that you do it right the first time. QRPD focuses a team on a powerful, focused objective, like the "put a man on the moon" Apollo missions in the 1960s. The power of this mission orientation is illustrated in a story about two stonecutters in medieval Europe. As the two craftsmen were methodically carving out blocks of stone one day, a bystander asked one "What are you doing?" He replied, "As you can see, I'm measuring out and carving these blocks of stone." The bystander asked the same question of the second stonecutter. His reverent reply: "I'm building a cathedral."

The second stonecutter understood his goal, his mission. Who do you think was more likely to work hard, contribute ideas for the betterment of the cathedral, and give the job his heart and soul?

In the same manner, motivated QRPD "volunteer" team members understand the customers' needs and thus the objectives of their project, creatively determine the best way to execute the mission, and synergistically work together to complete it quickly and with high quality. Teams on a mission to quickly deliver value to their customers can function effectively in the midst of seeming chaos and incredible demands.

Avoiding the Cost of Change

The cost of engineering changes increases drastically the later into the project you are. In the midst of intense global competition, it's essential that we Do It Right the First Time (DIRFT). We must deliver the product our customers need the first time, not the second or third time, and avoid costly late changes, to ensure that we achieve our desired ROI. QRPD is a comprehensive management strategy that will reveal to you the true cost of lateness, the value of front-end (QRPD phase I) concentration, and the power of a team-created Product Vision. With an emphasis on Rapid, QRPD accelerates the pace of the overall project while ensuring that sound decisions are made throughout, the right product is defined and designed, and costly late course corrections are not needed.

QRPD provides the practical skills and the "How to's" needed to achieve a 50% reduction in development time with improved overall quality. It presents proven techniques—including the best-practices currently employed by fast-growing companies, in agreement with today's textbook theories—for combining the fast paced innovation of start-up companies with some structure needed for every company's growth and continued success. This approach results in significantly increased ROI on research and development (R&D) expenditures.

© 1998 Global Brain, Inc.

QRPD: A Mission-Oriented Methodology for Product Development
QRPD's History

As Vice President of Engineering at Mountain Computer, Inc. in 1989, my staff of Engineering Managers and myself had noticed that some of our projects distinctly went better than others. I had started with this company which lay on the outskirts of California's Silicon Valley in 1984, a year out of college at Stanford University, where I had received my Electrical Engineering degree. From my first role as a Project Manager of a floppy disk certifier, responsible for a group of 10 developers, I had lived in the trenches with the challenges of attempting to engineer new technology-based products.

The certifier, a robotically-loaded tester of media, would eventually become IBM's standard for use in incoming inspection. This in turn would influence Japanese and other floppy disk manufacturers and users worldwide to buy it, and would help make it a very successful product for us for more than 5 years. On the day I arrived at the company however, we deluded ourselves with a champagne celebration as we shipped the first unit to a customer cross-country, and the 4'x2'x1' 110 lb. "engineering marvel" only started working about 9 months later. On the brighter side, several of us racked up frequent flier miles as we flew numerous times to make design modifications on the factory floor.... Nearly a year after we shipped the first unit we finally collected our $20,000 payment for it.

I'm sure many of you can relate to this experience. Happily, and somewhat amazingly—but not atypical in high-tech—that first customer eventually ordered large quantities of certifiers. Our innovative designs of digital and analog hardware, proprietary software, and highly reliable, patented, mechanical handling mechanisms would prove good enough. George, our brilliant software engineer, wrote an operating system from scratch to allow us to pioneer the first intelligent tester of its kind. He had returned from a mini-sabbatical in Europe 3 months before I was hired, and had been told that, "the product was almost done, it just needed an operating system".... Miracle after miracle, it wasn't always pretty, but somehow we made it work better and better, and kept our fledgling start-up afloat.

By 1988, as we had grown to over $50 million in yearly sales and 300 employees, we started wondering if there might exist a formula by which to develop products. Were there techniques or practices that consistently characterized the successful projects and differentiated them from the not-so-successful ones? We had plenty of both…yet overall enjoyed an excellent reputation for our technical prowess and for coming to market quickly with high quality products (not necessarily the cheapest ones, which is just fine).

Some of us had been blessed with reading Donald Reinertsen's 1985 article in *Electronic Business* on "Blitzkrieg product development: Cut development times in half." We tried using his checklist and found that it definitely helped. Donald had written this article while at McKinsey & Company in Palo Alto, California, where he was a close co-worker of Tom Peters and Robert Waterman of *In Search of Excellence* fame.

From Reinertsen's article and our own experiences—by now we had completed dozens of projects—we began compiling a "New Product Cycles Handbook for Project and Product Engineers" at the company. We had just completed a project we finally felt we "had really nailed," and thus proved our preliminary deductions on a formula. Based on this experience and other projects, we felt more confident, and issued Revision 1 of a 20-some page booklet on June 1, 1990. It is in my hands as I write, and it is from this that the book you hold in your hands evolved, with "a few" updates. (See the concept of incremental innovation under Commandment #1 in Part II Techniques: The QRPD Toolkit.)

© 1998 Global Brain, Inc.

I still believe in the accuracy of the Handbook's opening statement: "As part of the New Product Introduction Cycle it is critical that in Engineering (or more generally product development) we remember to enforce discipline into the Design Cycle of the product. Please follow the attached New Product Design Flow Chart as closely as possible. Let's Do It Right The First Time!" Experience had taught us that it wasn't all black magic, that we could abide by a process that didn't stymie creativity yet assured more consistent and faster results.

By this time I had joined and become chairman of the Silicon Valley IEEE Engineering Management Society (EMS) group. I found that many of my fellow engineering managers reported experiences not unlike my own: struggling painfully through getting products out, with incredible pressure from executives and especially sales and marketing. Many had, like me, tried to wade through the muck to learn in the school of hard knocks techniques they could apply time and again. Many of us were appalled at the process or lack thereof, and in particular, the lack of attention given to the greatest variables involved: the people and the risks. And no matter how hard we pressed our people and how far we kept pushing the limits of technology's state-of-the-art, it always came down to "it's all Engineering's fault," especially when our companies' financial results didn't meet expectations.

In early 1991 I semi-retired from Mountain Computer—we had sold it to Nakamichi of Japan and a number of us stood financially comfortable for at least a couple of years, and a few of the early founders were set for life. Our 32 consecutively profitable quarters and tenfold increase in sales, combined with a little luck, had paid off.

While roaming the beaches of the world I had the good fortune of being in touch with an old college friend of mine, Bill, with whom I still attended our alma mater's football games. He suggested to me that I might enjoy putting together a course for the University of California Berkeley Extension, where he taught in the evenings. I had always considered going back to school to get my M.B.A, and now had an interest in how technological-oriented products get developed rapidly.

Rather than enrolling somewhere myself, I opted to teach what I wanted to learn. My father, a world renowned Professor of Chemistry and Physics had taught me that, "he learned a lot from his teachers—some of whom even went on to receive Nobel prizes—more from his colleagues, and the most from his students." By the fall of 1991 I was teaching a class of 10 students a course on rapid product development. Over the ensuing years my students have taught me more than I probably ever could have learned at any program. Thank you!

The methodology, which by this time I had named Q*R*PD, kept developing. Each semester I updated the guidebook based on a combination of feedback from teaching and real-world experience with clients. Some of my students had seen the value of hiring me to share my insights with their management and teams, and this afforded me yet another proving ground for the material. Thus arose versions 1 to 6 of this guidebook, in spiral-bound form, a photocopied manual of class notes.

I founded Global Brain®, Inc. on January 2, 1992 as a corporation based in Palo Alto, California to promulgate Q*R*PD. I had become convinced that people could work together in wiser and more "conscious" ways and get a lot more done. A year earlier I had read the most influential book of my life, *The Global Brain*, published in 1983, and written by Peter Russell, a former student of Stephen Hawking. (We published an updated edition in 1995 called *The Global Brain Awakens)*. It further swayed me to believe that people synergistically working together could make miracles happen.

© 1998 Global Brain, Inc.

In the ensuing couple of years I taught 2-day workshops in Silicon Valley for the IEEE EMS that provided both invaluable feedback and a source of companies who believed enough in QRPD to try it out in-house. By 1994 I had compiled a substantial version of the guidebook, called the 7th edition. Some of you might even own one of these vintage binders. It includes articles I had published at various conferences where I had been invited to present. By now the methodology had really started to take form.

It got a huge push forward when Cinda Voegtli, with whom I had worked together years earlier at IEEE and who by this time had become chairman of the Silicon Valley EMS group, decided to join forces with me. My co-author, and an outstanding individual in every way, she recognized the inherent flaw that plagues most companies in developing products: They push everyone to work incredibly hard to get a project done, but often fail to intelligently manage their resources and risks and ensure that everyone works together in a harmonious way.

Together Cinda and I ventured out to teach QRPD at various companies of all sizes across the country, in a multitude of industries, ranging from aerospace to database software to medical devices to software games. We found that with some amount of tailoring, and by generalizing some of the terms we were using, we could help many companies make their projects much more effective.

By the mid-1990s, as many more industries began to recognize the foolishness of treating product development as magic—rather than a disciplined process where one could and should have predictable outcomes—we enjoyed even wider success with QRPD. We attracted attendees (and then clients) from a more diverse set of companies as we gave talks and workshops across the country at project management, product development, and technical conferences. These product types included desktop software, information technology and services (IT or IS), pharmaceuticals, other types of technology-based services, and more. Once we even had students in our Berkeley class from a company that makes various ice cream products for sale to airlines and others. They, too, found substantial use in QRPD. We weren't surprised!

You see, all these projects involve taking an idea, and rapidly transforming it through a maze of technological and resource risks into a product that you can deliver to a satisfied customer, who'll happily pay you money for the value you're providing them. You can overcome many of the common issues and challenges which plague these efforts with a set of wisdom, or a disciplined methodology for doing product development, that ensures results.

This edition culminates almost a decade of many peoples' struggle to find a formula for product development and make things easier and more pleasant for themselves and everyone else—not to mention more profitable. It encompasses updates to provide detailed explanations and examples of how QRPD can assist most if not all technology-related projects and product development (and arguably other types, too). It should serve as a comprehensive reference book or tool kit, chock full of information, and a cookbook for day-to-day pragmatic use by Project Leaders, other managers, and team members.

Even if you already think you know project management, we sincerely hope you'll never do any project without at least referring back to this book. If nothing else, it should help you countermand the tremendous temptation to fall back to old habits that create disorganized chaos and too often result in glacial product development. We believe that *organized* chaos is not only okay, but desirable. QRPD adds effective organization to creative, sometimes chaotic product development.

© 1998 Global Brain, Inc.

We further wish that you'll use this book to zoom forward at warp-speed, get to the future at "beyond light speed," and prove to yourself and others that there is a better way.

Cinda has put a lot of hard work into jointly developing Q*R*PD with me. She has a really solid understanding of the difficulties of implementation. We have often felt like parents who jointly gave birth to a baby that we hoped would do some real good in this world. I can never acknowledge her or thank her enough for how vital her contribution has been and for how much I've enjoyed co-creating and synergizing with her in this labor of love.

My thanks also go to Adam Josephs for the contributions he has made to this guidebook. Adam took the Q*R*PD course early in the 1990s and used its techniques at various companies. We were delighted to have him become part of Global Brain in 1997. He too understands the power of Q*R*PD principles in the hands of a project team, and the challenges of implementing new practices in companies. He is a valuable member of our team and his insights have been a great addition to this book.

I want to also thank Dr. Dick Tsina, Chairman of Continuing Education in Engineering at UC Berkeley Extension, who helped me get started with teaching, and with whom I've enjoyed a long-standing relationship filled with many good laughs—he's always got a good joke.

A special thanks goes out to some of the early believers in Q*R*PD who kept the momentum rolling as they were willing to pioneer it inside their companies. This took a lot of courage, as there's always massive resistance to change, and inertia in favor of doing things the old way—no matter how dysfunctional it may be. These include Doug King, Rex Peters, Tina Ohlhaver, Dave Paprocki, Jeff Abramowitz, Laurie Hewitt, Keith Williams, Neil Jablon, Bob Ohara, and others, I'm sorry to say, I may have forgotten. Their support and encouragement further fueled my faith and confidence in Q*R*PD and gave me strength to keep spreading it.

In general, it always seems to take an internal zealot who "sees the light," recognizes that there's a better way to do things that will result in both the company succeeding, and in peoples' lives being made more pleasant and fun. The above group all struggled hard to fight many battles and vindicate Q*R*PD.

Keith at NASA exemplified them all. A relatively young person, he worked among many 30-year veterans—some of whom had been present since the Apollo moon program days, had seen much, and bemoaned how people really used to get stuff done back then. Having had a chance to hear some of their stories, I would claim that they, like many other successful projects, had used Q*R*PD and its "mission-oriented" approach of best practices without having had a name for it.

Keith's battle cry should go down with Neil Armstrong's "One small step for man, one giant leap for mankind:" "We are just not going to do it that way any more!" He had to repeat it to many people as he went on his crusade. He and many other brave evangelists, willing to stick their necks out for what they believe was better for everyone, deserve a lot of credit.

I truly hope that many of you who read this are, or become, evangelists yourselves. Maybe we should start a support group... But please believe me, there really is a better way, one in which you *can* do projects in half the time, at half the cost, with double the profit, and double the fun. People have been doing it for a long time, well before we documented it as a set of best practices, gave them standard semantics, and called it Q*R*PD. It's just that they were doing it sporadically and inconsistently. That's why only perhaps one of ten or one of twenty projects got the results that now we can attain with Q*R*PD every time. May you use this guidebook to consistently "make it so!"

© 1998 Global Brain, Inc.

The Significance of the Q*R*PD Name

How did QRPD get named? After all, there are 24 different combinations of the letters Q, R, P, and D. The contents of the name, and their order, have significance.

- **Quality:** In Q*R*PD, quality means "value as perceived by the customer." Our projects all have customers: people who will use them and be affected by the outcome of our product development.

- **Rapid:** Speed is important for achieving our ROI goals. Q*R*PD focuses on the financial benefits of a time-based paradigm.

- **Product:** QRPD applies to consumer products, custom products, as well as services and processes. *All such efforts have a resulting, tangible "product."*

- **Development:** All such efforts involve "development": something is created by means of a series of tasks, activities, resources, and efforts.

Quality

The emphasis on "quality first" is no accident. Quality *has* to be first in the name of the methodology. Who cares about being fast-to-market if the resulting product quality is so poor that no one wants the product?

Doing it 'right' is defined by the quality of the final product. Customers base their purchases on both practicality and pleasure, and the range of needs and wants between the two is extremely varied. The renowned management expert on quality, Edward Deming Jr., showed us that customers aren't just satisfied with a minimum number of defects with the products that they buy. Rather, their evaluation is based on their overall experience from the product, including its presentation and design.

Quality is:

1) Value as perceived by the customer.
2) Improvement of the customers' experience.
3) Not a lack of things wrong, but the sense of overall presentation and design.

This is a distinction that remains clearly ingrained in the minds of many Detroit automobile executives. Regrettably, the 1980s were a time for the U.S. automakers to play catch up while they worked to eliminate an average of 13 manufacturing defects per vehicle. As American cars rolled off the assembly line, Japanese cars were capturing the U.S. consumer. By the time U.S. manufacturers remedied the defect issue, there was a new obstacle to surmount: the task of winning back the market from these foreign contenders.

© 1998 Global Brain, Inc.

Tom Peters and Nancy Austin in their management classic *Thriving On Chaos*, found that on average, those companies whose products scored in the top third on a 'relative perceived product quality' test, out-earned those in the bottom third by a 2-1 margin. Those are the rewards of DIRFT.

> "Quality must be judged as the customer perceives it."
> —Tom Peters, *Thriving on Chaos*, p. 100 [3]

The global corporate community has recognized this bounty for Quality. In response, the International Standards Organization (ISO) has issued guidelines for continuous improvement geared toward achieving higher quality products, called ISO-9000. Many high technology companies are now seeking to conform to ISO-9000. QRPD and the 5 keys to DIRFT discussed later in this book in no way conflict with ISO-9000, but rather augment it.

In fact, QRPD tenets are critical to ensuring that standards like ISO-9000 are implemented in such as way as to truly produce quality while not slowing development down.

> "With ISO-9000, you can still have terrible processes and products. You can certify a manufacturer that makes life jackets from concrete, as long as those jackets are made according to the documented processes and the company provides next of kin with instructions on how to complain about defects. That's absurd."
> —Richard Burstone, Motorola

QRPD is in sync with the foundations of Total Quality Management (TQM). TQM is a continuous improvement process where every employee participates, including management. The goal is to find failures and defects as early as possible, in contrast to the all-too-common sentiment "Do you want it good or fast? We don't have enough time to do it right now, but we have enough time to do it over again…."

Quality is Profitable

"When quality goes up, costs go down. *Quality improvement is the primary source of cost reduction.*" (usually due to simplification).

— Tom Peters, *Thriving on Chaos*, p. 97 [3]

"On average, those firms whose products score in the top third on relative perceived product quality outperform those in the bottom third by a two-to-one margin."

— Tom Peters, *Thriving on Chaos*, p. 82 [3]

"Savings are brought about by saving rework, reject items; repeat business generated from satisfied customers."

— Phillip Crosby, *Quality is Free* [4]

Benefits of Q*R*PD

The key benefits of the Q*R*PD methodology are:

- **Better product quality:** We can't sacrifice quality for speed. Q*R*PD ensures that we keep both in mind. In the 1980s many high technology companies enjoyed fantastic, sometimes overnight, success. In the 1990s however, as the market has matured, superior quality and high productivity have become just the price of admission for competing seriously. In the next century, quality will continue to grow as a primary differentiator of companies and their products.

- **Lower time to market by accelerating development times by up to 50%:** The emphasis however, now shifts to achieving quality much more *rapidly*. Concerned with national economic competitiveness, the late Ron Brown, U.S. Secretary of Commerce, noted at the first government-industry Technology Summit held in November 1993 in California, "An age in which change is the only constant requires unflagging, sustained (quick) innovation." To survive in a leapfrog world where even current products are here today and obsolete tomorrow, every project's result must turn into a successful new product seemingly overnight. Q*R*PD recognizes that time is of the essence.

  We plan projects to take a year, and what happens? They can actually take anywhere from 18 to 24 months. We have to find a way to plan and execute our projects such that we can achieve the aggressive schedules we need to set. Today at least 80 percent of the projects undertaken in Silicon Valley are supposed to take less than one year.

  Using Q*R*PD-like techniques, many companies have and are developing products in up to 50% less time than before, with lower overall spending levels. Recall the Xerox example at the beginning of this section. They reduced their average time-to-market company-wide by 50% on comparable products, with 50% less engineering resource dollars.

  As another example, management expert Peter Drucker reported that Toyota, Nissan, and Honda bring out a new automobile model now in only 18 months [5]. U.S. car makers have achieved a three year cycle, down from five years a decade ago. At Intevac, a mid-sized company in Sunnyvale, California, a newly formed team completed the latest Molecular Beam Epitaxy machine for depositing gallium arsenide on semiconductor wafers, in eight months instead of the usual year and a half. Rolm, a Siemens Company, developed a certain genre of voice mail products in successive cycle times of four years, two, and currently one. Other examples abound. (See the testimonials at the beginning of this guidebook.)

- **Increased R&D ROI.** Recently, both public and private shareholders have rightly expressed an increasing irritation about the lack of ROI from many high-tech companies' development expenditures.

  Past visible examples of failing to deliver sufficient ROI are IBM and Apple, but many other class action lawsuits have been filed, and executives removed. Do gargantuan R&D expenditures translate to commensurate returns to their investors on their equity? In some cases yes, in many no. We cannot allow the development and engineering disciplines to use play money to finance an expensive hobby. We must first and foremost focus on profitability, then on "doing neat stuff."

In the IT industry in 1996, 250 billion dollars were spent on IT projects. Only 16% of them completed on time and within budget; 33% of them were cancelled altogether. We have to do better than that! QRPD focuses on not only executing a project well, but maximizing the company's return on that development investment.

A word about costs: Experience tells us that project team sizes stay about the same, no matter how long a project lasts. This means that companies that develop products in up to half the time spend a lot less money overall, possibly even half. Consequently, they realize greater returns on their investments. That's why John Young, retired CEO and President of Hewlett-Packard, promotes the absolute importance of QRPD-like principles. In a phone conversation he remarked that, "improved new product development cycle time is not only free, it's profitable. It doesn't cost you anything, it's more fun for everybody, and you do it right the first time!"

- **Improved morale and fun:** Is your life in the technology arena what you thought it would be when you graduated from college? All too often the answer is "No." Our projects aren't fun anymore. QRPD recognizes that none of our other objectives are really consistently possible if we don't find a way to have fun and fulfillment during these challenging projects.

QRPD Benefits:
A *Mission-oriented* Methodology for Product Development

➡ Lower time to market by accelerating development times by up to 50%!

- Better product quality

- Increased R&D Return on Investment (ROI)

- Improved morale and fun

Have you been on at least one project that was considered successful, delivering the benefits above?

Repeatedly in QRPD workshops, less than half the class answers "Yes" to that question. Only a handful say they've been on two or more projects that meet those standards. Why is it so hard?

Consistently effective product development requires discipline, and a way to teach teams how to perform over and over. *Consistently rapid product development is much more a people problem than a technology problem!* The QRPD methodology is constructed to answer this challenge. If you're one of those people who answered "Yes" to the question above, we're sure you'll recognize in QRPD many of the practices you've used.

© 1998 Global Brain, Inc.

Elements of the Q*R*PD Methodology

All effective methodologies are broken down into key elements:

Assumption or paradigm: What is the basic underlying premise or perspective of the methodology? How are we trying to get people to see things and think? We must get that straight before trying to tell them to do things a certain way.

The "how-to's": What are the techniques, activities, documents, etc. we are telling people to do?

The process: What is the framework for integrating these how-to's into a set and sequence of work that forms a successful project?

The feedback loop: How do we make sure that we're really following the methodology effectively? What feedback is provided, and how do we make use of it?

Table 2. Elements of the Q*R*PD Methodology

All Methodologies	Q*R*PD
Assumption or Paradigm	Blitzkrieg
How To's	3 Secrets to Success
	10 Commandments
	150 Techniques
Process	13 Steps of Flow
Feedback Loop	5 Keys to DIRFT

In Q*R*PD these elements are:

- **The Blitzkrieg paradigm:** The blitzkrieg analogy converts the Project Leader and team's perspective to the time-based paradigm for product development. All project decisions are made with an understanding of the "late cost" of time-to-market. Make sure you understand that value! See Part I Blitzkrieg.

- **The 10 commandments and 150 techniques:** Consistent execution of excellent product development is a game of odds. The more things we do well each time, the higher our odds of achieving our most challenging goals. The commandments and techniques capture detailed best practices for day-to-day project tasks and perspectives. Develop the discipline to make sure you're using them on every project. See Part II Techniques: The Q*R*PD Toolkit.

- **The 13 steps of Flow:** Every project must have some kind of framework for its tasks to ensure most efficient and effective development. Q*R*PD concentrates on the most important steps you must execute, not creating a bureaucratic maze of "must-do" activities. Make sure you know and do these steps. See Part IV Flow.

- **The 5 Keys to DIRFT:** It's not enough to try any new methodology. How do we know we're "getting there?" Any well-performing system is closed-loop with ample feedback for optimum performance and stability. Make sure you know how well you're doing. See Part V DIRFT.

© 1998 Global Brain, Inc.

Cornerstones of Q*R*PD

The Director of Processes at a software company in Silicon Valley spoke about the challenges of implementing a product development process in an entrepreneurial software environment. In his company, "process" was equated with bureaucracy and a stifling of creativity. The most important message they delivered to their teams was this: "We are not trying to make you *do* things exactly a certain way each time. We just want you to learn to *think* a certain way, then execute your projects in a manner consistent with that."

This guidebook provides many tools for accomplishing product development. The important underlying assumptions for your teams to understand are:

1. **Obsessive, intelligent risk and resource management:** We cannot escape risk. Total risk avoidance is a sure path to uncompetitive offerings. It can also slow down projects, if fear of making mistakes leads to laborious decision-making processes or analysis paralysis in setting product objectives. However, we must pay incredible attention to properly managing the risks we take on. We have to get an innovative, valuable product out. How do we do that in the midst of rapid technological change, fierce competition, and scarce resources? We learn to understand and obsessively manage our risks.

   And unfortunately, the pressures on our resources today are intense. With the competitive pressures from our markets and users, we never have enough resources to do what everyone wants. We must learn to intelligently manage our resources as well, choosing the most important projects for our resources to work on and allowing teams to focus on these critical projects.

2. **Time-based paradigm based on Late Cost per Week (LCPW) means business as usual is out the window:** "Forget" everything you knew about product development. No, don't forget it, just learn to think outside the box. Understand the true cost of being late: for every week past a particular ship date, how much profit will you lose? How much money will your development team continue to burn? There are new ways to look at your product development efforts, new methods you haven't tried, that can help you get your product out as quickly as possible. There is no one "right" way to do things. Think in the time-based paradigm, then get creative!

3. **Volunteered Commitment and Responsibility:** "You cannot compel enthusiasm and commitment from knowledge workers. Only those who choose to opt in—who voluntarily make a commitment to their colleagues—can create a winning company." [6].

4. **Measured Accountability based on meeting milestones:** "What gets measured gets done." This is nowhere more true than in the complex world of competitive product development. We can't get rid of all the chaos, we can just make sure we are making progress, the right progress, and fast enough to make our goals. Everyone on the team is accountable for contributing to that progress. We'll set frequent milestones to make sure we get there. The entire team will understand and make decisions based on the LCPW for the project, the loss in potential profit and the extra project expenditures for every week the project misses its completion date.

© 1998 Global Brain, Inc.

Cornerstones of Q*R*PD

- Obsessive, intelligent risk and resource management

- Time-based paradigm based on Late Cost per Week (LCPW) means business as usual is out the window

- Volunteered commitment and responsibility

- Measured accountability based on meeting milestones

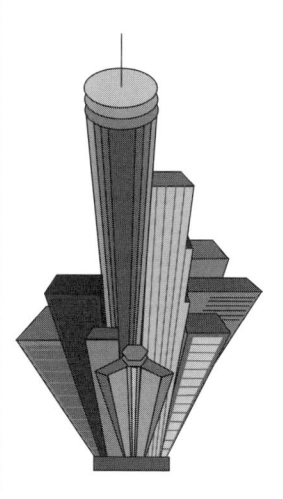

As you'll see as you learn the Q*R*PD methodology, these cornerstones will result in practices that are not necessarily intuitive—but are incredibly powerful principles for accelerating our mission.

1. **Do less sooner.** Focus on your company's *main* priorities. Understand each project's potential return to the company, and use your resources in a focused, conscious manner. Concentrate on getting a smaller number of projects to the market—more quickly than they'll get there if you dilute your resources across many projects.

2. **Slow down to speed up.** Spend more time up front to flush out risks, and issues that could become negative, project-delaying surprises later.

3. **Blow up early and often.** Don't be afraid to make mistakes. Just be sure to find your "mines" and mistakes as early as possible in the project.

4. **Spend now to save later.** The more eyes and tools you have looking at what might go wrong from every perspective, the greater the chance you'll arrive safely. Keep the time-based paradigm in mind: the more money you invest—in tools, risk mitigation, etc.—the more likely you'll be to reach completion as planned.

4 Q*R*PD "Oxymorons"

- Do Less Sooner

- Slow down to speed up

- Blow up early and often

- Spend now to save later

© 1998 Global Brain, Inc.

The QRPD Workshop

The QRPD course aims to help you meet the following objectives:

Objectives of the QRPD Workshop

- Make a paradigm shift to grasp the "Blitzkrieg" Product Development concept.

- Understand thoroughly the mission-oriented methodology that can accelerate projects by up to 50%: The 3 Secrets, 10 Commandments, 150 Techniques, and 13 Flow steps.

- Know which leadership skills are required to manage technical people and run projects in the fast-paced innovation environment of today and the future.

- Learn how to maintain or even improve overall product Quality despite accelerated schedules: 5 keys to Doing It Right the First Time (DIRFT).

- Analyze more and less successful case studies presented, and share experiences with fellow industry managers for mutual benefit.

- Return to your company with insights for how to actually start transforming your projects by implementing QRPD now.

The QRPD course bridges the gap between engineering and business management education. It teaches leadership skills for both effectively managing technical people *and* running technology projects for accelerated completion. It targets experienced developers and managers who want to grow with their companies and become star innovative engineers, Project Leaders, managers, and executives of the 21st century. In this guidebook you will learn how to successfully facilitate the Blitzkrie*g* development approach necessary to keep up with today's global market competition and racing pace of technology.

Patience for Speed

Now we've had an introduction to QRPD and indications of the kinds of results it can produce. It's critical to note, however, that there is no "silver bullet", no one easy solution that will make your product development issues disappear.

QRPD is a powerful methodology, one that team members and project leaders can "do themselves" in many ways. Gains and improvements will often be seen immediately. QRPD puts common sense into a common practice that's contagious and self-sustaining.

However, to reap the full benefits of QRPD inside a company, across all projects, will take time, commitment, and discipline:

"We feel strongly that the problem of shortening development cycles is complex and requires a full kit of tools."

—Reinertsen and Smith, in *Developing Products in Half the Time* [7]

© 1998 Global Brain, Inc.

QRPD is designed to provide a full kit of tools. But teams have to have the discipline to use as many as possible, to "stack the deck" in their favor in the game of odds that is product development. In the face of inevitable challenges, the team has to not abandon practices they know to be important, not bow to the expedient.

> "Simple solutions don't always work."
>
> —Reinertsen, in the article *The Mythology of Speed*

Every project will be different. No one solution or technique will be the key for a given project. Teams will have to truly understand the paradigm and cornerstones of QRPD, then determine how to best use them on their projects. The most important things to understand about a methodology are its key perspective and underlying principles. Then we can attack our product development in the correct spirit of the methodology, not blindly adhering to "the letter of the law."

> Beware of buzz words and acronyms: JIT, TQM, WCM, CE, QFD, DFM.

QRPD is not the latest management fad. The management approaches above, and QRPD, must be seen as pointing the way, and must be used intelligently and diligently. Beware the tendency to declare a new improvement program in name only! Don't treat any one initiative as the thing that will save the company.

> "Everybody has to go through this [QRPD] course. With the synergy it creates, 10 people who take it could do the work of 20 people. We met our demanding schedule, but could have been even further along on installing our satellite transceiver system in Brazil if everyone on the project team had taken the course a year ago."
>
> —Jim Barbera, Project Leader, Vitacom Corporation

Begin now to use QRPD to transform your company's product development engine into a JITPD organization. Turn your company into an information assembly line factory in this brave new world. As you "engage" at warp-speed, your new products will fly out the door, and your profits will soar as you zoom ahead to the future.

For a summary of how to use the combination of flexibility and structure embedded in the three secrets of QRPD, how to apply the principles and practices of the rest of the methodology, and how executives can participate in this transformation, see the next reading, "Executive Overview of QRPD Principles and Practices." For additional detailed information for day-to-day use of QRPD, read the rest of this book and use it as a reference as you execute your projects.

© 1998 Global Brain, Inc.

References

[1] Rushkoff, Douglas. 1994. *Cyberia: Life in the Trenches of Hyerspace*, Harper Collins.

[2] *Forbes ASAP, June* 2, 1997.

[3] Peters, Tom. 1987. *Thriving On Chaos: Handbook for a Management Revolution*, Harper and Row.

[4] Crosby, Phillip. 1980. *Quality is Free: The Art of Making Quality Certain*, Mentor.

[5] Drucker, Peter. "The New Society of Organizations," *Harvard Business Review*, September-October, 1992.

[6] *Fast Company*, Greatest Hits, vol. 1, pp. 94-95.

[7] Reinertsen, Donald and Smith, Preston. 1991. *Developing Products in Half the Time*. Van Nostrand Reinhold, p. 287.

Reading: Executive Overview of Q*R*PD® Principles and Practices

© 1998 Global Brain, Inc.

Executive Overview of QRPD Principles and Practices

Table of Contents

How Executives Can Help Speed Up Projects	45
The QRPD Blitzkrieg Paradigm	45
Putting Blitzkrieg into Action: Making Time-Based Project Decisions	47
The Objectives of Product Development	47
Understanding the Money Value of Time	48
Organizing Projects for Blitzkrieg Development	50
QRPD's Three secrets to JITPD success	50
QRPD "Concurrent Development" Flow	52
QRPD 10 Commandments and Toolkit of 150 Techniques	56
The QRPD "See-Saw Specifications and Scheduling" (SSSS) Process	57
Risk Assessment for Technological Innovations	58
Chicken Tests	58
5 Keys to DIRFT: Doing It Right The First Time	59
Implementing QRPD In An Organization	60
2 Phases and 4 Stages of QRPD "Absorption"	60
Recommended Full-Fledged Implementation Sequence	62
Critical Executive Roles and Responsibilities in Implementing QRPD	63

© 1998 Global Brain, Inc.

How Executives Can Help Speed Up Projects

This chapter should be useful for educating executives about QRPD and their role in its successful implementation. A basic understanding of QRPD will allow you to go beyond "lip service" to the support of more rapid development. You will be able to avoid accidentally impeding it and proactively take action to assist it.

The QRPD Blitzkrieg Paradigm

The term *Blitzkrieg,* meaning "lightning-fast war" was originally coined by Donald Reinertsen at McKinsey and Company in 1985 for use with product development:

> *Blitzkrieg Product Development:*
>
> Using new theories and methods (a paradigm shift), instead of an orthodox set of beliefs about how product development should be managed, that view projects from a time-based perspective and enable companies to cut product development times by one-half or more, compared to their standard approaches.

The use of the term Blitzkrieg became famous after a particular World War II battle. German General Heinz Guderian had a mission: to invade France. According to current military strategy and tactics, the French expected that it would take more than a week for Guderian to arrive, allowing them time to muster their defense. Unfortunately for the French, the general chose to change the ground-rules of the engagement. Instead of sending the infantry in ahead of his tanks as expected, he chose to send in his tank columns along with the infantry, saving precious time. Not only did Guderian change tactics, he added a new weapon to his arsenal—he used airplanes as an advance strike force and as air-cover for the advancing troops. In the end, he was able to invade France in only four days—less than half the expected time. The general won his battle using the Blitzkrieg approach.

Note that part of the general's time-saving approach was to send in tanks with the infantry instead of behind them. As a result, th*e general lost some tanks to the mines.* Essentially, he made an early investment to buy time. Overall, the battle ended in half the time, meaning less casualties overall, and most importantly, an overall, rapid victory.

In product development, we have to invest in our efforts to accelerate our development cycles. We may have to spend more money up front to ensure that we have adequate resources to get things done quickly enough. We have to be willing to make some mistakes—try out a new unknown technology, experiment with a new tool, try out prototype product ideas on a new customer base. That's acceptable, *as long as we make mistakes, and find those unknowns, early in the project!* As you can see in figure 1, *late* surprises and changes are what cost projects the most precious time and money and sometimes even threaten their completion. On average, the cost of recovering from mistakes increases by ten-fold for each subsequent stage in a project.

© 1998 Global Brain, Inc.

Figure 1. The Skyrocketing Cost of Development Changes
(major electronics product)

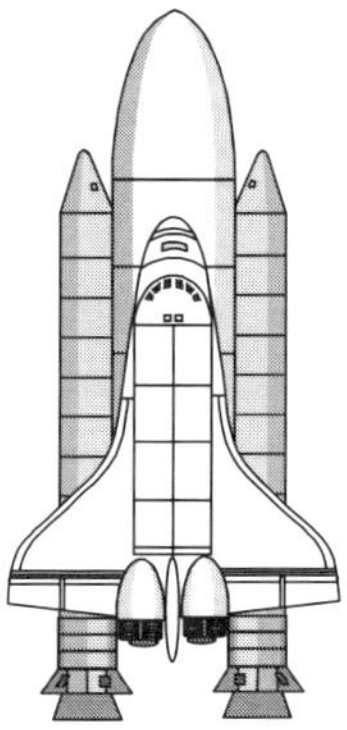

Time of Design Change	Cost
During final production	$10,000,000
During test production	$1,000,000
During process planning	$100,000
During design testing	$10,000
During design	$1,000

Source: "A Smarter Way to Manufacture; How Concurrent Engineering Can Reinvigorate American Industry," page 110, *Business Week*, April 30, 1990.

"Blow up" early and often.

Encourage mistakes in the early going, when they're still "cheap."

The benefits of the Blitzkrieg paradigm to product development are:

- months of extra sales life, revenue and profits
- increased market share
- higher profit margins, since the earliest entrant has the market to himself and can charge what the market will bear, and also has more time to cost-reduce the product as competition increases
- innovative company or department image
- customer loyalty
- an opportunity to develop more products

Putting Blitzkrieg into Action: Making Time-Based Project Decisions
The Objectives of Product Development

Figure 2 shows the four interrelated factors that must be optimized in making decisions about any project, in order to maximize profits for the company.

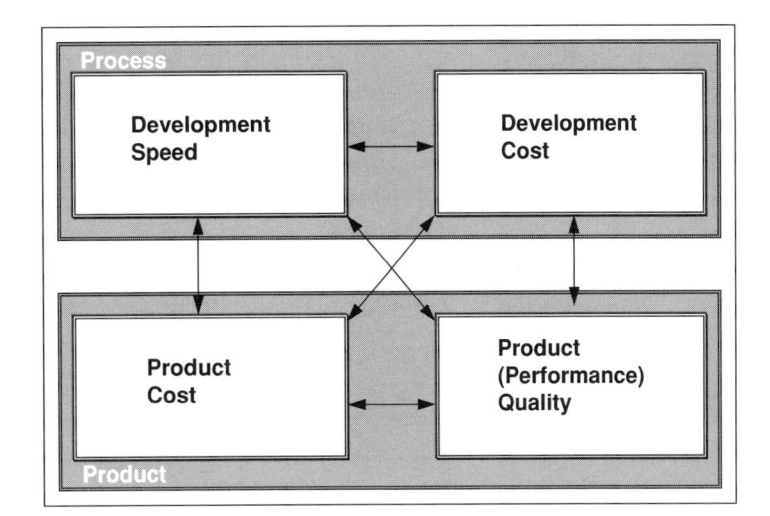

Figure 2. The Objectives of Product Development

[Diagram: Process box containing Development Speed and Development Cost; Product box containing Product Cost and Product (Performance) Quality; all four connected by bidirectional arrows]

Product performance (P): The features and functionality of the product and its quality, or "value as perceived by the customer."

Time-to-market (T): The amount of time the project can take to get the product out the door, to deliver the value to the customer as quickly as possible, and begin the economic benefits to the company.

Product cost (C): The unit cost of the product, as well as implications for life-cycle costs related to manufacture, installation, and maintenance.

Project cost (C): The amount of money the company will spend to bring the product to market, in salaries, equipment, and other non-recurring investments. Often referred to as the project budget.

We refer to these factors as the PTCC objectives of the project.

© 1998 Global Brain, Inc.

Understanding the Money Value of Time

A story from my days at Mountain Computer illustrates the power of this paradigm:

> In the mid-1980s a California company spent five years and $15 million to develop a printed circuit board that fit into a slot in a personal computer and provided 10 MB of hard disk storage to the then floppy-only systems. They developed their own electronics board, a thin hard disk that fit in one slot in these PCs, and the firmware. Mountain Computer decided to buy a commercially available 20 MB hard disk that took up one and a half slots and mate it to an off-the-shelf controller card. Nobody was using the 6 available slots anyway. By just writing some firmware, within only three months and for only $100,000, we were able to ship a product with double the capacity for the same price, ahead of the other company. It wasn't the sexiest technical product to be sure. But it made the company! We sold 50,000 cards in the next 6 months.
>
> The power of this kind of thinking has to pervade your teams. By making wiser tradeoffs, you can overcome seemingly insurmountable competition and constraints to deliver value to the customer and profits to your company.

How do we get to these wise trade-off decisions? Unfortunately, project decisions are all too often made unconsciously or without a full understanding of the ramifications. Perhaps a strong-willed team member insists on a pet feature that will result in a longer project schedule, regardless of whether this feature is really critical for the customer. Or a technical team insists on creating all the technology itself, regardless of the time and cost involved, rather than buying available technology outside the company. In either case, the resulting PTCC balance will not be optimum.

In contrast, Q*R*PD uses cost-benefit analyses to provide simple measures of monetary return of different product alternatives, with particular focus on understanding the basic costs and benefits of variations in time-to-market. The example below illustrates how to apply the concept.

In this example, a company's baseline assumption is that it can sell $100 million worth of product if it gets to market on the current schedule. As is often the case today, this is assumed to be a fixed market window. Thus, for every month the product is delayed to market, the company will lose $0.5 million in profit. Should the team delay the project by a month in order to add a feature that will get the company 1% more revenue over the life of the product? To figure it out, compare the costs of the delay in time with the benefit from the added performance and sales.

Figure 3. Simple Benefit-Cost Trade-off Analysis

Projected Product Sales in Market Window	$100 Million
Estimated profit lost per month delay	$1/2 Million
Incremental profit per additional sales dollars	15%

Should we add a feature that delays the project by two months, but adds one percent more revenue?

Figure 4. Simple Benefit-Cost Solution

COST		**BENEFIT**	
2 MONTH DELAY	$1,000,000	ADDITIONAL PROFIT	$150,000
($.5M/month x 2 months)		($100m X 1% X 15%)	
	───────		───────
	$1,000,000		$150,000

In the above example, the cost outweighs the benefit. The amount of profit we'd lose by delaying our entry to the market is not offset by the additional profit we'll realize from the added feature. We can still implement the feature later if we want that incremental profit. But we shouldn't delay getting an initial offering out the door.

What if the additional profit for the new feature were instead 10%? In that case, the benefit of adding the feature before initial shipment would be $1,500,000, compared to the cost of $1,000,000. The team may well choose to implement the feature in the first release of the product. In this example, the "break-even" point is around 6%: that new feature needs to result in at least 6% incremental profit before that additional profit begins to compensate for the cost of developing the feature.

What about the common objection that "it's impossible to have this kind of data" about exactly how much additional revenue a feature will cost or generate, or how long it will take to develop it. The fact is, the numbers don't need to be exact. Often a back-of-the-envelope comparison will lead you to an easy decision. An order-of-magnitude difference in cost vs. benefit may become evident. In general, it's possible to have only rudimentary financial data at the beginning of a project anyway; the simplicity of this cost-benefit analysis is in line with that fact. The numbers don't have to be exact to be meaningful.

The cost-benefit mindset can be extended to get a critical time-oriented project metric called Late Cost Per Week (LCPW), which we calculate to keep the importance of time foremost in our minds throughout the project. If we're late, how much will our profit be impacted? LCPW has two components:

- For every week we slip past our scheduled delivery date, how much product profit will we lose, by not being out in the market earning revenue?

- For every week past that delivery date, how much money is the project team still "burning" in salary and support costs?

Typical LCPW metrics range from $5000 to $250,000, numbers no company can afford to ignore. This number is a powerful tool for keeping team members focused on the benefits of speed.

© 1998 Global Brain, Inc.

Organizing Projects for Blitzkrieg Development
Q*R*PD's Three secrets to JITPD success

The concept of "just-in-time" (JIT) manufacturing provides a useful analogy for the kind of product development we want to achieve. JIT, an advanced manufacturing strategy widely practiced since the early 1980s, depends on getting the right materials to exactly the right place at the precise time required. Through a process of procurement, fabrication, assembly, and shipment, product assembly lines "add value to parts as rapidly as possible at each step, until they become a quality finished product ready to ship." JIT minimizes inventories and the costs associated with them.

Likewise, in a product development or information assembly line, teams start with inputs from the market, formulate product ideas, then proceed to add value to those ideas as they craft them into fully-defined products. To achieve just-in-time product development (JITPD), we have to improve the quality and timeliness of input materials at each step; eliminate variation and waste in the outputs of each step of our development work; and shorten the overall response time.

Q*R*PD calls for us to achieve efficiency, effectiveness, and quality in our product development efforts. The three secrets below are the keys. There's no rocket science behind these keys, and yet a majority of companies do not follow them.

Figure 5. The 3 Secrets to Successful Just-in-Time Product Development

1. Total company commitment to a concrete, well-defined *Product Vision*.

2. Obsessed Project Leader and a strong, synergistic, cross-functional core team on a *Mission* to "make it happen" and meet milestones.

3. Follow a new product development *Flow Process*, including testing working prototypes early on.

Success using Q*R*PD obviously depends on using many more techniques than just these three keys. Yet many organizations can realize increased JITPD by more carefully implementing the three secrets.

Secret #1, Product Vision: "The #1 reason for project schedule slippage is changing product definitions." [1] And yet, we don't have much time to convert information that we gather into each JITPD effort, or it becomes obsolete. The only remedy then is for the company to agree on a limited set of product objectives that everyone is committed to. Members participate in the process, then commit *whole-heartedly* and *knowingly* to a Vision and list of milestones. (See Commandment #1 in Part II Techniques, and Part IV Flow.)

Secret #2, Mission: Second, the company assigns an obsessed Project Leader and a strong cross-functional core team and launches them on a *Mission* to "make it happen" and meet the agreed-upon milestones. The choice of the right Project Leader is the most crucial decision upper management makes in managing accelerated product development. [3] Clearly, we want to select capable, experienced team members; and we need full cross-functional representation to ensure that our information assembly line will function optimally throughout the product development effort. Together the team and the Project Leader create and commit to a set of "do-or-die" milestones that embody the team's mission and create a sense of urgency.

Secret #3, Flow Process: And third, the team will follow a new product development *Flow Process*, including testing working prototypes early on. If we think of product development as an information assembly line, we clearly need plenty of in-line checks and inspections. This results in perceiving innovation as a *process*. As part of the process we test a working prototype early on, to verify the validity of our information before we spend too much money adding value to it. This prototype testing includes a "chicken tests," reality tests that verify the feasibility of the critical innovations and the overall design. (See more discussion later in this reading).

The Carnegie Mellon Software Engineering Institute developed the Capability Maturity Model to describe the different levels of process maturity observed in the software development process. These levels apply to many types of processes, including new product development.

Figure 6. Technology Process Maturity Levels

Maturity Level	Characterization
1. Initial	Ad-Hoc/chaotic
2. Repeatable	Intuitive, depends on individuals
3. Defined	Qualitative, independent of individuals
4. Managed	Quantitative, measured
5. Optimizing	Improvement fed back continuously

Source: Carnegie Mellon Software Engineering Institute

The majority of manufacturing organizations operate between levels four and five; they have streamlined production to a quantitative, managed, and continuously improving system. They know the percentage yields of defect-free products off the manufacturing line. They know how many products get returned. They understand their labor and materials costs and how to adjust their resources and processes to affect those costs.

Unfortunately, an educated guess predicts that over half of development efforts utilize levels one or two, about a quarter level three, and maybe 10% levels four and five. Most product development occurs in an ad-hoc manner that depends on certain key individuals. Even successfully completed projects seldom turn in repeat performances within the same company.

© 1998 Global Brain, Inc.

Q*R*PD "Concurrent Development" Flow

A Q*R*PD project is broken down into 4 concurrent-development-oriented phases to most effectively and efficiently accomplish our objectives. The concurrent development model incorporates the 13 steps of the Q*R*PD Flow process, whose overall goal is *quality of execution without sacrificing overall speed.* We want to focus on completeness, on quality at each step of the way, and especially on the important project decisions in the front end. Our goal is to find mistakes early, and even kill the project if appropriate.

Key points about the concurrent development model (see figure 7):

- No matter how your particular company is organized into departments, four functions" must be involved in concurrent development to make it thorough and successful: 1) Marketing, Management, and Planning; 2) Development; 3) Quality; and 4) Operations.

- The goal of the concurrent model is to avoid the "silo" effect prevalent in old-style development, where different functional groups do their piece of product development *sequentially*, receiving the output from the previous group "over the wall." That old approach has high probability for long timelines, misunderstandings, and rework. It is not an efficient information assembly line. Different functional groups must instead work in parallel as much as possible.

- Work within phases is overlapped as much as possible. What's the minimum amount someone needs from another team member to get their work going? The concept of Flow encourages us to look for ways to overlap work, pass off draft documents, and so forth, to allow others to get on with their own work.

- The phase boundaries are kept to a minimum to avoid bureaucracy, but they are important points for sanity checking synchronization among cross-functional groups and overall progress before proceeding with the next level of project work.

    One important note: These phase boundaries can be somewhat "fuzzy." In some companies, the end of a phase is a "gate," and no group or person can proceed through the gate even a small amount until everyone is ready to do so. Project work is seldom exactly aligned so perfectly. For example, a subsystem may be ready for approval testing slightly ahead of another subsystem, and there's definite time value to letting the test group have the first subsystem as quickly as possible. That subsystem is effectively starting phase III Approval sooner than the other. Such a fuzzy phase boundary is fine, as long as the team makes an intelligent and conscious decision to let this happen. So teams can use these phase boundaries in an intelligent way, accomplishing the appropriate sanity checks without unnecessarily halting or delaying anyone's work.

- The linear nature of the concurrent development diagram does *not* mean that Q*R*PD is limited to "waterfall" development. In a waterfall approach, a product progresses relatively straightforwardly from specification to design to prototyping to full testing and production, with little feedback, iterative work, or "looping" to previous phases. In other models, the product or pieces of the product may be developed more iteratively, with repeated cycles of design, prototyping, testing, and refinement before partial or full delivery to a customer. Q*R*PD phases can be used in this iterative manner.

© 1998 Global Brain, Inc.

Figure 7. QRPD 4 Phases and Functions of Concurrent Development

←——————————— Total Time-to-Market ———————————→

Company Function	Phase I: Kick-off	Phase II: Development	Phase III: Approval	Phase IV: Delivery
Planning and Marketing, Sales	1. Proposal, Business case 2. **New Project Evaluation request (NPER)** 3. Select team 4. Product Vision and See-saw Specifications and Schedules (including PDRs, milestones) 5. Announce internally	Sales forecast and pricing Begin marketing launch preparation	Introduction————> Sales support and launch materials	Selling————> Plan next cycle
Engineering or Development	Rough technical evaluation 4. Conceptualize solution (Architecture, technology, time & budget estimates)	6. **Detailed and Critical Design Reviews** 7. Final Design Review 8. Development Pre-releases *Iterative refinement...*	Fix bugs————> Minor redesign (tweaks) → 10. Release for Pilot	————> Final release (for production) Maintenance————>
Testing and Quality	Input to specs, plans, schedule, costs	Detailed test cases	9. Internal testing (Alpha) 11. External testing (Beta and Regulatory)	Customer feedback, quality analysis
Operations, Support	Input to specs, plans, schedule, costs.	Detailed planning and long-lead procurement.	Purchasing, manufacturing, customer support preparation	12. Pilot production/delivery 13. **Release to Full Production/delivery**

←——— *Customers, vendors involved throughout. Shading indicates an executive sign-off point* ———→

© 1998 Global Brain, Inc.

Executives should be involved at key decision points during the Flow process. These points provide a chance for sanity checking and go/no-go decisions. These decision points are:

    A. *Flow Step 2, approval of the New Project Evaluation Request.* Development is chartered to perform a full phase I investigation for this new product idea.

    B. *Flow Step 5, approval of the New Project Kick-off Announcement.* The project is now "real" and fully funded. PTCC objectives have been determined and agreed to, and the project team can proceed with development.

    C. *Flow Step 6, approval of the Critical Design Review results.* The system chicken test has passed, and all project technological risks have been mitigated. The project can proceed to completion.

    D. *Flow Step 13, approval of release to production and customer delivery.* The product can be shipped unrestricted to customers and produced in volume.

See table 1 for an overview of the phases and steps.

Table 1. The 13 Steps of New Product Development Flow

Phase	Objective
I. Kickoff 1) **New Project/Product Proposal (NPP)** 2) **New Project Evaluation Request (NPER)** 3) **Select Project Leader, Core team** 4) **Product Vision and See-Saw Specifications and Schedules process** (includes high-level design work, preliminary design review, schedule and milestones) 5) **New Project Kickoff Announcement,** internal	What is the new product (or service or process) idea? Is it worth pursuing further? If so, appoint a Project Leader and core team to investigate the idea further. What are the possible alternatives for implementing this product? Features, schedule, costs. Can we achieve acceptable return on a product development investment? If so, select the alternative, finish planning the project, get the whole team in place, and officially launch the project.
II. Development 6) **DDR and CDR** (Detailed design review meetings; Chicken tests and critical design review meetings) 7) **FDR** (Development testing and Final design review meetings) 8) **Development pre-releases**	Finish designing the product or service; review the design; build prototypes; and test it (development). Does it work, and does it meet requirements and its purpose? Release early versions of the product to other cross-functional groups for their work.
III. Approval 9) **Internal Approval** (Alpha testing and reviews) 10) **Development Release for Pilot** 11) **External Approval** (Beta and Regulatory Testing and reviews)	Let independent groups, both internal and external to the company, including customers, test the product. Does it work? Does it fulfill its purpose, meet its Vision and requirements? Release the product for pilot deliveries and pilot production.
IV. Delivery 12) **Pilot production/delivery** 13) **Release to Full production/delivery**	Do limited production and delivery to customers to test processes and readiness. Then release the product, produce it in volume, and deliver it to everyone.

© 1998 Global Brain, Inc.

QRPD 10 Commandments and Toolkit of 150 Techniques

Theory is useless without a reliable, effective way to make it a day-to-day tool. Teams need techniques for accomplishing the three secrets of QRPD. The 10 Commandments of QRPD provide that substance, the key to using the methodology on a daily basis. They provide detailed guidance for your organizational and product decisions. Everyone on the team can influence their use.

Vision	1.	**FOCUS**	**Focus** on a clear, limited, and on-target Vision.
Mission	2.	**TEAM/LEADER**	Assemble the right **team** and **leader(s)**.
	3.	**CROSS-FUNCTIONAL**	Initiate early **cross-functional** cooperation.
	4.	**SYNERGY**	Create a **synergistic**, mission-oriented, productive environment.
	5.	**REWARD**	**Reward** all participants commensurably.
Flow	6.	**INNOVATE**	Use **innovative**, parallel, iterative design strategies.
	7.	**INVEST**	**Invest** money to buy time and tools and minimize risk.
	8.	**PROTOTYPE**	**Prototype,** and test key design concepts early.
	9.	**FLOW**	Follow the **Flow** process to meet milestones, manage risk, and ensure quality.
	10.	**FEEDBACK**	Get early **feedback** and nail defects quickly.

The 150 techniques associated with these commandments give your teams a checklist for ensuring that they have the greatest chance to abide by these commandments and succeed on any project. The more of these techniques a team follows, the greater their odds of success.

The techniques checklists can be used as a planning tool during phase I: have we planned to use all the techniques we should? They can be used as a sanity-check during the project: especially if we think we may be off-track, what techniques have we followed and not followed? And finally, at the end of the project, the techniques checklists can be used as part of a "lessons learned" analysis: What were our project problems? What techniques did we not use, that could have prevented those problems? How do we use them on the next project?

The Q*R*PD Product Vision and "See-Saw Specifications and Scheduling" (SSSS) Process

The Product Vision is the key document for carrying out secret #1: Total company commitment to a concrete, well-defined vision. It is a one or two-page contract capturing what the team has committed to delivering to the company and customer.

Figure 8. See-Saw Specifications and Scheduling (SSSS)

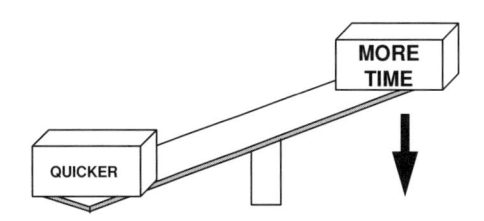

Marketing and Management

"We need all these features within X months or else!"

Technical Team

"What's-the-earliest-date-by which-we-can't-prove-we-won't-be finished?"

Kidder, *Soul of a New Machine*, p. 113 [4]

Goal of the Negotiation Process:

Find an optimal balance that everyone can live with and sign-up to:
a Product Vision (P), one Schedule with a set of Key Milestones (T),
product cost (C), and project costs (C).

During the SSSS process, the team considers various alternatives for achieving a balance of the four PTCC product development objectives, and negotiates trade-offs to achieve a balance that is best for the customer and the company. The Vision is created as an aligning document to capture the team's decisions, and then used throughout the project to keep the team focused on the concrete, limited goals.

Figure 9. Contents of the Product Vision

1. Target customers and how you are meeting their needs (problem, solutions, benefits)

2. Key, measurable factors customers will use to judge quality—the value of the product

3. Key technology and key features

4. Crucial product factors *as applicable* (use own list). I.e., safety, distribution, and the physical environment in which the product will be used.

5. Relevant financial numbers (Sales units, price, cost, market window, late cost per week, development cost)

© 1998 Global Brain, Inc.

Risk Assessment for Technological Innovations

As part of the SSSS process, the team must categorize the technological innovations inherent in their design alternatives. The team must ensure that they don't bite off too much in one project; and they must be prepared to test these risky areas as early as possible in the project. The higher the risk level, the more iterations it will typically take to wring out design issues and prove out the new technology or approach. The team can use this assessment to ensure that they plan appropriate testing and design iterations.

Table 2. Categorizing Innovations by Risk Level

RISK LEVEL	AMOUNT OF UNKNOWN	COST TO RECOVER
1. FLIRTING WITH DISASTER	Believed to have never been done by anyone, anywhere in the world!	INFINITE?
2. VERY MAJOR	Done by somebody, somewhere, once	VERY HIGH
3. MAJOR	Done elsewhere a few times, but never yet in-house	HIGH
4. MEDIUM	Done commonly or by people who now are in-house (but weren't at the time)	MEDIUM
5. MINOR	Done often, including in-house	LOW

Chicken Tests

> **What is a *chicken test*?** A reality test on a prototype that verifies the feasibility of the system, the critical parts, and the major innovations, of the design. Chicken tests should be performed within the first 25-50% of the overall schedule.

See Commandment #8 in the Techniques section for a description of how chicken testing got its name. Chicken tests on QRPD projects are done at two levels:

1) **Innovations chicken tests:** a test of each individual technological innovation that is a major or higher risk.

2) **System chicken test:** *the* critical risk mitigation event in the project, the point at which the fundamental overall design has been proven to hang together. This typically occurs early in the integration testing timeframe in phase II; it should occur no later than the 50% point of the project. Or by definition, history tells us that once you complete the system chicken test, you're really at the 50% point in your project, no matter where you think you are.

5 Keys to DIRFT: Doing It Right the First Time

The simple yet immensely effective individual and team management techniques of Q*R*PD help many high-tech companies bring successful products to market on time, the *first* time. The Q*R*PD commandments and techniques are geared to resolving risks as early as possible and investing money to speed up schedules, thereby eliminating standard sources of project delays.

The 5 Keys to DIRFT form the feedback loop for Q*R*PD, a standard part of any quality management approach. By monitoring these feedback keys during our project, we can be sure that we're really applying Q*R*PD sufficiently to achieve our objectives.

Table 3.   5 Keys to DIRFT

1.	**COMMITTED:**	Is everyone consistently committed, whole-heartedly and knowingly, to a limited, worthwhile Vision?
2.	**SENSE OF MISSION:**	Does everyone feels the sense of purpose and works urgently on a "put a man on the moon" Mission?
3.	**FOLLOW FLOW:**	Is everyone following and continuously improving a written Flow process?
4.	**TEST ENOUGH:**	Are we testing, testing, testing? Early, throughout, thoroughly?
5.	**PLUNGE:**	Are we plunging through the product development funnel, and micromanaging the last 10% to get it out?

See Part V DIRFT for tools to put this feedback loop into practice every day.

© 1998 Global Brain, Inc.

Implementing QRPD In An Organization

2 Phases and 4 Stages of QRPD "Absorption"

Product development improvements generally happen in two phases: *introduction* of a new process and management practices, and *absorption* of these practices into an organization. Overall, the stages within this process are marked by the state of the company's awareness of its issues, and the level of maturity in dealing with them and actually putting the process to work. The figure below shows the typical progression of a company through these stages and phases. The stages are explained on the following page.

Figure 10. The Absorption Curve

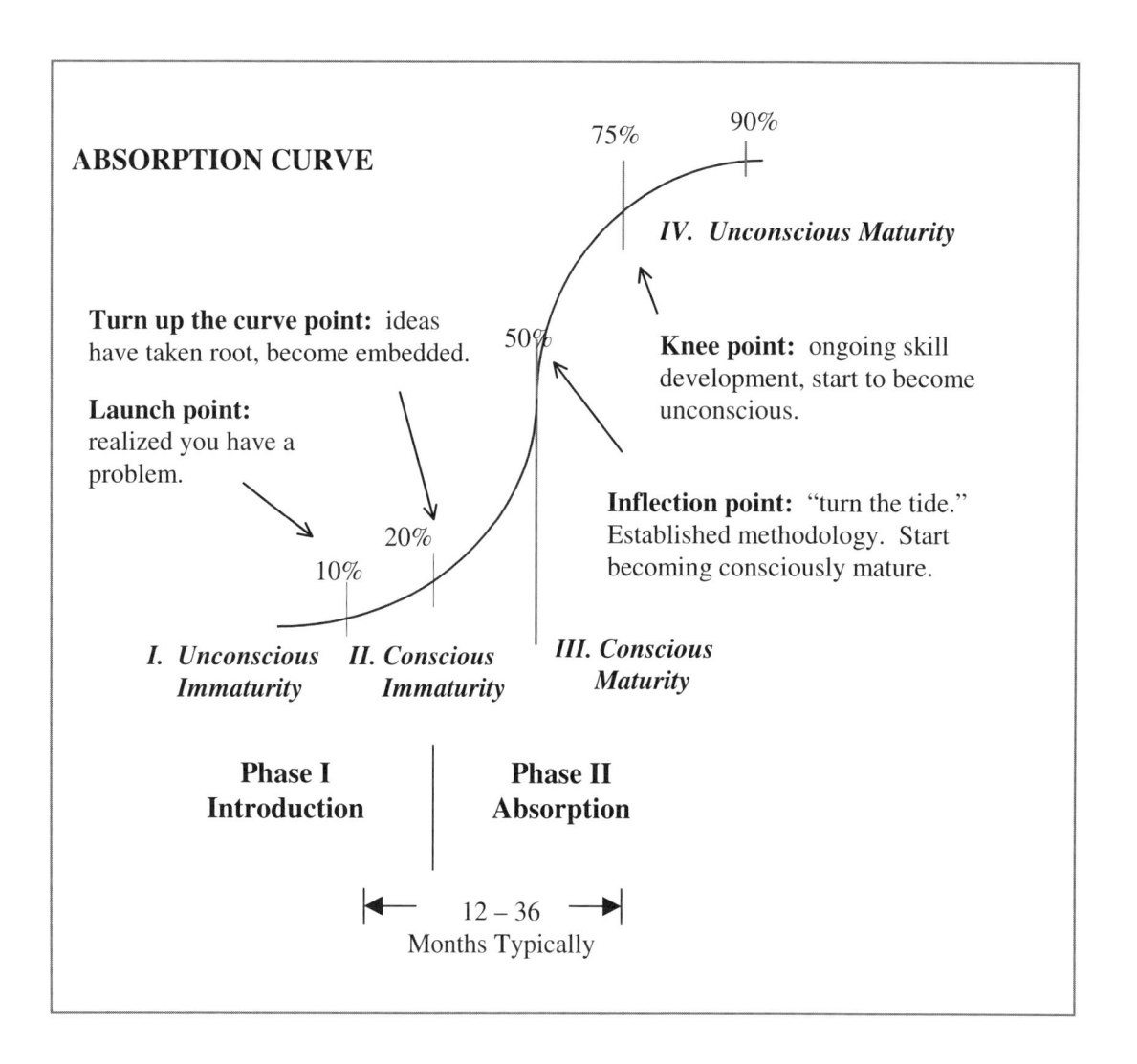

ABSORPTION CURVE

Turn up the curve point: ideas have taken root, become embedded.

Launch point: realized you have a problem.

Knee point: ongoing skill development, start to become unconscious.

Inflection point: "turn the tide." Established methodology. Start becoming consciously mature.

IV. Unconscious Maturity — 75%, 90%
III. Conscious Maturity — 50%
II. Conscious Immaturity — 20%
I. Unconscious Immaturity — 10%

Phase I: Introduction
Phase II: Absorption

12 – 36 Months Typically

© 1998 Global Brain, Inc.

I. Unconscious immaturity

Before introduction begins, an organization is in a state of "unconscious immaturity". The company doesn't really even know it has a problem!

II. Conscious immaturity

"Launch" point: A shift to a state of "conscious immaturity" occurs at around the 10% point, the "launch point", when the company realizes that it needs to improve its product development performance.

"Turn up the curve" point: At around 20%, a set of initial new principles for product development have taken root in the company culture. Now the company can make real progress on implementing these principles on projects. It has an established methodology, and has started to become consciously mature. The Introduction phase is complete.

III. Conscious maturity

"Inflection" point: This marks the point of "turning the tide." The absorption phase is now well underway. An initial degree of "conscious maturity" has been achieved: a defined process exists, one or more teams have had some success using it, and the organization in general agrees that the progress to-date is valid and important Now we must achieve "absorption" into the rest of the company.

"Knee" point: At this point, efforts now center on ongoing skill development of all team members, to make the changes truly sustainable and repeatable across projects. The organization starts to become unconsciously mature.

IV. Unconscious maturity

This last phase is achieved only after the fundamental principles behind the new process have been absorbed into the organization, are understood by the individuals contributing to the projects, have been used successfully by many teams, and are a natural part of daily practice throughout the company. It's almost as routine as brushing your teeth.

Companies often make admirable efforts to put in place a basically sound process framework, and thus complete a large portion of the introduction process. Often the main tasks remaining in the introduction phase are to (1) correct several basic process/methodology deficiencies that are critical to consistent time-to-market performance, and (2) ensure that executives understand and support the benefits of a process like Q*R*PD and the importance of the absorption phase.

The remaining absorption challenge then becomes to tune the process and adjust attitudes, skill levels, and management practices to (1) achieve consistent product development results throughout the company and over time, and (2) achieve not only predictable product development, but rapid product development.

Recommended Full-Fledged Implementation Sequence

A typical sequence of events for *launching* a QRPD implementation is:

- Someone recognizes a need for improvement of a company's development efforts.
- Someone champions QRPD and initiates in-house adoption.

To implement QRPD in the organization, we recommend the following steps:

Figure 11. Recommended Full-Fledged Implementation Sequence

1. Determine what "outside assistance" you will use: External consultants, internal experts, to gain an outside perspective and an objective assessment of the changes needed.

2. Define an implementation project and follow the QRPD methodology for it.

3. Educate top management, Project Leaders, and key personnel to affect a paradigm shift.

4. Assess the company's current product development methods and results against QRPD, to find key areas to improve upon.

5. Get top management commitment to facilitate and support a first attempt. They should:

    * Provide plenty of resources.
    * Contribute time and attention (not control).
    * Make major decisions only.
    * Establish MBO linked to performance appraisal process.
    * "Let the team run the team" (Reinertsen, p. 262)

6. Select the right pilot project (use QRPD from day 1 of this project).

7. Select the right (doubly "obsessed," i.e., about the project and the new process) Project Leader.

8. Train the whole team on QRPD and teach them new skills.

9. Learn from first attempts and improve and repeat this process on other projects.

10. Create a company guidebook/cookbook to practice QRPD consistently.

© 1998 Global Brain, Inc.

Critical Executive Roles and Responsibilities in Implementing QRPD

Executive management buy-in and ongoing support is critical to successfully absorption of QRPD in an organization.

Figure 12. Responsibilities of Executives During QRPD Implementation

1. Support—don't undermine—key concepts of QRPD. Use the terms, help establish the process and tools in the company's culture, and continue to communicate the value executive management sees in the methodology.
2. Support the team as they attempt to understand the business and financial aspects of project decisions.
3. Support the importance of Project Leader role. Help enforce the discipline to select Project Leaders judiciously, then support their authority in carrying out their role.
4. Reward teams and individuals. Ensure the company's performance appraisal and review structure rewards individuals for participating on project teams and meeting project goals.

Figure 13. General Roles of Executives and Management in QRPD Projects

General

Executives: (VPs)

1. Serve as product champion (see the glossary).
2. Participate in design reviews and project trade-off decisions.
3. Approve key project decision points.

Functional Directors and Managers:

1. Provide oversight of your technical area.
    * Ensure adherence to Commandment #6, sound and parallel design practices.
    * Ensure that good reviews of technical test data are done.
2. Participate in and ensure sound resource planning, technology roadmap planning, etc. (See the reading in Flow, "QRPD Phase I Project Evaluation and Project Portfolio Management.")

© 1998 Global Brain, Inc.

Figure 14. Responsibilities of Executives and Management by Project Phase

Phase I:

1. Approve New Product Proposals.
2. Assign one engineering person and one marketing person to do early investigation.
3. Provide information and ideas.
4. Approve project prioritization.
5. Minimize "fuzzy front end" issues to jump-start the project. Supply development and marketing person with any baseline scope boundaries (a "project box" or "marching orders").
6. Sign off the NPER (New Project Evaluation Request) approving (or not) the continuation of phase I.
7. Select appropriate Project Leader and product champion and allocate resources for completing a proper phase I.
8. Provide information and ideas, including input to the Product Vision.
9. Allocate resources appropriately. Don't under-staff the team.
10. Assist with "see-saw" negotiations.
11. Participate in Preliminary Design Reviews (PDR) and project trade-off decisions.
12. Kill the project if necessary.
13. Sign New Project Kickoff Authorization to approve the project.

Phases II-IV:

1. Approve completion of major milestones and design reviews and decision points as appropriate.
2. Monitor major milestones; make sure you agree the team is really on target.
3. Witness major chicken test demonstrations and congratulate team.
4. Approve project re-prioritization.
5. Kill the project?
6. Approve Vision or milestone changes.
7. Give rewards!

As you can see in the above checklists, executives have a golden opportunity to make concrete, positive contributions to the success of their teams' product development efforts. We encourage you to do everything in your power to help your teams achieve their ambitious bottom-line-oriented goals. It's up to you to help "make it so."

© 1998 Global Brain, Inc.

References:

[1] Patterson, Marvin. November 1992. *Accelerating Innovation.* Van Nostrand Reinhold. In a book endorsed by John Young, CEO of Hewlett Packard, and several other major CEO's, the author explains the innovation cycle time process. Particularly interesting use of metaphors between manufacturing and new product development processes.

[2] Patterson, *Accelerating Innovation*, p. 115.

[3] Reinertsen and Smith, 1991. *Developing Products in Half the Time, p. 112.* Van Nostrand Reinhold. An excellent and authoritative book on the subject; a precursor of Quality *Rapid* Product Development.

[4] Kidder, Tracy, 1981. *The Soul of a New Machine.* P. 113. Avon Books. Enjoyable reading about how one remarkable leader, Tom West, made it happen at Data General, a minicomputer company. Slightly outdated.

© 1998 Global Brain, Inc.

PART I. BLITZKRIEG

Blitzkrieg ("Lightning-Fast-War") Product Development

DEFINITION

> Using new theories and methods (a paradigm shift), instead of an orthodox set of beliefs about how product development should be managed, that view projects from a time-based perspective and enable companies to cut product development times by one-half or more, compared to their standard approaches.

Source: World War II German General Heinz Guderian's tank columns crossing into France in 4 days instead of the 9 days the French had expected based on standard tactics. *Blitzkrieg,* meaning "lightning-fast war" was originally coined by Donald Reinertsen at McKinsey and Company in 1985 for use in Product Development when he published an article called "Cut Development Times in Half."

BENEFITS

1. "X" months extra sales life, revenue and profits
2. Customer loyalty
3. Increased market share
4. Higher profit margins
   (beginning [higher prices] and end [manufacturing cost])
5. Innovative company image
6. Opportunity to develop more products

© 1998 Global Brain, Inc.

The Four Product Development Objectives: "PTCC"

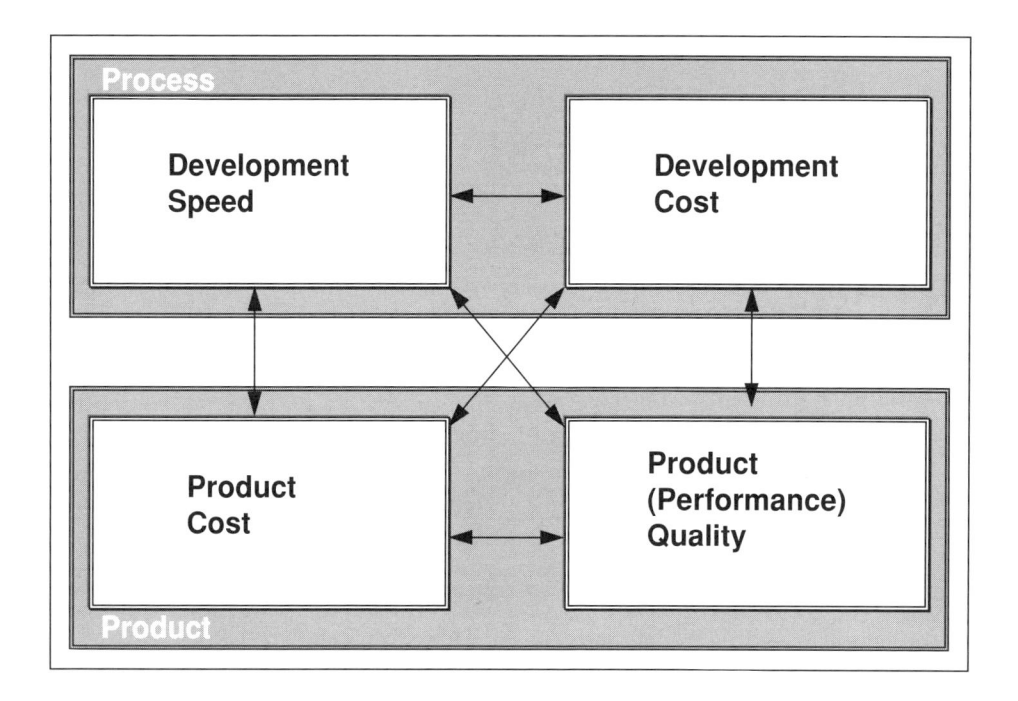

```
Process
  ┌─────────────────┐      ┌─────────────────┐
  │  Development    │ ←──→ │  Development    │
  │     Speed       │      │     Cost        │
  └─────────────────┘      └─────────────────┘

  ┌─────────────────┐      ┌─────────────────┐
  │    Product      │ ←──→ │    Product      │
  │     Cost        │      │  (Performance)  │
  │                 │      │    Quality      │
  └─────────────────┘      └─────────────────┘
Product
```

Product performance (P): The features and functionality of the product and its quality, or "value as perceived by the customer."

Time-to-market (T): The amount of time the project can take to get the product out the door, to deliver the value to the customer as quickly as possible, and begin the economic benefits to the company.

Product cost (C): The unit cost of the product, as well as implications for life-cycle costs related to manufacture, installation, and maintenance.

Project cost (C): The amount of money the company will spend to bring the product to market, in salaries, equipment, and other non-recurring investments. Often referred to as the project budget.

These four interrelated factors must be optimized in making decisions about any project, in order to maximize profits for the company. The following pages illustrate the PTCC trade-offs teams must make to achieve a suitable balance of these objectives.

Simple Benefit-Cost Trade-Off Analysis

A company's baseline assumption is that it can sell $100 million worth of product if it gets to market on the current schedule. As is often the case today, this is assumed to be a fixed market window. Thus, for every month the product is delayed to market, the company will lose $0.5 million in profit. Should the team delay the project by a month in order to add a feature that will get the company 1% more revenue over the life of the product?

To figure it out, compare the costs of the delay in time with the benefit from the added performance and sales.

Projected Product Sales in Market Window	$100 MILLION
Estimated Profit Lost per Month Delay	$1/2 MILLION
Incremental Profit per Additional Sales $$	15%

Should we add a feature that delays the project by two months, but adds one percent more revenue?

(Solutions in Appendix A.)

© 1998 Global Brain, Inc.

Benefit-Cost Trade-off Case Study: "Emebo" Cost Reduction

A company is developing a next generation version of its Emebo product line that uses molecular beam epitaxy (MBE) to deposit gallium arsenide on certain kinds of semiconductor wafers. This piece of equipment carries a price tag of about $500,000 each and the company expects to sell 50 over the next 4 years, at an average profit of 20% before tax. Since the product's market window of opportunity is about 4 years, every month delay may cost the company about $1/50^{th}$ of the life time sales of the product, i.e. one machine. The project leader estimates it will take 12 months to complete the development using QRPD, at a burn rate of $50k per month of R&D investment.

One of the brilliant engineers has come up with a way to save $5000 per unit off the material cost of the product (estimated to be $250,000 total). The engineering and testing required to substitute one metal for another in the ultra-high vacuum chamber will cost $20,000 of engineering labor, and delay the project by one month. It should also be noted that this procedure has only been tried by one other company in the world, but the engineer remains confident that it will work.

1. **Should this cost reduction be implemented?**
   If so, what's the additional net profit?

2. **How about if the cost reduction results in a three month delay?**

(Solutions in Appendix A.)

Benefit-Cost Trade-off:
"Faxit" Board Cost Reduction

A company is designing a new generation of a fax board that they expect will squeeze into a window of 10 months, in a hotly competitive market. The sales department has promised that in exchange for an on-time project completion they will deliver about $10 million in revenue by selling 10,000 boards per month at an average price of $100 each. The estimated material cost of each board rests in the neighborhood of $67, but the net profit to the company for each board sold is only $10. Engineering has committed to finishing the project in 6 months, and only spending $50,000 per month doing it. On average, an engineer costs the company about $5000 per month.

1. Should we design a gate-array chip to replace 5 other components on the board, if it saves $5 per board, but costs $100,000 in non-recurring engineering costs that must be paid to the gate-array vendor?

2. How about if doing this requires an additional engineer's time for the duration of the project, and delays product introduction by 1 month, in addition to the vendor's charge?

(Solutions in Appendix A.)

When To Emphasize Development Speed
Economic Calculation Approach

One method for systematically comparing trade-off possibilities is shown below.

1. Construct a base-case program profit and loss statement and balance sheet.

2. Calculate cumulative profits over the expected life of the product.

3. Define probable "what if" scenarios by making six possible trade-offs among the four product development objectives:

Development speed	<-->	Development cost
Development speed	<-->	Product cost
Development speed	<-->	Product performance
Development cost	<-->	Product performance
Development cost	<-->	Product cost
Product cost	<-->	Product performance

4. Recalculate pro-formas and cumulative profits for each "what if" scenario.

5. Weigh the financial benefit versus the cost to make decisions based on net profit, including whether development speed should be the most important development objective.

Source: *Developing Products in Half the Time*, Reinertsen and Smith, Van Nostrand, 1991, chapter 2.

Project LCPW and ROI Calculation

The cost-benefit analyses on the previous pages lead to a critical metric that will keep the importance of time foremost in the team's minds throughout the project. Each team must calculate the Late Cost Per Week (LCPW) metric for their project: If the project is late or delayed for added features, how much will the company's overall profit be impacted? LCPW keeps the team focused on the importance of time, keeps them focused on making their project milestones, and helps them resist the temptation to allow late changes that will delay project completion. Further, it gives them a tool for making fast and wise Blitzkrieg decisions during the project: where should they invest money to save time?

LCPW = Lost profit + development burn rate

- For every week we slip past our scheduled delivery date, how much product profit will we lose by not being out in the market earning revenue?

- For every week past that delivery date, how much money is the project team still "burning" in salary and support costs?

Further, to make the proper project decisions to balance performance, time, and costs, the team must also assess the potential profitability of the project. What is the potential revenue or savings from the product or service, compared to the development investment required? Is this project economically justified? Does one alternative yield a better return than others?

$$\text{ROI} = \frac{\text{Profit (or cost savings) to be gained}}{\text{Development cost}}$$

Organizations typically aim for an ROI of 3 to 10.

NOTE: These calculations ignore the time value of money, which often is fine for these simple assessments. More complex methods such as Net Present Value (NPV) can also be used.

ROI and LCPW are assessed by the team during the phase I See-Saw Specifications and Schedules process (Flow step 4). These metrics help them make the best decisions for balancing the four product development factors (performance, time-to-market, product cost and project cost—PTCC) and ultimately obtain the desired overall economic benefit from the project. See the Flow section for how these metrics fit into the SSSS process.

Since companies rarely, if ever, work on one project at a time, these numbers also play a role in an organization's project portfolio and resource management decisions. Which projects should get funded, based on potential economic value, the company's overall business strategy, and resource constraints? All these decisions need ROI, LCPW, and PTCC data from the phase I work of the various projects being considered. See the reading "QRPD Phase I Project Evaluation and Project Portfolio Management" in the Flow section.

© 1998 Global Brain, Inc.

The New Product Development Funnel

The metaphor of a funnel is sometimes used to represent a company's product development efforts. Information, ideas, and specifications for products enter the top of the funnel, but only some ideas can make it through the funnel to become actual products. Those ideas that make it should not encounter bottlenecks—they need to make it through the funnel as quickly as possible

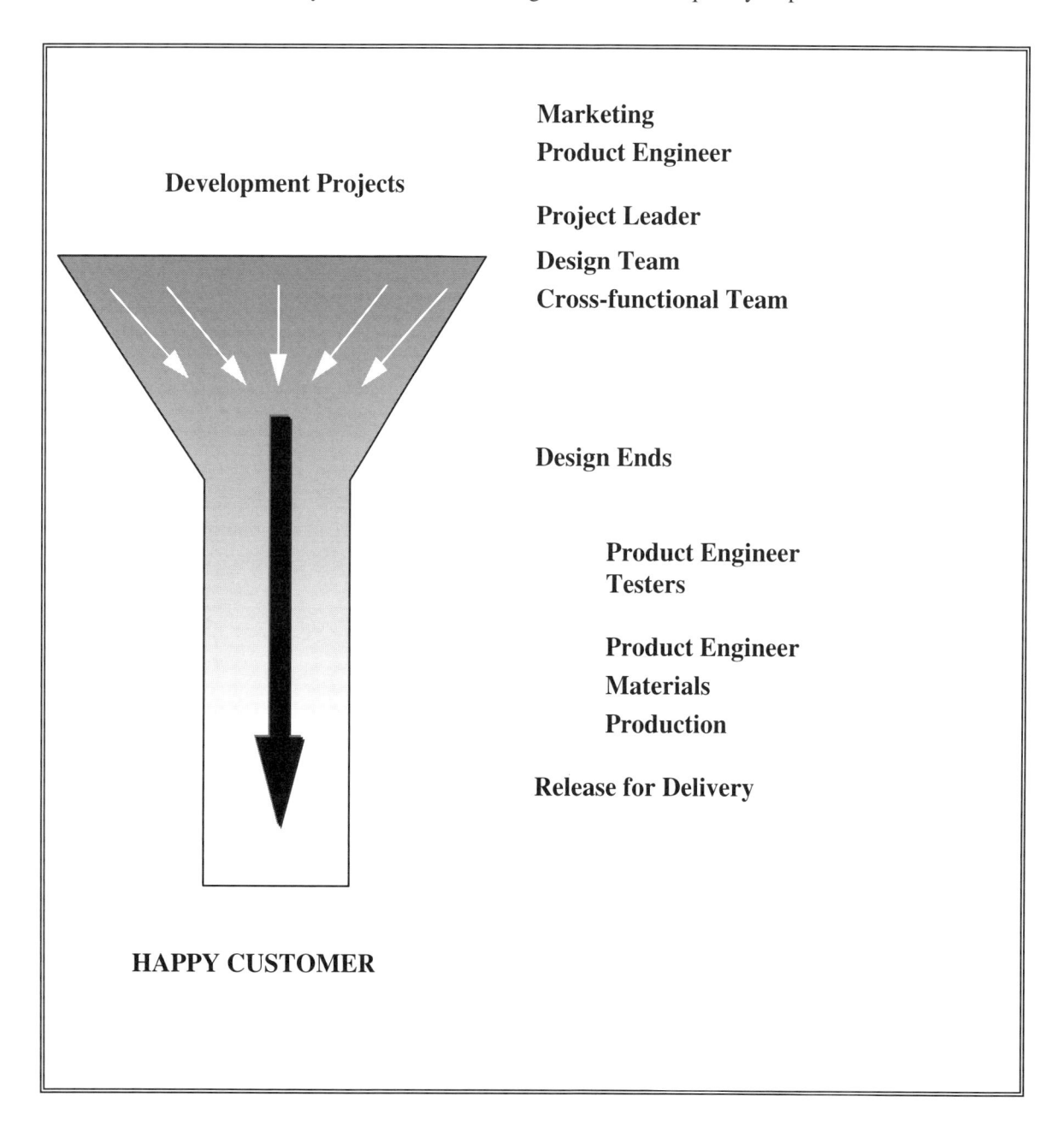

Development Projects

Marketing
Product Engineer

Project Leader
Design Team
Cross-functional Team

Design Ends

Product Engineer
Testers

Product Engineer
Materials
Production

Release for Delivery

HAPPY CUSTOMER

We need a way to structure and manage our development to ensure we do a good job selecting projects in the front end, then moving them quickly through the funnel to completion.

© 1998 Global Brain, Inc.

QRPD 4 Phases and Functions of Concurrent Development

←——— Total Time-to-Market ———→

Company Function	Phase I: Kick-off	Phase II: Development	Phase III: Approval	Phase IV: Delivery
Planning and Marketing, Sales	1. Proposal, Business case 2. **New Project Evaluation request (NPER)** 3. Select team 4. Product Vision and See-saw Specifications and Schedules (iterative process including PDRs, milestones) 5. **Announce internally**	Sales forecast and pricing Begin marketing launch preparation	Introduction————→ Sales support and launch materials	Selling————→ Plan next cycle
Engineering or Development	Rough technical evaluation 4. Conceptualize solution (Architecture, technology, time, budget estimates) *Iterative refinement…*	6. **Detailed and Critical Design Reviews** 7. Final Design Review 8. Development Pre-releases *Iterative refinement…*	Fix bugs————→ Minor redesign (tweaks) → 10. Release for Pilot	—→ Final release (for production) Maintenance————→
Testing and Quality	Input to specs, plans, schedule, costs	Detailed test cases	9. Internal testing (Alpha) 11. External testing (Beta and Regulatory)	Customer feedback, quality analysis
Operations, Support	Input to specs, plans, schedule, costs.	Detailed planning and long-lead procurement.	Purchasing, manufacturing, customer support preparation	12. Pilot production/ delivery 13. **Release to Full Production/ delivery**

←——— *Customers, vendors involved throughout. Shading indicates an executive sign-off point* ———→

© 1998 Global Brain, Inc.

3 Secrets To Successful Blitzkriegs:
Just-In-Time Product Development (JITPD)

Vision
1. Total company commitment to a concrete, well-defined Product **Vision.**

Mission
2. Obsessed Project Leader and a strong, synergistic, cross-functional team on a **Mission** to "make it happen" and meet milestones.

Flow
3. Follow a new product development **Flow** process, including testing working prototypes early on.

Vision	=	Structure	…to focus the team on the most important objectives, providing a critical bounding of their development efforts.
Mission	=	Flexibility	…to determine the best, creative way to complete the mission within the boundaries set by the Vision.
Flow	=	Structure + Experience (internal and industry)	…to add a minimum amount of necessary structure, including checks and inspections to ensure we meet the vision and achieve high product quality—taking advantage of both internal company and industry experience.

⇑

Q*R*PD success!

© 1998 Global Brain, Inc.

> "Improved new product development cycle time is not only free, it's profitable. It doesn't cost you anything, it's more fun for everybody, and you do it right the first time by investing up front!"
>
> —John Young, retired CEO and President of Hewlett Packard

How QRPD Teams Get LUCKy

S — Synergistic

C — Cross-Functional

O — Organized

R — Responsible

E — Enthusiastic

L — Laboring

U — Under

C — Correct

K — Knowledge

1. Ready. Aim. Fire. Instead of Ready. Aim. Aim. Aim.
2. Listen to everyone. Ideas come from everywhere.
3. Give out "Culture Scud Awards," Your best friend is the person who attacks corporate culture head on. Wish her well.
4. Spend 50% of your time with "outsiders." And 50% of your outsider time with wacko outsiders.
5. Make and encourage others to make lots of mistakes, but early.
6. Do a project twice or three times to get it done in half the time.
7. Spend twice or three times as much up front to spend half overall.

Source for #3 and #4: Peters, Tom. *Liberation Management: Necessary Disorganization for the Nanosecond Nineties.* New York: Excel, 1992.

© 1998 Global Brain, Inc.

Excerpted with permission from:
PROJECTWORLD® Winter 97 Proceedings

Article: Warp-Speed Product Development with QRPD®

© 1998 Global Brain, Inc.

Warp-Speed Product Development with QRPD®

Orion ("Ori") Kopelman, President
Global Brain®, Inc.
555 Bryant St. #369
Palo Alto, California 94301-1704 USA
Tel./Fax (650) 327-2012, (650) 327-2028
E-mail: missioncontrol@globalbrain.com
Web url: www.qrpd.com

Why Today's Environment Requires Moving at "Faster-than-Light" Speed, and How to Do It

Not long ago, Xerox used 600 engineers to design a 50 page/minute $150,000 color printer in only three years, while the previous black-and-white took them over six years to complete. Increasingly, companies today must perform this kind of miracle, as the pace of the acceleration of technology and global competition quickens. It's now estimated that the know-how we have in any given technology doubles every 12-18 months, creating a merciless environment in which to execute projects.

Xerox is not alone in adapting to it. GM's Buick division rolled out its "Park Avenue" in 36 months compared to 60 for a previous comparable model, HP developed a printer in 24 months versus 50, a small audio company in Florida did an in-home control panel, the "Intellipad", in 7 months rather than 18, and a project manager for Shell Services, Jon Hockenberry (a conference presenter), reports "delivering projects in months instead of years, and at costs far less than even a year ago." To compete, and not only survive but thrive today, we must clearly bend the rules of yesteryear (and physics) and thrust forward at warp speed.

Which new practices and management methodologies allow these companies to drastically reduce development times and costs? Do they work for all size companies? Is there a common formula of what one might call "global best-practices?"

This paper claims that there is. It presents the cornerstones of a management methodology that captures those best-practices, called Quality *Rapid* Product Development (QRPD) [1], which cuts development times and costs by typically 50 percent, while increasing quality, morale, and fun. It further explains how to "engage" the three secrets of QRPD and thereby develop products in half the time every time. "Make it so."

Speaker Biography

Orion ("Ori") Kopelman is President of Global Brain, the founder of QRPD, and one of America's leading product development experts. Global Brain provides "Warp speed development of technology, individuals, and organizations," and has helped many companies to significantly accelerate their projects through QRPD. Ori was VP of Engineering and co-founder of the Media Equipment Division at Mountain Computer, a company which grew from 50 to 500 people between 1984-1990, with 32 consecutively profitable quarters.

Kopelman's enthusiasm for quality and solid command of the product development cycle have made him a much sought after lecturer. He served for three years as Chairman of IEEE's Engineering Management Society in Silicon Valley, and teaches QRPD at UC Berkeley and to technology-driven companies world-wide such as NASA's Simulator Technology and Operations Division, Abbott Labs, CellNet Data Systems, and Niles Audio. He and his team of action-oriented experts plan to make QRPD an industry-wide standard by the year 2000. Ori earned his BSEE with distinction from Stanford University and lives in Palo Alto, CA and Maui, Hawaii.

© 1998 Global Brain, Inc.

Why The Q*R*PD Methodology ensures JITPD

We cannot allow the product development and engineering disciplines to deteriorate into using play money to finance an expensive hobby. We must first and foremost focus on profitability, and only second on having fun and "doing neat stuff."

Let's take a look at the analogies between JIT and JITPD. JIT, an advanced manufacturing strategy widely practiced since the early 1980s, depends on getting the right materials to exactly the right place at the precise time required. Through a process of procurement, fabrication, assembly, and shipment, product assembly lines "add value to parts as rapidly as possible at each step, until they become a quality finished product ready to ship." [2]

Similarly, JITPD occurs when we develop products in a way that inputs the right product specification information to the development group, and then stresses delivery of it to the right place, at the right time. This requires a process "for adding value to the information set as rapidly as possible until that information set describes the manufacture, support and use of a quality new product." [3]

Both JIT and JITPD address investing a lot of money and exerting large amounts of effort in a highly fluid and rapidly changing environment. Factories respond to swiftly varying market demands for product mix with flexible, JIT production. Likewise, product development groups must learn to ingest the latest information and turn it around into a value added product that sells profitably, using a methodology that fosters JITPD.

The Q*R*PD methodology ensures JITPD by accelerating new product development times by as much as 50%. First developed in the 1980s, it sprang from a conglomeration of theories and techniques experimented with by various organizations of all sizes, from startups to global giants. By distilling the methods and management wisdom that proved most successful, Q*R*PD provides a synthesis of the best-practices for the 1990s and beyond.

The "Q" in Q*R*PD reminds us to keep *Quality first* which means giving your customers value, as they perceive it. The "R" for *rapidly* allows us to survive in a leapfrog world where even current products are here today and obsolete tomorrow, and every project must turn into a successful new product overnight. Q*R*PD recognizes that time is of the essence.

Using Q*R*PD-like techniques, many companies have and are developing products in up to 50% less time, with lower overall spending levels. One example includes Xerox, who reduced their average time-to-market on comparable products company-wide by 50%, with 50% less engineering resource dollars.

As another example, management expert Peter Drucker [4] reports that Toyota, Nissan, and Honda bring out a new automobile model now in only 18 months. U.S. carmakers have achieved a three-year cycle, down from five years a decade ago. At Intevac, a mid-sized company in Sunnyvale, California, a newly formed team completed the latest Molecular Beam Epitaxy machine (for depositing gallium arsenide on semiconductor wafers), in eight months instead of the usual year and a half. Rolm, a Siemens Company, has developed a certain genre of voice mail products in successive cycle times of four years, two, and currently one. Other examples abound.

Experience tells us that project team sizes stay about the same, no matter how long a project lasts. This means that companies that develop products in up to half the time spend a lot less money overall. Consequently, they realize greater returns on their investments. That's why John Young, retired CEO and President of Hewlett-Packard, promotes the absolute importance of Q*R*PD-like principles. In a recent phone conversation he remarked that, "improved new product development cycle time is not only free, it's profitable. It doesn't cost you anything, it's more fun for everybody, and you do it right the first time!"

Q*R*PD facilitates this by combining the best of both startup and larger, more mature company environments. We've all heard and seen the swift successes achieved by many booming

© 1998 Global Brain, Inc.

startups. They took advantage of flexible, fast-paced, free-wheeling, entrepreneurial innovation. This spirit contributed significantly to Silicon Valley's mushrooming, and to that of other technology hotbeds around the world. And yet, many of these companies lacked the staying power to turn in repeat performances. They subsequently disappeared or declined almost as quickly as they appeared.

On the other hand, larger, more stable companies have suffered from stagnation and product development cycles that have slowed to a crawl, relative to the industry as a whole. On the positive side however, some of these giants have developed some structure necessary for every company's growth and long-term success in today's intense, global technology race. Q*R*PD blends the best of the startup and large company practices, thereby adapting to changes occurring at an accelerating pace around us, and enabling JITPD with quality.

Q*R*PD rests on the four philosophical cornerstones of:

1. Obsessive, intelligent risk and resource management is required.

2. The accelerating pace of technology calls for a time-based paradigm based on Late Cost per Week (LCPW); business as usual is out the window. LCPW refers to the cost to the company in lost profits and additional development "burn rate" if the project is not completed by a certain time.

3. Volunteered commitment and responsibility lead to the best results.

4. Measured accountability based on meeting milestones guarantees maximum return-on-investment to the company.

Q*R*PD's Three secrets to JITPD Success

There's no rocket science behind the strategies for implementing Q*R*PD, and yet a majority of companies don't even follow the three secrets or keys to *blitzkrieg* or "lightning-fast" product development! Success using Q*R*PD obviously depends on using many more techniques than just these three keys. Donald Reinertsen and Preston Smith in their classic book *Developing Products in Half the Time* remind us that "shortening development cycles is complex and requires a full kit of tools." [5]

Every product development effort must make trade-offs amongst the four main objectives of product performance or quality (P), development speed (T), development cost (C), and product cost (C). For example, if a company expects it can sell $100 million worth of product, and for every month the product is delayed to market the company will lose $0.5 million in profit, should it delay the project by a month in order to add a feature that will get the company 1% more revenue over the life of the product?

The correct answer is no. Making this type of PTCC trade-off leads us to the first secret in figure 1 called *Product Vision*. The other two are *Mission* and *Flow Process*.

---

3 Secrets to Successful *Blitzkriegs*

Just-in-time Product Development (*JITPD*)

1. Total company commitment to a concrete, well-defined *Product Vision*.

2. Obsessed Project Leader and a strong, synergistic, cross-functional core team on a *Mission* to "make it happen" and meet milestones.

3. Follow a new product development *Flow process*, including testing working prototypes early on.

Figure 1

Diverse groups of high tech executives and managers from every discipline support the validity of these three keys. In a facilitated discussion process on Q*R*PD, every workshop group reaches consensus on these three keys within half an hour. Everyone agrees that these are in fact the most important "tricks" that they've learned over the years. They concur that these keys separated their good project

© 1998 Global Brain, Inc.

experiences from their bad ones. Yet they surprise themselves and each other when they admit that even their current projects do not follow these three proven, known, and simple secrets. Are *you* adhering to them right now?

SECRET #1: PRODUCT VISION

"The #1 reason for project schedule slippage is changing product definitions." [6] And yet, we don't have much time to convert information that we gather into each JITPD effort (or it becomes obsolete). The only remedy then is to agree on a limited set of product objectives. So first of all, to successfully innovate incrementally and rapidly, the company must commit to a concrete and well-defined *Product Vision*.

All the functions involved in the project have to come together and hash out a one-page *Product Vision* that describes the major objectives. Everyone must participate in this negotiation process of trading-off product features, benefits, and costs for the resulting amount of time and budget required for design and production. The goal is to have all team members commit *wholeheartedly* and *knowingly* to a list of milestones that delivers a product to the customers just-in-time to make financial sense for everyone.

Recently, a robotics company decided to do this for a next generation platform it was developing. They were three years into the project and supposedly one year away from shipment. Many team members, the project leader, and upper management felt very surprised when they discovered what the consensus Vision really was. They revised the Vision to create a product that they could actually ship within a year, and re-committed to this more realistic mission.

A clear and concise product vision is your most powerful tool. A Hewlett-Packard engineer could remember word-for-word a Vision from a project he had worked on several years earlier. Obviously, he and the other team members had clear direction. The objectives described on a single page drove the nine-month software tools project for a CAD workstation to a successful, timely completion. Like many well-written Visions, it hadn't changed once for the duration of the project.

Once the Product Vision and milestones have been established and signed off, and sufficient funds appropriated, every effort should be made to strictly adhere to them. Try to leave them set in concrete. The Vision document should serve as an aligning set of objectives that guide all disciplines to make design, manufacturing, and other decisions as the project progresses. It leaves a lot of flexibility to the team, and yet bounds the project within a framework that everyone agrees up-front is more likely to have a worthwhile ROI.

If at all possible, feed new information that arrives during the project into added value in the next project. Changing the Vision disrupts the development work by creating a moving target for the team. Altering the Vision after its sign-off is most often necessary and justified for reliability, safety, or quality issues discovered during the project. Or once in a long while, a drastic change in the market really warrants a legitimate course adjustment in the product's development. Nonetheless, revising the Vision should require as much thought as amending the U.S. Constitution (it has only happened on average about once a decade for the last 200 years).

SECRET #2: MISSION

Second, the company assigns an obsessed Project Leader and a strong cross-functional core team and launches them on a *Mission* to "make it happen" and meet the agreed-upon milestones.

To do this, we should adhere to the four "propulsion wisdoms" to accelerate our mission:

1. **Do less sooner.** Focus on the main priorities.

2. **Slow down to speed up.** Spend a lot of time up front to find what may become negative surprises later.

3. **Blow up early and often.** Find your "mines" and mistakes as early as possible.

4. **Spend now to save later.** The more eyes and tools you have looking at what might go

wrong from every perspective, the greater the chance you'll arrive safely.

The Product Vision provides some structure to bound the team. Yet within that rather general specification, the team maintains tremendous latitude in executing its assignment. Teams and sub-teams of 8-10 people are ideal for allowing the kind of synergy to occur that speeds things along, with 4-5 an optimal group size.

Clearly, we want to select strong team members. Wherever possible, choose experienced, talented, and skilled people willing to volunteer and take responsibility for the completion of the mission. Look for a high sense of commitment to the cause, enthusiasm, and a readiness to participate in a conducive way in an atmosphere of team chemistry.

Synergy, or "synchronous energy," is most simply defined as 1 + 1 = 3—where the whole is greater than the sum of the parts. In the South Pacific, scientists have observed flocks of 50,000 birds turning in the same direction in 1/70th of a second, apparently with no leader. Imagine how spectacularly projects would succeed if all their team members were so tuned in to their overall goals (Vision), to fly together like this.

On a synergistic team, designers and others who obtain the pertinent information at a given decision-making time can make the best decision on the fly—very much like a start-up enterprise. As long as they stick to the Product Vision, we trust them to carry out their mission superbly.

Their Project Leader, an obsessed person, is one who tenaciously exercises interpersonal influence directed through communication, toward the attainment of the mission. They will mostly act as a supportive, trustworthy facilitator. At times however, when necessary, they may need to act uncompromisingly. This occurs particularly when major obstacles surface, as they often do in engineering—an inherent part of tackling risks and unknowns. They will not allow these obstacles to stymie progress and achievement of the overall goals. They will help to find a resolution, and continue to drive toward achieving the overall schedule and Product Vision.

The choice of the right Project Leader is the most crucial decision upper management makes in managing accelerated product development [7]. The ideal one is an obsessed leader who is confident (yet honest), technical, a model worker, a people person, and has high standards and management ability. While many managers do things right, only true leaders will do the right things. Only obsessed Project Leaders will pull-off the project.

Recently, a 30-year-old company experimented with the mission-oriented approach described here. They broke-off a small, crack team of half a dozen people. As a supplier of phone equipment, in years past their bureaucratic, ingrained, and functionally managed organization had earned them AT&T's *Quality Leadership Program* (QLP) award. However, it had also slowed-down new product development to almost a crawl by 1990s standards.

The results of their latest project however, were nothing less than outstanding. They managed to save a large customer's business by shipping a new product in nine months. This product went into production at the same time as a previous one with an almost identical component count. That project had begun nine months earlier, and had met its schedule using standard procedures. The new approach had provided conclusive proof. The project got done in half the time; 9 months instead of 18!

Gordon Simmons, the persistent Project Leader and a graduate of the Q*R*PD training program, says, "At times we ran counter to the accepted norms of doing things, but we met all expected customer deliverables. We could easily do this again and again, if management continues to clear the runway by giving us dedicated people from all departments, and says 'go!'"

SECRET #3: FLOW PROCESS

And third, the team will follow a new product development *Flow Process*, including testing working prototypes early on. This, once again, adds a minimal amount of necessary structure. If we think of product development as an information assembly line, we clearly need plenty of in-line checks and inspections. This results in perceiving innovation as a *process*.

© 1998 Global Brain, Inc.

Can development work be mapped as a process? Historically we have tended to think of the design process as mostly invention. One could hardly expect that Thomas Edison when he invented the light bulb, or Albert Einstein when he discovered the theory of relativity, followed a well-defined process. Or that anybody could repeat their inspiring works by trying to map them with a process and following it.

However, most design today relies on innovation that utilizes some amount of existing invention, while tackling a limited set of unknowns. This is intelligent risk taking, that one can comfortably build a business plan on (would you want to bet your company on making discoveries like Edison's or Einstein's?). Thinking of development as magic or artistry, where you throw a pizza at a group of people in a lab and eventually something pops out, is a mistake.

Technology Process Maturity Levels

Maturity	Characterization
1. Initial	Ad-Hoc/chaotic
2. Repeatable	Intuitive, depends on individuals
3. Defined	Qualitative, independent of individuals
4. Managed	Quantitative, measured
5. Optimizing	Improvement fed back continuously

Figure 2

At the same time, product development does have more unknowns than processes such as manufacturing. So mapping it with a process is a little more difficult, yet nonetheless doable.

The Carnegie Mellon Software Engineering Institute has observed five maturity levels in the software development process (see the table in figure 2). These can apply to many types of processes, including new product development. The majority of manufacturing organizations operate between levels four and five; they have streamlined production to a quantitative, managed, and continuously improving system.

Unfortunately, an educated guess predicts that over half of projects for development utilize levels one or two, about a quarter level three, and maybe 10% levels four and five. Most product development occurs in an ad-hoc manner that depends only on certain key individuals. Even successfully completed projects seldom turn in repeat performances within the same company.

A level two company with a repeatable but not yet defined new product development process can do many things right and still stumble into trouble. For example, a company developed a balloon catheter designed for coronary angioplasty, with a potential gross yearly sales of $100 million over a two year window. Despite use of a corporate plane, the project stalled while transferring it from California's engineering group to the manufacturing plant in Mexico. Production people only voiced concerns *after* equipment had arrived, not early in the project. The lack of a well defined process resulted in a three month delay that cost the company about $5.6 million in lost profit.

Meanwhile, organizations developing products with maturity level four or five are usually highly successful companies. Many companies at levels three and above create and use a guidebook. Much like cookbooks, these serve to follow the recipe more predictably every time (even master chefs use them, then improvise on the fly). While never assuring success, it does increase the odds of developing quality new products quickly.

As a very significant part of following a process, we might choose to verify the validity of our information that goes into it as early as possible, before we spend too much money adding value to it. We do this by testing a working prototype early in the development process. Doing this, plus using cross functional teams as described in secret #2 above, improves both product quality and time-to-market.

We can see why when we look at figure 3 below on the "Skyrocketing Cost of Engineering Changes" [8]. It suggests that the average cost of a change in the design increases tenfold at each later stage in a project. For example, a change during the liftoff or design phase may cost the company $1000, but that same change will debit

© 1998 Global Brain, Inc.

the company ten million dollars after all the boosters have fired, and final production is in progress. While the absolute monetary figures in the chart were gathered for large consumer electronic firms (such as TV, VCR, and appliance manufacturers), the proportions hold true for every company.

**Skyrocketing Cost of Engineering Changes
(for major electronics products)**

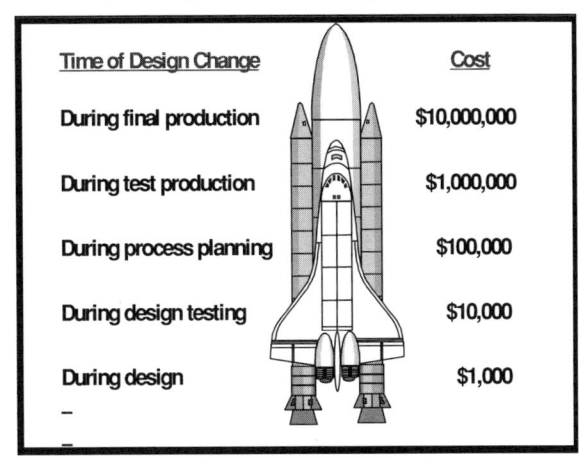

Time of Design Change	Cost
During final production	$10,000,000
During test production	$1,000,000
During process planning	$100,000
During design testing	$10,000
During design	$1,000

Figure 3

This exponentially rising costs curve points to the need to do a critical reality check on a working prototype in the early stages of the project, called the *chicken test* [9]. Typically it should occur within the first one-third to one-half of the schedule. It finally tells us if the essential technology actually functions as it should.

The chicken test gets its name from tests performed on airplane jet engines. Namely, in order to ascertain that during flight the engines can contend with the ingestion of flocks of birds, a barrel gun several feet in diameter fires chickens at them. This serves as an early warning system to uncover a possible fundamental flaw in the design, before spending the whole $250 million necessary to develop a new engine.

Every project must eventually undergo and pass a chicken test before it can really take off. The only question is how late in the project you will discover that you may need to take a different approach. Obviously, the earlier the better.

For example, a major mainframe computer manufacturer decided to re-package its systems into a new market application, telecommunications switching. Nine months into the one-year project they attempted system integration for the first time. Unfortunately, like many companies that hope for everything to just work out perfectly, many of the mechanical subsystems didn't fit together. Over 180 drawings had to be redone, causing a three month delay in a highly contested market.

To avoid this kind of late breaking bad news, you must simply have the courage to spend a little extra time and money early on in the project. Do your Chicken Test on a working prototype (even without having all the bells and whistles yet) within the first 25% of the schedule. This way you can find out if you're really on track, confirm many of your high-risk assumptions, and possibly decide to alter your course. With a typical one-year schedule, you could fail the test at the 90 day mark, start over, and still probably ship a product ahead of your competition, who had to do massive rework later in their project.

One last remark about the chicken test: The war archives of many companies reveal that on average, from the time you have passed this vital assessment point, you still have about 50% or half the project left to do. So don't kid yourself. Plan better, and leave plenty of time for system integration, testing, and debugging.

Many companies are working hard to leap up the maturity scale. ISO-9000, the emerging international quality standard, and market pressures, now mandate greater emphasis on a continuous process improvement effort. As organizations of all sizes and ages scramble to shake up their perhaps once adequate ways, only the swiftest to mutate survive.

One such company has been a leader in microwave electronic components for over 20 years. However, it lost its competitive edge mainly as a result of slow time to market. Consequently, the company set out to change their basic culture, and established a New Product Process (NPP). Tina Ohlhaver, the R&D Productivity Manager, says, "Q*R*PD identified the common success factors that maximize the probability of a successful product introduction. After implementing our *NPP*, with Q*R*PD as a key component of it, we saw an improvement not only in the timeliness of new product development, but also in the excitement and pride the participants in the process felt."

As many begin to use a disciplined *Flow process* we must bear in mind:

1. To work simultaneously on both the development process and the individual product projects, and not let one suffer at the expense of the other.

2. A process should be seen as a guideline, not a bible, and common sense and judgment in each set of circumstances should always rule the day.

SUMMARY

In a recent class on Q*R*PD at the University of California at Berkeley Extension, 24 students of greatly varying ages all agreed that during their whole careers they had participated in only one really great, successful *blitzkrieg* JITPD project. They also agreed that, often unconsciously, *that* one project unequivocally abided by the 3 secrets presented here. One of the students, Robert J. Russell, Sr., Manager of International Engineering Projects at VeriFone, and leader of a project of 10 people that completed in 11 months instead of 18, says "Does Q*R*PD work? Damn right it does. I just didn't know it had a name."

So begin now to use Q*R*PD to transform your company's product development engine into a JITPD organization. Use the combination of flexibility and structure embedded in the three secrets and the rest of the methodology. Turn your company into an information assembly line factory in this brave new world. As you "engage" at warp speed, your new products will fly out the door like hot cakes, and your profits will soar as you zoom ahead to the future.

REFERENCES

[1] Kopelman, Orion. And Voegtli, Cinda with Josephs, Adam, 1998. *Projects at Warp Speed with QRPD®: The Definitive Guidebook to Quality Rapid Product Development, 8th Edition.* Global Brain, Inc., Palo Alto, CA, USA.

[2] Patterson, Marvin. November 1992. *Accelerating Innovation*. Van Nostrand Reinhold.

[3] Patterson, *Accelerating Innovation*, p. 65.

[4] Drucker, Peter, "The New Society of Organizations," Harvard Business Review, September-October, 1992.

[5] Reinertsen, Donald and Smith, Preston. 1991. *Developing Products in Half the Time*. Van Nostrand Reinhold, P. 287.

[6] Patterson, *Accelerating Innovation*, p. 115.

[7] Reinertsen and Smith, *Developing Products in Half the Time*, p. 112.

[8] "A Smarter Way to Manufacture: How Concurrent Engineering Can Reinvigorate American Industry," *Business Week*, April 20, 1990, page 110.

[9] Peters, Tom and Austin, Nancy. 1985. *A Passion for Excellence, The Leadership Difference*. Random House, p. 130.

PART II. TECHNIQUES: THE QRPD TOOLKIT

10 Commandments and 150 Techniques: The Toolkit of Quality *Rapid* Product Development

This section provides teams with a toolkit of techniques to make the 3 secrets of Q*R*PD—Vision, Mission, and Flow—a day-to-day reality. Note that we haven't yet covered the steps of Flow in detail—for a very good reason. To use an analogy: When we were younger, before we could follow step-by-step instructions from our parents to build plywood creations or follow assembly instructions to put together a bicycle, we had to learn the basic tools such as hammers and screwdrivers—their purpose and how to use them. Likewise, to best put Q*R*PD into practice, we need to first learn the fundamental tools at our disposal. We'll start with the commandments—the critical principles—and techniques for each. In a later section we'll then cover the step-by-step Flow process of Q*R*PD.

1.	FOCUS	**Focus** on a clear, limited, and on-target Vision.
2.	TEAM/LEADER	Assemble the right **team** and **leader(s)**.
3.	CROSS-FUNCTIONAL	Initiate early **cross-functional** cooperation.
4.	SYNERGY	Create a **synergistic**, mission-oriented, productive environment.
5.	REWARD	**Reward** all participants commensurably.
6.	INNOVATE	Use **innovative**, parallel, iterative design strategies.
7.	INVEST	**Invest** money to buy time and tools and minimize risk.
8.	PROTOTYPE	**Prototype** and test key design concepts early.
9.	FLOW	Use the **Flow** process to meet milestones, manage risk, and ensure quality.
10.	FEEDBACK	Get early **feedback** and nail defects quickly.

> If you think you're too small to be effective,
>
> then you've never been in bed with a mosquito.

The following pages provide checklists of techniques for implementing each Q*R*PD commandment. A few of these techniques were adapted from Reinertsen's article on "Blitzkrieg Product Development," 1986.

⊃   On the following pages, this symbol denotes the importance of placing special emphasis on adhering to these techniques for time-to-market critical projects. Of course the other techniques all belong to the set of good project management practices.

© 1998 Global Brain, Inc.

#1. Focus on a Clear, Limited, and On-Target Vision

- The team needs a focused overall goal to make trade-offs.
- Have as few features as possible and no less to meet customers' needs.
- The vision is a document that all the team will memorize.

Figure 1A   Incremental Innovation

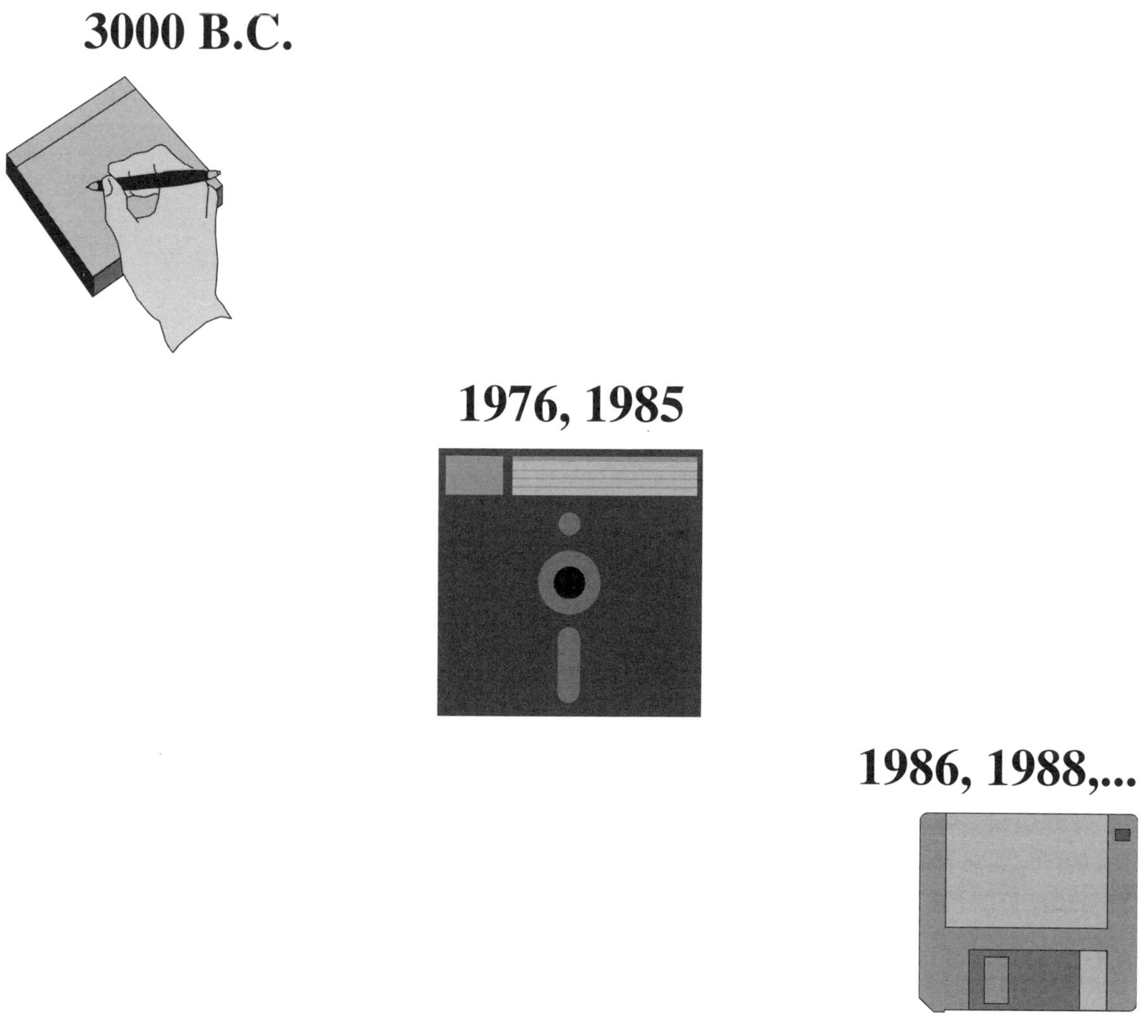

3000 B.C.

1976, 1985

1986, 1988,...

Commandment #1 Techniques:

Focus on a Clear, Limited, and On-Target Vision

⊃A)   Innovate incrementally. (Base hits, not homeruns)

⊃B)   Restrict each product to a manageable number of major innovations, typically three.

C)   Avoid breaking new ground simultaneously in (all 3): technology, applications, markets/customers.

D)   Justify all innovations (keep list) using benefit to cost to risk analysis.

E)   Quantify objectives and make them measurable wherever possible.

⊃F)   Strive for an adequate solution by finding an optimal balance of Performance (P), Time (T), and costs (C).

G)   Interview one or two leading-edge customers, and establish rapport and phone contact between them and the design team as beta sites.

H)   Also interview one or two target customers representing quantity buyers and/or the mass market (or survey it), and establish them as future beta sites.

I)   Satisfy the customer and end user needs before wants by being solution-oriented.

J)   Know the competition and their customers, including competing technologies.

K)   Restrict product requirements to necessary ones, and state them in the Product Vision as unambiguous criteria that allow shipments to begin.

⊃L)   Resist changing the Vision.

M)   Write a Product Vision iteratively during the SSSS process to align the team and ensure focus in the right direction throughout the project.

N)   Write a New Product/Project Proposal and rough business case to initiate a new product idea into the development cycle.

O)   Use trade-off tables to summarize information about project PTCC alternatives and facilitate rapid decisions.

P)   Have the entire team and upper management sign the Product Vision.

© 1998 Global Brain, Inc.

#2. Assemble the Right Team and Leader(s)

- One empowered "mad-person-on-a-mission" leader.
- Team should be full time and focused on Product Vision.
- Keep teams small and cross functional.
- Include essential experts.

⊃A) Select the Leader(s) very judiciously. See criteria in the Project Leader section.

⊃B) Have only *one* overall team leader.

C) Announce leader's and team's responsibilities formally and clearly.

⊃D) Assign team members to report directly to the leader(s), or to have their reviews heavily influenced by them.

⊃E) Use experienced, talented volunteers: committed, flexible, enthusiastic, eager to responsibly complete the mission.

⊃F) Strive for only full time members on the team.

G) For non full-time members, pre-determine their time allocated to the project for its duration.

H) Strive for teams and sub teams of up to 8 to 10 people (4-5 ideal).

⊃I) Find a champion with clout and authority.

J) Have a gatekeeper to inform the team on external technological news.

K) Enlist experts as adjunct members of the team.

L) Avoid changing people midstream, but early if necessary (during first half of the project).

⊃M) Keep members on the team from concept to production.

⊃N) Ensure that all key company functions are represented on the team.

O) Add all key team members before the halfway point, using a trapezoidal resource plan done in Phase I. See Figure 2O.

P) Prioritize company projects by quantified success metrics like ROI, late cost per week, or Net Present Value (NPV) to resolve resource conflicts quickly and appropriately.

Q) Treat contractors, vendors, partners, and third-party developers as part of the team, and select them judiciously.

R) Assess and select all team members for proper skills for the project, plan for mentoring, and account for learning curve time.

© 1998 Global Brain, Inc.

Figure 20. Resource Profiles

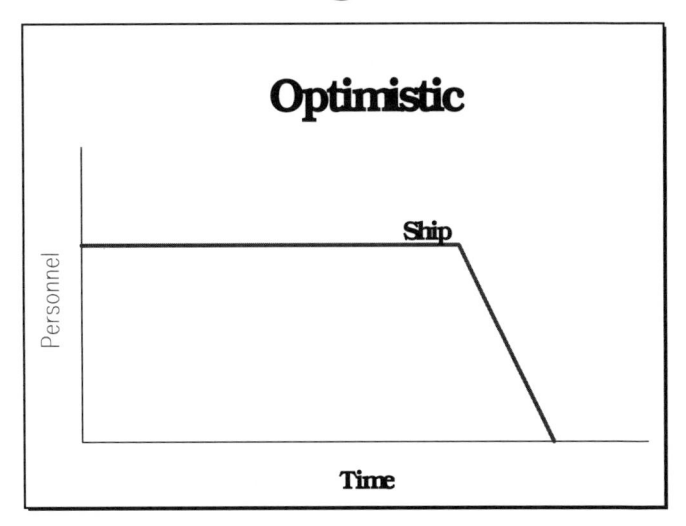

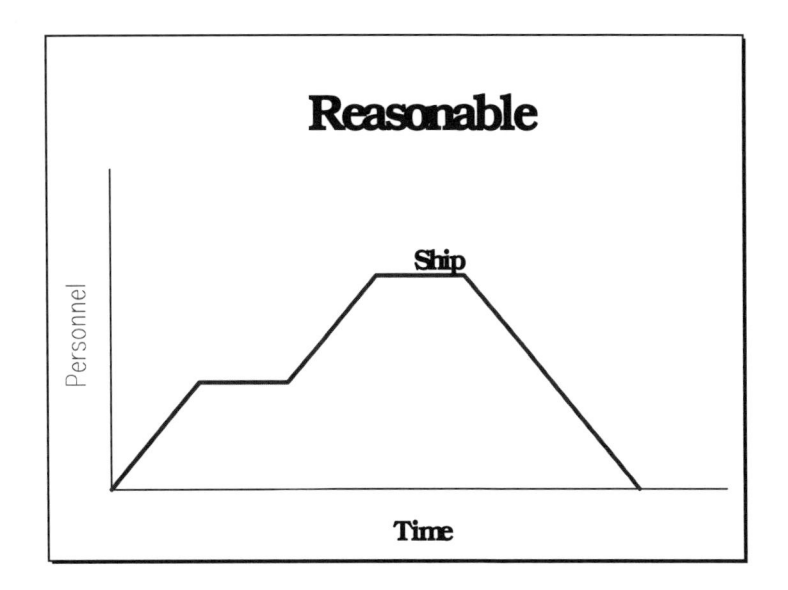

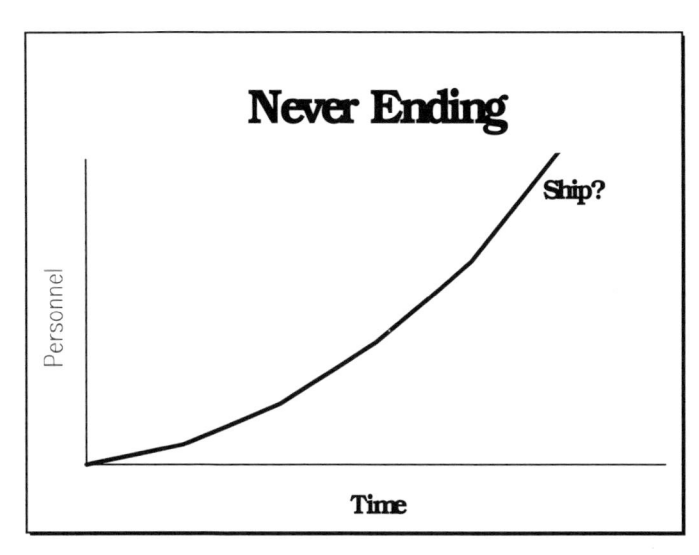

#3. Initiate Early Cross-Functional Cooperation

- Goal: get buy-in, avoid late changes.
- Get cross-functional commitment to Project Vision.
- Cover the entire lifecycle of the project.
- Establish clear roles and responsibilities.

Figure 3A. The Skyrocketing Cost of Development Changes
(major electronics product)

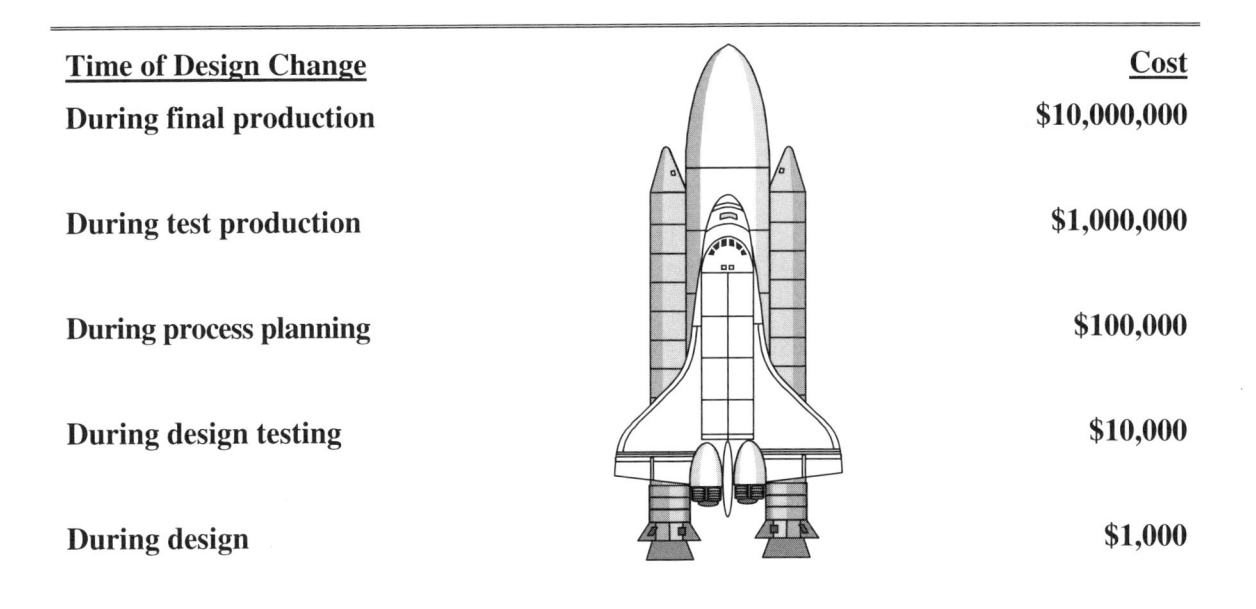

Time of Design Change	Cost
During final production	$10,000,000
During test production	$1,000,000
During process planning	$100,000
During design testing	$10,000
During design	$1,000

Source: "A Smarter Way to Manufacture; How Concurrent Engineering Can Reinvigorate American Industry," page 110, *Business Week*, April 30, 1990.

Typical Cross-functional Team Members

Research & Development / Engineering	Legal
Manufacturing/test/Reliability Engineering	Medical
Purchasing	Regulatory
Manufacturing/Operations	Vendors/Customers
Quality Assurance/ Control	Sales
Finance	Customer Support
Development partners, including distribution channels or end users	Technical support
Systems engineering (field pre-sales)	Marketing, including product management and marketing communications/public relations
Technical Publications	Shipping/Receiving

Commandment #3 Techniques: Early Cross-functional Cooperation

⊃A) All team members, including outside partners and contractors, involved and committed from day 1, and kept up to date.

⊃B) Concurrently work on putting in place and documenting the delivery process.

C) Concurrently work on improving and documenting the generic product development cycle process: "Flow".

D) No substitute for face-to-face communication.

⊃E) Design team especially close to front and back end of project: Customers/Sales/Marketing and production/delivery.

F) Design and build quality, safety, testability, and other "ility" attributes into the product and process early on by following "DFX" guidelines.

G) Document all major decisions and keep those decision records accessible.

© 1998 Global Brain, Inc.

#4: Create a Synergistic, Mission-oriented, Productive Environment.

- Keep clear focus on the Vision and the Mission and ensure communication.
- Have a "we're going to take the world by storm" attitude.
- Keep teams autonomous, empowered and responsible.
- Have fun!!!

Figure 4C. Communication vs. Distance

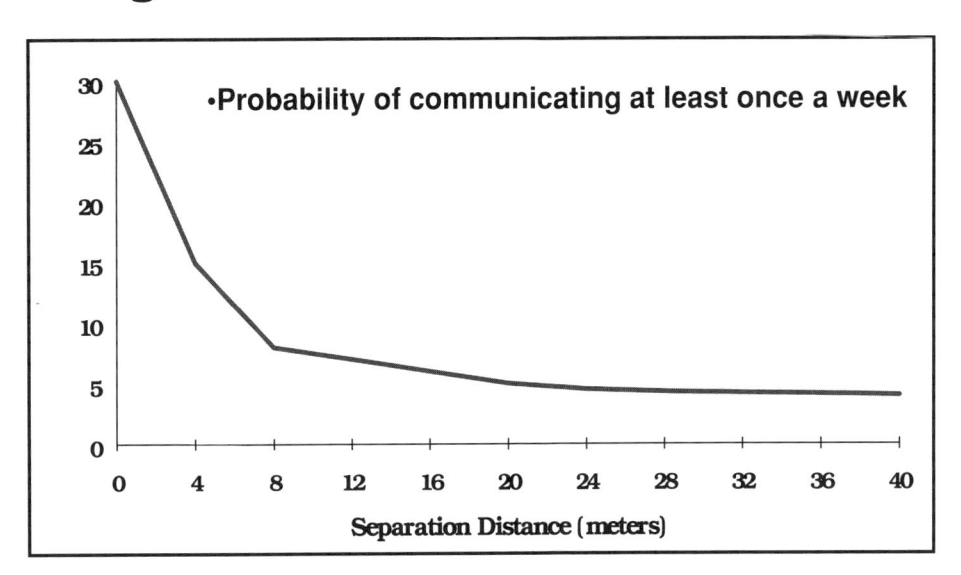

```
30 ┤•Probability of communicating at least once a week
25 ┤
20 ┤
15 ┤
10 ┤
 5 ┤
 0 ┤
   0   4   8  12  16  20  24  28  32  36  40
         Separation Distance (meters)
```

Source: Allen, *Managing the Flow of Technology*. MIT Press, p. 239.

Figure 4M. The Fuzzy Front End

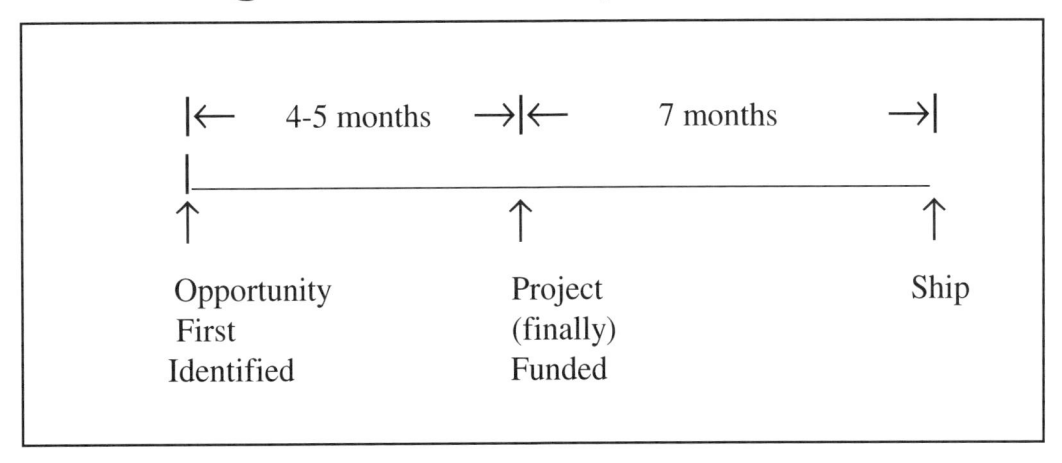

```
|←    4-5 months    →|←    7 months    →|
|_____|
↑                    ↑                    ↑
Opportunity          Project              Ship
First                (finally)
Identified           Funded
```

© 1998 Global Brain, Inc.

Commandment #4 Techniques:
Create a Synergistic, Mission-Oriented, Productive Environment

⊃A)   Create a shared sense of mission/purpose, *product* vision, and milestones.

B)   Define and publish a responsibility matrix. See *Flow* chapter.

⊃C)   Locate all team members together. See figure 4C.

D)   Ensure communication among team members regardless of location, including outside partners.

⊃E)   Insulate the team from the parent organization's culture ("skunkworks") only if the company is not Q*R*PD-like; or for a highly research oriented project.

⊃F)   Protect the team's autonomy.

⊃G)   Exercise team building processes, including off site meetings to gain buy in for the vision, schedule, and costs (PTCC).

⊃H)   Minimize and streamline administration and reporting requirements.

I)   Simplify the product specification process to a single page vision.

⊃J)   Restrict detailed front end planning to important items.

K)   Do not allow management reviews or decisions to delay work, including separating formal status reviews from technical meetings.

L)   Separate executive education sessions from reviews.

⊃M)   Spend time at the "fuzzy" front end of the project (top management especially, to "jump start" it). See figure 4M.

⊃N)   Ensure that all team members know/feel the cost of delay, using Late Cost Per Week.

⊃O)   Make excessive use of "hoopla" to build morale.

P)   Promote frequent, brief, open ad hoc meetings.

Q)   Hold a regularly scheduled team meeting.

R)   Invest in productivity tools that enhance communication (e-mail, video teleconferencing, etc.), and standardize the team on using them.

S)   Review the vision and measure against it for progress.

⊃T)   Work smarter and long hours using spurts to meet milestones and prevent burnout.

U)   Protect confidential information prudently.

V)   Have fun!

W)   Teach all team members collaboration skills such as meeting management and problem-solving techniques.

X)   Separate problem-solving versus status or informational meetings, and invite only the necessary people to each.

Y)   Find creative uses of "asynchronous communication" and establish team etiquette to allow team members un-interrupted productive time.

© 1998 Global Brain, Inc.

#5. Reward all Participants Commensurably

- Reward performance on projects.
- Recognize milestones and real progress.
- Ensure that rewards are perceived as fast and fair.

⊃A) Recognition at major milestones and other significant events.

B) Reward and recognize the team as a whole, some of its individuals, others, including in personnel reviews.

⊃C) Bonuses based on project and product success.

D) Use management by objectives (MBO) as a basis for rewards.

⊃E) Use rituals and celebrations.

⊃F) Special recognition for going the extra mile, beating milestones, saving costs.

G) Minimize alienating others, if possible.

H) Hold company parties for ongoing synergy.

I) Ensure recognition is cross-functional. Make certain people from all groups are recognized and all departments are aware of the individual and team accomplishments.

J) Make it easy for teams to do celebrations, rewards, and recognition, by planning ahead for these events and setting up the mechanisms.

K) Put a human face from top management on reward and recognition efforts.

> The leaders of tomorrow will be those who can
> create environments in which others feel empowered.
> This is the essence of good leadership.
>
> ~ Peter Russell, *The Creative Manager*

#6. Use Innovative, Parallel, Iterative Design Strategies

- Limit innovation and "beg, borrow or steal (legally)."
- Concentrate technical risk.
- Enable parallel development.
- Integrate early and often.

A) Partition into subsystems early at rigorously defined interfaces, using standards wherever possible.

B) Design subsystems to optimize system level performance.

⊃C) Accept less than optimal individual subsystems by priority, and leave generous design margins wherever possible.

⊃D) Concentrate technical risk in as few subsystems as possible. See figure 6D.

E) Organize to achieve minimum feasible team size for each subsystem.

⊃F) Invest in backup plans for critical technologies, tooling and parts, and be ready to implement them.

G) Have one key architect or "Evangelist"—sometimes Project Leader.

⊃H) "Beg, borrow, steal" or buy subsystems or expertise, and avoid "NIH:" The *Not Invented Here* Syndrome.

I) Plan to and start integrating modules and subsystems early and continuously.

J) Use a spiral or evolutionary (not waterfall) approach, especially for software.

Figure 6D. Concentrating Technical Risk

Technical risk evenly dispersed among all modules.

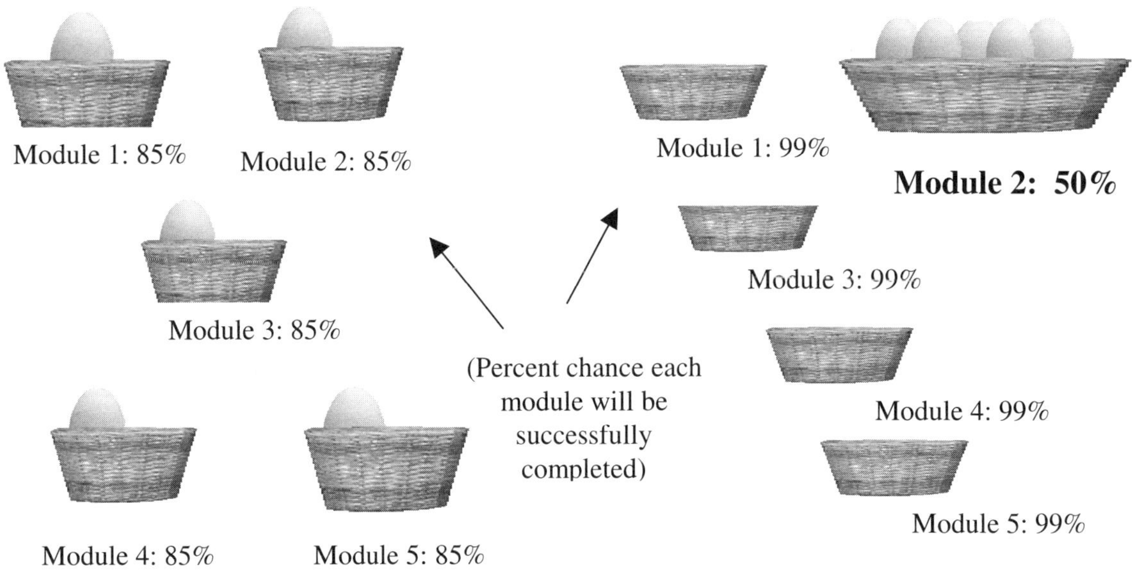

Module 1: 85% Module 2: 85%

Module 3: 85%

Module 4: 85% Module 5: 85%

Technical Risk concentrated in one "basket" or design module.

Module 1: 99%

Module 2: 50%

Module 3: 99%

Module 4: 99%

Module 5: 99%

(Percent chance each module will be successfully completed)

Percentage chance of project success
(on-time, on-cost, and it works):

85% x 85% x 85% x 85% x 85% =
44% overall

Percentage chance of project success

With no risk mitigation:

99% x 99% x 99% x 99% x **50%** =
48% overall

With backup plans:

99% x 99% x 99% x 99% x **85%** =
82% overall

The Message:
Keep your high risk "eggs" in <u>one</u> basket!

© 1998 Global Brain, Inc.

#7. Invest Money to Buy Time and Tools, and to Minimize Risks

- Get resources on board and trained early.
- Manage long lead items early.
- Reduce risk by spending money, justified by late cost per week.

A) Invest early and speculatively in long lead-time tooling.

B) Invest speculatively in long lead-time parts; create a *list* early on.

C) Utilize overtime and support personnel liberally, especially to meet key milestones.

D) Invest early and excessively in equipment, support, and training.

E) Make selective use of rapid turnaround outside services, and manage them well.

F) Computerize the process with CAD, software tools, quality tools, etc. If possible, learn to use them before a Blitzkrieg project.

G) Add resources judiciously if in any trouble, and as early as possible.

H) Actively manage the tools.

I) Invest in backup plans for critical designs, tooling and parts.

J) Set up more than enough prototypes, test and debug stations, and software build systems.

#8. Prototype and Test Key Design Concepts Early

- Do real world "chicken tests" early.
- Test creatively throughout the project.
- Review, track and resolve issues.
- Be able to kill a feature or project.

⟳A)   Do a reality check with real prototypes within about first 25% of the timeline: a "chicken test."

B)   Build a tall junk pile, real and abstract, of experimentation, analysis, and simulation tests throughout the project, especially at key milestones.

⟳C)   Prove out individual subsystems and interfaces early.

D)   Keep an updated list of critical issues and potential pitfalls: resources, sole sources, vendors, moves, tool availability, interdependencies with other projects, etc.

E)   Have a failure and test analysis program, and keep a central project logbook or defect tracking database.

F)   Take intelligent risks.

⟳G)   Stay flexible on unresolved issues, but set decision deadlines.

H)   Distinguish between testing technical and marketing concepts.

I)   Use company resources creatively to test throughout.

⟳J)   Know when to kill a project or feature, and do it.

"No, it wasn't pretty, but it was quick, and it got started without muss and fuss."

Tracy Kidder, *The Soul of A New Machine*, referring to an early prototype.

© 1998 Global Brain, Inc.

What is a Chicken Test?

> A reality test on a prototype that verifies the feasibility of the system, the critical parts, and major innovations, of the design. Should be performed within 25-50% of the overall schedule.

As a very significant part of following a process, we might choose to verify the validity of our information that goes into it as early as possible, before we spend too much money adding value to it. We do this by testing a working prototype early in the development process. Doing this improves both product quality and time-to-market.

We can see why when we look back at figure 3A on the "Skyrocketing Cost of Development Changes." It suggests that the average cost of a change in the design increases tenfold at each later stage in a project. For example, a change during the liftoff or design phase may cost the company $1000, but that same change will debit the company ten million dollars after all the boosters have fired, and final production is in progress. While the absolute monetary figures in the chart were gathered for large consumer electronic firms (such as TV, VCR, and appliance manufacturers), the proportions hold true for every company.

This exponentially rising costs curve points to the need to do a critical reality check on a working prototype in the early stages of the project, called the *chicken test*.[1] Typically it should occur within the first one-third to one-half of the schedule. It finally tells us if the essential technology actually functions as it should.

The chicken test gets its name from tests performed on airplane jet engines. Namely, in order to ascertain that during flight the engines can contend with the ingestion of flocks of birds, a barrel gun several feet in diameter fires chickens at them. This serves as an early warning system to uncover a possible fundamental flaw in the design, before spending the whole $250 million necessary to develop a new engine.

Every project must eventually undergo and pass a chicken test before it can really take off. The only question is how late in the project you will discover that you may need to take a different approach. Obviously, the earlier the better.

For example, a major mainframe computer manufacturer decided to re-package its systems into a new market application, telecommunications switching. Nine months into the one year project they attempted system integration for the first time. Unfortunately, like many companies that hope for everything to just work out perfectly, many of the mechanical subsystems didn't fit together. Over 180 drawings had to be redone, causing a three month delay in a highly contested market.

To avoid this kind of late breaking bad news, you must simply have the courage to spend a little extra time and money early on in the project. Do your chicken test on a working prototype (even without having all the bells and whistles yet) within the first 25% of the schedule. This way you can find out if you're really on track, confirm many of your high risk assumptions, and possibly decide to alter your course. With a typical one year schedule, you could fail the test at the 90 day mark, start over, and still probably ship a product ahead of your competition, who had to do massive rework later in their project.

One last remark about the chicken test: The war archives of many companies reveal that on average, from the time you have passed this vital assessment point, you still have about 50% or half the project left to do. So don't kid yourself. Plan better, and leave plenty of time for system integration, testing, and debugging.

---

[1] Peters, Tom and Austin, Nancy. 1985. *A Passion for Excellence, The Leadership Difference*. Random House, p. 130. Insightful information on innovation and "Skunkworks."

© 1998 Global Brain, Inc.

#9. Follow a Flow Process to Meet Milestones, Manage Risk, and Ensure Quality

- Agree on Vision, including Performance, Time, Development Cost, & Product Cost (PTCC).
- Define and manage to short milestones.
- Use simple tools to plan and execute well: checklists, historical data, rules of thumb...
- Resist change, but change quickly and clearly when necessary.

Commandment #9 Techniques:
Follow a Flow process to meet milestones, manage risk, and ensure quality

A) Agree on a reasonable *see-saw schedule.*

B) Use project management computer software to plan tasks and resources, set milestones, and re-plan if missed milestones.

⊃C) Post the milestones, and track to them.

D) Have a *written* product development Flow process and selective sign-off for the 13 defined steps of Flow.

E) Use checklists as structural guidelines for each step, including a list of deliverables to clearly define each milestone.

F) Encourage creativity and "Golden Moments"- find shortcuts.

⊃G) Project Leader identifies major problems early, and jumps in to facilitate breakthroughs and avoid delays.

H) Top management personally involved in and convinced of achievement of major milestones.

⊃I) Technically respected outside observer reviews key designs, problems.

J) Practice occasional pause and evaluate.

⊃K) Freeze conceptual design as early as possible—change later only for safety, reliability reasons.

L) Use evolving functional design outline document, not rigid requirements specification.

M) Create and adhere to meeting schedules and guidelines.

⊃N) Avoid "creeping elegance" (excessive perfection) and feature creep and "ship it".

O) Use work breakdown structures and industry and company specific planning and estimating checklists to ensure the work is sized and sequenced appropriately.

P) Avoid using software to track or update actuals, except for historical data for future estimates.

Q) Decide up front which development model you'll use and review which deliverables make sense to do for this project in each phase.

R) Negotiate elements of your Flow process with outside partners.

S) Individuals on the team must estimate their own work and help assess dependencies to ensure accuracy and buy-in.

T) Do early test, manufacturing, documentation, and deployment planning to ensure that late project milestones are accurately set.

U) Use action item tracking to pace detailed team tasks.

V) Define quality goals for Flow steps and deliverables where it makes sense, and review against them before proceeding.

W) Use MBWA and iterative and informal design reviews to pace work and catch mistakes as early as possible; don't wait for formal phase reviews.

X) Use progressively tighter change control as the project proceeds to properly handle or avoid late changes and undesired rework.

Y) Use trend analysis judiciously to understand true project progress.

Z) Plunge through the product development funnel by micro-managing the last 10% of the project.

© 1998 Global Brain, Inc.

#10. Get Early Feedback and Nail Defects Quickly

- Keep close ties between team and strategic/first customers.
- Be able to tell when you're done.
- Transition intelligently.

A)	Question, listen, admit and respond to key customers; include lead and target customers, and other departments within the company.
⊃B)	Particularly close tie between Engineering, Manufacturing, Quality, Field/Customer Support, and customers for first shipments.
C)	Don't move key team members on to new projects too early.
D)	Use beta sites to weed out defects *before* release.
⊃E)	Create a company wide sense of urgency mode to solve major defects once discovered.
F)	Use alpha system testing to test new functionality and regression test old functionality.
G)	Involve customers (internal and external) in reviews and testing to find issues and defects before beta, track them, and use an early adopter program to ensure proper translation of customer feedback.
H)	Do pilot runs to test the process and product before volume manufacturing and shipment, and to slowly introduce the product to customers.

© 1998 Global Brain, Inc.

#11. Learn From and Improve the Above Process

➲A) Hold lessons-learned reviews during and after the project.

➲B) "Start talking and get to work."

C) Remember to see the process as an ever improving guideline.

D) Hold Project Leader "best practice" forums and issues meetings to cross-fertilize between projects.

E) Identify root-causes of schedule slips and cost overruns and their quantitative impacts to help justify ongoing improvement efforts.

F) Record causes of product defects as they are discovered to improve the process next time.

If you think education is expensive,

try ignorance!

Exercises: Techniques and Case Studies

Exercises Using Techniques

The power of the commandments and techniques come when the team is aware of those past projects have followed, and those that have been violated. Analyze a past or current project to gain further insight into your current capabilities, and where Q*R*PD techniques can be put to use to accelerate your development.

1. **Think back to a project you were involved with (or knew a lot about) that was considered a *successful* blitzkrieg, especially for meeting schedule.**

    1) Describe it briefly, but with important details about the kind of product, the schedule, team size, etc. Then explain why it was considered successful.

    2) Make a list of the five (5) most important Q*R*PD techniques that were followed that made the project successful overall. Refer to them by Commandment number and technique, for example: 5G. <u>After each technique</u> in the list, briefly explain why and how following that technique resulted in a positive impact to the project's objectives.

    3) Speculate on the positive effect, cumulatively, that following these Q*R*PD practices had on making the project successful. For example, did it complete 30% faster than a comparable project? This is obviously just an estimate, but try to think it through, and make a succinct case for your answer.

2. **Think back to a project you were involved with (or knew a lot about) that was considered *less successful*, especially for <u>not</u> meeting schedule.**

    1) Describe it briefly, but with sufficient details about the kind of product, the schedule, team size, etc. Then explain why it was considered less successful.

    2) Make a list of two columns: one of three or more Q*R*PD techniques that were followed, the other of three or more that were violated (refer to them by Commandment number and technique, for example: 5G).

    3) For each violated technique in the list, briefly explain why and how and speculate on the consequent cost to the project (time, money, etc.).

    4) Armed with the knowledge from Q*R*PD, estimate what percent of the project's duration could have been saved?

© 1998 Global Brain, Inc.

A Less Successful Blitzkrieg: "BlownBalloon" Case Study

Good Heart News (GHN), a leading company in the field of surgical tools for cardiovascular applications, decided to design a balloon catheter designed for coronary angioplasty. This product, the "BlownBalloon," was regarded as a platform technology and deemed critical in order to maintain market share.

The product's potential gross yearly sales were about $100 million, with a gross profit margin of about 60%. It sold in a very competitive market, where each market share point was worth $1.6 million.

A focused effort on this platform project burned R&D investment at a rate of about $41,000 per month. The BlownBalloon was on a schedule that reflected a normal product life cycle for GHN of about 18 months, although total development time, including FDA approval, was expected to consume approximately two years.

The project team consisted of seven core members representing various functional areas: R&D, reliability engineering, regulatory affairs, clinical research, marketing, manufacturing, and quality engineering. The de facto project leader was the R&D engineer who not only had responsibility for developing the project, but also for organizing team meetings, and tracking progress. He also presented results regularly to senior management, especially at key milestones. They supported the project wholeheartedly, and recognized milestone accomplishments publicly, including with lavish bonuses.

To have the greatest potential of success however, the project depended on three major areas of technology, all categorized as major risk areas whose processes had not been proven in-house: a new lubricious coating, metal alloy (kink-resistant) shaft, and a higher pressure balloon material. At least three months and $50,000 were spent doing feasibility testing and trying to justify to senior management that the product was still viable even without all three of these major technological innovations. This could have been avoided if a clear, limited objective had been set that defined the customer benefits required, and a backup plan existed for the worst-case contingency. As it turned out, two of these innovations were implemented with the help of some outside consultants with direct expertise in these areas.

Once engineering got through these design hurdles, the BlownBalloon had to be manufacturable in quantity. And yet, unfortunately, during crucial phases in Pilot and transfer to Production, two key personnel were either promoted or transferred to a different group. While done for personal and career growth reasons, these transfers came at a critical time in terms of handing off knowledge, and did not allow an overlap period for replacements to come up to speed on project issues. An estimated four months and $40,000 were lost in retraining and opportunity cost of having earlier manufacturing involvement in process issues.

Furthermore, despite use of a corporate plane, the project stalled while transferring it from the engineering group's location to the manufacturing plant some 500 miles further south. It was difficult to obtain early manufacturing involvement in the project. Whether it was due to physical separation or a simple lack of resources, manufacturing voiced concerns only after equipment and processes were transferred from Pilot to Production. This resulted in some equipment and fixturing redesign that caused a three-month delay and $30,000 worth of machine shop time/materials. Earlier interdisciplinary cooperation would have avoided this delay.

The product was eventually filed with the FDA, who pointed out numerous deficiencies in the product. Consequently, the engineering group remained involved and close to the field support engineers who worked with the

© 1998 Global Brain, Inc.

FDA's reviewers. However, the organization's conservative consensus decision-making culture inhibited the team from quickly responding to technological and regulatory issues, as well as obtaining permission to release product for initial clinical trials. The additive effect of these bureaucratic delays was probably about two months with an approximate cost of $20,000.

Overall the project was considered less successful because of the delayed filing, the deficiencies it received from the FDA, and delays in manufacturing ramp-up. Each month the project was delayed caused GHN's market share to erode due to increased competition and the fact that current products did not perform as good as the competition's.

Daniel Iman, one of the team members, says that he "would estimate that at least 6 out of 24 total months could have been saved, resulting in a 25% reduction in project duration." Over the total project duration the company lost 15% on market share to the competition, and assuming that the release of this project would have stopped or maybe even reversed this decline, the opportunity cost of the 6-month delay was as follows:

.25 (15%) market share pts. x $1.6 million/pt.

≥$5.6 million

Any delay in market release is financially detrimental to product revenue (shorter lifetime) and profit margins (higher prices and lower manufacturing cost). In addition, GHN's company image suffered along with market share.

Which techniques from the QRPD checklist of techniques were violated, and contributed to this project's problems?

A Successful Blitzkrieg
"Verichina" Case Study:

In March 1992, in the Asia Pacific region, a local competitor to Verifone announced a breakthrough product—a credit card point of sale (POS) terminal that had a Chinese character graphic display interface. Verifone's two larger customers immediately announced that this feature was now required for their POS terminals, and thus they would begin purchasing units from this competitor.

Verifone had no product to offer that supported this feature. All of their current products were based on a 1X16 VF segment display technology, which did not lend itself at all to adaptation for Chinese character support.

Verifone's sales force then struck a deal with the customers—if Verifone could deliver functional prototypes for field testing by July 15 (1992!) and volume production units by October, they would continue with Verifone as their single source POS terminal supplier.

Everyone knew that meeting this aggressive schedule would require some special techniques, as that was about one-half the normal development cycle time for this type product.

Desperate, Product Marketing decide to approach Douglas Encke, at the time the Director of a small R&D group (10 engineers) in Paris, France. They offered him and his team to "become heroes" and accept responsibility for the project.... As in most smaller companies, all engineering resources were already over-committed to priority projects. The Paris team was selected because prioritizing them onto the VeriChina project would have the least painful impact to the company overall.

Another advantage in having the Paris development group do this project was that they did not have a lot of overhead with managers, or constant status reports and design reviews. When Doug took on the project, he asked (insisted) that the development group be left alone by senior management to "go make it happen." That request was respected. This autonomy to make decisions quickly, with minimal second-guessing and analysis paralysis, was a contributing factor to the success.

Putting together the right team to attack this project turned out to be one of the most important decisions. Because Verifone had no graphic LCD expertise in our company (and no time to learn), they contracted an outside consultant to join the team for the project duration and design this subsystem. They also made certain to assign firmware, test, and manufacturing engineers that were experienced with product development at Verifone. The engineers selected were also highly committed people, available to do "fun" and challenging tasks.

As an example, one of the committed and flexible engineers was asked to jump onto an airplane to fly to London to integrate prototype hardware and software (where he labored until 3 am to get it to work), then get on an airplane 3 hours later and fly to Taiwan to integrate with vacuum-cast plastic case prototypes and LCD samples, then fly that night to Hong Kong for a press release and beta site installation. None other was present at that demonstration than the CEO of American Express, who watched to see if the product worked. While this sounds hard to believe, it's a true story. What a classical example of JITPD, or Just-In-Time Product Development!

Rather than designing a new product, the team leveraged heavily off of existing products. This included the main processor PCB Assembly and the industrial design and packaging. They also re-used existing components and microcontrollers, wherever

© 1998 Global Brain, Inc.

possible. That minimized the work to select and qualify and release new components; and leveraged knowledge base and tools that were already in place.

Doug also made sure that his team did a lot of early, rapid prototyping of the product up front. This helped to determine early on what was the minimum size display and optimal keyboard layout, and which existing packaging design the team could leverage from most effectively. In fact,

this technique led them to make a mid-point decision to switch from one packaging approach to another. Given how the product exceeded the expectations of everyone, that decision proved to be a critical one for the success and profitability of the VeriChina.

Despite the incredible demands of this project, Doug realized the importance of making sure that everyone was having fun, too. Recently, he was quoted as saying, "I am more and more learning as a leader how important this truly is to doing successful new product development. Keeping the development team charged up, the energy level high, having people laugh at themselves, etc.—this all keeps people wanting to work hard for the team effort. We did this during the VeriChina Blitzkrieg project by having cartoons hanging in the office; having TGIF each Friday afternoon; periodic off-site picnics, and more that I'm sure I've forgotten about by now."

On the more serious side, he goes on to say that, "above all, the project required me as the leader to keep a clear vision and address any politics or runaway ego's or problem performers quickly and effectively. Sometimes I even had to humble myself and act like a bit of a clown, and be the first one to laugh and set the example/tone for everyone."

This project is today considered one of the most successful in Verifone's history, for several reasons. The first is, of course, revenue/profit. The product exceeded all targets, and has had the fastest ramp-to-volume of any of their our products: over 40,000 units in less than one year from release. The "COGS" (Cost of Goods Sold) came in under target: $128 per unit actual versus $135 target.

This project was also completed mostly on schedule. The first field test installation date was slipped to July 27 from the original request of July 15, but revenue deliveries occurred on time. Also, the product has been very reliable with high quality. And although the focus of the product was for the Chinese character set in Asia Pacific, the design of the graphic display system had the flexibility to support other user interfaces and languages. This resulted in the product being spun off into 25+ different countries around the world (Saudi Arabia, Thailand, UK, Czechoslovakia, Mexico, USA, Israel, Brazil, etc.)—again, in record-breaking time.

Doug summarizes the cumulative effect of using QRPD techniques on the VeriChina project's success by saying: "I believe that if we had followed the Verifone traditional development approach and schedule, the time-to-market would have increased by 40-50%. This is arrived at by examining other similar development efforts done before, during, and after this one. In terms of impact to profitability, it is even greater than just losing 4-6 months of revenue—because we would have opened the door to our competitor in the region, allowing them to gain market share, credibility, and financial strength. We also would have lost our two largest customers in the Asia Pacific sales region, thus adversely impacting our business plan and strategy. I would estimate this impact alone at something like $10-20M lost revenue annually."

Ironically, this blitzkrieg project succeeded near the very battlefields (France) where the German army first demonstrated the power of using new methods and techniques to surprise and overwhelm the competition. It obviously demonstrates the stuff heroes are made of, and that very successful products *can* be developed in half the time by using QRPD techniques.

Which techniques from the QRPD checklist made this project a success?

(Solutions in Appendix A.)

© 1998 Global Brain, Inc.

Reading: QRPD® Techniques Detailed Explanations and Examples

QRPD Techniques
Detailed Explanations and Examples

Table of Contents

#1: Focus on a clear, limited, and on-target vision 123

#2: Assemble the right team and leaders 135

#3: Initiate early cross-functional cooperation 145

#4: Create a synergistic, mission-oriented, productive environment 151

#5: Reward all participants commensurably 163

#6: Use innovative, parallel, iterative design strategies 169

#7: Invest money to buy time and tools and to minimize risk 177

#8: Prototype and test key design concepts early 183

#9: Follow a flow process to meet milestones, manage risk, and ensure quality. 191

#10: Get early feedback and nail defects quickly 205

#11: Learn from and improve the above process 211

© 1998 Global Brain, Inc.

Commandment #1.

FOCUS ON A CLEAR, ON-TARGET, AND LIMITED VISION

In managing projects and developing products, the number one reason for schedule slippage is changing requirements, or lack of well-defined requirements. These schedule delays indicate a lack of critical understanding of the important purpose of a product and a lack of continued focus on the most important goals.

Aggressive time-to-market targets first and foremost mandate a crystal-clear understanding of what you're trying to accomplish for your customers, and an unwavering commitment to achieving it. These techniques provide the tools.

⊃A) **Innovate incrementally (Base hits, not homeruns).**

What happens in baseball when you try to hit a homerun? You strike out—often. Once in a while you get lucky.

Incremental innovation helps conquer one of the typical pitfalls of product development—long projects geared to producing the "it-can-do-it-all" product. These projects take the "long bomb" strategy, where the company lobs a long-range assault toward a distant product objective. If the market changes in the middle of such a long development—which now often happens within a year or 6 months or 3 months— you stand a great chance of getting to the target only to discover that the market has moved. You may try to respond to the shifts along the way by constantly course-correcting, and in the end you may never finish a product at all.

Incremental innovation forces you to define the most important benefits to the customer, and to deliver those as quickly as possible to meet customer needs in the right timeframe. By definition, you try to deliver quickly enough that market shifts during development are minimized, and you are able to produce an on-target beneficial product. By introducing successive generations regularly, a practice perfected by many Japanese companies, you can lower overall risk while learning more about the market and the technology and continuously refining your products. You begin to construct a product strategy and project portfolio that will allow you to continue to satisfy your customers over time through successive product releases. Best of all, you rarely strike out completely, and always get paid by the customers along the way. They win, too, since you presumably provide them with value and a better way to do something.

Mitsubishi Electric provides a good example of how a company can use the incremental innovation technique. In improving a 3 horse power heat pump product, Mitsubishi made essential step-by-step changes over a five year period instead of attempting the improvements all at once. In the first year the company added integrated circuits. Microprocessors were added in year two. Improving condenser efficiency was the target in year three by replacing the reciprocating compressor with a rotary version. In year four the company enhanced the control system by adding sensors that used the microprocessor's power. Finally, by adding an automatic motor speed control for the compressor in year five, the

Commandment #1. Focus on a Clear, On-Target, and Limited Vision

company achieved even greater efficiency. Mitsubishi's focus on base hits and not homeruns helped them to maximize their product's returns, kept the product continually up to date and fresh, and cost a minimal investment each year. It also allowed their customers to essentially keep financing their continuing product improvement, so that after 5 years they had a brand new, state-of-the-art product.

A type of project that absolutely requires incremental innovation is web site development. Web production tends to involve a much greater level of subjective criteria than traditional development projects. Users do not care as much about the technical aspects of a site—with the notable exception of download time—but rather value a web page according to content, multimedia interest, and general layout. By first implementing the basic structure and content of the site, evaluating the results both technically and subjectively, then proceeding to add advanced features in stages, the risk of creating a technically adept site that no one wants to visit is minimized. You can save money and time by using an iterative process. You ensure that each iteration meets the needs of the perceived user, both technically and in content, before proceeding.

As another example, a start-up integrated circuit (IC) manufacturing company needed to install new software to automate its operations. Within any company there are many processes and operations that can be automated: the manufacturing line, parts procurement, payroll, other human resources functions, etc. Implementing all of them can take years. The company had two choices: It could do it the old way and implement everything at once. Or it could follow the dictum of the information technology (IT) industry for rapid implementation projects: get the company running on the new software within 3 to 12 months, *implementing only what is absolutely needed* in the first round. The company decided to get the critical manufacturing line operational first, and left the payroll system and everything else for later. It made its aggressive 4 month target and was ready to supply the market with its new leading edge integrated circuits.

Incidentally, you may have to educate your customers about the concept of incremental innovation. The head of Cambridge Technology Partners, a firm that creates large software systems for clients such as Microsoft, said "Users ask for every feature they can think of because they think if they don't get it now, they never will." ("Speed Kills the Competition," *Fast Company*. Aug-Sept. 1996, p. 85) Until more customers buy the concept of incremental innovation, we'll have trouble satisfying them, and keeping our projects small and iterative enough. Cambridge Technology Partners therefore spends time educating their customers on the economic benefits (or lack of benefits) of the projects and features they are considering.

"Innovation is 1 new idea and 100 old ones."

© 1998 Global Brain, Inc.

Commandment #1. Focus on a Clear, On-Target, and Limited Vision

⊃B) **Restrict each product to a manageable number of major innovations, typically three.**

This is a rule of thumb for achieving incremental innovation. A major innovation is defined as something "done elsewhere a few times, but never yet in-house." See the table below. These innovations are inherently risky; the more you have on your project, the higher your odds that something will go wrong. During phase I of the project, assess technical risks and ensure that you aren't biting off more than you can chew.

One project to update a custom computer placed a high priority on size reduction of the overall package, a decrease in its weight, and an increase in processor performance. To get to the most desired size, the engineers determined that they would need to use a totally new switching power supply design from an outside vendor, construct a new chassis of a lightweight material never previously tried within the company, implement 3 existing hardware designs in ASICs, and switch to a new microprocessor family never before used in the company. These changes were all considered major innovations. The team determined that this project was too big for one iteration; they decided to focus on the performance upgrade and slight weight reductions first, and approved a project to implement the new microprocessor design and power supply.

Categorize a List of Innovations by Risk Level

RISK LEVEL	AMOUNT OF UNKNOWN	COST TO RECOVER
1. FLIRTING WITH DISASTER	Believed to have never been done by anyone, anywhere in the world!	INFINITE?
2. VERY MAJOR	Done by somebody, somewhere, once	VERY HIGH
3. MAJOR	Done elsewhere a few times, but never yet in-house	HIGH
4. MEDIUM	Done commonly or by people who now are in-house (but weren't at the time)	MEDIUM
5. MINOR	Done often, including in-house	LOW

© 1998 Global Brain, Inc.

Commandment #1. Focus on a Clear, On-Target, and Limited Vision

C) **Avoid breaking new ground simultaneously in (all 3): technology, applications, markets/customers.**

This is another rule of thumb for appropriately limiting innovation and risk in a particular project. Trying to create a product which is new for your company in technology, the markets or customers it's intended for, and the applications you're delivering to those customers, adds incredible "unknowns" relative to your experience.

A particular medical device manufacturer decided to get into a new type of application: patient information management systems, typically software databases running on off-the-shelf computers. After starting out with a 486-based PC running standard driver software, the engineers became concerned about performance. They didn't believe the system would run fast enough. The 7 engineers decided to write their own faster software drivers and other tool kits and use a faster hardware platform, a Sun workstation. All these decisions were fatal. The customer segment for this product was different than that buying their costly monitoring devices; and these new customers could not handle the cost of the faster platform, which were double the original plan. Delivery time slipped out 6 months (added to an original 12 month schedule) since the new driver and toolkit technology took the engineers much longer than expected to implement. In short, the company's risk went through the roof, and the project failed.

D) **Justify all innovations (keep list) using benefit to cost to risk analysis.**

For every innovation identified, perform a cost-benefit analysis to be sure that this innovation is truly needed and thus worth the increased risk. See the example cost-benefit exercises in the Blitzkrieg section.

Teams often include innovations just to create a "hot" product. These innovations, which are inherently risky, may or may not be justified by the customer's real needs. The true financial benefit associated with each innovation must be understood. Does the innovation provide features or capabilities that will be responsible for 80% of revenue? or 10% of revenue? or 1%? If only 10% or 1%, is it worth taking that extra time and risk to include the innovation in the first incremental innovation of the product?

E) **Quantify objectives and make them measurable wherever possible.**

Make the requirements for your product, system, or service crystal clear through the use of quantifiable descriptions and outcomes. For example, rather than saying that a software application must have a "user friendly interface", state "any function can be performed within 3 keystrokes" or "any function can be learned by a new user within 15 minutes."

A project involved the design of a patient information management system for a hospital. The users of PC software had never used a Windows-based system before, much less a database management system with a graphical user interface. The vision for the product stipulated that the product must be sufficiently easy to

© 1998 Global Brain, Inc.

Commandment #1. Focus on a Clear, On-Target, and Limited Vision

use. Development fashioned a user interface they thought would fit the bill; Marketing reviewed it; all seemed well.

However, during the coding period, Marketing continued to request numerous changes to the graphical user interface to make the product easier to use. This resulted in arguments with Development: were the changes really necessary, or was it already easy enough to use? Days and days of changes and arguments ensued. The arguments (and the change requests) didn't stop until the team jointly came up with a *quantitative* specification for ease of use: "the administrator must not have to use more than 3 keystrokes or mouse clicks to access any major program function." The design was changed to accommodate this definition and work progressed without further delays.

⊃F) **Strive for an adequate solution by finding an optimal balance of Performance (P), Time (T), and costs (C).**

As described in the Blitzkrieg chapter, the goal of ROI-oriented product development is to balance the four product development factors:

- **Product performance (P):** Quality, or perceived value by the customer, including features and functionality of the product.
- **Time-to-market (T):** the amount of time the project takes to get the product out the door, deliver the value to the customer, and begin the economic benefits to the company.
- **Product cost (C):** the cost of delivery, including any unit cost to manufacture the product, as well as implications for life-cycle costs related to manufacture, installation, and maintenance.
- **Project cost (C):** the project budget, including the amount of money the company will spend to bring the product to market, in salaries, equipment, and other non-recurring investments.

The Flow section describes how this PTCC balance is arrived at during phase I of the project, using the process of "see-saw specifications and schedules."

In the example of the new patient information management system in Technique C above, it turns out that the faster performance was not really needed in the first release of the product. These engineers made a common mistake, assuming that an optimal product would be "best." The switch to the workstation platform provided an optimal technical product, but not an optimal solution to the customer's problems. In this case, the cost of the platform was much more important, and the optimal technical approach was actually much too expensive for the customer. The engineers could have stayed with the 486 and off-the-shelf drivers for the first release of the product—an adequate product that provided a good solution for their customers.

© 1998 Global Brain, Inc.

Commandment #1. Focus on a Clear, On-Target, and Limited Vision

G) **Interview one or two leading-edge customers, and establish rapport and phone contact between them and the design team as future beta sites.**

> *Leading-edge customers:* those customers who give you valuable design input not only for the current generation product you're working on, but also give you ideas in which direction your future products should go.

The key to a "quality" product is intimate understanding of the customer. To end up with an on-target product, you must get actual input from, and form relationships with, your most sophisticated, "early adopter" customers. Start this relationship at the beginning of the project during the Vision process.

Conner Peripherals, a new disk drive manufacturer at the time, benefited from a close union with Compaq Computer Corporation, getting valuable feedback on performance and customer needs to consistently create high quality marketable products. Conner's business was, in fact, built to its ultimate prominence by its highly profitable relationship with Compaq. Many great products have been created by such strategic alliances.

- Encourage relationships with members of the design team, not just Marketing, so that the team can get quick, open, thorough feedback on requirements and design options throughout the project.

- Involve these leading-edge customers in many ways throughout the project, such as participating in design reviews, prototype testing, and usability testing, well before time for the formal beta testing. Set the expectation in your team and with these customers that *any team member* can call that customer to bounce ideas off them or ask questions.

- Establish these customers as beta sites early on, rather than waiting until close to beta test time to get a commitment.

Consider a new printer such as the HP DeskJet. Such printers have to take into account the needs of leading-edge customers, those who are concerned with amount of memory, font support, and advanced graphics capability for their applications. And HP has certainly done very well meeting the needs of this type of customer. But to sell a high volume of printers as HP has done, the vast numbers of target customers must also be taken into account. Read on to Technique H.

© 1998 Global Brain, Inc.

Commandment #1. Focus on a Clear, On-Target, and Limited Vision

H) **Also interview one or two typical customers representing quantity buyers and/or the mass market (or survey it), and establish them as future beta sites.**

> *Typical customers:* those who are generally not the first to adopt your product, but will form more of the quantity or mass market later. These customers are "typical" users, perhaps less sophisticated than leading-edge customers—they expect to turn on the product, or start using the service, and be able to begin using it to advantage quickly and naturally.

Typical customers will often have very different needs, expectations, and constraints than leading-edge customers (see Technique G). For instance, they might be less sophisticated users and thus would require a simpler user interface for a computer product. They might require a different price point. They might require much more user documentation or special training programs. They might have to be reached through different sales channels.

One typical customer group for the new HP DeskJet printer discussed in Technique G was secretarial personnel who were fairly new to computer use. When the product first started shipping, issues arose when a number of these customers thought their products did not work. Actually, the product worked fine—once the user found the power switch! It was located in a new spot, on the bottom of the printer, out of sight. Not used to experimenting with their tools, these users assumed that the printer should just work when they plugged it into the wall, and called HP when it didn't. Leading-edge customers probably would have played with the product, rather than making quick assumptions, until they discovered the location of the switch.

As with leading-edge customers, identify and form relationships with your typical customers, to get feedback during requirements, design, prototyping, and later, beta testing. Set the expectation in your team and with these customers that *any team member* can call that customer to bounce ideas off them or ask questions. Establish them as a future beta site early in the project.

To further illustrate the power of following Techniques G and H regarding leading-edge and typical customers:

When Mountain Computer sought customer input on its floppy disk certifier, IBM provided many useful suggestions for not only designing the hardware and software, but even additional software features and tests that many floppy disk manufacturers subsequently found valuable. In contrast, Lotus and Microsoft wanted to use this same floppy disk certifier in just a go/no-go manner, i.e. to tell them if the millions of disks they bought were good or bad. In response Mountain provided two configurations: a two-bin certifier for companies like Lotus and Microsoft that just sorted for good and bad, and the original 6-bin model that allowed manufacturers such as BASF and IBM to sort disks for more subtle levels of differences. Both types of customers gave valuable but different input.

© 1998 Global Brain, Inc.

Commandment #1. Focus on a Clear, On-Target, and Limited Vision

Many companies do marketing surveys of thousands of customers to get such feedback. In some cases that may be not only justified but mandatory. But many times we have found that close contact with only a handful of leading-edge and typical customers provides as much, if not more, useful input for product design as those vastly more time consuming and expensive market studies.

One more example: When Microsoft started design of its C++ compiler, the natural reaction was to develop a product to satisfy the leading-edge programmers already using C++. But in the course of talking with a number of typical customers at a software conference, one of the team members realized that these people didn't want all the fancy templates, exception handling, and neat features the advanced programmers did. The benefit of the product to the typical customer would be the ability to become a hot-shot programmer making $90,000 per year as quickly as possible. To satisfy these customers, the first iteration of the compiler focused on creating simple wizards that would generate code "at the push of a button" and fulfill the wildest dreams of the mass market.

To ensure the rapid development and rapid success of your product, be sure to identify the most important customer segments for your first iteration, and form relationships that will help you understand exactly what they need.

I) **Satisfy the customer and end user needs before wants by being solution-oriented.**

If we are to limit the scope of our projects for best risk management and time-to-market, we must make sure we include the solutions to our customers' most important problems. Don't lose this focus on understanding their problems and devising solutions when making your early implementation decisions: the "what" to build must not come before the "why".

To achieve the best PTCC balance you obviously have to have an accurate understanding of your customers and their needs. Who are the customers, or buyers, of your product? Who are the users? The customers and users may be two totally different groups of people, and the product must address the needs of both.

To answer those questions you must find ways to get real data and make decent decisions: by interviewing lead or innovative users as well as later typical or mass-market customers; by getting engineers close to the customer as early as possible; by forming strong ongoing relationships with key customers that provide continual insight into their needs.

A project to miniaturize a customized special-purpose computer got bogged down in debates about making it as small as possible in order to give the customer maximum flexibility to fit all possible mounting applications, and because "we ought to be able to make it this small". The *real* need was a computer no taller than 9", to allow mounting it in the majority of locations (but not all) the customer was concerned about.

Apple Computer, when originally creating a graphic interface based computer, didn't understand the needs of its market when it created the Lisa computer for business users, priced at over $10,000 per machine back in the 1980s. Businesses

Commandment #1. Focus on a Clear, On-Target, and Limited Vision

could not reconcile this price with the perceived benefit of the graphical interface. Learning from its mistake, however, Apple then developed a low cost graphical interface computer for consumer use and introduced the wildly successful Macintosh Computer in 1984.

J) **Know the competition and their customers, including competing technologies.**

What hurt the railroad companies the most during the 20th century? It wasn't competition from other railroad companies, it was the advent of the jet airplane. They didn't see it coming! In a similar vein, at Mountain Computer we prided ourselves on our high quality tape drives made of metal. We dismissed the entry of a low cost competitor to the market, CMS, with their junky looking plastic tape drive. So we failed to invest the necessary dollars in developing a product for that segment of the market which CMS had correctly identified—the single non-networked PC. It took us a couple of years to recognize this market, launch our effort, and catch up. Meanwhile CMS boomed and far surpassed our company's sales.

Make sure to always keep your eyes open for the best ways to meet current and future customers' needs, including understanding the best technology for the purpose.

K) **Restrict product requirements to necessary ones, and state them in the Product Vision as unambiguous criteria that allow shipments to begin.**

We've already discussed that through understanding of your customers and how your product will provide value to them you should limit each project to the most important features and "incremental innovations". It's critical then to not "overspecify" the product with requirements that don't really contribute to the customer value. One of the benefits of the Vision process is that, properly executed, it eliminates time unnecessarily spent by cross-functional teams reviewing highly-detailed specifications line by line. Teams typically argue over details that do not require cross-functional approval, details of the features or implementation that are not critical to whether the product truly delivers value to the customer, and details which often cannot be figured out before some phase II detailed design work takes place. A medical device manufacturer's project post-mortem survey found that only 122 of the over 600 requirements line items were actually critical to the customer. Yet the entire team had spent precious time reviewing and negotiating all 600 of these items.

It is also critical to clearly specify the requirements that allow shipments to begin. For instance, the ultimate cost target for a product to be manufactured in volume might be $1000. But if your financial position will allow you to ship a certain volume at a cost of $1200, state both numbers in the Vision and ensure you get that product out to customers as soon as you can.

© 1998 Global Brain, Inc.

Commandment #1. Focus on a Clear, On-Target, and Limited Vision

⊃L) **Resist changing the Vision.**

The Vision process is critical to the ongoing focus of the team as well: once the early definition phase is "completed", suggestions for improvements inevitably arise. New information becomes available, someone who didn't speak up before becomes vocal about the need for a feature or attribute, or perhaps the market changes. But if requirements are allowed to change capriciously mid-stream or late in a project, engineering work will have to be redone, and the project will slip. In some cases, it will slip numerous times—when there is no sense of product purpose, there is no corresponding fierce control of product requirements, and a knee-jerk change mentality will rule the day. The Product Vision is a mechanism for both achieving and *maintaining* team alignment.

According to an engineer at a video game company, if his team had given in to all the requirements changes asked for during the project, or even spent time discussing them as they used to, their one-year project would have slipped an additional 3 months. But it didn't, because the team resisted changing the Vision.

M) **Write a Product Vision document iteratively during the SSSS process to align the team and ensure focus in the right direction throughout the project.**

The Product Vision is a one to two-page document capturing the reasons for the project and the most important aspects of the product. It is written during phase I of the project as part of the "see-saw specifications and scheduling" process. The Vision identifies the customers for the product and its benefits to them; critical factors the customer will use to judge quality or value; key technology and features; crucial product factors; and relevant financial information. This information reflects the PTCC balance chosen by the team.

The Vision is an absolutely critical aligning document that focuses the team and forms a contract between the team and Management: we'll give you a product fast, if you won't make us keep shooting at a moving target. The process of creating the Vision is critical to getting team alignment.

N) **Write a New Product/Project Proposal and rough business case to initiate a new product idea into the development cycle.**

The New Product Proposal (NPP) kicks off a potential Q*R*PD project. Anyone in the company can submit one. Rough business case information accompanying the NPP immediately focuses everyone on the potential benefits of the idea to the company. The NPP encourages company-wide formulation of good product ideas, and a company-wide attention to bottom-line benefits. See the Flow section for more details on the NPP.

© 1998 Global Brain, Inc.

Commandment #1. Focus on a Clear, On-Target, and Limited Vision

O) **Use trade-off tables to summarize information about project PTCC alternatives and facilitate rapid decisions.**

One of the most difficult parts of the early days of a project is simply getting through all the decisions—which features to provide, which technologies to use, which risks to take—to identify that clear, on-target, limited vision for the product. Always use a trade-off table to compare technical, schedule, cost, risk, and resource alternatives for your project. These tables speed up decision-making by putting all the data in black and white on one piece of paper. Incremental innovations become obvious; a risky "do it all" project screams out from the page; endless arguments can be put to rest more quickly.

P) **Have the entire team and upper management sign the Product Vision.**

The Product Vision is the contract among team members and between the team and management. We use the ritual of signing the Vision at the end of QRPD phase I to formally underscore the incredible importance of sticking to it throughout the project. No one adds features on the sly at their desks. Management doesn't stick their heads into a developer's office and add new items. Everyone agrees that "this is the product".

© 1998 Global Brain, Inc.

Commandment #1. Focus on a Clear, On-Target, and Limited Vision

Commandment #2.

ASSEMBLE THE RIGHT TEAM AND LEADER(S)

Q*R*PD Secret #2 requires "An obsessed Project Leader and strong, synergistic cross-functional team on a mission to make it happen and meet milestones." We have to invest time and effort into selecting and right leader and team members for the particular project, and structure the team in a way that sets them up for success.

⊃A) **Select the Leader(s) very judiciously. (See Selection Criteria in the Part III, Project Leader and Team.)**

A key word here is SELECT. "Of all the decisions management makes in managing accelerated new product development, none is more crucial to success than the choice of a team leader. A strong one will be able to overcome many other shortcomings and imperfect management decisions, but a mediocre one will be stymied by even the smallest obstacles." (Reinertsen p. 112)

When companies select a leader for a new project, they often anoint someone who's a good technical contributor, or a good functional manager—or whoever happens to have the time. Needless to say, this person may not necessarily be the best Project Leader! You must get your company into the mindset *of consciously selecting the best person for the job*. Go out and hire that person if need be, even if it's a contractor who has the skills and will make the commitment.

Q*R*PD Project Leaders fill a special role requiring a range of critical skills and experience. They perform the functions of traditional project managers, but they are much more than schedule creators and trackers. Many companies do not yet understand this distinction. At a PC-based game development company, the chosen software development Project Leader did all those normal project manager jobs: created schedules, tracked progress, reported milestone status to the customer. However, he couldn't resolve issues with the lead programmer, deal with some technical uncertainties that called for iterative development, realize that the lack of assigned staff rendered the schedule virtually meaningless, or gel some competing factions into a synergistic team. Sounds incredible: how could this company think the person was right for the job? Yet it happens all the time. He was doing the outward mechanistic functions of the role, but not much else!

The team member who recounted the odyssey of the patient information management system mentioned in Techniques 1C and 1F laid the schedule slip at the feet of the Project Leader— who didn't exercise the oversight to keep these schedule-killing decisions from getting made. The leader who "couldn't say no" was responsible for a 6 month schedule slip.

Having the right leader puts your competitors at an immediate extreme disadvantage. If you're playing 5 card poker and on the first deal you already hold 3 aces in your hand, before you even draw you already stand a fairly good chance of winning the hand. The cards you draw in the rest of the project—the team, the process, technical difficulties—will influence the outcome, but you already stand a very high chance of success.

© 1998 Global Brain, Inc.

Commandment #2. Assemble The Right Team and Leader(s)

However, a caution: The Project Leader is critical, but can never be expected to carry the full load. At Abbott Laboratories, a manufacturer of sophisticated hospital devices, management expressed concerns about the role of Project Leader: if achieving rapid product development truly depends to such a great extent on a single person, doesn't too much ride on this one person's shoulders? The company can't expect a single Project Leader to handle every detail, solve every problem alone, or worry about every single possible software bug which might have the potential of harming a patient in a medical application. High-performance teams absolutely require a strong leader—but not a lone hero. Just like a star quarterback, a strong Project Leader may take you to the playoffs. But to get to the Superbowl, everyone must participate, the correct plays must be used, and everyone must play their role optimally, down to the last blocker holding his block for that half second longer. And you must be following a best-practices process.

⊃B) **Have only *one* overall team leader.**

A project team must report to *only one leader.* Not only must you appoint one overall Project Leader; you must ensure that there are no de-facto extra leaders either—such as that executive who countermands decisions or directs activities or decisions behind the scenes.

On a medical device manufacturer's project to create a laser for eye surgery, three different team members essentially acted as the leader: the hardware engineer, the mechanical engineer, and the laser specialist. They each made product feature decisions independently; they gave conflicting schedule instructions to other team members. The software eventually got three months behind schedule because no single person owned complete responsibility for the project and noticed that the software effort was short-staffed.

With a single Project Leader it is clear who has the authority to make decisions, resolve differences, and direct the project.

C) **Announce leader's and team's responsibilities formally and clearly.**

Everyone must be absolutely clear about who has responsibility for the project and for each of its components. Why? The purpose is not to institute a "command and control" project atmosphere, but in fact 180 degrees the opposite. The more clearly team members understand how everyone fits into the project, the more smoothly the project will function, with a minimum of second-guessing, in-fighting, and lost time. Team members will "get" the importance of their roles and be absolutely certain of their specific responsibilities. Others will see the team structure as sacred, including team member's authorization to speak for their functional groups and make technical decisions. Bureaucratic, top-down management will not be required.

Use a team roles list and responsibilities matrix to make everything clear to each team member. Publish these documents to formally announce, and give weight to, these roles to those outside the team. (See the sample forms in Flow.)

© 1998 Global Brain, Inc.

Commandment #2. Assemble The Right Team and Leader(s)

⊃D) **Assign team members to report directly to the leader(s), or to have their reviews heavily influenced by them.**

Project leadership must be a position of authority and responsibility. You can accomplish this with various organizational structures. If your company is organized by "matrix," where people work on project teams but report to and are reviewed by functional managers, institute a method for Project Leaders to provide inputs to each team member's performance appraisal, and for team members to provide input for the Project Leader's appraisal. Note that although this approach gives the Project Leader leverage for dealing with performance problems with a team member, it has a positive side as well. If your company explicitly rewards people for their performance on their project teams, it sends the message that projects and *results* are important, and reinforces people's attention to their project commitments.

⊃E) **Use experienced, talented volunteers: committed, flexible, enthusiastic, eager to responsibly complete the mission.**

Does everyone get to volunteer for which project they want to work on? Not always. But the volunteer spirit is very real. Think of an organization outside your job that you volunteer time to. What makes you do it? Typically, you believe in the goals of the organization and so do those you work with there. And it's important enough to you that you're willing to work through challenges, go the extra mile to help the group reach its goals.

In the classic book *Soul of a New Machine* about the development of a new computer, teams used a ritual of "signing-up": a formal statement by each team member that they were "on-board" and ready to go.

⊃F) **Strive for only full-time members on the team.**

It is not always possible to have only full-time members on the team, but strive for it. When people can focus on the project, you will avoid lost time, misunderstandings, and dropped information. If people have one primary task that they are responsible for, and every task has one person with primary responsibility for it, things will get done: there are no excuses and distractions are self-limiting. When people or tasks are shared, it's very difficult to hold people accountable. Furthermore, people work more efficiently if they are full-time on one project rather than switching back and forth between goals, tasks, and teams.

Companies routinely undertake multiple projects, with resources split across those projects, because "they're all important." They even add new projects when the organization is already running at full capacity, which rarely results in extra profit to the company. [Reinertsen p. 198] Spreading available resources across multiple projects ensures that none of the projects will get out as quickly as it could if it was staffed full-time. The reality is that it may be better for the company if the projects get worked on more sequentially, with the most important one finishing first, rather than all of them coming out later. The late cost per week for each project, and other valuation methods, can help with these decisions.

Commandment #2. Assemble The Right Team and Leader(s)

When a consumer audio manufacturer first started using Q*R*PD, the company had 12 engineers spread across 15 projects. The engineers couldn't figure out what to work on; they reported that they usually just worked on what seemed fun that day. The message to this company: DO LESS SOONER! The company subsequently reduced their number of projects to 5 and prioritized them. They got their next major product out within 7 months instead of the 18 months it had taken them to get out the previous, comparable product.

G) **For non-full-time members, pre-determine their time allocated to the project for its duration.**

If you can't have a particular team member full-time, you still must have a clear, agreed-upon time commitment from them and their functional manager. You cannot plan accurately and execute effectively without it.

For a new consumer electronics project, you might plan for a customer service person to be available half-time in phase I to participate in the Vision definition and planning; quarter time in phase II to attend design reviews and plan testing; half-time in phase III for training and execution of alpha and beta tests; and full-time in phase IV for delivery to customers. For an information technology project, a business leader might be available half-time in phase I for requirements definition, half-time for several different weeks in phase II for prototype testing, three-quarters time for several weeks in phase III for acceptance testing, and half-time during deployment to the user population.

Think through and specifically identify the time you will need from different part-time team members. Then get commitments from them and their managers.

H) **Strive for teams and sub-teams of up to 8 to 10 people (4-5 ideal).**

Logically group the work into small enough sub-teams to achieve tight day-to-day communication and synergy. When multiple people work together on closely-related aspects of a project, frequent and detailed communication is required. The more people involved in those details, the more chance you have for inefficient communication, dropped information, and ultimately project delays. And the more time you'll spend in meetings sharing information. Doubling a team's size can more than quadruple the overall communication burden [Reinertsen].

Set up the project such that the maximum amount of work can be done and decisions made without communication required across the smaller sub-teams. For instance, set up sub-teams according to the functional or technical sub-systems of the product. The larger projects at a network communications device developer usually have sub-teams for each hardware and software subsystem. Game development projects usually have a lead and sub-team of artists, a lead and sub-team of programmers, and a lead and sub-team of testers. Large software releases are divided into sub-projects according to feature sets. Any size project can be broken into logical sub-teams that will greatly enhance everyone's ability to move quickly.

© 1998 Global Brain, Inc.

Commandment #2. Assemble The Right Team and Leader(s)

I) **Find a "champion" with clout and authority.**

The product champion is a major corporate supporter or sponsor of the project who provides an extra edge for moving quickly, most often an executive or high-level manager.

The champion helps overcome large obstacles, especially resource or financial ones. He helps ensure major project decisions are made for best benefit to the company. For instance, the champion will participate in Preliminary Design Reviews in phase I to contribute to trade-off decisions. The champion can always be consulted informally as well.

When the original Hewlett-Packard HP-35 calculator was developed, Marketing was convinced that only 10,000 units would be sold. Bill Hewlett, one of two HP's founders, thought otherwise. He acted as the champion for the product, even helping out nights and weekends by getting resistors out of the stockroom for the engineers. In the end, of course, over a million of these calculators were sold. The champion believed and acted!

Also at HP, a project to develop a system to electronically distribute new software updates to users avoided a hit while everyone else took a budget cut—because the champion went into action and kept this project off the chopping block.

At a wireless network equipment manufacturer, one CEO effectively acted as a champion for a new ASIC project. He stated, "I'll be the biggest Santa Claus you've ever seen at Christmas if the product is shipping at or below the cost target." And he backed up his words with hands-on support during the project: he authorized large expenditures for risk-reducing parallel design efforts; he reinforced the importance of the project with all the functional vice-presidents to ensure their support; and he encouraged the team and its leader.

Criteria for selecting the Champion (select at beginning of phase I):
- Someone who has clout and authority, and budget control, usually the president, a vice-president, or a director.
- The executive who has the most direct, clear interest and stake in the successful outcome of this project.

J) **Have a "gatekeeper" to inform the team on external technological news.**

Unfortunately it may be difficult for each individual members of a fast-moving project team to stay abreast of every technical advance or news of interest. A gatekeeper is a person who stays tuned to technological news, understands the needs of this particular team, and keeps the busy team members informed of developments. Those developments can then often be brought into the project to enhance the product, speed up development, or reduce costs.

Commandment #2. Assemble The Right Team and Leader(s)

K) **Enlist "experts" as adjunct members of the team.**

The adjunct expert is a team member who is not full-time but whose contribution can have a critical impact on quality and time. When you identify your project's technological innovations, all the technical areas in which you may not have adequate company or team expertise are candidates for an outside expert. Find someone, inside or outside company, to fill in the gaps. Sign them up as adjunct member, and involve them enough in the project to have them feel a stake in the outcome.

For instance, for a company new to wireless technology—a notoriously "black magic" area of electrical engineering—an experienced RF (radio frequency) design engineer is key until the company develops in-house expertise. And even if the company has in-house RF engineers for the project, an outside expert provides another set of eyes to look for problems.

A company using a new software development tool or trying object-oriented development for this first time can likewise use outside experts to advantage.

An applications engineer from Siemens told us that his goal in life was to have engineers feel comfortable calling him up to attend design reviews for their products that would include Siemens parts. He knows that he can find issues in their designs—he sees them all the time at numerous customers—and he wants to be the outside expert who saves them critical time on their projects.

A company called Quintiles acts as an outside expert for pharmaceutical companies; they run clinical trials for new drugs trying to enter the market. For example, the company has done most of the existing testing of drugs for Alzheimer's disease. They therefore have access to a patient population and a knowledge of past tests and pitfalls, and can save drug companies incredible time.

Remember, we're looking to find mistakes as early as possible. Another expert set of eyes is great insurance.

L) **Avoid changing people midstream, but early if necessary (during the first half of the project).**

Changing team members during a project can lead to dropped information, additional time to bring the new members "up-to-speed," and consequently lost project time. The synergy developed within the team during the early phases can be disrupted and even destroyed when new members come on board. During phase I, plan the project to minimize the need to change people later. If changes are required, strive to make them before the half-way point of the project.

One software development vice-president stated from his experience, "Once you are past the early design phases of a project and are into implementation, the impact of losing one team member is at least one calendar month—regardless of how you re-jigger the schedule and responsibilities."

Commandment #2. Assemble The Right Team and Leader(s)

⊃M) **Keep members on the team from concept to production.**

Non-development people think they aren't needed until late in the project. Development staff think they are no longer needed once the product goes to beta testing or production. In the former case, manufacturing or customer support people will miss out on the chance to make important contributions to product definition and design decisions. In the latter case, the development staff will be scarce when problems need to be solved quickly, and will miss the opportunity to gain first-hand knowledge of operations and customer issues.

Every team member has a contribution to make at each stage of the project, that will ultimately affect the speed of the development effort, the costs, and the value delivered to the customer. They may contribute different percentages of their time in different phases of the project, but they must be tied in to the team to make contributions at the right time.

⊃N) **Ensure that all key company functions are represented on the team.**

A Q*R*PD team is a fully cross-functional team.

Even if it seems at first glance that a particular function doesn't really have any work on a project, include a representative from that area in early planning to ensure no impact is overlooked. If hardware and software engineers don't include field service people early on, the product's diagnostic capabilities may not be fully developed. Teams plan to outsource manufacturing but then don't include their own or outside manufacturing people on the team. to ensure manufacturability. Finance people can help the team truly understand product costs and benefit-cost trade-off decisions. Effective cross-functional participation gives your team the best shot at finding those project mines early. See also Commandment #3.

O) **Add all key team members before the halfway point, using a trapezoidal resource plan done in phase I.**

Optimistically, we want our full staff right at the beginning of the project, and want to keep them throughout the project, as shown in the "optimistic" staffing curve in the Resource Profiles below. Unfortunately, this usually doesn't happen. All too often our projects are staffed according to the "never-ending" profile on the right in the figure. We try to just get by, only adding staff when we're getting in trouble again. Projects staffed in this manner limp along and may never really finish.

We should recognize that the trapezoidal resource curve below meets our key requirements in the face of reality:

- Remember, 80% of project and product costs and feature performance are set in the first 20% of the project, and we must have at least key team members on board early to participate in those decisions.

- Then we need to be fully staffed around the beginning of phase II. Note: Not only should the team be fully staffed by the beginning of phase II; schedules

Commandment #2. Assemble The Right Team and Leader(s)

are inherently risky if the end-date is dependent upon anyone who is not on board at the time the scheduling is completed.

- And finally, we must understand that people will ramp off the project slowly, not immediately after the product ships or deploys.

In the pharmaceutical world, the clinical trials company Quintiles practices this technique in a unique way. When a client is preparing a new drug to test, Quintiles mobilizes its network of hundreds of health care professionals, and gets them busy signing up doctors and patients for the upcoming trials. They don't wait until the product is ready for testing; they get the testing effort staffed well before that, so that the entire "team" is on board early as the trapezoidal resource profile recommends.

Resource Profiles

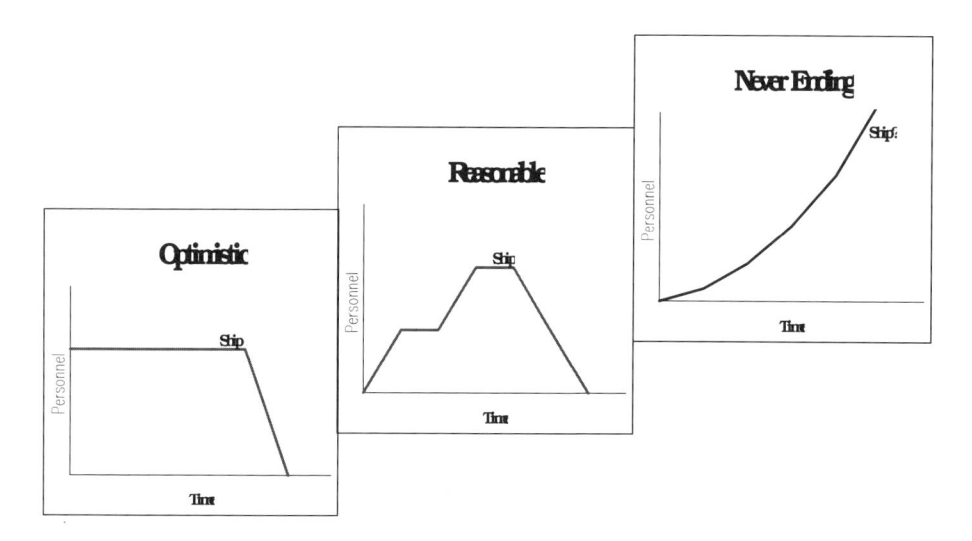

© 1998 Global Brain, Inc.

Commandment #2. Assemble The Right Team and Leader(s)

P) **Prioritize all company projects by quantified success metrics like ROI, LCPW, or NPV to resolve resource conflicts quickly and appropriately.**

The world is not perfect. Projects often compete for resources. Decision-makers must stay clear on the relative priorities of projects within the company. If these priorities are not set via a smooth, rational decision making process, and kept clear within the company, then teams are subject to "thrashing" from continual resource changes between projects. The result can be horrific hits to schedules, not to mention team morale and productivity.

Marketing, financial, or product management team members own the responsibility for helping understand the relative importance of projects to make wise company wide resource allocation decisions. Projects may be important from an immediate return-on-investment standpoint, for meeting contractual requirements with a prime customer, or for strategic positioning of the company. The business cases developed in phase I for each project provide this input.

ROI calculations compare the projected sales of the product and the resulting profits to the investment required to develop it. Late cost per week metrics show how much profit is lost for every week a product is late getting to market. NPV calculations provide a more refined comparison between projects by adjusting their projected profits to account for the time value of money over their period of execution.

Multiple projects often rely on the same software resource, documentation person, or PC board designer. When one or more of the projects falls behind schedule, and more work is required from the shared resource, we have found it very important to have an overall ranking of projects within the company. This ranking allows the shared team member to determine automatically which project they should spend their time on first, instead of having to elevate the decision to a functional manager.

Executives can always make a conscious choice to overrule and shuffle the numbers-based priorities, i.e., to invoke their gut feeling or factor in more "qualitative" or complex considerations. For example, Marketing initially applied a #20 ranking to an IC-development project using its weighted scoring method for projects. The president bumped the project to #1, based on its strategic importance and impact on the future costs of the company's product line.

The quantitative approaches provide important baseline numbers, and allow the resource allocation process to be generally sane and automatic.

Q) **Treat contractors, vendors, partners, and third-party developers as part of the team, and select them judiciously.**

The outcome of your project depends upon how well all of these "outside" people perform, meet commitments, and meet quality standards. *They are part of your team.* The buy-in of outside team members is just as important as that for in-house members. In fact, it can be more important because you have less control over outside members   Therefore, interact with them and include them appropriately:

Commandment #2. Assemble The Right Team and Leader(s)

- Include them in phase I activities that determine the course of the project.

- Form relationships with suppliers early to facilitate clear understanding of their products and ensure timely support from them throughout the project.

- Include development partners in the Product Vision and milestone creation and sign-off.

- Include them in design reviews.

- Make sure developer partners follow the steps of Q*R*PD Flow or other legitimate, effective development processes. A consumer audio manufacturer required that their turnkey manufacturer buy in Q*R*PD so that they would participate effectively throughout the project.

- Make sure these partners have compatible and appropriate tools for the job. One company out-sourced a transceiver design to a company that didn't have a compatible CAD tool. The result was a number of related delays.

- Forge common incentives for completing the project on time and at the cost targets.

Furthermore, the skills, attitudes, and priorities of these team members will be critical to their level of commitment and performance. Are they committed to your dates, or is some other client a higher priority? Are they financially stable or might they close up shop if their other contract goes away?

R) **Assess and select all team members for proper skills for the project, plan for mentoring, and account for learning curve time.**

Just as Project Leader selection is critical, so it is for team members. To accomplish a project fast, you must get the right people on the team. Does your product's complexity or your schedule's urgency call for the most senior people possible? Is your schedule accurate considering the ability levels of those on the team? Do you have cross-functional team members with adequate experience participating in design reviews? Ask the same questions for outside team members as well, such as strategic partners, third-party developers, and contractors.

Identify where team members need education or mentoring: Technical skills? Meeting management or design review techniques? Tools training? Allocate time for such training and/or coaching. Estimate the learning curve you expect, the time it will take them to become fully productive members of the team. Make sure the schedules account for this time!

Commandment #3.

INITIATE EARLY CROSS-FUNCTIONAL COOPERATION

In *Thriving on Chaos*, Tom Peters states that "the single most important reason for delays in development activities is the absence of multifunction (and outsider) representation on development projects from the start."

Beyond this time impact, early cross-functional team participation can make or break your ability to achieve your product and project performance and cost targets: *80% of a product's performance and its cost (including cost to build, test, install, and service) is set in the first 20% of the project.* It is imperative: we must get cross-functional team members involved early!

Here are typical representatives who should participate from the beginning:

Research and Development or Engineering	Legal
Manufacturing, test, and reliability engineering	Medical
Purchasing	Regulatory
Manufacturing or Operations	Vendors, outside partners, contractors
Quality assurance, quality control	Sales, Marketing
Systems administration	Business leaders, customers, users
Finance	Customer support
Technical publications	Shipping and receiving, purchasing

⊃A) **All team members, including outside partners and contractors, involved and committed from day 1, and kept up to date.**

What's the difference between involvement and commitment? One analogy is the difference between ham and eggs for breakfast: the chicken was involved, but the pig was committed. We are not implying that being committed requires dying for your project! But it is absolutely true that all team members must have some "skin in the game." The Project Leader must make sure that the commitment is there.

- Make sure all team members are *involved.* Include them in project discussions and correspondence from the beginning.

- Make sure they're *committed:* they must buy into the fact that they must play a role on the team, even if they are part time, and even if the majority of their hours of work come later in the project.

© 1998 Global Brain, Inc.

Commandment #3. Initiate Early Cross-Functional Participation

Why do we need this involvement and commitment from the beginning? As noted above, 80% of the product's costs are set in the first 20% of the schedule. And as shown in the figure below, the average cost of a change in the design increases tenfold at each later stage in a project. For example, a change during the design phase may cost the company $1000, but that same change will debit the company ten million dollars after final production is in progress. While the absolute monetary figures in the chart were gathered for large consumer electronic firms (such as TV, VCR, and appliance manufacturers), the exponential increase holds true for every company.

An example of the cost of leaving out a team member: An embedded systems company, which held daily coffee break meetings, failed to include a project consultant at one of these morning meetings to discuss software development issues. As a result, the consultant did not catch a specification update that limited him to a specific (small) amount of ROM space. By the time he did find out, it was too late. It's hard enough squeezing code into a small number of bytes when you know the limitations ahead of time. It can be virtually impossible to shoe-horn code into a smaller space once it's written. The company lost time and money trying to reorganize entire sections of code to fit.

An important note: Sometimes education of the non-development functional groups is required to get the right participation. These groups are often not used to being included. Initially, they will be thrilled to even be invited to meetings. But you may then have to teach them *specifically* what they are to contribute. For instance, they must speak up about critical dependencies, provide thorough inputs to requirements and designs, and plan their testing and other work ahead of time to help create an accurate overall project schedule.

The Skyrocketing Cost of Development Changes
(major electronics product)

Time of Design Change	Cost
During final production	$10,000,000
During test production	$1,000,000
During process planning	$100,000
During design testing	$10,000
During design	$1,000

Source: "A Smarter Way to Manufacture; How Concurrent Engineering Can Reinvigorate American Industry," page 110, *Business Week*, April 30, 1990.

Commandment #3. Initiate Early Cross-Functional Participation

B) **Concurrently work on putting in place and documenting the production and delivery processes.**

When you think about how to build a product, you *will* find design issues. When you think about how to deploy new software to 1000 internal users, you *will* find issues.

A software company began development of a major new capability for specialized computers in the field. The upgrade would require a one-time replacement of all the computers in the field. The team didn't start thinking about the deployment process until half-way through the project. Much to their horror, as soon as they wrote a first draft of the installation procedure, they realized that they would need a totally new tool to do the installation: They needed an application that could retrieve and temporarily store the data currently in the computers, then load it back into the new computers. This tool ended up taking 2 resources 6 months to create (they had to be shared with another hot project). Needless to say, this company now writes first draft installation plans very early in their projects.

A vice-president of software development at a database company reported a case where they were going to deliver early releases to two to three customers to get critical feedback. A team member astutely asked "So are these customers going to have the hardware ready for our delivery when we get there to start our tests?" The answer was "No," and the result was some fast attention to this issue and a just-in-time correction of this potential schedule killer.

C) **Concurrently work on improving and documenting the generic product development cycle process: "Flow".**

Every project is different. Every project is an opportunity to continuously enhance the development process. The best way to do it—document decisions and recommendations for best practices as you go along in the project. This is especially effective if you're having process buy-in problems: when a snag is hit, the team can identify something that could be done better next time, and tools to do it. Voila! You have instant process improvement, done by the team itself.

A major software development effort started with a virulently anti-process team, but ended with the same team assigning its members action items for the following: a) documenting what level of detail an architecture specification should contain in the future to ensure that all the work had been identified and the schedule was therefore accurate; b) writing up an estimating checklist; and c) documenting the most efficient ways to do code reviews. During the project, they had learned where the lack of important process steps had cost them previous time, and together they determined how to avoid those problems the next time.

These are concrete examples of how an eye to improving process flow and overall productivity can make life easier for everyone without bureaucracy. Such involvement helps developers buy into the process. They impact it, they shape it—then they'll use it.

© 1998 Global Brain, Inc.

Commandment #3. Initiate Early Cross-Functional Participation

D) **No substitute sometimes for face-to-face communication.**

These days, with increasing globalization, we have to operate with remote team members, especially in large corporations with scattered divisions. But we *must* plan for face-to-face team meetings and reviews during a project.

The most important time for face-to-face communication is early in the project, when such interaction is critical for team building and alignment. It will also greatly facilitate phone and email communication later on: once you can associate a face with a name, it's a whole different ballgame. Remote interactions are made much more comfortable by those earlier personal encounters. Off-site meetings are great, even if you have to fly those London and California team members to the Caribbean.

In the IT organization of a large oil company, the Project Leaders and customers for a data warehouse project were in one region of the country, the development team in another. The team had a number of team meetings over the phone, but they held Vision meetings and design reviews face to face. A large data and telecommunication concern held some paper-based design reviews over their in-house video-conferencing facilities. However, the manufacturing staff traveled for prototype and mock-up reviews, so that they could physically handle the hardware and resolve issues directly with the engineers.

E) **Design team especially close to front and back end of project: Customers/Sales/Marketing and production/delivery.**

"In the interests of time" teams unfortunately tend to keep developers away from anything that is not pure design work. In reality, to save time overall, the design team should get lots of exposure to the customer, the requirements creation process, and the process of building, installing, deploying, servicing, and supporting a product.

A medical company in Silicon Valley designs and produces heart catheters for use in microscopic viewing during surgery. As you can imagine, steps of the manufacturing process are critical: for example, curing the tips at the correct temperature so that they do not fall off during surgery. This company always sends their design teams south to San Diego factory during pilot production. Their job is to ensure that all processes are clear, understood, documented correctly, and stand up during early volume manufacturing.

NASA astronauts work closely with the contractors designing the training facilities that will step-by-step simulate their operations in space. This contact, in many cases with astronauts who have already been in space, bring up 'real-world'—actually, out of this world—issues that the designers would not otherwise be familiar with.

A manufacturer of specialized pole-mounted computers for the utility industry instituted a standard trip to the field early in each project. The company found that its hardware designers gained incredible design insight by personally driving around and viewing various mounting locations. They learned the most by watching a 6-foot-tall person up in a bucket truck servicing the company's

© 1998 Global Brain, Inc.

Commandment #3. Initiate Early Cross-Functional Participation

small computer, mounted 50 feet up a pole, in 10 degree F. snowy weather, wearing heavy gloves!

F) **Design and build quality, safety, testability, and other "ility" attributes (see list below) into the product and process early on by following "DFX" guidelines.**

The "ilities" listed above must be designed in. "DFX" means Design For Manufacturability, Design for Serviceability, etc. These attributes profoundly affect the product, materials, labor, and life-cycle costs. And remember, 80% of the product cost is set within the first 20% of the schedule. Build these attributes into the product by having cross-functional team members intimately involved with requirements definition and design reviews.

Typical "ilities" include:
- Usability
- Serviceability
- Manufacturability
- Installability
- Maintainability
- Testability
- Quality
- Availability
- Reliability
- Scalability
- Re-usability

See also the Product Vision section 4, Crucial Product Factors, in Part IV Flow.

G) **Document all major decisions and keep those decision records accessible.**

Devise a system to create a critical team memory of decisions. This record will save you time—you won't have to second-guess past decisions or lose valuable related information. And of course it's always O.K. to change the decision if new information warrants it.

These critical decisions must be kept accessible or they don't do anyone any good. Key team decisions should be highly visible in team minutes. Keep a decision folder, a file on the internal web, or a binder, for a detailed history of technical decisions. Use email as a software development team did to document hallway design decisions. Record these decisions crisply, with the following information: the date of the decision, who was involved, the alternatives considered, rationale for the decision, other designs and people affected, etc.

© 1998 Global Brain, Inc.

Commandment #3. Initiate Early Cross-Functional Participation

Commandment #4.

CREATE A SYNERGISTIC, MISSION-ORIENTED, PRODUCTIVE ENVIRONMENT

In Microsoft's multi-media division, the creators of the Encarta CD-ROM encyclopedia, the Program Manager's mantra to teams was: "Everyone in the unit has the same job: to SHIP PRODUCTS. ...not to code, not to test, not to manage..... to ship products exactly on time." (Moody, p. 17) This is the start of a mission-oriented environment. We further encourage it with really solid communication and attention to the environment, tools, and morale to get the best possible results from our teams.

> What is synergy? Common definitions include:
>
> "The whole is greater than the sum of its parts."
>
> "1 + 1 = 3, or 4, or 5."
>
> "Synchronous energy."

Scientists in South America have observed flocks of over 50,000 birds turning in unison in 1/70th of a second—without a single visible leader. This is truly a team synergy to strive for, team members tuned into each other as they fly toward the same destination together.

The tools under Commandment #4 give us the means for creating and maintaining incredible team synergy.

⊃A) **Create a shared sense of mission/purpose, Product Vision, and milestones.**

The first key to creating the proper team environment: make sure everyone knows what we're doing, why, and by when! The Product Vision and Milestones list are key tools.

Note: You must include your contractors and development partners in the creation of the Vision and Milestones; they must be as committed as your other team members to the outcome of the mission.

B) **Define and publish a responsibility matrix.**

Teams work best when their responsibilities are crystal-clear. The responsibility matrix concisely identifies team member's critical areas of responsibility. It doesn't, however, list every project task. See the Flow section for examples.

These charts are especially useful for spelling out which tasks cross-functional team members must be involved in, and shows their type of involvement: input to a specification, review of a design document, or primary responsibility for writing test plans, for instance. A partial example is shown on the next page:

© 1998 Global Brain, Inc.

Commandment #4. Create a Synergistic Mission-Oriented Environment

Partial Responsibility Matrix

Area	Mktg/John	Dev/Susan	SQA Lead/Tim	SQA tester/Pam
Functional specifications	Review	Primary		Review
Design documents		Primary	Review	
Test plans	Review	Review	Review	Primary

⊃C) **Locate all team members together.**

The figure below is the result of a 1960s MIT research study into the communication of 512 technical professionals. The study showed that colleagues sitting 40 meters apart had only a 5% probability of communicating at least once a week. That percentage didn't increase until the separation distance was reduced to around 8 meters. Even sitting right next to each other, the probability of communicating once per week was only 30 percent. Even with today's use of voice mail and email, the distance between team members affects their interactions, and the general message of the MIT study still holds. People end up communicating more with those they sit near. Co-located team members overhear information, join in impromptu discussions, and end up collaborating more closely.

At Hewlett Packard, employees who are working on the same project sometimes share a common work space or "war room," in some cases even a rented apartment. The war room may contain not only all the tools and equipment required to design the product, but also competitors' workstations or products. By locating all team members together, HP creates an atmosphere conducive to employee communication and team collaboration.

Similarly, at Intel, employees working on the same product are purposely placed at the same office location. In designing the Pentium, Intel used engineers from its California offices. The 686 team members were all located in Oregon.

Office furniture companies on the leading edge are even creating special mobile "offices" that let individuals move their equipment and materials to where the team action is, and fast-moving companies are embracing the idea of moving people each time a new project starts.

© 1998 Global Brain, Inc.

Commandment #4. Create a Synergistic, Mission-Oriented Environment

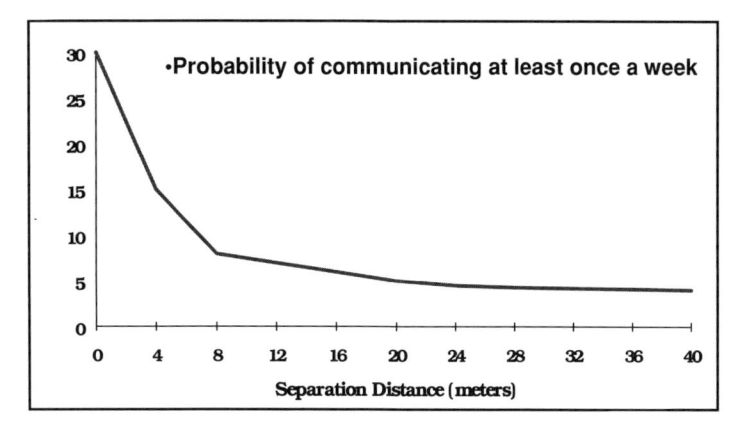

Communication vs. Distance

[Chart: Probability of communicating at least once a week vs. Separation Distance (meters), ranging from 0 to 40 meters, showing a sharp decline from ~30 at 0m to ~8 at 8m, leveling off near 5 at larger distances.]

Source: Allen, *Managing the Flow of Technology*. MIT Press, p. 239.

D) **Ensure communication among team members regardless of location, including with outside partners.**

Whether or not team members are located together, the Project Leader must ensure that effective communication takes place by creating opportunities and monitoring participation and effectiveness.

Team meetings must have consistent, full team attendance. Team minutes must be published with key decisions and action items documented concisely. The team must have an adequate number of design meetings and reviews. And watch for good hallway conversations, one big sign of a synergistic team!

Teams with geographically-separated members simply have to work harder at communication. Visa involves all their regions by phone for input. In the Hong Kong and London office, for example, team members work late at night or early in the morning so they can all be present for team phone conversations with the people at headquarters in California. Some international companies "spread the pain", with U.S. team members pulling the night-shift now and then for such cross-time-zone calls.

In joint development or partnership situations, be sure to assess corporate cultural differences and use the forms of communication that work the best. Outside team members must stay tightly connected to the flow of information on your project. Are they used to using email or voice mail or memos? How will you have to impart information to them to make sure they stay abreast and committed? If the outside company's communication style is very different, you may have to establish highly-structured communication, like regimented meetings or conference calls with published updates to ensure that communication takes place.

© 1998 Global Brain, Inc.

Commandment #4. Create a Synergistic Mission-Oriented Environment

⊃E) **Insulate the team from the parent organization's culture (skunkworks) only if the company is not Q*R*PD like, or for a highly research-oriented project.**

A classic example of a skunkworks project was the creation of the original IBM PC. The team was originally located in a warehouse in Boca Raton, since IBM culture at that time was not particularly conducive to the fast-moving entrepreneurial approach needed to get the PC out to market.

The team that created the Apple Macintosh was housed in a separate facility and flew a skull and cross-bones flag with an apple in the middle.

⊃F) **Protect the team's autonomy.**

The project team must be empowered to make decisions free from second-guessing or micro-management from executives or functional managers. If this one is tough in your company, notice and remember when it happens, note the impact on your schedules—then educate your management!

⊃G) **Exercise team building processes, including off-site meetings to gain buy-in for the vision, schedule, and costs (PTCC).**

"Off-site" meetings get you full team attention in a relaxed, focused environment. They provide a great boost to synergy and energize the team. Getting outside development partners at an off-site meeting can be especially beneficial since it is a neutral environment away from both corporations.

Off-site meetings can be used to discuss process issues or work on particular project issues. For instance, we typically do Product Vision meetings in day-long to half-day off-site increments.

One of the most enjoyable off-site meetings I was involved in was a meeting held by Rolm to figure out how to design a voice-mail system in 11 months. Their previous system had taken 2 years; the one before that took 4 years. The whole team—about 15 people, including a couple of functional managers and a director of engineering—met for 2 days at a beautiful ocean-side resort called Strawberry Ranch, on a cliff about 50 miles south of San Francisco. I spent a few hours briefing the team on the Q*R*PD best practices for rapid product development. The rest of the session they hashed out the vision and the schedule for the ambitious project. In the evening we had dinner all together with Hans, the vice president from the parent company, Siemens in Germany, and shared the results and our excitement. In the end the cost of putting the whole team up for two nights at a lodge were inconsequential compared to the profit they stood to realize from cutting their development time in half.

I was later told that the team felt so motivated by the meeting and so confident that they could pull this off, that they actually planned to work to a schedule *shorter* by one month than the official published schedule. (They also had some financial incentives. See Technique 5C). As it turned out they shipped exactly on the original schedule and the vice president was quite pleased. "The

© 1998 Global Brain, Inc.

Commandment #4. Create a Synergistic, Mission-Oriented Environment

off-site at Strawberry Ranch, and following the rest of Q*R*PD allowed us to ship our latest voice mail system in 10 months—on our vice president's birthday—right on schedule, and in half the time of previous, comparable systems." (Pedro Rump, Director of Engineering at Rolm.)

We cannot emphasize enough the importance of the esprit-de-corps that such team building meetings create, along with the resulting enthusiasm, alignment, and the belief that, "yes, we can do it!"

⊃H) **Minimize and streamline administration and reporting requirements.**

Having a process doesn't have to translate to bureaucracy. Use the 80/20 rule for identifying high-leverage activities. For instance, meeting minutes don't need a full transcript of the discussion, or the details of everyone's status. In fact, the more information you have, the less likely people are to read them. Create highly effective meeting minutes by recording the key decisions made and all action items with names and dates.

Likewise, use executive review sessions wisely. Executives don't need detailed project status every week; they don't need to be aware of all project decisions. Don't waste the team's time on meetings and reports that aren't beneficial to the project.

Such streamlining helps development proceed rapidly for several reasons. First, of course, it keeps team members' time from getting drained writing status reports and going to meetings. Beyond that, it keeps team energy up overall because contributors feel their time is spent on project-specific, valuable work.

The figure below illustrates the potential differences between reporting requirements.

Streamlined Administrative and Reporting Scenarios

Possible weekly administrative scenario in non-Q*R*PD environment	Scenario in Q*R*PD environment
Written status report to boss every week.	Monthly project review meetings, 10 minutes on the overall state of the project.
Detailed formal schedule updates from every person each week.	Quick email status from team members: progress toward milestones, any critical issues.
3-hour team meeting with round-robin status.	1-hour team meeting to share information, celebrate progress, deal with issues that require the whole team.

© 1998 Global Brain, Inc.

Commandment #4. Create a Synergistic Mission-Oriented Environment

I) **Simplify the product specification process to a single page vision.**

Why a Vision? As stated in Commandment #1, the Vision is an aligning document, absolutely critical to the project. The Vision is not a Marketing Product description, or a detailed engineering specification. It captures the essence of the product—its customers, the benefits it will provide, the high-level technology and feature decisions, crucial factors, and relevant financial constraints.

Why one page? A one-page vision is *memorable*. The team must be able to easily stay aligned to the overall goals of the product. People doubt that a one-page vision can be done. They sometimes ask if they can use 8 point type to get everything on one page (not recommended!) The concerns fade away once the team zeroes in on the core benefits, features, and attributes of the product.

Of course many projects will still create detailed engineering or functional specifications. But the Vision must be done first—to ensure that the why of the product is determined before all the details of how are addressed.

J) **Restrict detailed front-end planning to important items.**

Front-end planning should concentrate on anticipating and attacking the big issues and finding places to make big positive impacts on our project. What technological innovations are risky, and what are the back-up plans for them? What resources are needed and when, and what issues must be addressed? What chicken tests will be performed and when? What tools and equipment should be invested in? See the list of phase I deliverables in Flow.

Front-end time should not be spent planning in minute detail work that cannot accurately be determined at this point.

K) **Do not allow management reviews or decisions to delay work, including separating formal status reviews from technical meetings.**

Management oversight has its place on any project, but too often management's decision-making role slows down projects unnecessarily. A team is ready to choose a design alternative and zoom ahead, but it takes three weeks to get all the executives into a review meeting to sign off on the decision. Or management's signoff is simply needed, but when management and technical subjects are covered in the same meeting, management unnecessarily gets involved in technical decisions.

Q*R*PD teams are empowered to make many decisions about the project themselves. This Q*R*PD technique calls for teams to consciously and creatively avoid delays related to management's role, and keep them in line so the team can jet ahead.

Commandment #4. Create a Synergistic, Mission-Oriented Environment

L) **Separate executive education sessions from reviews.**

Review meetings generally involve a number of people needed to review and approve a design or a course of action. Such meetings should be kept efficient and effective. An executive who is not up-to-speed on the project should *not* be allowed to slow down the meeting for his education process. Do the education off-line. Your team and other managers and executives will thank you for it.

M) **Spend time at the "Fuzzy" front end of the project (top management especially, to "jump start" it).**

What happens if a company thinks about doing a project for 6 months before even launching a team on phase I work to explore alternatives? They've used up a significant percentage of their time-to-market. The figure below shows how 40% of a team's intended time-to-market was used up making these fuzzy front-end decisions.

The phase I trade-off process for PTCC is new to teams. Teams are used to taking an end-date and/or a feature list unquestioningly and blindly moving forward. The freedom to do the right thing for the customer and the company adds complexity and uncertainty to Phase I decisions. Some teams get a bad case of "analysis paralysis." They spend long periods of time in phase I analyzing requirements and possible design alternatives, and are unable to prioritize and make trade-off decisions.

Phase I is intended to be an iterative process. Teach the team to identify big-ticket trade-off items first. Will a particular new feature or capability add three months to the schedule? It may be the first to go. Teach the team to set a target for phase I of no more than 25% of the hoped-for schedule. Then learn to "Arbitrate, escalate, terminate" (even the project, if necessary) to get through the decision process. An important factor is your choice of product champion, who should stand ready to assist this process.

The Fuzzy Front End

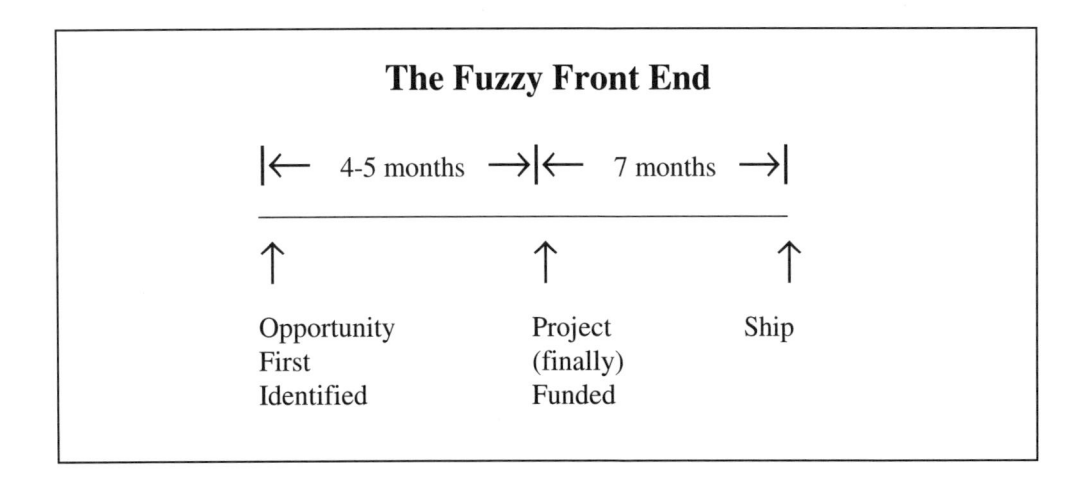

|← 4-5 months →|← 7 months →|

↑   ↑   ↑

Opportunity   Project   Ship
First   (finally)
Identified   Funded

© 1998 Global Brain, Inc.

Commandment #4. Create a Synergistic Mission-Oriented Environment

N) **Ensure that all team members know/feel the cost of delay, using Late Cost Per Week.**

Every day counts. Every project should calculate its late cost per week, the amount of potential lost profit for every week the product is late shipping. Typically we see at least a $35,000 LCPW for a project of medium importance. They've run up to $250,000 for a high-volume cost-reduction project, and sometimes much higher. Team members armed with such numbers are more likely to personally avoid inefficiencies, take the initiative to keep the entire team cranking, and make the wisest decisions for the company's bottom line.

When Digital Equipment Corporation decided to develop the Alpha RISC microprocessor, it faced an uphill battle getting buy-in from even the project managers involved. The project was huge, daunting: not only the chip itself, but application software, compilers, and developers kits. To help get the project kick-started, DEC managers determined that the late cost would be $1 million per hour! They used this number as an education and motivation tool to get all the Project Leaders signed up to the mission.

In a database systems start-up company, an engineering vice-president had to explain to his team that *one person* being late a week would cost the project the entire expense of the team for a week, since people couldn't be released for other work until the product was done. This loss, of course, was in addition to revenue/market opportunities that would never occur again. This is the education and perspective we need all team members, including other parties in our joint development arrangements, to have.

O) **Make excessive use of "hoopla" to build morale.**

Hoopla is a team tool: a means of making a big deal of progress, achievements, and just the fact that we're a team. Hoopla promotes synergy by keeping the team's identity strong and by recognizing progress every step of the way. It continually tells the team that what they are doing is vitally important, helps keep that sense of enthusiasm and mission alive, and therefore keeps the team charging forward toward their goals.

Excessive means use more than you might think you need. Have a motivating team name and logo. Create an identity within the company. Get everyone T-shirts or polo shirts. Crow loudly, via voice mail, email, the company newsletter, etc., about team and individual achievements throughout the project. Invite the president to the demonstration. Create team mottoes that lead the charge. A project called the Bi-ASIC Meter Module, or "BAMM," coined the phrase "for BAMM sure" to remind themselves of their commitments to making their milestone dates and cost targets.

Be sure to include development partners in hoopla events. And take the opportunity to draw in non-full-time team members, so people have a chance to get to know them better. See also Commandment #5 for related recognition ideas.

© 1998 Global Brain, Inc.

Commandment #4. Create a Synergistic, Mission-Oriented Environment

P) **Promote frequent, brief, open ad hoc meetings.**

The cry for lots of team communication does not mean that everything has to happen in big meetings! Get the team to talk often, ad-hoc. Just be sure to document any decisions made or actions assigned.

Q) **Hold a regularly scheduled team meeting.**

The purpose of team meetings is to keep everyone up-to-date and uncover issues, and make sure those issues get resolved. However, note that you should actually resolve the issues outside the meeting if at all possible. For example, do not attempt to work on an issue that involves 2 people in the 10-person team meeting; instead, record the issue and take care of it "off-line." Team meetings must stay efficient and effective, or their value to team synergy could well be lost, as team members decide that those meetings just aren't worth their time.

Team meetings also keep team identity, spirit, and communication alive. The call for team meetings is not a call for long-winded, round-robin status, excruciatingly given by each team member. Each Project Leader can use judgment about what to include. Just keep it effective. See the Flow section for more tips for handling team meetings.

R) **Invest in productivity tools that enhance communication (email, video teleconferencing, etc.), and standardize the team on using them.**

The best money you'll ever spend is whatever keeps your team communicating and sharing all kinds of information as easily as possible. Easy, continual information exchange is the best way to find mines early and avoid nasty project surprises and the added project costs that go with them. Use the following types of tools: Email. Email filters to keep team members organized in the midst of potential email floods from multiple projects and people. Team email lists. Voice mail group lists for easy team announcements. Good-quality speaker phones for team meetings by phone. Videoconferencing and collaboration capability, on the desktop if possible. Groupware tools such as Lotus Notes to keep project documents and discussions organized, living, and accessible. Web-based project and company information repositories for project documents, best-practices information, guidebooks, and templates. Electronic whiteboards for instant translation of team meeting scribbling. They're out there and they're a great investment. Note: Ask team members what they need to be more productive!

© 1998 Global Brain, Inc.

Commandment #4. Create a Synergistic Mission-Oriented Environment

S) **Review the vision and measure against it for progress.**

If the Vision is the alignment tool and a chief means of establishing our synergistic environment, we have to keep it visible! Make it a habit to review the vision—at team meetings, at design reviews. Are we still meeting it? Are we making progress—do we see the elements of the Vision coming to life in the product? Does anyone have any discrepancies to discuss that may affect where we as a team are going?

T) **Work smarter and long hours using spurts to meet milestones and prevent burnout.**

The goal is to not have to work long hours to get our projects done. But the reality is that it often becomes necessary, for instance to hold a milestone. It's critical that long hours in such cases be done only in "spurts", not for long periods of consecutive time. For example, don't plan the scheduled tasks and milestones assuming that team members will work long hours throughout the project. But when a milestone approaches, kick into higher gear if necessary to hold that date. The team will feel good about accomplishing the milestone and staying on track, but they won't feel overwhelmed, knowing they just "spurted" temporarily to make it. Avoid burn-out of your team members, for the long-term good of your project.

U) **Protect confidential information prudently.**

We need to have empowered, in-the-know teams. But we also may need to avoid free-flow sharing of all project information to ensure confidentiality is adequately protected.

When a project involves joint development, the team will work together and move fastest if the two sides can freely exchange information, but of course each company has legitimate confidentiality concerns. Structure your partnerships to make information exchange as easy as possible in the areas where it's needed, and get the agreements in place as quickly as possible. Then ensure that team members are aware of what their obligations are with respect to intellectual property or other secrets deemed vital to the company.

A high-priority software integration project got off to an unexpectedly slow start when the engineers at the main company and the outside partner were raring to go, but couldn't even talk to each other about critical high-level design decisions. Why? Because their respective executives had not yet gotten a contract in place.

© 1998 Global Brain, Inc.

Commandment #4. Create a Synergistic, Mission-Oriented Environment

V) **Have Fun!**

If you aren't having fun, you haven't achieved the synergistic, mission-oriented environment. People want to do what they love, and love to do what they enjoy. When people are doing challenging work, they achieve their greatest satisfaction and happiness. Make it possible!

W) **Teach all team members collaboration skills such as meeting management and problem-solving techniques.**

We send our managers to "meeting management" classes. We need to send our team members too. Individuals need to understand how critical their personal behavior, skills, and actions are to the effectiveness of the team; then they need the tools to help them improve. Important aspects for them to know include the mechanics of preparing for, running, or participating in meetings; and group tools for issues exploration and resolution.

Team members can also benefit from understanding their own personalities and abilities, using tools such as the enneagram, Meyers-Briggs Type Indicators (MTBI), and other aids to self-assessment. (See the Project Leader and Team section for more on MTBI.)

X) **Separate problem solving versus status or informational meetings, and invite only the necessary people to each.**

It's generally desirable to have all team members present at periodic project status and information dissemination meetings. These meetings provide "face time" and a chance to build rapport, keep everyone on the same page, and reinforce team synergy. However, if the meeting degenerates into one where 3 people out of 10 are working out the details to a particular problem, with everyone else drumming their fingers on the table, guess what—soon your team members may stop attending the status meetings.

When issues arise in a meeting, and they don't require everyone's input, save them until the end when those not required to solve the issue can leave, or assign an action item to deal with them later.

Y) **Find creative uses of "asynchronous communication" and establish team etiquette to allow team members un-interrupted productive time.**

The advent of cubicles has definitely impacted productivity. People see you in your office, think of something they'd like to say, and interrupt you. There goes that state of concentration and optimal productivity on the task at hand. "Asynchronous communication" refers to interactions that happen via voice mail, email, or other indirect means. The two parties are not directly talking with each other at one point in time. When teams make the most of this indirect communication, they are able to avoid interrupting each other.

Teams develop all kinds of coping strategies to avoid interruptions:

© 1998 Global Brain, Inc.

Commandment #4. Create a Synergistic Mission-Oriented Environment

- A software game developer gives each new-hire a big laminated sign to post on the wall outside their cubicle. One side says "I am interruptible." The other side says "I am working; please don't interrupt. I'll be free again at ____."

- Some teams set aside a time period each morning for mandated "leave each other alone" time. Only voice mail or email communication is allowed during this time.

- One of the best deterrents is to simply turn your desk to face *away* from the door. If people make eye contact with you as they walk by, they'll probably interrupt you. Interestingly, a turned back is a very effective deterrent.

I am always amazed at the results that happen

when a group of pro-active, self-directing individuals

are turned loose on a task.

~ Stephen Covey

Commandment #5.

REWARD ALL PARTICIPANTS COMMENSURABLY

A few years ago, when I was teaching a two day QRPD workshop for IEEE's Engineering Management Society, I asked the class if they new why it was so important to give rewards. "Because we're human," said Jim Boyden, former laboratory director at HP labs in Palo Alto and developer of their ink jet and laser jet printer technologies. (He was taking the course to polish up on the latest bench-marking and semantics for rapid product development). All agreed. It's so important that people feel treated like real human beings and not merely cogs in a wheel. It's the only way to keep their interest level and motivation high.

Often when we get to this commandment in class, we get told that the only reward people can realistically hope for at their companies is to get to work on another project—a project which is already behind schedule before even getting started. People do not thrive or excel in the long run in such environments.

Take note: Surveys have shown that people's biggest motivation in the long run is not necessarily money, but professional respect, development, and recognition. QRPD teams must make use of all kinds of rewards and recognition to make team members fulfilled and happy on even the most challenging project. And members must be rewarded commensurably with, or in accordance with, their individual efforts. Be sure to fairly acknowledge the contributions of each individual, and in the process you'll highlight and reinforce the desirable team member performance.

⊃A)   **Recognition at major milestones and other significant events.**

Recognize the team for their *specific* achievements at major points in the project. True recognition is not just a bland "they met the alpha start milestone", but a personalized acknowledgment of the tangible achievements and the odds overcome.

At a communications company, the software team gave demonstrations of important technology as it was chicken tested (see Technique 8A). The Project Leader invited top executives in the company to those demonstrations. To everyone's surprise, the President came to every one. The team knew they were doing something important.

One company developed the recognition culture of mentioning people's accomplishments individually in status emails. The email list went not only to team members, but also to "interested parties" in the company. In this same company, whenever a new product shipped, the Product Manager sent a company-wide email alerting everyone as to the achievement, and thanking team members by name.

To recap, often even small tokens of acknowledgement and appreciation go a long, long way.

© 1998 Global Brain, Inc.

Commandment #5. Reward all Participants Commensurably

B) **Reward and recognize the team as a whole, some of its individuals, others, including in personnel reviews.**

If you want a team to perform, reward them for being part of the team. Also reward individuals for taking responsibility and contributing to a project's success. Ensure that the Project Leader is rewarded for performance in their role.

Be sure to recognize the contributions of individuals, teams, and others:

Individual recognition: This is what companies are usually best at: rewarding and recognizing individual efforts and achievements.

Team recognition: This often requires a powerful shift in culture, requiring executives and managers to explicitly recognize the results a team produced together.

Others: Don't forget those people who faithfully supported the core team: the Product Champion, part-time support personnel, and anyone else who may have helped. Recognizing those people helps the overall Q*R*PD company culture evolve. When you reward non-core team members, and thereby encourage them to participate synergistically, you remove one of the typical obstacles to implementing improved product development—lack of effective participation from outside Development.

Performance appraisals: When a team member's performance review is approaching, have the Project Leader fill out a simple appraisal of how the team member performed on the project, review it with the team member, then pass it along to the functional manager. When it's time for the Project Leader's appraisal, have the team members do likewise. (This can and should be only a 5-10 minute process for each team member.) At the end of the project, evaluate everyone. See the Project Leader and Team section for a description of the evaluation process and example forms.

C) **Bonuses based on project and product success.**

Look for ways to tie rewards to project and product *results*.

- A computer manufacturer gave a $1500 cash bonus to each team member when the product ship date was met.

- A telecommunications company set up a bonus incentive of $4000 if the project was a month early, $3000 each if it shipped on time, $2000 if only a month late. (See the project story in Commandment 4, Technique G). The team secretly worked to a schedule that would let them ship a month early, so they could make that maximum bonus. They drove hard, and ended up being a month behind their clandestine aggressive schedule—meaning they shipped right on time.

- A computer manufacturer gave each team member a $1000 travel voucher at the end of a successful project. Their in-house travel agency arranged for 8 exciting trip destinations, and worked out heavily discounted package prices so that the $1000 could buy each family a significant trip.

© 1998 Global Brain, Inc.

Commandment #5. Reward all Participants Commensurably

- An entire team of 27 people at a Silicon Valley company finished a custom multi-media integrated circuit. The company sent them to Disneyland for the day—flew them down, paid for meals, and provided tickets. Sounds extravagant, but when you do the math, you discover that it only cost about $5000, on a project with a late cost per week of $100,000!

D) **Use Management by Objectives (MBO) as a basis for rewards.**

MBO is a system of performance measurement whereby employees set their own goals, one quarter at a time, creating a sense of empowerment. These goals then get mutually agreed upon with their manager. This system is based on a quarterly score of 0 to 100 points maximum and can quite powerfully be linked to project performance.

Pioneered for use as a form of self-appraisal in the 1960s, it grew out of favor by the 1980s because it had the unfortunate consequence of creating excessive competition among individuals on a project team. Each would excel only to achieve their own score, often at the expense of the whole team's performance. Many companies have now remedied this by setting half of the 100 points based on the whole team's performance, and half on the individual's performance. Cadence, the large CAD software company, has used this MBO successfully for many years. See DIRFT for more details on using MBO.

E) **Use rituals and celebrations.**

As in religion, shared rituals strengthen bonds among a group of people. Project teams often create standard rituals and celebrations, such as Thursday bagel day, or a half-day off at the movies each time a major milestone is achieved. Here are some ideas from actual project teams:

- Plan periodic team lunches or outings. And since it is sometimes hard to find an activity or food that everyone likes, plan lots of different outings to hit everyone's tastes. Plan these activities during phase I of the project, so that the time is allocated and the team has time to generate good ideas.

- Have a team lunch at the end of each phase, and be sure to invite those "unseen" part-time members who might otherwise not feel enough part of the team.

- Fly virtual reality airplanes at Silicon Valley's "Magic Edge," or your local equivalent of this highly-exciting and harmless dogfight simulator, or play team laser tag.

- At the end of phase I of a project, take the entire team to a "brew it yourself" beer brewery. Then throughout the project, as key milestones are hit, the team can brew the next batch. For example, on the BAMM project mentioned previously, the team brewed several batches, including "Beta Brew", "Alpha Ale", "Production Pilsner". The team can even make a custom label for the beer. The BAMM team's label says "WARNING: CellNet Data Systems along with the Global Brain have determined that excessive consumption of BAMM Brew products may result in one or

© 1998 Global Brain, Inc.

Commandment #5. Reward all Participants Commensurably

> several of the following conditions: intermittent loss of lock, increased bit error rates, undesirable phase noise, schedule slippage, reduced carrier suppression, dropped packets, the annoyance of the CEO, and potentially the generation of a last-gasp packet" Seem silly? Perhaps on the surface, but this team had an incredible sense of spirit and had a great deal of fun as they accomplished their intense company mission.
>
> - Other ideas for outings: a night at the Comedy Club or jazz concerts, a trip to the aquarium with families in tow, team shirts with a designated "wear it" day, trips to horse racing events, and so on.
>
> The above activities might seem to some like a frivolous waste of good work time. They are actually worth their weight in gold. The synergy they create actually improves a team's productivity, enables them to meet those time-to-market goals, and ultimately produces a high return on the development investment.

F) **Special recognition for going the extra mile, beating milestones, saving costs.**

> Don't take super efforts for granted—that's a recipe for declining contributions. Don't even take little special efforts for granted—they add up.
>
> An IC design company holds monthly "all-hands" meetings, at which individuals are recognized for super efforts to meet particular deadlines, volunteering for unassigned tasks, etc. They get Post-it note pads personalized with their names, gift certificates to the next Macy's sale, and dinners for two at a nice restaurant.

G) **Minimize alienating others, if possible.**

> After a successful project completion, company executives took out a full-page ad in the Wall Street Journal to celebrate and recognize the accomplishment. The problem? They put the names and pictures of the three project leaders. The team received no mention. Guess who probably had a little less energy to perform the next time around.
>
> Note that it may be impossible to avoid alienating someone. Do your best to take others into account, but don't use a fear of alienating someone as an excuse for not rewarding at all.

© 1998 Global Brain, Inc.

Commandment #5. Reward all Participants Commensurably

H) **Hold company parties for ongoing synergy.**

Team synergy is influenced by company atmosphere and strengthened by strong cooperation among departments. So make sure to include opportunities to build "company spirit".

- One company in Silicon Valley rented out the Monterey Bay aquarium on a Saturday night, and provided food, drinks, a band, and special aquarium shows. The entire company turned out, kids and all. The company also provided busses to get there, discount hotel rates if people wanted to stay overnight, and a golf tournament the next day. Many Silicon Valley companies know how to do these events superbly.

- Silicon Graphics, a Silicon Valley computer company, is known for its elaborate theme parties. At Mardi Gras employees were treated to a Dixieland band and costumed parades. Employees feel appreciated and believe companies like this are a "cool place to work." They feel compensated for the high-pressure times and tend to stay loyal to the company.

I) **Ensure recognition is cross-functional: people from all groups are recognized; all departments are aware of the individual and team accomplishments.**

Part of implementing QRPD successfully is breaking down barriers or mistrust between functional groups. Recognition can help—so take the opportunity to acknowledge and learn to appreciate each others' unique contributions. Some companies give an award once per month to someone on the team, with widespread recognition: a notice in the company newsletter, mention in department meetings, etc.

J) **Make it easy for teams to do celebrations, rewards, and recognition, by planning ahead for these events and setting up the mechanisms.**

Projects on a mission are focused, busy. Don't let the opportunities for "feel-good" events and synergy-building slip by from lack of attention.

- To avoid people not attending team outings due to work pressure or being busy in "spurt" mode, plan outings ahead to set expectations and ensure time is in the project schedule.

- Establish guidelines for how much Project Leaders can spend on rewards, recognition, and celebrations. Get clear on what approvals are necessary so requests are easy. Have a good discretionary budget for this as part of the project.

- At Johnson & Johnson, any employee in the company can give $20 gift certificates to anyone, anytime at their discretion. A QRPD student at UC Berkeley said that she had given out hundreds per year, and other Project Leaders tend to use them heavily as well. These mechanisms provide a great way to say "thank you" at a small cost.

© 1998 Global Brain, Inc.

Commandment #5. Reward all Participants Commensurably

- Get administrative help for planning outings, especially if the team is large. One company created a list of standard nice lunch places and group "play" outings. An administrative assistant kept the master list and could set any of them up easily with one call from a team leader.

K) **Put a human face from top management on reward and recognition efforts.**

People want their work to be appreciated. Feeling true appreciation is often far more important than the exact form of the "reward" given. The more Management shows that it understands the challenges their teams face, the sacrifices they make, and the intelligence and skills they apply to get the job done, the better people will feel about the value of their efforts. And the more they feel understood and appreciated, the more likely they'll be to "step up to the plate" the next time.

Commandment #6.

USE INNOVATIVE, PARALLEL, ITERATIVE DESIGN STRATEGIES

Commandment #6 speaks to the profound positive impact that sound system engineering and development practices, technical risk management, and flexible use of iterations can have on a project schedule.

A) **Partition into subsystems early at rigorously-defined interfaces, using standards wherever possible.**

Divide the technical work into logical pieces as quickly as possible so that the detailed work on each subsystem can be done in parallel. Define interfaces well so that each subsystem's work is clearly understood, and once completed, the pieces will play together with minimal rework.

This technique is particularly important for implementing Q*R*PD incremental innovation cycles. Poorly designed systems cannot be modified easily and therefore rapidly. For example, a medical equipment manufacturer enjoyed very early success with its core patient monitoring products for hospitals. However, as time wore on, projects were more and more hampered by the difficulty of modifying the original software—it truly deserved the old moniker of "spaghetti code." Eventually an engineer was assigned full-time to reverse-engineer the code and document it so that future projects would not be slowed down by the poor design.

Use standard interfaces wherever possible to save time and headaches. For example, RS-232 interfaces are the standard for serial communication. Chips, cables, and software can be bought off-the-shelf; no need to design this type of interface from scratch! And the idiosyncracies of standard interfaces have become known over time, providing teams with a valuable knowledge base that will usually speed up not only development, but later testing and delivery as well. Standards exist for computer busses, software communication protocols, and so forth. Use them wherever possible.

B) **Design subsystems to optimize system level performance.**

Do not allow engineers or designers to develop their sub-systems outside the context of the overall system's performance requirements. Over-engineering of individual designs is a common cause of slipped schedules, out-of-line product costs, and missed system performance goals. Remember, our definition of Q*R*PD performance includes "quality," or value as perceived by the customer, not how neat or whiz-bang some of the designs may be.

The medical company discussed in Technique 1C broke this rule. They changed from a 486 PC to a Sun workstation platform and developed code from scratch to gain higher performance of the user interface. But that higher performance wasn't necessary in the first iteration. Going to the workstation and roll-your-own code caused a 6-month schedule slip and a system too

Commandment #6. Use Innovative, Parallel, Iterative Design Strategies

costly for its target customers. They optimized one subsystem at the expense of the overall value of the product.

⊃C) **Accept less than optimal individual subsystems by priority, and leave generous design margins wherever possible.**

Less than optimal sub-systems: To make overall system feature and performance goals, some subsystems may use less than the most "elegant" solution. The system design should indicate which subsystems are most important to optimize in order to fulfill the requirements in the Vision.

When cable TV first became available, the channel-select box placed on top of our television sets used to get very hot. The manufacturer had two concerns: Would consumers balk at this heat, and would the electronics degrade with time due to overheating? In order to begin shipping much earlier than the months required to find the answer to these two questions, they came up with what seemed like a 'kludge' solution: they put the power supply in a separate box from the decoder box. The decoder sat on top of the TV, and a cable ran to the power supply box, which could sit on the floor. This inelegant solution bought them the time they needed for testing and gaining consumer acceptance. They subsequently combined the two boxes into one and many of us today have some version of this product. Incidentally, the boxes that sit on our TVs still generate a lot of heat, but this does not seem to cause a problem.

Generous design margins: Design margins refer to extra capacity or "room for variation" in elements of a design. Margins are important for overall reliability, especially in the face of uncertain, high-load operating environments and for products that will be manufactured in high volume with multiple parts suppliers and multiple configurations. For example, good hardware design practice mandates that the cumulative delay through any one circuit can use no more than 98% of the available clock cycle time, leaving margin for timing variations in different physical parts. In embedded hardware/firmware systems, the available memory for code should never be cut too close, leaving room for the uncertainties of actual final code size. In real-time software, every interrupt service routine should leave more than enough time for operating system-related tasks.

In addition, leaving generous design margins allows you to design more subsystems in parallel in the face of uncertainty. For instance, say you're designing a multi-board system and power-supply. If you want the supply to be no bigger in capacity than it has to be to support the boards, you can't finalize its design until the power draw of each board is well-known. In short, you can't fully parallelize the design of the power supply to gain time to market. However, if you're willing to allow some extra capacity in the power supply, you can go ahead and finish its design in parallel with that of the boards.

© 1998 Global Brain, Inc.

Commandment #6. Use Innovative, Parallel, Iterative Design Strategies

System architecture and sub-system design documents should make clear the sub-system priorities and design margin guidelines. Do not leave these important system design elements to chance; think them through and provide detailed guidelines to all developers.

⊃D) **Concentrate technical risk in as few subsystems as possible.**

Although we've all been told to "spread risk around," it actually is not the best approach for technological risk management. As shown below, the percentage probability of successfully meeting project design goals—functionality, cost, and schedule—increases the more a design concentrates the technical risk in one area.

As the following picture shows, if all 5 subsystems or modules in a system have an 85% probability of successful completion, the overall system has only a 44% chance. Probability theory tells us that we can calculate this by multiplying together the percent chance of success for all the modules in the system. If instead all but one of the modules has a 99% chance of success, and the fifth module has a 50% chance of success, the overall system now has a 48% chance. Then if that last module can be brought up to a 85% probability—for instance by reducing the technological risks and by creating backup plans—your overall system now has jumped up to an 82% chance of success. Remarkable!

Why is this? One relatively risky area of a design is actually much easier to manage than multiple risks. It can receive intense technical scrutiny, back-up planning, cross-group communication (which has risks of its own) and ongoing management. If every module or sub-system is risky, proper risk management will require considerable effort. It's just too hard to keep your eyes on that many eggs. So put as many as possible of your eggs—your project technical risks—into one basket.

© 1998 Global Brain, Inc.

Commandment #6. Use Innovative, Parallel, Iterative Design Strategies

Concentrating Technical Risk

Technical risk evenly dispersed among all modules.

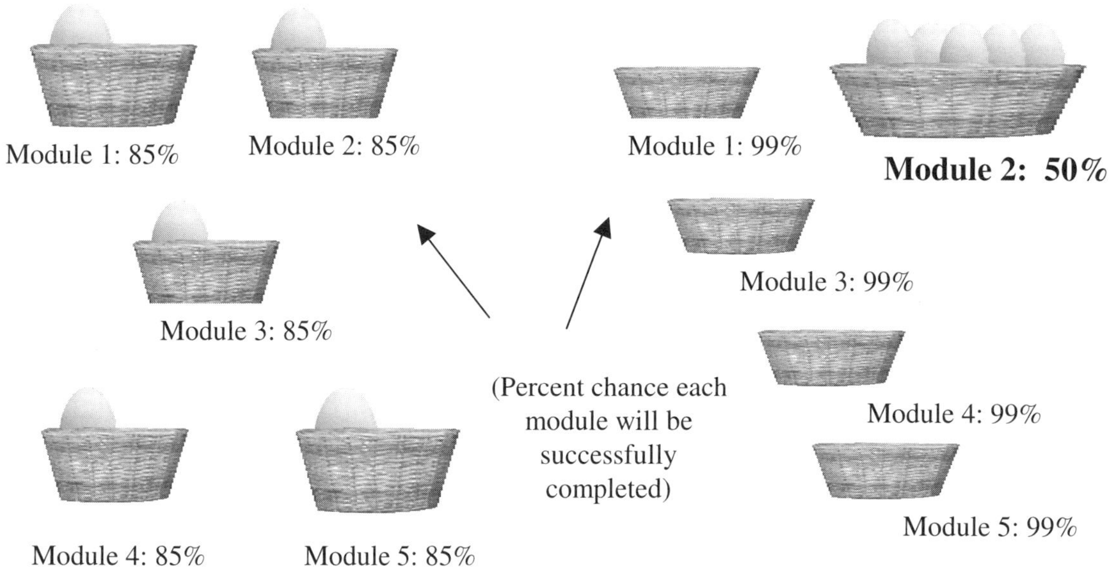

Module 1: 85%   Module 2: 85%

Module 3: 85%

Module 4: 85%   Module 5: 85%

Technical Risk concentrated in one "basket" or design module.

Module 1: 99%   **Module 2: 50%**

Module 3: 99%

Module 4: 99%

Module 5: 99%

(Percent chance each module will be successfully completed)

Percentage chance of project success
(on-time, on-cost, and it works):

85% x 85% x 85% x 85% x 85% =
44% overall

Percentage chance of project success

With no risk mitigation:

99% x 99% x 99% x 99% x *50%* =
48% overall

With backup plans:

99% x 99% x 99% x 99% x *85%* =
82% overall

The Message:

Keep your high risk "eggs" in <u>one</u> basket!

© 1998 Global Brain, Inc.

Commandment #6. Use Innovative, Parallel, Iterative Design Strategies

E) **Organize to achieve minimum feasible team size for each subsystem.**

The smaller the team, the better the communication will be. (See also Technique 2H.) A small sub-team working on a well-defined subsystem will be nimble: able to efficiently design, review, and make decisions with a minimum of overhead and misunderstandings.

F) **Invest in backup plans for critical technologies, tooling and parts, and be ready to implement them.**

Do not "assume" that a new technology will work. Find out as early as possible whether it will, then have a second, and possibly even third, implementation alternative. To be ready to implement the alternatives, plan ahead sufficiently: identify the resources and perhaps even do parallel work on them just in case.

Planning for and possibly even carrying out multiple options in parallel is viewed as an expensive proposition that should only be done if absolutely necessary. In reality, it's far more expensive to the project to wait until problems occur with a design, tooling, or parts acquisition, then try to recover and lose time-to-market and revenue. Money spent on backup planning and alternatives implementation is an investment.

For a critical and risky high-speed RF circuit design, even though a wireless company had full expertise in-house, it was worried about their ability to make this innovation work. It decided to invest in 3 designs in parallel: $15,000 to a consultant to design one, $20,000 to an outside vendor to buy a finished module, and the salary of the full-time in-house RF designer. At the 25% point in the project, none of the designs worked! At 50%, one did. By the end of the project, two of the designs worked, and the team was able to pick the more cost-effective alternative.

One company had a very high volume product already shipping which contained a board with many components. The team calculated that by redesigning this board and combining many of the components into a single ASIC (application specific integrated circuit) they could save approximately $8.00 per board, which would translate into an additional $200,000 of profit per week! They launched a new project and worked with a vendor to help them design and manufacture the ASIC. Unfortunately, the vendor consistently missed milestone dates on the schedule and seemed uncooperative, and an early prototype test showed their quality left something to be desired. The company's decision was a no–brainer: they contracted an additional ASIC house to independently and in parallel work on an equivalent chip and spent several hundred thousand dollars on this backup plan.

In the end, the company used the chips from their original supplier. But having the back up plan not only bought them peace of mind, it also allowed them to put more pressure on the vendor, knowing that they had another one in the works. Furthermore, when it came to buying large manufacturing

© 1998 Global Brain, Inc.

Commandment #6. Use Innovative, Parallel, Iterative Design Strategies

quantities, they had more negotiating leverage on the price they would pay per ASIC, because they had the second supplier in their hip pocket.

Incidentally, this company gave the original vendor an additional substantial payment for agreeing to accelerate the project. Having to do this angered several of the executives at the company. They ultimately reasoned that even with having the backup vendor, if they could save just one week of time, it was worth making this payment based on the large late cost per week.

G) **Have one key architect or evangelist—sometimes the Project Leader.**

For a coherent system design that will enable the team to work the most efficiently technically, have a single person responsible for the completeness and consistency of the subsystem and interface designs, at least at the highest level interfaces. This person must have the time to devote to thorough system design up front, and time to attend later subsystem and module design reviews to ensure that everything is holding together.

⊃H) **Beg, borrow, steal or buy subsystems or expertise and avoid NIH—the *not-invented-here* syndrome.**

What work have others done that is useful to your project? Is there a subsystem you can buy from another vendor? Is there a prototype or technology somewhere within your company from a similar project that you can re-use or adapt? If you have to buy that technology or expertise, remember cost-benefit analyses: if you gain profit by getting to market faster, it will more than make up for the money you spend.

Innovation can be defined as introducing novelty (new know-how) into practical use (technology) to increase the customer value and satisfaction obtained from the seller's or manufacturer's resources. Lots of technology already exists, untapped—and more and more gets invented at a shocking pace. The US Issues over 300 patents per day. Over 200 million scientists and technologists go to work everyday, more than the number of people that lived on the whole planet 2000 years ago. Why not package available inventions as a subsystem in your product?

When originally producing the PC, IBM used Intel's 8088 microprocessor and Microsoft's OS instead of creating their own versions. This was a highly unusual move for IBM; they normally design everything in house. This decision allowed the IBM PC to come to market faster than any other competitor and capture over 90% of the market initially and over 50% of the market afterwards.

Note that you may not want to use outside sources for areas of core competency technology unless you acquire all the rights to the design, or assure that your market position will not be compromised by not owning the technology outright.

© 1998 Global Brain, Inc.

Commandment #6. Use Innovative, Parallel, Iterative Design Strategies

Before the innovative Huggies Pull-Ups diapers were launched, the frustrated team couldn't make the diapers pull up without tearing— until they borrowed a material from another part of the company, designed for a different use.

By using "hand-me-downs" from an F-15 guidance system and fuel tanks from another program, McDonnell Douglas was able to develop a reusable rocket prototype in only 18 months and at a total cost of $60M. Considering that a specially designed toilet for the space shuttle cost $23M to develop, the use of existing parts and technology drastically reduced the cost McDonnell Douglas might have incurred, had they done things "as usual."

An IT sales force automation project at a major oil company chose to use the Lotus Notes database as its engine rather than invent one from scratch. Buying technology was a tough sell; the Project Leader had to put together a white paper and invite the skeptics to a demonstration and discussion. It was worth the investment of his time and the project's money: this use of a purchased, existing, external system was a major contributor to the success of this project: it finished in 9 months, half the time of previous similar efforts.

NIH takes on many insidious forms, including *creeping elegance* (wanting to do it perfectly to show-up the others), and pride of ownership issues. For example, recently a top notch, senior software engineer working on a Motorola 68000 platform was doing object-oriented code for the first time. He claimed it would take him longer to bring several helpers up to speed than to do it all by himself. After they were added (the project had plenty of money, but lacks time), he agreed that only then did he have a reasonable chance of actually making the aggressive schedule.

I) **Plan to and start integrating modules and subsystems early and continuously.**

The sooner you find out if your modules and subsystems work together as planned, the longer you'll have to correct any problems you find. Unfortunately, people may not be used to letting other people see and use their work "in the rough". Help the team get over those concerns and find the mines early. Identify the most critical or complex interfaces, determine the earliest in the schedule you can get a first look, and schedule accordingly.

J) **Use a spiral or evolutionary (not waterfall) approach, especially for software.**

According to Boehm, the father of the spiral model, "A primary source of difficulty with the waterfall model has been its emphasis on fully elaborated documents as completion criteria for early requirements and design phases. For some classes of software, such as compilers or secure operating systems, this is the best way to proceed. However, it does not work well for many

Commandment #6. Use Innovative, Parallel, Iterative Design Strategies

classes of software, particularly interactive end-user applications." [Boehm, "A Spiral Model of Software Development and Enhancement," *IEEE Computer*, May 1988, p. 62.]

The waterfall model assumes a fairly straight-line progression through the stages of development work: requirements, design, prototyping, testing, delivery. The spiral model of development is geared to making successive passes at a system design and prototyping, targeting the riskiest areas first. Evolutionary development is a variation where features are developed iteratively in order to let designers and users implement particular features, test them, modify them, and perhaps even informally deliver them, before going on to the next set of features.

As an example of where the spiral model might be used, developers of certain types of networking systems often have to face uncertainty about performance (throughput and response time) of their software under heaviest traffic loads. In such situations, the developers might choose to work only on the communication part of the system first, develop prototype code, and test the performance of different approaches using test data. When those risks are understood, and the design alternative selected, the team could then specify more of the entire system.

These models work well when there is benefit to an iterative process: someone can look at prototype, discern issues, change things, and test to see that the change is better before proceeding. However, iterative models are not best for all projects, even all software projects.

Commandment #7.

INVEST MONEY TO BUY TIME AND TOOLS, AND TO MINIMIZE RISK

All too often teams miss the opportunity to speed up their projects because they are working according to old definitions of what project costs are "justified." Spending $5000 on fast turnaround service is too expensive. But when we shift to the Blitzkrieg paradigm, we see that many expenditures are really investments in the success of our project: they help us save time, and thereby gain money by getting to our customers earlier, and freeing our teams to move on to the next project sooner.

➲A)   **Invest early and speculatively in long lead-time tooling.**

Q*R*PD projects have a late cost per week ranging from $5000 to $ 500,000, with many in the $20,000 to $100,000 range. The cost of spending money early on tooling that might have to be reworked or even thrown away is cheap compared to the cost of lost time on the project. Make a bet on the future and identify places where you can purchase long lead tooling aggressively to have a chance of saving project time later.

A typical example: the tooling to create molds for plastic enclosures often take a vendor 12 to 16 weeks to produce. If the mold costing $60,000 can be released earlier than normal, the schedule can be sped up significantly, since the full 12 to 16 weeks will no longer be the "long pole in the tent" on the schedule. At worst, if the design changes before that mold is finished, it might have to be scrapped and a new one commissioned. But if releasing it early has a high probability of saving the project weeks of time, it's generally worth the risk.

➲B)   **Invest speculatively in long-lead-time parts; create a <u>list</u> early on.**

Again, the cost of spending money early on materials that might have to be thrown away is cheap compared to the cost of lost time on the project. Make a bet on the future and identify places where you can purchase long lead parts aggressively to have a chance of saving project time later. Such a list would include the following information:

Part.....Date needed ...Lead time...Risk that we won't need it...When we'll be certain.... Quantity to buy on speculation...Potential project savings if we buy on speculation and are right... Average cost if we're wrong.

At Mountain Computer, just before the 3.5 inch floppy disk format came out, we wanted to get a jump on selling the testers, or certifiers, for this new size. We took our 5 and 1/4 inch model, a rather large unit, and cut and hacked it to make a prototype that worked on the smaller disk. Based on this prototype, or mock-up, and having never proved that a purchase of the parts from the mechanical drawings would be accurate, we took a risk. The president approved buying 180 sets of parts at an approximate cost of $1000 per unit so that we would be in a position to deliver. These parts had very long lead times, typically two to four months.

© 1998 Global Brain, Inc.

Commandment #7. Invest Money to Buy Time and Tools, and to Minimize Risk

When the parts arrived they required a total of about $20,000 of rework. This cost paled in comparison to what we gained by being prepared when IBM announced introduction of its PS/2, which hastened the world's acceptance of the 3.5 inch disk format.

⊃C) **Utilize overtime and support personnel liberally, especially to meet key milestones.**

The cost of overtime pay or extra support personnel can be low compared to the financial impact of lost time-to-market. As outlined in Technique 6F, a team chose to pay consultants a total of $35,000 to develop alternate designs for an RF circuit, just to be sure they'd have an alternative that worked on schedule. A lot of money? Yes, but the late cost *per week* for this project was $50,000. The $35,000 insurance was a good investment.

⊃D) **Invest early and excessively in equipment, support, and training.**

"Excessively" means more than you think you really need. Proactively go after "hidden" items that tend to slow projects down unexpectedly.

- *Equipment:* Have extra computers on-hand so you don't lose time if one goes down or someone needs one at home. Have plenty of lab tools, too.

- *Support:* Have extra technicians and other support personnel up-to-speed on your project in case your main team member is unavailable unexpectedly.

- *Training:* Train developers on new tools *during phase I*. Train field test personnel well before sending them away with your product.

It's also critical to invest *early*. These items have lead time, too.

⊃E) **Make selective use of third party and rapid turnaround services, and manage them well.**

If rapid turn on a PC board costs $5000 to save a week on a project with a $20,000 late cost per week, why wouldn't you do it? If a consultant costing $15,000 per month can help with software coding on a project with a $15,000 late cost per *week*, consider it. If a graphic design firm can do a rush job that saves you a week and costs an extra $2000 on a $10,000 late-cost-per-week project, do it. This is the attitude we want to instill in all team members. We may not always use these services, but every team member should be looking for opportunities to buy time. Make wise, informed, conscious decisions.

That being said, it does no good to pay for rapid turnaround services if they don't deliver as promised. Outside organizations are staffed with humans, often with other priorities and customers as well. Commitments from outside vendors must be taken as seriously as internal team commitments to the goals of the project. Manage your outside services by:

© 1998 Global Brain, Inc.

Commandment #7. Invest Money to Buy Time and Tools, and to Minimize Risk

- including due dates in the contract.
- using incentives and penalties to get best performance.
- understanding their other commitments.
- selecting them for their true skills related to your project.
- setting interim deadlines for measuring progress and getting tangible evidence of it.

Here's an example of what can go wrong. A well-known mainframe computer company designed a new telephone central switching system. Although the mechanical design was basically a re-packaging of existing products, the company decided to use an outside firm to develop the product to save their internal resources for other projects. Unfortunately, the outside firm was left unmanaged—and each of 180 drawings had to be re-done, causing a 3-month delay.

F) **Computerize the process with CAD, software tools, quality tools, etc. If possible, learn to use them before a Blitzkrieg project.**

Use new tools to your advantage. For hardware projects there are emulators, simulation tools, automatic PC board and IC layout tools. For software quality management, there are tools for memory leakage, code coverage, complexity measurement, configuration management, defect tracking, call tracking, enhancement tracking. The list, of course, goes on. It's really amazing—almost any automated assistance you can think of is available somewhere.

If you take on new tools during a project, your schedule will be affected by the learning curve. Find ways to get training on and experience with the tools before the project if possible, or during phase I of the project at the latest.

A network management system project decided to use off-the-shelf software for a trouble-reporting subsystem. This lessened technical work dramatically, and made the project easier. However, they underestimated the difficulty of learning to use and interface to this system and sacrificed 3 weeks of time stumbling with the tool. In a lessons learned meeting they determined that they should have learned to use this subsystem way back in phase I.

The Varian Traveling Wave Tube Product group reduced a 2-3 year cycle time to 2-3 months by creating a spreadsheet that would analyze customer criteria by variable. Field engineers were able to take a laptop to the customer site, input the necessary information, and have the spreadsheet generate product specifications. As a result, labor costs also decreased with fewer development engineers necessary. Many went on to implement other cost reductions in the company.

G) **Add resources judiciously if in trouble, and as early as possible.**

It's possible that adding resources too late can actually lengthen the schedule. New people must be brought up to speed; communication overhead increases. If you take on these resources, plan to educate them on your process and on the

© 1998 Global Brain, Inc.

Commandment #7. Invest Money to Buy Time and Tools, and to Minimize Risk

design, and don't underestimate that learning curve. Remember the trapezoidal resource curve in Technique 2O and strive to have all resource on board by the beginning of phase II.

As a rule of thumb, adding a key team member after the midway (roughly 50%) of the project tends to hurt you as much as it might help you. Each new person must be brought up to speed—usually by the already-overworked team members they are supposed to be helping—thereby decreasing productivity instead of increasing the team's output. A new team member may be more prone to mistakes due to their newness to the work. And if the person is not a good "fit" with the rest of the members, important team synergy may be lost just at the time you need it most. As Frederick Brooks opinioned many years ago in *The Mythical Manmonth*, adding resources to a late project will just make it later.

H) **Actively manage the tools.**

Proactively ensure that the tools you've invested in actually produce benefit for your project. This includes configuration management and build systems, internal networks, automated testing tools, simulation and design tools.

- Are your licenses up to date? One IC design team in a start-up company lost 3 days of schedule time when the licenses on their verification software expired on a Friday; they couldn't use their systems again until Tuesday, after management had negotiated new agreements.
- Do you have licenses/authorization for the number of users you'll have?
- Does someone have responsibility for monitoring defects reported on the tools, both in-house and by other customers, and do they disseminate that information to your teams? Do you know the upgrade schedule for your tools and have time scheduled in for them?
- Has any configuration work for the tools been scheduled, and does it occur early enough?
- Are you going to be using the tools in a new way on this project, and should you therefore test your new approach before you actually need the tool on the project?

I) **Invest in backup plans for critical designs, tooling, and parts.**

See 6F.

J) **Set up more than enough prototypes, test and debug stations, and software build systems.**

This is not a place for your project to skimp! The logistics involved with sharing equipment among developers on a project or even among different projects causes real schedule hits. Those slips are insidious: day by day, there isn't enough equipment to keep up with test case execution; developers have to wait to test new code or defect fixes. And we've seen Project Leaders or test leaders spend 50% of their time during the testing period just managing

Commandment #7. Invest Money to Buy Time and Tools, and to Minimize Risk

equipment flow in the lab because everyone thought it was more efficient to skimp; this is *not* an effective use of those leaders' time.

Have independent test setups in the lab, even if you think two projects can share effectively. Then when one project hits a problem, the other can keep going without impact. Have extra equipment in case you experience hardware failures or come up with new test ideas.

And on the positive side, plan for enough equipment to find problems as early as possible. Provide enough equipment and plan your software systems such that developers can start "building" their code incrementally as early as possible. They're sure to find problems that can be resolved before system build and integration efforts get complex and time-consuming. Find ways to test early, even if extra equipment will be involved. One software team knew that their field environment would involve running their software in a network of over 200 devices. A typical approach before Q*R*PD would have been for this company to wait until beta testing to try the software in such an environment. In this case the proactive Project Leader fought to get a lab setup of 100 systems, and early access to the Services group's test network in the field. As a result, the team found several important software problems well before beta. They even found problems in existing code in the field that had never been seen before. The engineers had plenty of time to fix their problems; and the trouble and expense of encountering problems in the field were avoided. The team for the next major software project in this company decided to "make do" with a limited lab setup, and paid the penalty—they discovered a major problem on the first day of beta testing in the field, severely disrupting their test schedule and the customer's opinion of them. The Project Leader subsequently admitted that he should have followed the model of the earlier project, *not* hoped for the best, and fought hard for adequate testing resources to minimize risks.

Commandment #7. Invest Money to Buy Time and Tools, and to Minimize Risk

Commandment #8.

PROTOTYPE, AND TEST KEY DESIGN CONCEPTS EARLY

The more frequently we test design iterations, the more likely we are to find those hidden "mines" early, when they are easier to correct, and when we have more time to correct them. Scale up your testing efforts commensurate with the uncertainty of the situation, the complexity of the system, and the amount of technical risk in the design. Frequent testing also provides concrete means of evaluating true project progress and provides team satisfaction and higher morale through the very tangible results. It also creates many small opportunities for the team to learn and refine its approach on the fly. Commandment #8 provides ways to put this philosophy to work.

⊃A) **Do a reality check with real prototypes within about first 25% of the timeline: a "chicken test."**

> What is a *chicken test*? A reality test on a prototype that verifies the feasibility of the system, the critical parts, and the major innovations, of the design. Chicken tests should be performed within 25-50% of the overall schedule.

One of our most powerful risk mitigation strategies is to test working prototypes early in the development process. Faithful attention to chicken tests will ultimately improving both product quality and time-to-market.

The diagram "Skyrocketing Cost of Engineering Changes" under Commandment #3 suggests that the average cost of a design change increases tenfold at each later stage in a project. This exponentially rising costs curve points to the need to do chicken tests, critical reality checks on working prototypes, in the early stages of the project. Typically these tests should occur within the first one-quarter to one-half of the schedule, to tell us as early as possible whether the essential technology actually functions as it should.

The chicken test gets its name from tests performed on airplane jet engines. In order to ascertain that during flight the engines can contend with the ingestion of flocks of birds while in flight, a barrel gun fires chickens at the engines in a wind tunnel. This test serves as an early warning system to uncover a possible fundamental flaw in the rotor design before spending the whole $250 million necessary to develop an entire new engine. [Peters, Tom and Austin, Nancy. 1985. *A Passion for Excellence, The Leadership Difference*. Random House, p. 130. Insightful information on innovation and "Skunkworks."]

Chicken tests on QRPD projects are done at two levels:

1) Innovations chicken tests: a test of each individual technological innovation that is a major or higher risk. A "major" technological innovation is one that has been implemented elsewhere only a few times, and never yet in-house. See the risk assessment table under Commandment #1.

Commandment #8. Prototype and Test Key Design Concepts Early

2) The *system* chicken test is *the* critical point in the project: the point at which the fundamental overall design has been proven to hang together. This typically occurs early in the integration testing timeframe in phase II; it should occur no later than the 50% point of the project.

Every project must eventually undergo and pass a system-level chicken test before you know that your major technical risks are past. The only question is how late in the project you will discover that you may need to take a different technological approach. Obviously, the earlier the better.

For example, a major mainframe computer manufacturer decided to re-package its systems into a new market application, telecommunications switching. Nine months into the one- year project, they attempted system integration for the first time. Unfortunately, like many companies that just hope for everything to just work out perfectly, many of the mechanical subsystems didn't fit together. Over 180 drawings had to be redone, causing a three-month delay in a highly contested market.

To avoid late surprises, do your chicken tests on working prototypes (even without having all the bells and whistles yet) within the first 25% of the schedule, even if you have to "throw them away." This way you can find out if you're really on track, confirm your high-risk assumptions, and possibly decide to alter your course. With a typical one-year schedule, you could fail the test at the 90-day mark, start over or go to your back-up plan, and still probably ship a product ahead of a competitor who had to do massive rework later in their project. That's why we often say that you may "do a project twice to deliver it in half the time:" once to get to the point of passing the system chicken test, and the second time to finish the real product that fully meets the Vision.

On average, from the time you have passed this vital assessment point—where all of your individual innovations chicken tests have been performed, and your system chicken test has passed—you still have about 50% or half the project left to do.

Chicken Test examples:

- A developer of networking software needed to create new code that would allow them to send software upgrades "over the air" to remote computers on telephone poles (for the utility industry). The major elements of this transfer were breaking the software to be sent into chunks, sending it out over the network, and receiving it and loading it at the pole-mounted computer. The team didn't wait to make sure their design would work until the end of total integration testing with all the code in place. Instead, they did a system chicken test as soon as they had enough code to break down a fake new software build, send it out to computers in another part of their lab, and receive it into these test-bed computers. They proved early that their basic design held together.

- IT data warehousing projects focus on getting information out of existing corporate computer systems, such as order entry or customer service

Commandment #8. Prototype, and Test Key Design Concepts Early

systems; storing that data in a central repository; and providing end users such as business analysts with ways to get at the data for making corporate strategic decisions. The primary innovations chicken test for one such project was to determine the ability to get at particular pieces of data from within the legacy order entry processing system: no one was at all sure that the necessary data field was stored properly there or easily accessed from outside! The ultimate system chicken test for this product was the point at which prototype programs were used to automatically extract that data, transform it, and transfer and display it to the user at his desk. To accomplish this system chicken test, the team didn't have to extract and transfer all the data or have all of the user interface completed. But the whole basic path had to be executed in a rudimentary fashion.

- Radio-frequency designs often face emissions challenges: can a new system be produced that meets the Federal Communication Commission's radiated emissions standards? Critical chicken tests for these systems involve many early probes of PC board and other layouts, packaging alternatives with mock circuit boards, and antenna cabling configurations to ensure the design concept will pass. Such early testing can be critical to many different types of electronics systems, especially when new enclosure designs are involved.

- A creator of a new ASIC for use inside standard PCs realized that they had never before tested the ability of their computers to handle the heat generated by their new chips—until they had the final chassis design. Unfortunately, this point was too late in the project for quick design changes if they discovered a problem. Early in the project they now use computer simulation programs, and tests with mock heat-generating devices and a mock chassis, to conduct this important innovations chicken test.

- Hewlett Packard did not chicken test its oximeter, an earlobe clip device that detects the oxygen level in blood, on people already sick. Unfortunately, the product as originally conceived did not work for anyone except the healthy, since blood doesn't flow as well to extremities when we're sick. An earlier chicken test of this product—trying the earlobe clip and perhaps other attachment methods on patients—could have saved this expensive-to-develop product from its false start.

- The Mars Pathfinder team made headlines with its low-cost, quickly developed rover vehicle for exploring Mars. This team credited much of the rover's success to their attention to early testing. For instance, they made sure the lander's petals would open up at landing, even with it up against a boulder, by making the motors strong enough to flip the rover. Then they tested those motors in their "Mars yard" site behind the development facility.

It *is* important that your chicken tests be accurate and therefore meaningful. When the British high-speed rail was developed, testers took a page from the original chicken test concept to make sure the windshield of the train would be strong enough to withstand hitting airborne birds. They borrowed the FAA's machine for testing airplane windshields, reset it to approximate the maximum

© 1998 Global Brain, Inc.

Commandment #8. Prototype and Test Key Design Concepts Early

speed of the locomotive, and shot chickens at the new train's windshield. Unfortunately, the bird went through the windshield, broke the engineer's chair, and made a major dent in the back wall of the engine cab. They were quite surprised with this result, and totally stumped as to its cause, so they asked the FAA to make sure they had done the test correctly. A fax came back from the FAA with a single suggestion: "Try using thawed chickens."

B) **Build a tall junk pile, real and abstract, of experimentation, analysis, and simulation tests throughout the project, especially at key milestones.**

Every phase of the project should have testing of concepts, whether by physical prototypes, computer simulations etc., that constitute the best, truest indicators of technical progress. Completion of real-life tests is much more meaningful than checking off a less concrete milestone on a piece of paper. These items may or may not be used in the final product—they may be "throw-away" (hence the term "junk-pile"). Encourage the team to find creative ways to test as many aspects of the design in as many ways as possible as early as possible. "Make mistakes early".

David Kelly designed the Apple mouse by building and discarding many models, the first of which was made of a plastic butter dish. He then built 100 more, checking for feel and number of buttons. Often creating "quick and dirty" prototypes gives valuable information much more quickly than thinking things through on paper.

A manufacturer of equipment for the consumer market used to wait until the end of a project to submit to the UL (Underwriter's Laboratory) for safety testing. The company now submits twice, paying an extra $20,000, but saving valuable market time, to find any problems early. Similarly, biomedical firms submit products that they are still developing to the FDA. This early analysis and experimentation helps save the companies dollars and time in the long run.

C) **Prove out individual subsystems and interfaces early.**

Test whatever you've got as you go: make sure features work, subsystems communicate properly, performance is adequate. Build and integration your software components and systems early and continuously to flush out problems.

The Mars Pathfinder mission team mentioned in Technique 8A identified a critical new attitude on this project: the understanding of the need to test, test, test! The team leader related that they broke new ground by testing and testing and testing their components as they went along, rather than waiting until the whole craft was put together, a new concept for teams used to having years and large amounts of money to throw at their projects.

© 1998 Global Brain, Inc.

Commandment #8. Prototype, and Test Key Design Concepts Early

D) **Keep an updated <u>list</u> of critical issues and potential pitfalls: resources, sole sources, vendors, moves, tool availability, interdependencies with other projects, etc.**

A critical issues and dependencies list is a risk management tool that focuses attention on the project's important dependencies. The list should identify each issue, indicate who is responsible for monitoring it, and the date by which the part or tools is needed, and/or the date by which any decision is to be made or back-up plan is to be invoked. This list should be kept accessible: for instance, attached to the weekly team meeting minutes. The list is no good as a management tool if it's buried in a notebook!

E) **Have a failure and test analysis program, and keep a central project logbook or defect tracking database.**

Let there be no misperceptions about how much testing has been done and how good or not so good the results have been! The team must have the full picture. By the time products enter integration with other components, it's typical to use a defect tracking database program. In earlier testing by the individual engineer, results tracking can be less formal. But even individual testing efforts such as unit test should have some specified completion criteria and documentation of results. Issues encountered while "bringing up" multiple copies of a new hardware design must be recorded also.

F) **Take intelligent risks.**

Very few projects these days involve no risk. The world is moving too quickly and product development is too competitive for easy or tried solutions to be sufficient. The goal here is to make sure all risks have been thought through, assessed for their probability of occurrence and severity if they do, and taken on with fully-informed decisions made about mitigation.

On the IBM PC, one early question was whether the computer should include a tape port or a floppy drive. Not knowing the answer, IBM decided to allow for both, and put a place for a data cassette tape port and a floppy port on its first motherboard. They didn't decide until the near the end of design that they would use the floppy disk drive.

© 1998 Global Brain, Inc.

Commandment #8. Prototype and Test Key Design Concepts Early

G) **Stay flexible on unresolved issues, but set decision deadlines.**

Q*R*PD encourages flexibility to work iteratively on risky areas. However, work can spiral on forever without an understanding of when a decision must be made to allow the schedule to progress to completion. Document these issues in a Critical Issues and Dependencies List, with ownership and their "drop dead" decision deadline dates listed.

Black & Decker couldn't decide on whether consumers would want a square or a round handle for its cordless screwdriver. They decided to make handle molds that worked with both models. Due to marketing feedback, the company switched to the smaller, round handle after having started pilot production with the square handle.

A software team decided to use object-oriented (OO) development for a portion of their system. It was their first experience with OO. They decided early on to set a date by which they would go back to a more conventional software design if the OO design wasn't getting done on schedule.

H) **Distinguish between testing technical and marketing concepts.**

Both types of testing must occur, but they are often confused. If the two types of testing are combined, often the goals of one type of testing will obscure or push aside the needs of the other. Test the technical completeness and performance of your system or product. This is an acid test of your product's viability, using the actual product. Separately, test the product's usability, the market's response to its feature set, packaging, and so forth. These tests can use "smoke and mirrors;" i.e., often they can be accomplished without having the actual product in hand yet. See Commandment #10 for a discussion of various types of feedback to get from your testing.

I) **Use company resources creatively to test throughout.**

All testing does not have to be accomplished by a so-called "test group"!

A team creating a new PC program for medical record manipulation enlisted the support of an administrative assistant in the engineering department. Her computer skills were in-line with those of the expected user base; she made a great tester and in fact carried out a test effort for the rest of the project.

A networking company got Field Service involved with integration testing to give them the earliest possible head start on understanding and using and configuring the system. It's extremely motivating to the tech support people who get to play with the products. It also gives you the added advantage of having them trained on the product, in advance of its shipping, so that they will be able to better support it.

© 1998 Global Brain, Inc.

Commandment #8. Prototype, and Test Key Design Concepts Early

⊃J) **Know when to kill a project or feature, and do it.**

A $50 million dollar project at IBM got canceled. The next day the project manager went into his boss' office expecting to be demoted, but got a big surprise. He was in fact promoted. His boss told him that it was no fault of his own that the project got canceled, and that in fact he had done an excellent job running it. IBM had simply decided that this product no longer made financial sense for them.

It is hard to let go of a project or feature once a team has invested time, effort, and care into its development. But technical and business viability must take precedence over emotions: if the product no longer makes sense, or if a feature has proven technically problematic or unnecessary, make the call.

No, it wasn't pretty, but it was quick,

and it got started without muss and fuss.

~Tracy Kidder, *The Soul of A New Machine*,

referring to an early prototype

© 1998 Global Brain, Inc.

Commandment #8. Prototype and Test Key Design Concepts Early

Commandment #9.

FOLLOW A FLOW PROCESS TO MEET MILESTONES, MANAGE RISK, AND ENSURE QUALITY

The Flow process is a framework for integrating the work of the entire Q*R*PD project team. It is simply a systematic, but not bureaucratic, approach to product development. The goal is to set the project up for success from the start, and ensure timeliness and quality of execution. The following techniques are all part of having a useful product development process to accomplish the work of the project and achieve its challenging goals, while in no way stifling creativity, innovation, or productivity.

A) **Agree on a "reasonable"** *see-saw schedule.*

To have the best chance of meeting a project's milestones, the schedule must be reasonable, and the whole team must be committed to it. Your process will be meaningless and useless without that commitment. The "see-saw specification and scheduling" process (see Flow) is used to arrive at a Product Vision, schedule and milestones, and project and product cost targets that everyone believes in and signs up to.

B) **Use project management computer software to plan tasks and resources, set milestones, and re-plan if missed milestones.**

A good tool will be invaluable for getting complete, accurate schedules.

However, use caution in deciding how complex to get about the scheduling. Schedule at a low enough level of task granularity to get good bottom-up estimates, but plan to do tracking by milestones extracted from this schedule. These milestones should be set no more than 3 weeks apart, and closer together if the schedule is less than 6 months long.

C) **Post the milestones, and track to them.**

Milestones should be no further than three weeks apart. The purpose is to keep high visibility into the progress of very tangible project activities and deliverables. The milestones should be posted prominently in the company, and kept visible in other ways, such as attaching them to the team meeting minutes each week.

Actual completion dates vs. planned dates must be indicated for easy visibility of schedule slips. One simple trick for visibility is to mark all met milestones in green, all those made within a week of their planned dates in yellow, and all those missed by more than a week in red. Not only does this method keep the team honest about how they're doing, it provides big benefits in promoting "hype" and internal competition. Try posting all your teams' milestone charts; watch everyone start actively avoiding those red dates; and watch for an upsurge in friendly competition among teams. (See Flow for a milestone table format.)

© 1998 Global Brain, Inc.

Commandment #9.   Follow a Flow Process to Meet Milestones, Manage Risk, and Ensure Quality

D)   **Have a *written* product development Flow process and selective sign-off for the 13 defined steps of Flow.**

Your company should have a defined product development process in some form. What are your phases of development, Flow steps, and related deliverables? You don't need a bureaucratic process definition, just agreed-upon guidelines that teams can use and tailor.

Then, identify which steps of the process should receive a sign-off from team members and/or executives. The purpose of each sign-off is to impart a bit of formality to the completion of the critical step. This insures that everyone pays attention: when you ask someone to sign something, they usually get pretty serious about making sure they agree! Sign-offs from executives provide visibility into, and a sanity check of, the decisions being made by the project team and the reality of purported progress.

We recommend that some form of team sign-off occur for all 13 steps of QRPD Flow. Executive sign-off is required only for major project decision points.

E)   **Use checklists as structural guidelines for each step, including a list of deliverables to clearly define each milestone.**

Using checklists is an effective way to monitor progress toward frequent milestones. The checklist concept allows flexibility in tracking progress; it allows you to monitor progress without tracking the detailed time and exact completion dates of the small tasks that lead to the milestone. (See Technique 9P).

Track deliverables rather than just tasks; it is much easier to determine that a deliverable is complete than a more abstract work task without a physical deliverable.

A checklist of deliverables can be extracted from the schedule created with computer software and included on an actual physical checklist, or deliverables on the computerized schedule can simply be checked off to confirm satisfaction of the milestone. The team can determine how to define true milestone completion. For instance, if you've completed 80% of the deliverables associated with a milestone, have you completed the milestone? In general it is safest to hold yourself to the checklist and complete all of the work associated with it. Teams may exercise some judgment here; the important thing is that you are sure that the detailed project work is actually being accomplished in support of the overall plan, and you aren't fooling yourselves about real progress.

Caution: Be sure to include schedule draft or interim versions of deliverables to ensure that the team gets an early look and can iteratively correct issues.

© 1998 Global Brain, Inc.

Commandment #9. Follow a Flow Process to Meet Milestones, Manage Risk, and Ensure Quality

F) **Encourage creativity and "Golden Moments"—find shortcuts.**

Encourage team members to think "outside the box" when solving tough problems. Management and engineering discipline does not have to obliterate creativity! Recognize that the best ideas can come at the strangest times, and help the team find unstructured times for this type of thinking. Use group creativity tools as well, such as brainstorming techniques in problem-solving meetings.

The book *What a Great Idea! Key Steps Creative People Take* (Thompson pp. 12-13) cites the top 10 idea-friendly times (determined from surveys taken in the author's creativity workshops) as:

10. While performing manual labor.

9. While listening to a church sermon.

8. On waking up in the middle of the night.

7. While exercising.

6. During leisure reading.

5. During a boring meeting.

4. While falling asleep or waking up.

3. While commuting to work.

2. While showering or shaving.

1. While sitting on the toilet!

The term "golden moments" refers to the moment when the scales fall from the eyes of a developer—often in the unlikeliest of places, such as the shower—and they suddenly see the solution to the design problem they've been battling. In *Soul of a New Machine*, the architect had a golden moment, also called "an epiphany," that produced an elegant new memory management approach for the Eagle, a Data General mini-computer. Often these types of "aha's," which come after weeks of working on a problem, make it all worthwhile.

⊃G) **Project Leader identifies major problems early, and jumps in to <u>facilitate</u> breakthroughs and avoid delays.**

Project Leaders don't sit on the sidelines waiting for team members to report bad news. They look for warning signs of trouble: a low percentage (under 80%) of action items completed on time, milestones not made, unanticipated design iterations needed, poor early test results. Then they ensure that the real causes of trouble are being rooted out, that problem solution investigation isn't dragging out, and so forth. They are proactive!

In the midst of a 3-week-old design problem at Mountain Computer, I finally one night bought pizza and told the team that "we're not going home until the

© 1998 Global Brain, Inc.

Commandment #9.   Follow a Flow Process to Meet Milestones, Manage Risk, and Ensure Quality

problem is solved". It was solved at midnight, and many of us didn't come in again until late the next morning. There were no complaints about staying late to get that problem solved.

H)   **Top management personally involved in, and convinced of the achievement of, major milestones.**

Let management provide a sanity check of progress at key points in the project. An outside observer will be much less likely to rationalize partial progress to a milestone as being sufficient; they'll want to see sharp, bottom-line progress.

Asking management to take this role will also help maintain their interest in and support of the project.

I)   **Technically respected outside observer reviews key designs, problems.**

A fresh perspective helps avoid team blinders or unfounded optimism. Find a respected expert either inside or outside your company to objectively review designs, schedule estimates, test results. Even if you have to pay a bit for it, it's cheap in the long run, certainly compared to a week or two, or even a day, of schedule slip.

J)   **Practice occasional pause and evaluate.**

The team should be tuned in to realistically evaluating their project's performance. When projects get into trouble, or even slightly off-course, typical response is denial! "We'll catch up somehow." Especially in phase II, Development, step back occasionally and ask: Are we on schedule? Is our product going to meet the Vision we agreed to at the beginning? Are costs still in line? If yes, great! If not, why have the problems occurred? What Q*R*PD techniques have we violated? What do we need to do differently? As a team, review alternatives for getting back on track. If it's not possible to do so, the phase II see-saw process may have to be repeated, and schedule, cost, or features re-negotiated.

Ask these questions in an actual "pause and evaluate" meeting. Scheduling specific time for this lends weight to its importance. Consider using off-site meetings to get away and have a candid team discussion away from the pressure of daily activities and deadlines.

In the ASIC project mentioned earlier, due to the delays (caused in part by the vendor) the company decided approximately 2/3 of the way through the original schedule to have a "pause and evaluate" to decide on the best plan for completing the project. About a dozen people went off-site to a meeting room in a hotel nearby and spent a good part of the day hashing out how to proceed. By the end of the day they had made slight changes to the Vision, revised the cost targets, and redefined the milestones through the end of the project, which was now targeted to complete two months later than the original schedule. The two-month delay, which amounted to 13 percent of the project, was deemed

© 1998 Global Brain, Inc.

Commandment #9. Follow a Flow Process to Meet Milestones, Manage Risk, and Ensure Quality

relatively acceptable, even by the executives, since the project involved a very major innovation. However, it was critical to set a very realistic, aggressive, yet achievable new game plan to which everyone could recommit and march forward.

At every point in a project, scrutinize the plan for moving forward, and make sure that it is still the best plan. As long as the Vision, the costs, and the end date are held, it's often important that the team exercise its latitude to make timely split-second decisions in the battlefield. Happily, due in part to having held this pause and evaluate meeting, the ASIC product shipped on the exact revised date, 6 months after the meeting.

K) **Freeze conceptual design as early as possible — change later only for safety and reliability reasons.**

Although you may use the spiral approach (see Technique 6J) to work on risky or uncertain areas iteratively, this approach must not give license to the team to change the design on a whim. Changes to the high-level design ripple throughout the system, potentially affecting any detailed work that has already been done. Understand the goals of the project and avoid unnecessary design changes. See also 9N.

The same principle applies to freezing the implementation, especially setting a "code freeze" date for software.

The project must define change control mechanisms to ensure this happens. See the Flow section for a discussion of QRPD change control and releases.

L) **Use an evolving functional design outline document, not a rigid requirements specification.**

The Product Vision is the contract and alignment document created early on by the team. See Commandment #1 and the SSSS process in Flow. The Vision captures the critical aspects and parameters of the product or system that the entire team must agree upon. With the Vision in place, the functional specification and design process can be much more streamlined: the Development staff has the Vision as a guiding document.

Functional specifications can elaborate on areas of the Vision to more fully describe features for the technical team as needed. They can evolve during the design phase as appropriate, and without the overhead of unnecessary discussion of every item by the entire cross-functional team. Design documents can then capture the technical approaches and decisions regarding the actual implementation as they are made. At the end of the project you have an as-is description of the design.

To illustrate the importance of putting the Vision process before that of traditional detailed functional or requirements specifications: Such requirements typically go quickly to the details of all the features a product must implement and all the specifications it must meet. They have been

Commandment #9.   Follow a Flow Process to Meet Milestones, Manage Risk, and Ensure Quality

viewed as a good tool for guiding detailed development work, since they closely specify what the product is supposed to do. If a lot of time is spent writing down and trying to agree upon these details before a Vision is done, the resulting product may not even be on target for satisfying the customers' needs. And the rigid listing of requirements may even remove the chance for creative innovations of unexpected features that "wow" the customer. For instance, when the F-22 fighter plane was developed, the Air Force took a new approach to managing its subcontractors. Rather than dictate the detailed specifications up front, they commissioned a prototype that simply had to fly. The subcontractors were free to explore solutions and innovate a new machine. In the end, freed from rigid specifications, the team came up with a mechanism that would allow the plane to take off almost vertically, opening up vast new possibilities for effective aerial maneuvers and combat advantage.

Now an example of *not* following this technique: A large aerospace project involving over 200 software engineers and programmers was scheduled to complete over a period of 10 years. For the first 5 years, the team put most of its effort into writing a complete detailed set of specifications, without developing anything. At the end of this time, they discovered that 1) by then the hardware platform had changed completely, and 2) so had the system with which the software was going to operate. The people had spent their time writing hundreds of pages of documents, some of which went to waste when the vision had to change. A combination of incremental innovation or iterative development, along with evolving functional specifications during development, could have saved this wasted time and money.

A large medical equipment company did an after-shipment analysis on a product which had 600 requirement line items. Out of curiosity they asked their customer how many of those designed-in line items were actually needed. The answer? Only about 120, or about 20 percent. The point is this: at the very start of a project, it can be extremely hard to accurately define all the details of the features to meet customer needs. To try to exactly specify the details of the product, nail all those details down in a document before doing any design work, and hold people to those details, is foolish. Rather, spend a quarter of the project setting the Vision in concrete and work iteratively and continuously to update documents as the detailed requirements and designs evolve.

Commandment #9. Follow a Flow Process to Meet Milestones, Manage Risk, and Ensure Quality

M) **Create and adhere to meeting schedules and guidelines.**

Project work is paced along by individual efforts and communication among team members. All projects need meetings to ensure that issues are surfacing and technical decisions are understood. Don't write off meetings as an unproductive waste of time. Instead, early in the project, define what kinds of meetings will be needed, and set ground-rules about how to prepare for and conduct those meetings to best use team members' time. Then, don't abandon this critical team communication method during the project to "speed up" the work. Ultimately something will fall through the cracks and delay the project. See the Flow section for a discussion of Q*R*PD meetings and this deliverable.

N) **Avoid "creeping elegance" (excessive perfection) and feature creep and ship it.**

Be clear on the benefits the product or system is designed to provide the customer (as documented in the Product Vision). Design the system up front to meet those needs, identify the most important features, and clearly set the time, budget, and cost targets. Then avoid finding new things to improve technically, or new features to add, that are not needed to meet the customer needs. To guard against such design "enhancements", use increasingly tighter change management processes as the project progresses.

A Project Leader at a consumer audio company did a great job at holding the line. When the inevitable "great ideas" for something to add or change came up, he always emphasized: "I want to deliver units by Christmas, and if nobody can prove this added feature will amount to a higher percentage of sales, then I don't want to jeopardize that end date!" He kept all those great ideas from becoming the kind of schedule nightmare that had plagued past projects at the company.

O) **Use work breakdown structures and industry and company specific planning and estimating checklists to ensure the work is sized and sequenced appropriately.**

Make good use of basic project management techniques to break down the work the project will involve, and estimate all the pieces to get an overall accurate schedule. And make sure you don't repeat scheduling mistakes of the past! A checklist of planning and estimating considerations is invaluable.

© 1998 Global Brain, Inc.

Commandment #9. Follow a Flow Process to Meet Milestones, Manage Risk, and Ensure Quality

P) **Avoid using software to track or update actuals, except to capture historical data for future estimating.**

You don't want to use detailed scheduling to micro-manage people. 3-week-apart milestones are extracted from the detailed schedule, and the project tracked to those. What's critical is that each milestone be finished by the assigned date, to pace the project forward, but it's not necessarily important that each of the tasks leading up to the milestone be finished on exactly the date the schedule shows.

The reality is that the schedule is a concrete representation of the amount of work we have to do, and some basic dependencies, but exactly how we accomplish our work each day will vary. It's hard for scheduling software to exactly show reality, and where you really are in the project, especially when you're trying to parallelize and overlap work as much as possible. And tasks will get added as the project moves on. Trying to track at that level can create a rigid "fear-based" environment, and kill feelings of creativity, when team members feel hemmed in and judged by whether they make each little task completion date. And finally, tracking to a lot of detail takes a lot of time.

When might it make sense to do detailed tracking?

1) When a contract requires reporting of detailed actual costs.

2) To accumulate project cost data and some historical data on how much time different areas of work took.

3) Near the end of the project, when there are few technical unknowns, and much coordination among groups required.

For all of these cases, just make sure you track only to the granularity that's really necessary, track with a tool only if you need to, and make sure your team includes support personnel to do any time-consuming tool manipulation.

As an example of using a tool to track task actuals only if you need to: a software team did a lessons learned meeting at the end of their development phase. They were behind schedule and wanted to figure out where the slip had really come from. They hadn't tracked all their actual work in their scheduling program, but the team members were able to easily sketch out roughly how much time they had spent on the various major sub-systems in the last 6 months. And they were able in 30 minutes to determine that the cause of their schedule slip was incomplete software design work early in the project, which led them to leave several software modules worth of work out of the original schedule. Daily tracking in a tool wasn't necessary to get enough information to make a major improvement in the next project!

© 1998 Global Brain, Inc.

Commandment #9. Follow a Flow Process to Meet Milestones, Manage Risk, and Ensure Quality

Q) **Decide up front which development model you'll use and review which deliverables make sense to do for this project in each phase.**

The Flow process is a guideline. Your process shouldn't become a bureaucratic nightmare! At the beginning of each project your team should sit down with your company guidelines and decide how this project will be run via that process. Will you use spiral or evolutionary development? (See Technique 6J). Which deliverables will be needed?

At a fast-growing data communications company, the initial introduction of a formal product development process brought the predictable backlash—complaints that the process would slow work down and kill creativity. Finally the founder and CTO added his own personal support to the idea of wisely using the process: as the first page of the guidebook, he wrote:

"The Product Life Cycle captures best practices and lessons learned to provide Project Leaders and teams with guidelines for managing projects. The PLC promotes rapid time-to-market and maximizes economic benefit to the company."

"PLC is not a form of bureaucracy and should not stifle entrepreneurial drive. Rather, it is a tool to help project teams communicate and structure the project effort. Each Project Leader and team must decide the best use of PLC on their project. In guiding the project forward, the team leader should reflect on the spirit of the company culture: It is better to overstep the bounds of authority than never to push them."

R) **Negotiate elements of your Flow process with outside partners.**

In situations where you are working with an outside developer, discuss your development process with them up front and get agreement on the key phases, Flow steps, and deliverables each side will use.

S) **Individuals on the team must estimate their own work and help assess dependencies to ensure accuracy and buy-in.**

Project Leaders don't create the schedule! They facilitate team creation of an overall schedule. Each individual on the team should estimate their work during QRPD phase I. Project Leaders and functional managers should sanity check it, as some people are overly optimistic, some overly pessimistic, etc.

The Project Leader then creates the integrated schedule. They should have team members examine it for correct and complete dependencies.

© 1998 Global Brain, Inc.

Commandment #9. Follow a Flow Process to Meet Milestones, Manage Risk, and Ensure Quality

T) **Do early test, manufacturing, documentation, and deployment planning to ensure that late project milestones are accurately set.**

The QRPD concurrent development model and just-in-time mentality tells us to look ahead and do cross-functional work in parallel throughout the project. During phase I, all cross-functional team members should provide their own inputs to the schedule: when should test planning happen so that equipment can be ordered in time, testers trained, and real testing start on day 1 of the test period? When should manufacturing get its processes and procedures drafted in case they illuminate design problems that you'll need time to fix, hopefully even before any units are constructed? What are the steps leading up to deploying the product or service to the customer?

If this kind of planning isn't done early, your Flow process will leave out critical activities, and your schedule could blow up during the end game.

U) **Use action item tracking to pace detailed team tasks.**

What gets measured gets done! Teams have their scheduled tasks and deliverables to work on, but there are always many little things to get done, and issues to get resolved, that don't belong in the actual schedule. You need to write them down, assign them to someone with a due date, and make sure they happen. Action item lists were made for this purpose.

We use a special Excel macro that provides convenient reports with action items organized by due dates and reports statistics on your team's completion rates. The rule of thumb: if your team is not maintaining at least an 80% on-time completion rate each week, something is wrong: too much work, not enough commitment, etc.

V) **Define quality goals for Flow steps and deliverables where it makes sense, and review against them before proceeding.**

The QRPD Flow steps are important places to judge our progress and the quality of our work to-date. We have to consciously use them that way. To ensure we don't move on into a next phase prematurely, be clear about what state the product or service design has to be in before proceeding.

A typical software quality goal is that phase III alpha testing can't start until there are no "crash" bugs. No customer shipments can happen until there are no major defects in any feature. Pilot hardware builds can't start until all defects found in alpha, beta, and regulatory have been reviewed, and fixes determined and implemented.

Likewise, quality goals can be associated with deliverables: what is a "complete," or "complete enough" functional specification or design document or interface document? Iterative development often involves moving forward with incomplete information. But if multiple software designs capriciously, rather than consciously, proceed forward based on an incomplete interface

Commandment #9. Follow a Flow Process to Meet Milestones, Manage Risk, and Ensure Quality

specification, there could be serious rework at either design review, or worse yet, integration time, to work out the disconnects between all the designs based on that flawed interface document. Manage your deliverables creation efficiently, but also effectively to both move ahead quickly but avoid later rework.

W) **Use MBWA and iterative and informal design reviews to pace work and catch mistakes as early as possible; don't wait for formal phase reviews.**

Q*R*PD Flow provides design review guidelines for preliminary design reviews, detailed design reviews, critical design reviews, and final design reviews. There must be at least one instance of each design review per project, and usually there are multiple. We want to review our work iteratively and informally to catch mistakes.

Many reviews can actually be accomplished very informally using management by walking around. (MBWA). This is what is really happening when team members get into informal conversations as they work. In situations like this, you hear "how are you designing that interface again?"

One danger with traditional phase gate processes is that teams will wait until a formal end-of-phase big review meeting with management to really take hard looks and dig for progress. Don't do it! Q*R*PD puts emphasis on the design reviews during the phases. Find the mistakes then, correct them, and the major project decision points will be no-brainers.

X) **Use progressively tighter change control as the project proceeds to properly handle or avoid late changes and undesired rework.**

To make sure we don't capriciously change the Vision during our project, or even introduce lower-level feature changes that cause re-work and project delays, we have to build some change control into our Flow process. Each design review, development release, and testing period provides the opportunity for managing changes. Teams review what they've done, discuss issues, decide and agree upon what should get changed or fixed. Those agreements get progressively more formal later in the project. See the Flow section for a discussion of change control.

For instance, software developers use configuration management systems to manage their code once it is time to start integrating with other developers' code. These tools ensure that changes made by various developers don't get introduced into the system in an ad-hoc way, possibly disrupting testing, but rather get added to the overall software build in a controlled manner.

Later in a project formal change review groups usually review the defects being discovered during testing, prioritize them for correction, and approve that work.

Hardware groups generally institute engineering change control once they've built more than one prototype, with revision numbering and a formal process for documenting changes and updating hardware accordingly. Processes and

© 1998 Global Brain, Inc.

Commandment #9.   Follow a Flow Process to Meet Milestones, Manage Risk, and Ensure Quality

other "paper" products such as technical manuals are generally put under some type of control once they are distributed beyond the primary development group for review.

Y)   **Use trend analysis judiciously to understand true project progress.**

Trend analysis refers to a method of using various metrics for judging progress. For instance, testing is one of those areas where teams often just say, "OK, one month for testing", then don't have a good sense of whether they're actually doing well enough to finish on time.

So use some trend analysis: for instance, if you know that your testers have to execute 500 test cases in two weeks (10 working days), and there are 2 testers, you can use that information to determine whether things are staying on track. Each tester would have to execute roughly 25 test cases per day. If at the end of the first week, half their scheduled time, they've executed less than half their test cases, then they aren't keeping up. If you plot the number executed each day on a graph, you can see the trend: are they increasing the number completed each day, so that you might have a chance of recovering? Or is the line flat or declining, meaning that the "we'll catch up" mantra has no basis in reality?

One networking team had scheduled 3 months for a major software testing effort. Progress was definitely being made, and the reports to management always said so. But as the supposed end date approached, there was still plenty of work to do. And no one could really predict the end date, until an outside expert was brought in to show the young test group how to do testing planning and trend analysis. Graphing the test case execution rate, incoming bug discovery rate, and how fast the developers were able to fix the problems, the team got a handle on the actual time it would take to finish—and it was 4 months later than planned. They were then able to use these graphs to see where they could apply more testing resources to speed things up and where they might be able to use more development help to reduce the biggest bottleneck, the developers' bug fix time. Based on this information, the company reset the project end date, committed to it, and applied more resources to make the new schedule. They made the date within a couple of weeks of the re-planned date; and along the way management had confidence that the project was actually getting finished.

© 1998 Global Brain, Inc.

Commandment #9. Follow a Flow Process to Meet Milestones, Manage Risk, and Ensure Quality

Z) **Plunge through the product development funnel by micro-managing the last 10% of the project.**

Projects can fall apart in the end game. No matter how well you've done until now, don't underestimate the importance of, or the potential of, looming pitfalls at the end of the project.

This is the only part of the project where we want to micro-manage. We recommend daily quick team meetings each morning, 10 minutes, where everyone gets clear on the priorities of the day, looks for remaining issues to tackle, and agrees on who has responsibility for what. They reconvene the next morning, review progress quickly, then set the goals for the coming day. This kind of attention near the detail-ridden end helps ensure that nothing falls through the cracks.

© 1998 Global Brain, Inc.

Commandment #9.   Follow a Flow Process to Meet Milestones, Manage Risk, and Ensure Quality

Commandment #10.

GET EARLY FEEDBACK AND NAIL DEFECTS QUICKLY

We want to ensure quality, including the value as perceived by the customer, throughout the project. And if problems occur, we have to attack and resolve them quickly to avoid impacting our schedules. We need to get as much feedback on our product as possible, both internally and externally, as early as possible.

One natural tendency is to avoid showing customers an incomplete product. We're afraid it would damage our image or make the customers think we don't know what we're doing. We must have the opposite attitude, and understand that our customers will want to contribute to creating the highest-value product. The way to accomplish that? Involve them every step of the way.

A) **Question, listen, admit problems and respond to key lead and target customers and other departments within the company.**

Once the finished product gets out to the customer, get feedback from as many places as possible. Don't just wait for bad news to be reported; seek out the users. Are they using the product? Are they using it as you expected they would? You must confirm that you have truly delivered "value" to the customer.

When Intuit experienced problems with TurboTax in 1995, they announced the problem quickly, took responsibility, and shipped customers notices and updates quickly. By contrast, when Intel's Pentium chip was revealed to make floating point math calculation errors, Intel tried to ignore the issue at first, severely alienating their customers. Note that the problem was relatively insignificant to most customers. But Intel's handling of the problem caused customer mistrust. When IBM's customers for the original IBM PC AT complained of having hard disk problems, IBM ignored the issue. As a result, IBM clone makers gained significant market share by addressing this consumer need.

Note that the Pentium problem above became such a big issue because of the Internet's pervasiveness. The problem was originally discovered by one researcher and posted on the Internet. This wide distribution of the problem, and subsequent world-wide discussion of Intel's response, greatly amplified the seriousness of the entire episode. This technique becomes increasingly important as customers gain the ability to broadcast your product's "dirty laundry" to the world. When you hear a new joke one day in New York and the next day in San Francisco, it's a fun sign of our interconnected world. When you hear your customer's complaint around the world all in the same week, it's a sure sign you'd better learn to find those problems before shipment, with your customers' help if necessary.

Netscape has used the Internet positively to make the process of getting customer feedback almost instantaneous and effortless. Their home page has an electronic bug report form through which users can submit their problems,

Commandment #10. Get Early Feedback and Nail Defects Quickly

the severity level, how they encountered it, and whether they can reproduce it. They can also ask for future features. Netscape engineers thus get that information straight from the customer! Netscape has also created a users group on the Web, an interactive forum where users and engineers can discuss issues and priorities, and share tips. As one observer said, "It's a free-for-all of ideas, with all the ideas dedicated to upgrading the company's products as rapidly as possible."

B) **Particularly close tie between Engineering, Manufacturing, Quality, Field/Customer Support, and customers for first shipments.**

For best efficiency and effectiveness at the end of a schedule, all cross-functional groups must work closely together to get the product out the door. Use a single status board to identify and review all obstacles to shipping. Make sure everyone agrees as to the criteria for starting shipments! And formally sign-off together the approval to ship.

The end-game is all details; your schedule can still get trashed at this late date.

Note: This closeness provides the opportunity for a development of cross-functional rapport and joint learning that should be taken advantage of for the next project.

C) **Don't move key team members on to new projects too early.**

An all-too-typical scenario: By the time the product is rolling off the manufacturing line and into the hands of customers, engineers are long-gone to another project. This greatly reduces the chance of getting valuable feedback to fold into the next incremental innovation of the product. It also negatively impacts the ability to quickly respond to customer concerns with fixes.

On a wireless networking project, the team was raided before the end. Engineers were on to new projects. Field Service didn't know that the product had started shipping off the manufacturing line. The system software didn't totally work. The end game was a disaster. The product did not reach volume manufacture anywhere near its target date.

It isn't over until it's over. Use your Vision to define the true "end" of the project: the target volume, target cost, installed base. Use your milestones and schedule to show when resources are really done, and available to the next project waiting in the wings.

© 1998 Global Brain, Inc.

Commandment #10. Get Early Feedback and Nail Defects Quickly

D) **Use Beta Sites to weed out defects *before* release.**

Beta testing should include use of the product in an operational (or close to operational) environment. For some reason, problems that you'll never see in-house tend to crop up here. You can count on surprise visits from Mr. Murphy at your customers. Both lead and target customers should be included. This testing will find the problems that you couldn't find in the lab environment, or those that weren't uncovered by the in-house testers.

Mountain Computer sold a floppy disk duplication system called the ImageCopier. The disks were robotically loaded, and copy counts kept on each machine by a microprocessor. We had developed an Ethernet network system that allowed a single computer on the production floor to keep cumulative counts of the number of disks duplicated, as well as other important production data for a number of ImageCopiers.

One of our beta test-sites was Lotus in Boston, Massachusetts. When Lotus started running the network, they found that all their ImageCopiers would hang once a day, most often during the night shift. Since no technicians on duty at night were capable of restarting all the machines, Lotus lost thousands of disks of throughput until 8:00 a.m. when the machines could be brought back online. We tried to replicate the exact configuration back at our company headquarters in California, and no matter what we did we could not get the units to exhibit this hang. We were particularly suspicious because it was the night-shift and we thought it might be operator error. We also suspected that maybe power brown-outs or low voltage situations might be causing the problems. After weeks of searching we had convinced ourselves that this was a site-specific situation that the customer would have to solve—until one day we got a call from the Vice President of all of operations at Lotus. He not-so-subtly suggested that we "take back all our boxes" unless we fixed this problem immediately.

Needless to say, since our reputation, a key customer, and a lot of money were at stake, I sent one of our software engineers to Boston on the next flight. She carried with her all the tools she might need to look for the problem, such as an emulator and PC, to make sure she could figure out what was going on. She wasn't particularly fond of traveling or getting on airplanes but agreed to in this case, and I promised her that she could return just as soon as the problem was solved.

She came back home in less than 24 hours from the time she got to Boston. Sure enough she had found that there were brown-outs and low voltage situations at night, which caused an intermittent Ethernet card in one of the units to stop working. She also found a software bug which caused this error condition to not be properly identified.

This type of situation can drive a team crazy but nonetheless really helps to shake out the product. Our in-house testing would most likely not have encountered this problem. Customers understand that some of these problems may be "wrung out" in the field. The key is to respond quickly!

© 1998 Global Brain, Inc.

Commandment #10. Get Early Feedback and Nail Defects Quickly

E) **Create a company wide sense of urgency mode to solve <u>major</u> defects once discovered.**

It's not over until it's really over! Major defects after release mean that the customer is not yet satisfied, so the project has not yet completed successfully. Maintain intensity, ensure that the problems are closed out—and the project work really finished.

Once defects are discovered, handle them with a sense of urgency using methods like HP's probable cause committees, and the use of "stop-ship" orders. HP maintains committees that are responsible for immediately identifying the source of each customer problem, to ensure both that they are fixed quickly and the lessons transferred to other teams. In one company, the VP of manufacturing over and over again resorted to a stop shipment order to focus company attention on the manufacturing problems affecting yield. These orders were enough to send the President into the VP of Engineering's office to ask why the problem wasn't solved yet. Quick progress was virtually assured.

Intensity and vigilance regarding customer feedback can be maintained by:

- Setting a target date some time after release, by which you expect customer reporting of defects to have dwindled.

- Holding daily or weekly customer comment and defect review meetings with representatives from all functional areas required to attend.

- Publishing "stop-ship" status and progress via email notices company-wide.

F) **Use alpha system testing to test new functionality and regression test old functionality.**

Alpha testing is testing of your product or service by a group inside your company but independent of those who developed it. It is done at a "black box" level, meaning the goal is to test the functionality from the user's point of view. Testers try to do all of the operations a user might, in different combinations, to find areas that don't work, and to verify that system features and performance meets the Vision and detailed requirements.

Regression testing refers to the need to re-test previous functionality when you introduce new features or sub-systems, to make sure that these changes have not disturbed other elements, and to make sure the entire system will really still work together. This is particularly important when your product is an incremental innovation of an existing shipping product.

One communications company didn't put their new modem design through a full alpha (software QA) test with the entire existing system. When they went to the field they experienced communications problems between the modem and the system, a result of a software bug in the existing software system that hadn't come to light before.

(See Flow and DIRFT for further discussion of Alpha.)

Commandment #10.   Get Early Feedback and Nail Defects Quickly

G) **Involve customers (internal and external) in reviews and testing to find issues and defects before beta, track them, and use an early adopter program to ensure proper translation of customer feedback.**

Testing should not just look for bugs or defects, places where the product doesn't work according to the detailed specification. Throughout the project, make sure that your testing takes a hard look at whether you're meeting your Vision. Customers should be involved throughout to help accomplish this. Beta testing will ultimately test the product in the customer's operating environment; in the meantime, use customer feedback creatively!

And don't just track "bugs" in your tracking databases. Track opinions, enhancement requests for next time, whatever valuable information and requests your customers give.

H) **Do pilot runs to test the process and product before volume manufacturing and shipment, and to slowly introduce the product to customers.**

Pilot is a step of Q*R*PD Flow. The purpose of pilot is to start ramping up production or deployment of your systems before opening the floodgates. It gives you a chance to test how well your manufacturing processes will work and whether any hardware design issues show up when more units are built. You can deploy a new IT application to a small group of users and test whether your training program and documentation were adequate to get them started quickly. You can roll out a new cellular phone service plan to a small group of customers and test your order entry and customer service processes. There are often mines waiting for you at this stage of the project, and they are very expensive to fix if you go straight to volume manufacture or installation.

© 1998 Global Brain, Inc.

Commandment #10.   Get Early Feedback and Nail Defects Quickly

Commandment #11.

LEARN FROM AND IMPROVE THE ABOVE PROCESS

The extra commandment: Continually look for ways to improve on everything you're doing.

⊃A)   **Hold "lessons-learned" reviews during and after the project.**

Hold a team review to discuss how the project is going, and at the end, how it went. What did you do well? What did you not do so well? What was the bottom-line result for the project? What can you learn for next time that will help you and others on other projects?

Lessons learned meetings are your best weapon for implementing continuous improvement. These reviews give everyone a chance to freely discuss the good and bad aspects of the project so that good practices are repeated and bad practices are eliminated. They should be held at or near the end of a project, and can also be useful at key interim points during longer projects, such as after phase II in a major software project. These reviews are attended by the entire core team. Key functional managers may sit in but should not impede the process.

Review project results by asking questions like did we do what we said we would in terms of PTCC? What were the cost issues, feature issues, schedule issues?

⊃B)   **"Start talking and get to work."**

Tom Peters, who coined this phrase above, recognizes that the best team synergy comes from team communication. Synergistic interaction should be encouraged.

In prior days of "command and control" style management, talking was often viewed as time-wasting. Not so with Q*R*PD. Teach team members the value of pro-active, ongoing, open discussion of not only project details, but process details. Encourage people to speak up with suggestions for positive change.

Back in 1980 an AT&T manager saw an engineer with his feet up on his desk. He asked him, "What are you doing?" "I'm thinking about a problem," answered the engineer. "Well do that on your own time!" barked the manager. We've come a long way from those days. Knowledge workers need to think, communicate, and synergize. Our products and processes are complex, competition is fierce, and time is short. Individuals will always contribute their knowledge and skills and innovations. But our overall success will come from these team members collaborating, refining ideas, building off of each others' breakthroughs, and working together to creatively bring projects to completion.

© 1998 Global Brain, Inc.

Commandment #11   Learn From and Improve the Above Process

C) **Remember to see the process as an ever-improving guideline, not a static set of rules set in concrete.**

Team members should learn to view your development process as a guideline that they have responsibility for using <u>and</u> improving.

Every project is different, every team is different. An initial attempt at establishing a new product development process will never capture everything the first time. The most successful organizations learn to improve their tools and techniques as they work. This is also useful for getting rid of resistance to the process. When process-phobic groups see something as Bible "handed down" from someone else, they tend to rebel and over-react every time they believe that the documented process is "deficient" or restrictive. If they, however, see the process as a guideline meant to simply steer by means of best practices, and feel free to include their suggestions at any time, they are more apt to buy in to using and contributing to it. This is the mark of a "learning organization:" one where each individual is engaged in learning from experience, and building that wisdom back into the knowledge base of the entire company.

Organizations use internal email discussion groups and a mechanism for ongoing "updates" to accomplish this ongoing process improvement. They also ensure that each project's "lessons learned" get reviewed for impacts on the process, and suitable enhancements get folded in right then and there.

D) **Hold Project Leader "best practice" forums and issues meetings to cross-fertilize between projects.**

Project Leaders often have the best advice for other Project Leaders. Give them regular forums for exchanging information. If you don't, everyone is often so busy that the great lessons from the past won't be passed on.

One major creator of desktop PC software schedules quarterly manager training weeks where their development and project managers from around the country converge at Headquarters for intensive interaction. They attend project-related training together, and schedule a best-practices forum where Project Leaders can share their experiences.

A fast-growing wireless company growing a large number of Project Leaders "from scratch" decided to implement Project Leader meetings every 6 weeks to create an "esprit-de-corps" and a regular opportunity for cross-project synergy. Project Leaders air problems and get advice, share techniques that have worked, train other Project Leaders on custom tools they've created, and give group feedback to management on their project management issues and needs.

© 1998 Global Brain, Inc.

Commandment #11 Learn From and Improve the Above Process

E) **Identify root-causes of schedule slips and cost overruns and their quantitative impacts to help justify ongoing improvement efforts.**

Lessons learned meetings result in some hard data about not just how much a project slipped, but why, and how much it cost the company. These results are powerful for convincing management to fund that extra tool, bring in that new training program, give teams time and money to use off-site meetings; in short, invest more to buy time next time.

F) **Record causes of product defects as they are discovered to help improve the process the next time.**

Many companies track defects in the product as they test it and after they release it. But when they fix the problem, they don't necessarily figure out or write down why the problem happened. Was a design review skipped that would have caught the problem? Or was a particular technical expert absent from that review? Was an area of the product not tested thoroughly enough? Was a detailed specification item wrong? Was the customer's need misunderstood and not tested with a prototype during the project?

Asking these kinds of questions as you go gives the team immediate improvement ideas for next time and helps ensure that you capture information before it is lost; the real root causes of these problems may be forgotten by the time you get to an end-of-project "lessons learned" meeting. So include "what happened here" questions on each design review checklist; schedule interim "lessons learned" meetings to discuss problems. Record the team's findings and distribute them by email, Web, or whatever mechanism ensures that all projects will get to take advantage of them.

If you think education is expensive,

try ignorance!

© 1998 Global Brain, Inc.

Commandment #11   Learn From and Improve the Above Process

PART III. PROJECT LEADER AND TEAM

Project Leader Selection Criteria I: Personality Traits

> *Leadership is interpersonal influence, exercised in situations and directed through the communication process, toward attainment of a specified goal or goals.*

An *OBSESSED* **LEADER** that is **CONFIDENT and HONEST, TECHNICAL**, a **MODEL WORKER**, a **PEOPLE PERSON**, and has **HIGH STANDARDS** and **MANAGEMENT ABILITY**.

The Project leader "Hat"

In the workplace, as in all aspects of our life, we find ourselves wearing different "Hats". Leading a team requires specific skills that are distinct from those used to solve a technical or marketing problem as a team member. It may also require different communication skills. The mastering of these skills and the recognition of when to use them is the sign an effective project leader.

Project Leaders Must	And the Traits Required are:
• **Drive the Project**	Obsessed
	Leader
• **Deal with People**	"People person"
	Understanding Styles
	Communication and Listening
	Motivating and Rewarding
	Managing and Resolving Conflict
• **Deal with Work**	Technical skills: knowledgeable, perceptive
	Work habits: Time management
	Management skills: Delegation, organization
	High standards for work products
	Good project management skills: Process, planning, tracking…

© 1998 Global Brain, Inc.

Project Leader Traits and Behaviors

TRAITS	BEHAVIORS: What it Looks Like
OBSESSED: • "A good man in a storm." Trustworthy. • On a mission, "fearless," firm, uncompromising at times • Determined, persistent, tenacious, persevering	• Continually accepts "buck stops here" responsibility. • Handles the problems rather than building the excuse list. The assignment is to get the job done NOT getting it done unless it gets difficult. • Observers know what you are working on. You are seen as an advocate for the project and the team. The organization empowers you to act in that role.
MANAGEMENT ABILITY: • Well-organized administratively • Delegates, manages time • Project management skills: requirements, planning, tracking...	• Details don't fall through the cracks, but the PL doesn't do it all. People feel trusted. • The planning is thorough, the tracking is useful without being overwhelming…
PEOPLE PERSON: • Sensitive to personality styles, issues • Communicates and listens accordingly • Recognizes, Rewards, Motivates • Manages and resolves conflict	• People feel understood and heard. They voice their opinions. • People feel appreciated. • Even tough tasks are worth doing. • Constructive conflict feels comfortable to everyone; but unconstructive conflict is not allowed to fester.

Project Leader Traits and Behaviors (continued)

TRAITS	BEHAVIORS: What it Looks Like
LEADER: • Motivator, dynamic, creates drama and hype • Visionary, grasp of "big picture" • Project "adult" • Performance-oriented, pragmatic • **CONFIDENT**, not overly egotistic	• When you walk around, you personify the project. • You stand in the front of the room and remind the team about the whats and whys. What the goals are and why we are doing them. • Remind individuals that they are part of a team and what their roles are. • You pat people on the back. • Theatrical leadership. Tell the team "what they need to hear from you at any given time" (and always tell the truth). • Everyone gets to act like a prima donna but you…. • Have the team agree to a doable project and then continue to reassure the team that they can do it. • Turn issues into actionable problems. • Believe in the team and make sure they know it. Continue to reassure them that they can do it. • Eagle eye always for effort vs. results.
TECHNICAL/ Knowledgeable, perceptive: • Analytical/technical, not necessarily a genius or expert • Calculated risk-taker • Understands how to adapt the process.	• Sure that assumptions are tested, that decisions are credible. • Knows how to get the right information into the decision process. • Good "BS" detector. • Willing to ask the dumb questions. • Content leads feel they have to have their act together before they propose. • The process is used appropriately for the project, technology, risk, etc. No one feels mired in bureaucratic mess.
LEADS BY EXAMPLE (Model Worker): • Hard-working, doer, not a taker • Time management	• The leader and team are in this together. • No us vs. them, worker vs. non-worker.
HIGH STANDARDS, values: • Setting the bar on deliverables	• The project work is useful, meaningful, thorough; work doesn't have to be redone.

© 1998 Global Brain, Inc.

Project Leader Selection Criteria II: Experience

> "Unlike the managers of old, they won't take charge and give orders to subordinates. Instead, they'll subtly lead, guide, challenge, and support their team members."
>
> ~ Tom Peters, *Liberation Management*

EXPERIENCE AREA	ASSETS
Ability to deliver results	• Track record • Vision: Market/Company/Business perspective
Cross functional understanding of the project area	• Broad/relevant technical background • Abreast of recent technology • Financial understanding • Relevant educational background
Understands people, organizations and process	• Good rapport with upper management • Management of engineers, other people • Familiarity with workings of company • Knowledge of computer systems and tools • Understanding, respect for process

> "If you want to get the best out of a man,
> you must look for what is best in him."
> ~ Bernard Haldane

Ways to Gain Experience

The list on the previous page might lead you to ask: If I'm not an experienced Project Leader, how can I ever successfully lead a rapid development effort? Keep in mind that there are additional ways to gain knowledge that will be invaluable. The following tables give several pointers.

Ability to Deliver Results

Type of Experience	Impact on Project	Source of Additional Knowledge
Proven track record of projects with results	Provides you with a personal history of how-to and how-not-to. Ensures that you have practice making decisions, judgment calls, etc.	Lessons learned from other projects (yours and others) Respected Project Leaders inside or outside the company Functional managers Conference papers and project case studies
Vision: Market, company, business perspective	This experience helps you: • ensure that what the team is delivering is what the customers need. • understand overall company strategy and how a particular project fits in. • understand the competition. • be able to fold this information into trade-off decisions for the project.	Form a relationship with your team's marketing group/representative, and work with them on the side to understand their perspectives. Bring an executive or marketing person to team meetings and Vision meetings to explain their perspectives and market knowledge to the team. Go on customer visits with executives or marketing person. Read trade magazines.

© 1998 Global Brain, Inc.

Ways to Gain Experience:
Cross-functional Understanding

Type of Experience	Impact on Project	Source of Additional Experience
Broad/relevant technical background, **Abreast of recent Technology,** **Relevant educational background**	Helps you understand project risks. Helps you make good decisions about what risks to take on. Provides understanding of the interplay between elements of your system and helps ensure that you know how to take advantage of Commandment #6 design techniques. Ensures a solid understanding of thorough cross-functional work and what "done" means in each area. Ensures you understand the role you and others should play during different parts of project, are able to assess team member skills in each area, and successfully staff the team.	Get personal tutoring by an expert. Encourage and attend brown bag seminars at your company. Attend continuing education courses. Expert participates in design reviews, especially early systems design. Team members get specific role assignment to be "sanity check" on this. Have functional team representatives check schedules for proper durations, all work there, etc. Added step, have their functional managers check too. Gets buy-in. Learn from their changes. Ask team members in each functional area where the risks are, where their concerns are. Make sure someone is assigned to cover all of them; decide if you need extra help. Get help from functional managers. Appoint an expert to act as an adjunct member of your team. Find a gatekeeper in your company to keep the team informed.
Financial understanding.	Provides you with an understanding of where true project costs and product costs are, including life-cycle costs, so that the true cost and benefit of the project will be understood.	Involve all functions in project budgeting and product costing. Have finance person on team to sanity check the thoroughness of project and product costing. Have them define a template for costing if company doesn't have one.

© 1998 Global Brain, Inc.

Ways to Gain Experience:
Understanding of Organization, People, Processes

Type of experience	Impact on project	Source of Additional Knowledge
Knowledge of computer systems and tools	Aids personal productivity. Allows understanding of project impacts from possible tools and equipment glitches; costs due to equipment needs; need for training during the project…Development tools, testing tools, etc.	Attend lessons learned meetings for other projects or read their reports. These reports should consistently mention where tools and equipment issues caused a project problem.
Good rapport with upper management	Management trusts your assessments, will be more likely to provide resources without second guessing you, and will support you even when times are tough. This rapport includes understanding executives' styles, the information they want, and a reputation for being honest about the state of the project.	Obtain mentoring from a respected person in the company who knows the executives involved: what are their styles? Their perspectives and usual issues? Attend managerial reviews, learn what questions upper management members ask.
Management of engineers and other people	People in functional groups make up the team. If you have experience managing their work, you're more likely to understand their particular issues, their ways of working, and the risks in their areas. This experience also helps you understand and address motivation issues.	Cultivate relationships with functional managers. Read publications targeted at the workers for the particular technical area. I.e. EE Times for electrical engineers.
Familiarity with workings of company	Allows visibility into particular roadblocks to getting work done. Conversely you'll know where to find people who get things done.	Obtain advice from those who've been around the company. Learn on your projects.
Understanding and respect for process	The process provides the framework and communication tools for getting things done. If you understand it and respect it, you'll be able to help the team understand what to do and why; you'll be able to improve it as you go along; and you'll be less likely to leave out an important step.	Seek explanations of how the company's development process has helped, or not helped, from more experienced Project Leaders and functional managers. Understand how other Project Leaders have adapted the process on their projects.

© 1998 Global Brain, Inc.

Project Leader Responsibilities

COMMUNICATION

        LEADERSHIP

                MANAGEMENT

                        RESULTS

Communication
- Keep the interdisciplinary participants motivated and informed.
- Measure performance and results accurately, then take appropriate action in response.
- Give clever, constructive, helpful criticism.
- Accurately report project progress and problems to superiors.

Leadership
- Build the project team; motivate for synergy.
- Focus everyone toward common vision; resolve conflicts.
- Do everything on Quality *Rapid* Product Development Checklist.

Management
- Initiate and complete each item of development Flow on schedule.
- Worry about <u>all</u> the details (prioritize, delegate).
- Resolve problems, conflicts, delays.

Results
- Meet product specification, on schedule and within budget. (Performance, Time, Costs).
- Do It Right The First Time (DIRFT)!

Project Leader Success Wisdoms

COMMUNICATION:
- LISTEN! ASK OPEN-ENDED QUESTIONS!
- "Seek first to understand, then to be understood." (Covey)
- Understand the styles of those on your team.
- "Ninety-nine percent of all surprises in business are negative." Encourage open communication, mistakes are okay.
- Get objective, "unshakable facts" (Geneen, p. 98, 102); Whenever possible... (Ori)
- Learn who to take advice from, and on what.
- Let people come up with your idea and solutions (ask questions).

LEADERSHIP:
- Heart attack vs. cancer—both will kill you eventually.
- Okay to lose some battles and win the war.
- Shortest distance between two points may be a zigzag.

MANAGEMENT:
- "Management must manage!" (Geneen)
- "Manage means to get something done, to accomplish something...you set out to do." (Geneen, p. 111)
- "...the significant difference between one manager and another is what standards each of them sets." (Geneen, p. 129)
- Loose/Tight management: delegate but stay very involved. (Complete trust, but cut the deck.)

RESULTS:
- Don't "go on accepting inadequate results and explaining them." (Geneen, p. 129)
- Don't confuse effort with results!
- Step back and say, "Bullshit!" when appropriate. Change things.
- "Not Everything Worth Doing Is Worth Doing Well." (West in *The Soul of a New Machine*)
- Know when to say, "Okay. It's right. Ship it."

  "... often the most talented engineers have the hardest time knowing when to stop striving for perfection." (West, *Soul*, p. 119)

© 1998 Global Brain, Inc.

Listening Effectively

> A manager should spend about 80% of his/her time communicating!

Excuses for Not Listening (that may lead to project failure)

- Not interested (seems less important than current problems)
- Pre-judgment
- Lack of concentration (bad timing)
- Material is too complex
- Attention to note taking
- Pretending to be interested (tired, etc.)
- Delivery not interesting, or difficult to follow
- Listening speed (can think faster than people talk)

"Go ahead, I'm listening now"

How to Improve Listening Ability

- **Show the speaker that you are interested** by demonstrating active, supportive attention to what he has to say.

- Even though you are busy and have your problems, **listen.**

- **Don't constantly interrupt the speaker or try to finish his sentences** by leaping ahead with your own thoughts, and don't occupy yourself with busywork or fidgeting while you are supposed to be listening.

- **Listen for the concepts and the ideas** being presented by the speaker. Don't concentrate exclusively on the facts he is using to support his arguments.

- **Make sure that there is sufficient feedback** on both sides to assure that the points being made are clearly understood.

Source: p. 303-304, Meredith, Jack R. and Mantel, Samuel J. Jr. 1989. *Project Management: A Managerial Approach*, John Wiley and Sons

Dealing with People: Personality Types

People view the world differently. They differ in the way they:

- Perceive and organize information
- Communicate
- Make decisions

Understanding the differences is critical to leading a team successfully. Differences in team members' personal styles are often at the root of conflicts or misunderstandings. If the Project Leader and team members recognize this fact, such conflicts can be more easily resolved and pose less difficulty to the team's performance. The Myers-Briggs Type Indicator system provides one way to describe and understand the above differences.

Myers-Briggs Type Indicator® (MBTI)

The MTBI system of personality assessment is based on four basic aspects of human personality:

- **Extrovert vs. Intravert:** Describes how we interact with the world and where we direct our energy. Extroverts focus their energy and attention on the world outside themselves, enjoying lots of interaction and working out problems in groups. Introverts focus their energy within themselves, preferring to spend more time alone, for instance, thinking about problems alone before discussing them in a group.

- **Sensing vs. Intuitive:** Describes the type of information we usually notice. Sensors concentrate on data they gather with their senses. They trust whatever can be measured or documented and focus on what is real and concrete; they focus on the present. Intuitives focus on implications and inferences. They value imagination and trust inspirations and hunches; they are oriented toward the future.

- **Thinking vs. Feeling:** Describes how we make decisions. Thinkers prefer decisions that make sense logically, priding themselves on their ability to be objective and analytical in the decision-making process. Feelers make decisions based on how much they care or what they feel is right, priding themselves on their ability to be empathetic and compassionate.

- **Perceiving vs. Judging:** Describes whether we prefer to live in a more structured way (making decisions) or in a more spontaneous way (taking in information). Judgers like to do things in an orderly way and are happiest when their lives are structured and matters are settled. Perceivers like to be spontaneous and are happiest when things are flexible; they like to stay open to all kinds of possibilities.

Impact of Team Member Personality Types

While most individuals tend to have a preference for one of each of the following pairs, we all must develop skills from both parts of each pair to be successful.

How we interact with the world	**Extrovert (E)**	• talk first, think later • talk through problems • find it easy to talk to people • like lots of feedback
	Introvert (I)	• prefer to think through problems before answering • do not interrupt others and hope they will reciprocate • often perceived as shy • need time alone to recharge
How we gather and organize data	**Sensing (S)**	• prefer specifics • look for tangible results • master the details • rather do than plan
	iNtutive (N)	• Prefer "Big Picture" to the details • seek out creativity and innovation • future oriented • time is elastic
How we make decisions	**Thinking (T)**	• the "truth" is most important • cost/benefit decision making • more important to be right than liked • remember facts and ideas more than people
	Feeling (F)	• good decisions take the people into account • empathize with other people • prefer harmony over clarity
How we organize	**Judging (J)**	• like activities to drive to a decision/conclusion • like having a plan and sticking to it • sometimes perceived as angry when you're not • like to finish things
	Perceiving (P)	• prefer spontaneity • work in spurts • enjoy generating alternatives • love diversity

© 1998 Global Brain, Inc.

Covey's Four Activity Quadrants:
A Time Management Matrix for Effective Teams

It is the Project Leader's responsibility to make sure each individual, and the team as a whole, practices effective time management. It is especially critical that adequate time is spent in quadrant II below—working on important issues and plans, before they become urgent "fires."

Activity Type	Urgent	Not Urgent
Important	**I** "HEART ATTACKS:" Crises Pressing problems Deadline-driven projects	**II** "HEART ATTACK AND CANCER PREVENTION": Prevention, "PC" activities Relationship building Recognizing new opportunities Planning, recreation
Not Important	**III** Interruptions, some calls Some mail, some reports Some meetings Proximate, pressing matters Popular activities	**IV** Trivia, busy work Some mail Some phone calls Time wasters Pleasant activities

Adapted from Covey, Stephen. *The 7 Habits of Highly Effective People.* New York: Fireside, 1990, p. 151.

© 1998 Global Brain, Inc.

The 4 Stages of Team Development:
"Form, Storm, Norm, Perform"

STAGE OF DEVELOPMENT	CHARACTERISTICS
1. FORMING	• Agreeing on common goals • Developing trust • Establishing base-level expectations • Getting to know each other • Members dependent
2. STORMING	• Struggle for power and control • Identifying who's doing what, how, when • Learning how to communicate with each other • Expressing differences: ideas, feelings, opinions • Reacting to leadership • Members independent
3. NORMING	• Members agree about roles and processes for problem solving • Decisions made through negotiation, consensus building
4. PERFORMING	• Things happen: effective and satisfying results • Solutions found appropriately • Team work: collaboration, mutual caring • Unique group identity established • Members are interdependent

Notes about behaviors:

- Each step builds on the previous one, and prepares for the performing stage.
- Skipping any step affects performing negatively.
- With every new challenge, the process repeats.

Building and Motivating Technical Teams

> Strong lives are motivated by dynamic purposes.
> ~ Kenneth Hildebrand

- Make vision visible: post, with milestone charts

- Hold team meetings to portray the big picture

AVOID ACTING	ACT
FEARSOME	COMPETENT
CRITICAL	SUPPORTIVE
ARBITRARY	RATIONAL
DEMANDING	ENCOURAGE INVOLVEMENT
of hard work, no humor, no play, no fun, no spending	based on passion, fun

- Promote career building opportunities

- Conduct "one-on-ones" regularly with team members

- Provoke interest and inter-member dialog ("nose-poking" in lab, "stupid" questions, etc.)

- Encourage team to participate in creating and improving the new product development process

The Cross-Functional Team
And the Power of Asking Questions

At the core of QRPD is the importance of providing projects with clear goals and committed cross-functional teams.

- Create in Phase I the Product Vision and Team Responsibility Matrix, and use them to manage the project.

- Use questions to keep the team focused on the Vision and their individual roles.

On the road to meeting the Vision, team members inevitably besiege Project Leaders with problems looking for solutions. There are two dangers to avoid when a Project Leader is discussing solutions:

1. How can I be sure that everyone in the conversation is trying to solve the same problem?

2. How can I assist while ensuring the team member retains ownership of the problem and is committed to the solution?

**Try asking your team member these three questions.
They hold the secret to the "meaning of life" for your project:**

You can post these questions on your wall. When the next stressed team member comes running into your office, point to the questions, give them a piece of candy or a cookie, and ask them to start with question 1.

1. What is your understanding of the goals of this project?

2. What is your understanding of your role in meeting these goals?

3. What is in your way and how can I help?

Make sure they get each question right before going on to the next one.

What's so special about these questions?

- They require the person answering to confirm that they are on the same page as the project. By asking for the person's understanding you can uncover any unspoken, incorrect assumptions. People often spend a great deal of time solving the wrong problem.

- The third question asks them to translate their stress and frustration into specific issues that you can help them address. Keep asking the third question until they run out of answers (and excuses).

© 1998 Global Brain, Inc.

Project Leader Survival/Sanity Wisdoms

- Believe in yourself and what you're doing.

- Hang in there; accept implicit appreciation (until later).

- Higher responsibility requires more strength from within.

- Put something physical in your office to make you smile, believe in the dream.

Zigzagging From Point A To Point B

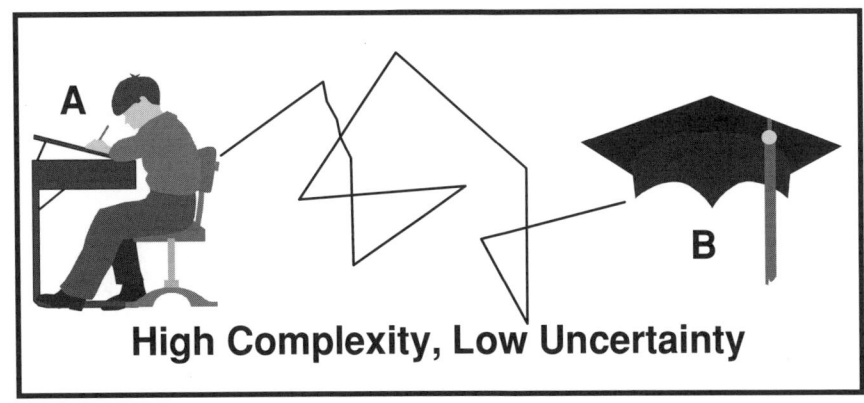

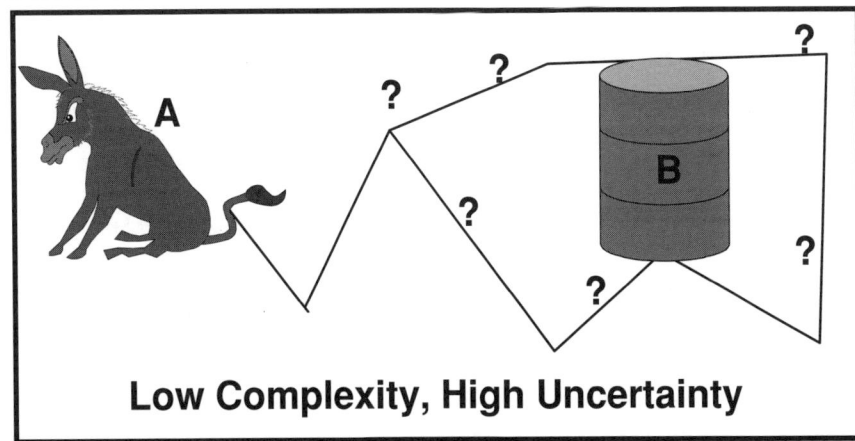

High Complexity, Low Uncertainty

Low Complexity, High Uncertainty

Typical Q*R*PD Team Players

> There is no comradeship, except through union in the same high effort.
> ~ Antoine de Saint Exupery

Team Member	Responsibilities	Job Description
Project Leader or Team Leader	Lead cross-functional team to achieve all project objectives by acting as team leader and manager.	An obsessed leader that is confident yet honest, technical, a model worker, a people person, and has high standards and management ability.
Project Architect or "Evangelist"	Mastermind the technical design. Have overall responsibility for how it will all work together.	Top technical person on the project. Highly experienced, and respected by team.
Project Engineer(s) or Project Lead(s)	Each one spearheads one aspect of the design: software, hardware, mechanical, etc.	Qualified engineering design professionals capable of some leadership, too.
Product Champion or Sponsor	Major corporate supporter, and intervenes to help overcome large obstacles, especially resource or financially-related.	A godfather and believer in the project, who has significant organizational clout and authority; usually a member of top management.
Product Engineer	"Cradle to grave" liaison between team and rest of the world, inside and outside the company. May have primary responsibility for coordinating all testing.	A jack-of-all-trades, and project troubleshooter. Sufficiently technical to know how to solve any problem that arises, often by finding who to go to for help. Strong communicator.
Manufacturing Engineer	Representative from Operations who will facilitate product introduction into manufacturing.	Technical person that assists production in all ways that facilitate manufacturing (tools, methods, etc.)
Marketing Product Manager	Composes the initial and ongoing market requirements.	Understands the market and customers, yet sufficiently technical and visionary to give input to product design.
Buyer	Provide rapid response for purchasing parts, tools for engineering, etc.	Purchasing person familiar with many types of vendors and comfortable with working with engineering personnel.
Design Engineer(s)	Design portions of the project.	Qualified engineering design professionals.
Technician(s), Machinist(s), Drafter(s), Documenter(s)	Provide support as necessary.	Vocationalists happy to respond quickly with quality work.

© 1998 Global Brain, Inc.

Typical Q*R*PD Team Players for IT and Software Projects

IT Team Member	Responsibilities	Job Description
Business analyst	Speaks for the customer of particular IT systems and processes.	Leader on the business side: involved with day-to-day company operation, key processes related to customers, etc.
System analyst	Helps define detailed user requirements and system/process design to meet those requirements	Technical person who understands both the corporate computing environment and the business it supports.
Programmer	Creates new applications or other code for the new product	Technical person/software engineer.
System administrator	Responsible for ongoing systems support; ensures new products and services work well in current environment and will be well-supported.	Technical person who understands and administers the corporate computing environment.
User training	Defines and creates the training necessary to ensure the product/service is effectively used by customers.	User-oriented person with training design and development abilities.

Software Team Member	Responsibilities	Job Description
Usability engineer	Defines requirements and user interfaces for the product to ensure it will be used effectively by the entire customer community. May help with testing the product for usability.	User-oriented technical person. May have a formal "human factors" educational background.
Localization engineer	Defines requirements and sometimes manages and/or executes the work to adapt a core product for international markets.	Technical person familiar with international markets.

Web Team Member	Responsibilities	Job Description
Asset manager	Coordinates configuration control of all multimedia "assets": graphics, sound clips, movies, etc.	Organized person with database and configuration management experience.

© 1998 Global Brain, Inc.

Virtual Team Checklist

Project Goals:	
• Do the outside developers understand the "return on investment" goals of this project and the feature, technical and cost trade-offs that are acceptable?	
• Will they commit to your project schedule and deliver?	
• Are they interested in a long-term relationship with you? Are they interested in participating in your industry in the long term?	
• Are they truly interested in the type of technical work required by this project, or are they taking this project as a stop-gap until they find the work they actually want to do?	
Skills, experience, capabilities:	
• Have they done this kind of work before? Do they have the appropriate technical skills? Do they have extensive experience using these technical skills, and a track record of related on-time projects and high-quality products? Do they have experience *in your industry*?	
• Do you have a say in what level person works on your project, e.g. junior engineer vs. senior engineer? For third-party development organizations, the skill level and experience required by the individuals should be defined in the contract.	
• What are the communication skills of the individuals, both verbal and written? Will they be able to communicate both technical and management information?	
• Do they have experience with the development and testing tools to be used on this project?	
• Do they produce usable, complete technical documentation?	
• What are the technical and project management skills of the managers in the outside organization and can they be counted on to manage their aspects of the project? Do they know how to estimate project work; can you count on the accuracy of their project bid?	
Priorities:	
• Is the group or individual dedicated to your project or spread among projects? What is the company's workload?	
• Will the team members be available in the right timeframe? Will they be able to work on early planning and design or will they "come in at the last minute"?	
• Are other projects they're working on higher priority than yours?	
Product Development Processes:	
• Do they understand how to use a development life-cycle for risk management and predictability?	
• Do they know how to define product requirements?	
• Do they routinely perform design reviews? Do they understand design for manufacturability, serviceability, etc. and take a cross-functional, concurrent approach to product development?	
• Do they have established configuration management processes and systems?	
• Do they understand and perform all levels of testing, such as unit testing, integration, system testing, usability testing?	
• Do they have defect tracking systems and do they use them during product development?	
• Do they have significant experience using a development process on different types of projects, especially ones like yours?	

© 1998 Global Brain, Inc.

Process and Forms for Project-based Performance Appraisal Input

The processes below and the forms on the following pages can be used to provide functional managers with input on the performance of the Project Leader and team members on the project.

- These forms will be filled out not necessarily at the very end of the project, but when the particular team member is leaving the team. Performance will therefore be fresh in the Project Leader's mind.
- The expectation will be set with functional managers that they must incorporate feedback from Project Leaders in people's annual review, and from individual team members in any Project Leader's review.

They would have these forms on file for already-completed projects in the last year.

They would be expected to solicit some kind of input from Project Leaders or team members of current projects the person is on.

Process for Team Member Performance Appraisal by Project Leader:

1. When the person is about to leave the project, the Project Leader will fill out the form.
2. The Project Leader will then give a copy to the person and give them the option to schedule time to discuss it. (If it is negative, it is assumed that they will discuss it.) The discussion could be a three-way meeting with the functional manager and Project Leader.
3. The person will sign to indicate that they have seen the form and had a chance to review it (or selected not to review it) with the Project Leader.
4. The Project Leader will give a copy of the signed form to the functional manager to be filed for the person's next review (and for any current issues to be addressed in the near term).

Process for Project Leader Performance Appraisal Input

1. When the person is about to leave the project, they will fill out a form on the Project Leader. The form can be anonymous.
2. The person will give the form to the Project Leader's functional manager.
3. The functional manager will review the forms with the Project Leader. (The functional manager will be responsible for protecting the anonymity of the team member.)
4. The Project Leader will sign indicating they've reviewed the forms, and they will be filed for the next performance review.

© 1998 Global Brain, Inc.

Project Leader Performance Appraisal Input Form

Project Leader being Appraised: _____ **Team member (optional):** _____ **Project:** _____ **Date:** _____

Introduction: The purpose of this form is to solicit your feedback for this individual's annual performance appraisal. Please rate and comment upon his/her work on the above project. Provide enough detail to allow the person's functional manager to commend the individual on strengths and accomplishments, and to point out specific areas for improvement in the next year. NOTE: The intent is for you to spend only 5 to 10 minutes doing this basic assessment.

	Poor	Fair	Good	Very Good	Excellent	n/a or no opinion	Comment specifically on strengths/accomplishments, or weaknesses/shortcomings in this area.
Project results: degree to which Product Vision, schedule, and costs were met.	__	__	__	__	__	__	_____
Leadership of a synergistic team							
Effective use of Q*R*PD; continuous improvement of technical/team processes	__	__	__	__	__	__	_____
Success at obtaining adequate cross-functional participation.	__	__	__	__	__	__	_____
"People skills" demonstrated in working with individuals and motivating the team.	__	__	__	__	__	__	_____
Ability to apply technical skills and other knowledge to make right project decisions.	__	__	__	__	__	__	_____
Management Skills							
Accurate and thorough planning, scheduling	__	__	__	__	__	__	_____
Ability to keep the project on course.	__	__	__	__	__	__	_____
Open, accurate, and timely communication of objectives, progress, status, issues	__	__	__	__	__	__	_____
Ability to run effective meetings	__	__	__	__	__	__	_____
Overall performance as Project Leader	__	__	__	__	__	__	_____

Particularly commendable contributions/strengths: _____

Major dissatisfactions (major areas for improvement): _____

Other comments: _____

© 1998 Global Brain, Inc.

Team Member Performance Appraisal Input Form

Team member being appraised: _____ **Project Leader:** _____ **Project:** _____ **Date:** _____

Introduction: The purpose of this form is to solicit your feedback for this individual's annual performance appraisal. Please rate and comment upon his/her work on the above project. Please provide enough detail to allow the person's functional manager to commend the individual on strengths and accomplishments, and to point out specific areas for improvement in the next year. You may leave an item blank if you do not have an opinion. NOTE: The intent is for you to spend only 5 to 10 minutes doing this basic assessment.

	Poor	Fair	Good	Very Good	Excel-lent	n/a or no opinion	Comment specifically on strengths/accomplishments, or weaknesses/shortcomings in this area.
Quality of work performed on project	___	___	___	___	___	___	_____
Timeliness of project task completion	___	___	___	___	___	___	_____
Timeliness of action item completion	___	___	___	___	___	___	_____
Contribution to meeting product cost and project budget targets	___	___	___	___	___	___	_____
Participation as a synergistic team member (rate each sub-category)							
Cooperation with other team members	___	___	___	___	___	___	_____
Communication of progress, status, issues	___	___	___	___	___	___	_____
Communication on technical matters	___	___	___	___	___	___	_____
Contribution to continuous improvement of development, technical, team processes	___	___	___	___	___	___	_____
Overall performance on project	___	___	___	___	___	___	_____

Particularly commendable contributions/strengths: _____

Major dissatisfactions (major areas for improvement): _____

Other comments: _____

© 1998 Global Brain, Inc.

A Special Team Role: The Product Engineer's Responsibilities During Product Life Cycle

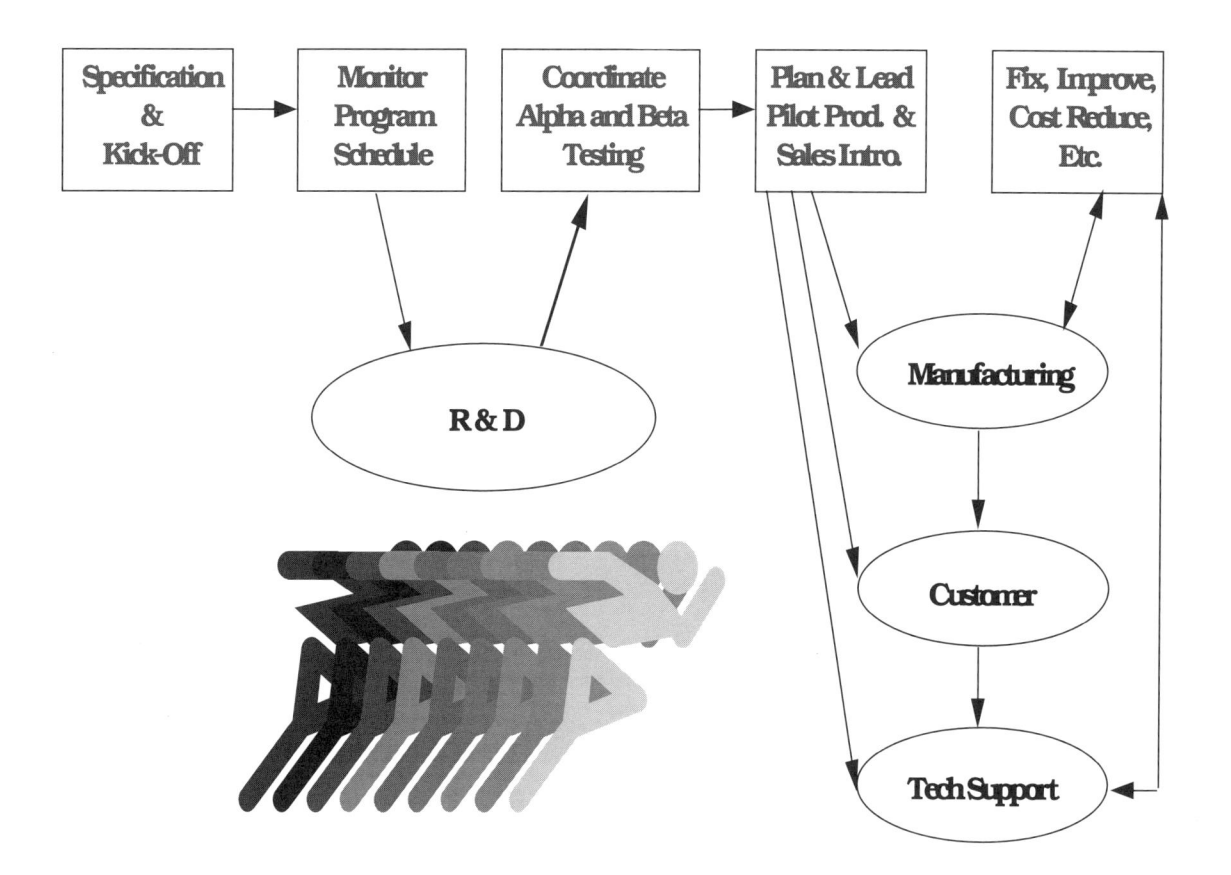

```
[Specification & Kick-Off] → [Monitor Program Schedule] → [Coordinate Alpha and Beta Testing] → [Plan & Lead Pilot Prod. & Sales Intro.] → [Fix, Improve, Cost Reduce, Etc.]
```

- R & D
- Manufacturing
- Customer
- Tech Support

Product Engineering Advantages

- **Creates a technical resource pool outside Development**

    (May include: Customer and Field Service, Manufacturing Engineering, Training, Documentation, Testing, Engineering)

- **Owns all company technical problems**

    No more finger pointing

    Faster solutions to customer problems (internal and external)

- **Versatility and multi-functions (jack-of-all-trades) saves $:**

    Customer Service may conduct Design Verification Testing

    May eliminate a separate Manufacturing Engineering group

    Training manager may write technical publications

- **Improved intra-company and external technical communications**

- **More Effective, independent design verification testing and beta test coordinating**

- **Accelerated new product introductions (streamlined into company)**

- **Effective, more rapid response to customer problems**

    Top ten design complaints

    improved technical documents and field updates

- **Continued technical training (Internal and External)**

- **Can include proactive technical specialists to keep a finger on the pulse of the business.**

© 1998 Global Brain, Inc.

Product Engineer Candidates

1. Burnt out design engineer

2. Ace technical support person

3. Marketing engineer yearning to be technical

4. Top manufacturing engineer

> In the business world, everyone is paid in two coins:
> cash and experience.
> Take the experience first, the cash will come later.
> ~ Harold Geneen

Product Engineering Sample Charter

I. FULFILL A ROLE AS COMPANY TECHNICAL LIAISONS:

- Insure customer satisfaction within and outside the company.

- Create excellent/effective lines of communications between Sales, Operations, and R&D.

- Create a sense of ownership whereby each Engineer is fully aware of their products from conception to customer use.

- Attend all design review meetings acting as a key team player in design approval and introduction.

- Prioritize top design complaints (from customers, manufacturing, or any where), marshal fixes (assist R&D), track to completion, and then send updates to the field.

- Send a representative to all ECO (Engineering Change Order) meetings to insure that Product Engineers respond in a timely manner.

II. TAKE PRIMARY RESPONSIBILITY FOR PRODUCT <u>TESTING</u>:

- Assist R&D with design verification testing throughout new projects.

- Serve as the company Alpha test site, issue report.

- Coordinate with Sales/Marketing/Customer the Beta testing, compile reports, and assist R&D to implement necessary changes.

- Submit new products to company's main Product Test Lab, get reports, respond effectively.

III. MANUFACTURING SUPPORT FOR TECHNICAL ISSUES:

- Assume full responsibility for all technical issues on new products, and strong support for mature products.

- Assist purchasing with component issues, including testing of multiple or cheaper sources, etc.

- Aid in the timely disposition of suspect materials at inventory scrapping meetings.

© 1998 Global Brain, Inc.

Sample Product Engineering Charter
(Continued)

IV. CREATE AND UPDATE TECHNICAL PUBLICATIONS:

- Manuals, including ongoing improvements and sending updated printings and addenda to customers.

- Trouble shooting guides.

- Write Field Change Notices in a detailed manner and insure full distribution to the field.

V. PROVIDE TECHNICAL/FIELD SUPPORT TO CUSTOMERS:

- Supply technical assistance and fixes utilizing effective links between Product Engineer and Project Leader/R&D.

- Insure quick and effective reaction to spare parts requests (create lists with detailed indexes).

- Establish a phone coverage rotation to extend total time available to customer, but avoid long hours for individuals.

- Categorize and track calls to allow more effective prioritizing of areas of concern.

- Log and track serial numbers by customer for all product sales, to facilitate traceability, assistance and updates.

- Identify a key person as the direct contact for field representatives who can then obtain corrective action to problems from the appropriate Product Engineer.

VI. PROVIDE CONTINUING TECHNICAL TRAINING:

- For mature and new products.

- To customers, salespeople, customer support, and others.

© 1998 Global Brain, Inc.

Adapted from original article in

Proceedings of IEMC '96
International Engineering Management Conference

Article: Using Virtual Teams and QRPD® to Do Projects at Warp-Speed

© 1998 Global Brain, Inc.

Using Virtual Teams and Q*R*PD® to Do Projects at Warp-Speed

Cinda Voegtli
Consulting Partner, Global Brain, Inc.
555 Bryant St. #369
Palo Alto, CA 94301
(650) 327-2012   Fax (650) 327-2028

Abstract

By building a "virtual team" to achieve their product development goals, high-technology companies can stay financially and technologically competitive in today's markets. The company concentrates "in-house" on core competencies, keeps its permanent staffing at an optimum level, and turns to the outside for expertise and resources of organizations and individuals on an as-needed basis. The resulting virtual project teams often include individuals or sub-groups such as independent consultants, contractors, and third-party development organizations, many of them often located far away.

Don't overlook the difficulties of actually achieving truly synergistic partnerships—and ultimately successful projects—using these team members outside the corporation. If not created and managed properly, these teams actually can seriously threaten a firm's critical time-to-market goals. The Project Leader must understand how to assess and select team members, plan a project in detail considering the specific ramifications of remote members, and manage the project to its successful completion.

Q*R*PD, a methodology and toolkit for Quality *Rapid* Product Development [1], provides critical guidelines for selecting and managing any project team. A Q*R*PD project team is a cross-functional group of people working together to develop a product and introduce it to the market. This paper explains several "alignment factors," based on Q*R*PD principles, which are especially crucial for virtual teams. The lack of these factors is then illustrated by examples from two actual projects. The paper finally explains the actions the Project Leader must take to properly plan and manage such projects using Q*R*PD techniques, including questions for assessing and selecting virtual project team members.

Critical Alignment Factors

Q*R*PD includes 10 "Commandments" which outline critical principles for achieving rapid product development.

Q*R*PD 10 Commandments
1. **Focus** on a clear, limited, and on-target Vision.
2. Assemble the right **team** and **leader(s)**.
3. Initiate early **cross-functional** cooperation.
4. Create a **synergistic**, mission-oriented, productive environment.
5. **Reward** all participants commensurably.
6. Use **innovative**, parallel, iterative design strategies.
7. **Invest** money to buy time and tools and minimize risk.
8. **Prototype** and test key design concepts early.
9. Follow the **Flow** process to meet milestones, manage risk, and ensure quality.
10. Get early **feedback** and nail defects quickly.

All 10 commandments apply to any product development effort, but three in particular

© 1998 Global Brain, Inc.

warrant special attention here: commandments 1, 2, and 9. In our experience, the success of virtual teams depends upon the degree to which these various members are aligned in the following areas:

- **The goals of the project:** Commandment #1, Focus on a clear, limited, and on-target Vision.

- **Team members' skills, experience, and capabilities:** Commandment #2, Assemble the right team and leader.

- **Team members' time priorities:** Commandment #2, Assemble the right team and leader: full-time members and prioritized projects.

- **The product development process to be used:** Commandment #9, Follow a flow process to meet milestones, manage risk, and ensure quality.

The following sections explain these factors.

The Goals of the Project.

QRPD Commandment #1 says to "Focus on a clear, limited, and on-target vision." Are all your team members committed to the same goals for the project, both to its outcome and to the means of getting successfully to that end?

The answer might surprise you. Virtual team members tend to operate more autonomously, and have their own particular personal goals, driven by their own values and needs or those of their organization. The result? An increased risk of differing perspectives and misunderstandings which can seriously undermine your project.

It is important to remember that the overall *goal* of developing products is return on investment to the company. Achieving maximum ROI depends upon a company's ability to correctly balance among four factors when defining a product and planning a project [1,2]:

- **Product performance (P):** including features and functionality of the product and its quality.

- **Time-to-market (T):** the amount of time the project can take to get the product out the door, to deliver the value to the customer as quickly as possible and begin the economic benefits to the company.

- **Product cost (C):** the unit cost of the product, as well as implications for life-cycle costs related to manufacture, installation, and maintenance.

- **Project cost (C):** the amount of money the company will spend to bring the product to market, in salaries, equipment, and other non-recurring investments.

Together these factors are referred to in QRPD as the PTCC balance. All members of a team, including those outside your company, must understand how the factors contribute to the return goal, and must commit to making decisions about the product and project that support that goal.

Team members' values, the relative worth or importance they attach to different elements of product development, influence how they make PTCC trade-offs to accomplish the project goal. Incompatible values can sabotage the return on investment of a project. For instance, a developer may be faced with "make vs. buy" decisions for the product element they are creating. The "not invented here" syndrome is very common among high-technology firms: they value their ability to create a product from scratch, without regard to the time and money consequences. Other organizations exalt the ability to create complex, full-featured, technologically sophisticated products over the expediency of getting to market with a simpler product that would adequately satisfy customers. QRPD says to find an *adequate* solution that provides the optimal balance of PTCC.

Skills, Experience and Capabilities:

Webster's New Collegiate Dictionary defines skills as "The ability to use one's knowledge effectively and readily in execution or performance; a learned power of doing something competently." [3]

Commandment #2 says to "Assemble the right team and leader." The ability of the virtual team member to do the job in the required timeframe, with the required quality, is critical. But we don't always act as if this is true when selecting development partners. For instance, do you perform as much due diligence when hiring consultants and development organizations as when hiring permanent employees? Be sure to assess potential team members for skill level, experience, and track record in these areas:

- technological or other functional expertise;
- estimating, risk management, and other project management skills;
- verbal and written communication.

Research into risks in software development projects using outside contractors found that among the most prevalent sources of friction between team members were bidding on projects where the contractor has no skills or capabilities, promising delivery dates that are impossible, and inaccurate and inadequate status reports. [4]

Priority:

Priority, according to Webster's definition, is "A preferential rating, especially one that allocates rights to goods and services usually in short supply." [3]. In QRPD commandment #2, part of having the right team is ensuring that team members' are full time as much as possible; that part-time responsibilities are clearly delineated and committed to; and that the priority of the various development projects in an organization are clearly ranked and resources assigned accordingly.

The same factors apply with outside team members. The priority of your project with the outside team member is critical. Consultants and third-party organizations often take on multiple simultaneous projects with different clients. Resources can be pulled from your project, or your project unexpectedly left with less-capable engineers, if another endeavor has nearer-term deadlines or is of higher priority to the development organization's or consultant's financial success.

Product Development Processes:

Webster defines a process as "the series of actions or operations conducing to an end." [3] By defining the steps to develop a product, a process helps teams accomplish "known" project activities more predictably (without unnecessary mistakes), and helps them identify and manage the unknown, risky areas. Consultants and small development firms may prefer an ad-hoc style to more orderly, process-oriented development, which can increase your risk of technical problems and missed schedules.

QRPD Commandment #9 says "Follow a Flow process to meet milestones, manage risk, and ensure quality." The QRPD 13 steps of Flow, along with the 10 commandments, frame interactions between disparate groups, pace their work throughout the project, and help build common project language and values. Techniques for commandment #9 include defining deliverables in detail, setting frequent milestones to track progress, using defect metrics to judge completeness, and performing design reviews and testing throughout the project to ensure quality.

Steps of QRPD Flow
1. New Product/Project Proposal
2. New Product Engineering Request
3. Select Project Leader and Core team
4. Product Vision, See-Saw specifications and schedules
5. New Project Kick-off Announcement
6. Detailed and Critical Design Reviews
7. Final Design Review
8. Development Pre-releases
9. Internal verification (alpha testing)
10. Release for pilot
11. External verification (beta, regulatory testing)
12. Pre-production/delivery
13. Full production/delivery

© 1998 Global Brain, Inc.

The QRPD process provides enough structure and "checklists" to enable more predictable, focused product development, while still allowing teams to work in an innovative, flexible manner. The hiring company can use the QRPD framework very effectively to show virtual team members the advantages of a good process, help them adopt any missing elements, and follow through during the project.

Example Projects

In our experience, lack of alignment in the above areas often leads to significant project delays and serious product design problems. The following vignettes from projects illustrate typical impacts.

Example 1: Multimedia development

A publisher of CD-ROM based multimedia education and entertainment titles contracted with a small development firm to develop a new entertainment title. The publisher was new at using outside developers. The development firm was contracted to produce a game based upon a prototype that met the publisher's vision of what their next title should be: a fun flight-simulator for kids, with funny scripts for adults. Payments were to be based on the publisher's receipt of specific deliverables such as documents and prototypes at monthly milestone intervals.

After 4 months the development house communicated that they were approaching a schedule problem. The publisher ultimately realized that, although the previous contract milestones had apparently been satisfied, the developers were now late. They had spent most of their time so far defining and creating the movies that would be played at different points in the game. The game was becoming a story, not a flight-simulator.

The movies were not of high importance to the publisher; the game-play of the product was, and the publisher realized that the game definitions were almost non-existent. The publisher had an in-house development process that emphasized early definition of game vision and design, but assumed developers would be self-policing in this area, so the early project milestones had not stipulated review of game design documents. The developer viewed the game design as something that would creatively evolve over time and did not have a development process that emphasized early game definition.

This mismatch in project goals and product development processes resulted in a massive contract re-negotiation when it became apparent that the developers had gotten off-track. Schedule time was lost putting effort into the game designs mid-stream and overhauling the scripts to make the product match the publisher's vision. In addition, it became clear that current staffing was not sufficient to make the original schedule, and possibly not even the drop-dead date for delivery in time for the next Christmas season. The young development organization simply had very little project management and risk management skill and experience.

Ultimately project management consultants were brought in to help replan the rest of the project and provide the publisher with weekly visibility into progress. The milestones were redefined, much more specifically, to ensure that monthly progress shown was not "artificial". Consultants were brought in to assist with proper detailed game design. The publisher imposed a definition for format and content of a complete game design document. After the final re-planning the project was projected to be 5 months late but was expected to finish in time for the Christmas season. The total project cost increased by 50%.

Example 2: Outsourced Hardware Design

An outside development organization was contracted to create a hardware module for a wireless communications company. The developers' expertise was digital signal processing for radio-frequency applications. The contract was basically handed over to the outside house with little technical oversight. The developer delivered a "complete" design, along with test data, to the company. However, the design proved to not be manufacturable in quantity.

It turned out the development organization had never developed hardware for mass production; they were oriented to research and development and in the past had always let someone else improve their designs for volume manufacture. The design verification tests had not been complete because they had not considered "corners" testing for environmental factors or testing of an adequate number of modules. This R&D orientation also led to a design that Underwriter's Laboratory (UL) would not approve, leading to scrapping of several hundred units, a re-design of part of the board, and a very late beginning of beta testing. Completion of the project required the company to invest in-house engineering resources to modify the design and shepherd the board through production ramp-up, and in the end this product was a year late coming to market.

Project Leader Actions

To avoid scenarios like those above, Project Leaders must take the following actions to assess, plan, and manage consultants and third-party development organizations as virtual team members.

1. Assessing virtual team members

The virtual team members must be fully assessed against the alignment factors for their suitability for this job. For each factor the Project Leader must identify possible issues, discuss them with the potential team member, and make a conscious decision at to whether to go forward with the relationship. Note that product development using virtual teams requires an experienced Project Leader who is willing and able to deal with the complexity and uncertainty of these situations. The following questions can aid the Project Leader in his assessment:

Project Goals:

- Do the outside developers understand the "return on investment" goals of this project and the feature, technical and cost trade-offs that are acceptable?
- Will they commit to your project schedule and deliver?
- Are they interested in a long-term relationship with you? Are they interested in participating in your industry in the long term?
- Are they truly interested in the type of technical work required by this project, or are they taking this project as a stop-gap until they find the work they actually want to do?

Skills, Experience and Capabilities:

- Have they done this kind of work before? Do they have the appropriate technical skills? Do they have extensive experience using these technical skills, and a track record of related on-time projects and high-quality products? Do they have experience putting these skills to use *in your industry*?
- Do you have a say in what level person works on your project, e.g. junior engineer vs. senior engineer? For third-party development organizations, the skill level and experience required by the individuals should be defined in the contract.
- What are the communication skills of the individuals, both verbal and written? Will they be able to communicate both technical and management information?
- Do they have experience with the development and testing tools you want used on this project?
- Do they produce usable, complete technical documentation?
- What are the technical and project management skills of the managers in the outside organization and can they be counted on to manage their aspects of the project? Do they know how to estimate project work and can you count on the accuracy of their bid for the project?

Priorities:

- Is the group or individual dedicated to your project or spread among projects? What is the company's workload?
- Will the team members be available in the right timeframe? Will they be able to work on early planning and design or will they "come in at the last minute"?

© 1998 Global Brain, Inc.

- Are other projects they're working on higher priority than yours?

Product Development Processes:
- Do they understand the concept of using a product development life-cycle for risk management and predictability?
- Do they know how to define product requirements?
- Do they routinely perform design reviews? Do they understand design for manufacturability, serviceability, etc. and take a cross-functional, concurrent engineering approach to product development?
- Do they have established configuration management processes and systems?
- Do they understand and perform all levels of testing, such as unit testing, integration, system testing, usability testing?
- Do they have defect tracking systems and do they use them during product development?
- Do they have significant experience using a development process on different types of projects, especially ones like yours?

2. *Plan the project in detail*

After deciding to include a consultant or third-party development organization on the project team, the Project Leader must plan the project in detail, with special attention to minimizing the risks inherent in dealing with these virtual team members.

a. Agree on the product vision.

Both parties must participate in a definition of the vision of the product.

1. Who is the customer? What benefits are being provided?
2. What factors will the customer use to judge the quality of the product (what most dictates the products value to the customer?)
3. What key technologies and features are to be included?
4. What crucial product factors must be considered, such as usability, regulatory certifications, environmental constraints, and user documentation?
5. What are the agreed-upon financials: cost and price targets, perceived market window, allowable development cost, etc.?

b. Negotiate and define the elements of the Q*R*PD process you'll both use, and define the specific deliverables.

A project is a continual exchange of information. The team must analyze and plan their interactions to avoid misunderstandings and unnecessary delays. Specifically define the manner in which the steps of Q*R*PD Flow will be used, including major design reviews and overall status checkpoints during the project, and identify the deliverables or documents which you'll exchange. The Project Leader may have to apply considerable effort and salesmanship to obtain cooperation if the outside organization is averse to "process".

On the technical side, pay special attention to defining the content for requirements specifications, design specifications, test plans, and final design documentation. On the management side, the in-house Project Leader must identify the responsible manager within the outside organization and reach agreement upon the project plan elements, including the level of detail for estimating and planning and the methods for tracking and communicating status.

- Will they work with you to define all deliverables in detail, to ensure that the information is on target and provides value, and to make sure that team members have clear concrete goals for small incremental project progress? What is the purpose of each deliverable? What content must it have to be considered complete, and when in the project should it be complete to minimize risk?
- Will they participate in concrete detailed planning, produce status reports as

© 1998 Global Brain, Inc.

necessary, attend team meetings if required, and work hours that allow you to reach them quickly and predictably?

c. Plan the work and communication.

All members of the team must make accurate estimates of project work, especially considering the possible inefficiencies inherent in working with a remote outside consultant or organization. The Project Leader should analyze communication risks as well as technical risks, looking for areas where the physical exchange of information could break down or be delayed due to tool incompatibilities or distance. The Project Leader must pay special attention to technical and communication risks and form detailed contingency plans. These plans must address any weaknesses identified in the assessment of the team members against the alignment factors. Q*R*PD includes a deliverable called a "Critical Issues and Dependencies List" where these items can be recorded and monitored.

Team member responsibilities should be explicitly defined and made visible using Q*R*PD deliverables such as a team roles list and a responsibility matrix. In addition, everyone on the team must be given the big picture, so that they know how their individual work fits within the entire plan. The complete project schedule should be built to provide this task and resource information, and to make clear the dependencies between groups.

3. Manage to Conclusion.

During the project the leader must continue to treat the outside organization as part of the team, keeping them informed and closely coupled with the in-house team members. The leader must continue to highlight to the team upcoming dependencies between groups.

The Project Leader must promote frequent exchanges of information that will show what progress is being made and highlight immediately any misunderstandings regarding project or product goals. Outside organizations or individuals should be included in normal team status meetings. Frequent interim informal reviews should be held on works in progress such as requirements specifications and designs, to uncover misunderstandings as early as possible. Even if an organization is providing a "turn-key" solution, where the company is delivering a final product, the contract should include the right to review engineering specifications. The Project Leader should also determine whether pre-releases of prototypes from the outside developer would be beneficial for spot checking quality and completeness. In short, the Project Leader must be especially proactive in promoting communication and identifying and managing risky areas.

Conclusion

The use of outside consultants and development organizations can provide companies with effective avenues for competitive product development. However, any endeavor making use of virtual project teams must be managed appropriately to ensure that the desired return on investment is actually achieved. Applying the principles of Q*R*PD, attention must be paid to the alignment of the team members' project goals; their skills, experience, and capabilities; their time priorities; and their product development processes. Assessment of these factors will provide the Project Leader with criteria for selecting outside development organizations, insight into potential problem areas, and an understanding of the special planning and management necessary to make the virtual team and project a success.

© 1998 Global Brain, Inc.

References

(1) Kopelman, Orion and Voegtli, Cinda with Josephs, Adam. *Projects at Warp Speed with QRPD: The Definitive Guidebook to Quality Rapid Product Development, 8th Edition.* Global Brain Inc.: Palo Alto, CA, 1998

(2) Smith, Preston G. and Reinertsen, Donald G. *Developing Products in Half the Time.* Van Nostrand Reinhold: New York, NY 1991.

(3) Woolf, Henry (Ed.). *Webster's New Collegiate Dictionary.* Merriam-Webster: Springfield, MA, 1977.

(4) Jones, Capers. *Assessment and Control of Software Risks.* Prentice Hall: Englewood Cliffs, NJ, 1994.

Reading: Using QRPD® to Manage a Strategic Partnership

W. Bradley Stewart, Program Manager, CellNet Data Systems

Using QRPD® to Manage a Strategic Partnership

W. Bradley Stewart
Program Manager
CellNet Data Systems
San Carlos, CA

Introduction

This article describes how to use QRPD to ensure success when facing the unique challenges of a project involving a strategic partnership.

Sometimes the result of a union can be greater than the sum of its parts; this is the value of a strategic partnership. Two independent companies can join forces to create something that neither company could individually create as efficiently, or with equivalent results. A strategic partnership is just such a union. Each partner company brings its own unique capabilities and expertise, and together they produce something of value for each participant.

What Makes Strategic Partnerships Different?

Strategic partnerships usually involve two companies. This creates risks and challenges beyond those in traditional single-company project.

The partner companies frequently have different philosophies, different processes, different standards, different expectations, and generally different ways of doing things. Much of the "common perspective" we take for granted when working within a single company can be missing in a strategic partnership. Since strategic partnerships are frequently created for a single project and subsequently disbanded, these projects cannot necessarily depend on previous projects to provide a common reference as an example to follow.

Resolving problems in a strategic partnership can be far more difficult than in traditional projects, because there is usually a longer escalation path to follow in order to reach a resolution. Decisions that could be made by a manager or Director on an internal project, may have to be resolved between Vice Presidents or even the CEOs or Presidents of the partner companies.

When working on a project contained within a single company, one can generally assume that all participants share the same fundamental goal: to do what is best for the company. When a project spans two companies, this assumption may no longer be valid. The partner companies may have very different goals and motivations. When they do, unique challenges for the Project Leader may arise.

Another factor that differentiates projects by strategic partnerships from single-company projects is the likelihood that there will be two Project Leaders, one from each company. In the traditional arrangement with a single Project Leader, it is usually clear that he has the authority to make decisions, resolve differences, and direct the project. When two leaders are involved this area can become murky and problematic.

The following sections of this chapter describe how to use QRPD to successfully manage a project by a strategic partnership in light of these unique conditions.

Unique Risks and How to Manage Them

In every phase of a QRPD project, challenges can be found that arise from the unique conditions of working within a strategic partnership. By recognizing these challenges

© 1998 Global Brain, Inc.

and the conditions that give rise to them, one can use the principles of Q*R*PD to avoid potentially be severe problems.

Common Incentives

Strategic partnerships are most effective, when both partners face the same incentive to succeed. Q*R*PD commandment #5 is "Reward all Participants Commensurately." Participants should be considered to include partner companies as well as individual team members. If there is a sizable disparity between what the partner companies stand to gain from a project, it may become difficult for the companies to agree on important issues. For example, Commandment #7 suggests to "Invest money to buy time and tools, and to minimize risk." If one partner company has very little to gain from timely project completion they may be reluctant to invest much to improve their time-to-market, while the other partner may have far more to gain from bringing in their first customer ship date. To avoid these problems, projects by strategic partnerships should be defined so as to make both partners are equally motivated by common incentives.

Communication

Effective communication within a team can be significantly more difficult to foster when a project spans two companies. Usually a company develops its own culture. This culture helps to define how project teams communicate. Some companies rely heavily on e-mail or voice mail, others use intranets or internal bulletin boards, some depend on water-cooler exchanges, while others leverage formal group meetings. All of these methods can be effective when team members are familiar with how they are used in their environment, and understand what form of communication will best achieve their purpose in a given situation. When two companies attempt to work together they can experience culture clash if their native environments are not very similar. When setting up a project by a strategic partnership, it is important to assess the cultural differences between the companies, and plan to facilitate the form of communication that will work the best. If the two companies communicate very differently, highly structured communication, like regimented meetings, conference calls, or published updates help ensure that required communication takes place.

Even if the communication styles of the partner companies are similar, some simple techniques can go a long way to facilitate the sharing of knowledge within the project team.

- Set up email and voicemail lists that include appropriate team members from both companies.

- Publish roles and responsibility lists and phone lists that include all team members from both companies.

- Hold frequent regularly-scheduled meetings and/or conference calls including key participants from both companies.

- Encourage ad-hoc phone calls and e-mails between team members from different companies.

- Encourage "visiting hours," when team members can work on-site at the other company to learn more about their culture and how they communicate.

Team Building

Team building can be more difficult when team members do not all come from the same company. Q*R*PD commandment #4 recommends creating a synergistic mission-oriented environment. To do this try getting the team members together face-to-face as much as possible, and when together focus on the project, not the companies. Include team members from both companies in all celebrations and hoopla around the project. The more the team members feel committed to the project over their companies, the fewer difficulties you will experience due to difference in corporate goals, incentives, and motivations.

© 1998 Global Brain, Inc.

Intellectual Property

When team members are exposed to the intellectual property of another company, care must be taken to ensure it is treated with appropriate discretion. Progress will be fastest and easiest if information can be freely exchanged between team members regardless of for which company they work. Strive to structure the partnership to facilitate this to as great an extent as possible. Then, ensure that all team members are aware of what their obligations are with respect to intellectual property, and set the expectation that these obligations must be met.

Important Elements of Phase I: Kickoff

Product Vision

The Product Vision takes on additional importance in a project by a strategic partnership. Since the team comprises members from multiple companies, all team members probably do not report directly to the Project Leader. In such a team how can one ensure that the team members from both companies will do the right thing, and all the parts will work together in the end? Not all technical details can practically be worked out and agreed to before work on the project begins. Even if one attempted to write specifications that cover every technical detail of the project before work began, there is a high likelihood that either they would have errors or take an unacceptably long time to generate. An effective way to address this is for the entire team to agree on, and commit to, a Vision at the beginning of the project. Then, when questions need to be answered or designs need to be modified, it is easy for every team member to ensure that their decisions are consistent with the Vision.

Choosing Team Members

QRPD Commandment #2 is "Assemble the right team and leader(s)." This task can be difficult in any project, but in a strategic partnership it is compounded by lack of knowledge about the candidates. Since there is no easily tapped source of information about candidates from the partner company, extra steps must be taken to ensure that all team members have the required experience and expertise called for by the tasks at hand. Here are some suggestions for how to do that:

- Hold formal or informal interviews of all candidates by the key responsible managers from both companies.
- Request performance records or resumes of candidates from the partner company.
- Get permission to talk with coworkers of a candidate at the partner company.

Any potential team member not from within the Project Leader's company should be reviewed as thoroughly as a new-hire candidate would be.

Even if ideal candidates cannot be found to assign to the project, having a good understanding of the team members' strengths and weaknesses will enable the Project Leader to anticipate and avoid potential problems down the road.

Roles and Responsibilities

Clearly defining the roles and responsibilities of the team members and the partner companies early in the project is critical in a strategic partnership for two reasons:

1. Making adjustments later will be more difficult than in a traditional single-company project.

2. How the two companies are sharing the work must be well understood.

In all projects it is important to estimate the amount of work required, in order to make an informed ROI estimate; you need to determine if the project is worth doing. In a strategic partnership you have to consider not only the total amount of work required, but also the split of that work between companies. The project has to be worth doing for *both* companies.

Creating a detailed project schedule that identifies all project related tasks and names a specific team member who will be responsible for that task will help address both of these requirements. Having this detailed schedule will allow both companies to understand how the work load will be shared, and will help all

© 1998 Global Brain, Inc.

team members to knowingly commit to doing their part. To ensure that both companies remain committed to the project through to completion, key milestones should be linked to contractual obligations. Separate milestones should be chosen that represent completion of significant amount of development effort by each of the partner companies. These milestones should be explicitly called out in the development agreement, and explicit penalties or incentives should be associated with them.

Important Elements of Phase II: Development

Open Design Reviews

Over the course of development in a project by a strategic partnership, both companies must be confident that work is progressing as planned and quality meets their standards. Open design reviews can help achieve that goal. By putting work-to-date on display for open review by representatives of both companies, all parties can be assured that design and development is on track.

Since it is likely that the two companies will have different approaches to the type of design work being done, it is important to have a respected, independent, objective expert included in the review. This outside expert can help differentiate between what may be just different ways of doing things, and what may be serious risks or potential problems.

Tracking Progress

Through design and development phases, a mechanism must be put in place to track progress. This will ensure that issues or delays are recognized early in the project and can be addressed quickly.

There are many ways of doing this, including, milestone tracking, schedule tracking, status reporting, and frequent design reviews or progress reviews. Whatever mechanism is adopted, both partners must agree to use it and it must be focused on identifying (and resolving) the critical issues of the project.

Important Elements of Phase III: Approval

The Approval Phase of a QRPD project by a strategic partnership can have a unique problem: who says "ship it." Traditional projects contained within one company usually benefit from an established process for determining when a product is adequately tested and ready to ship. If this process is lacking, they at least have a clear chain of command within which that decision can be made. This is not so straightforward for a strategic partnership.

The best solution for this problem is to agree on how release will be handled while still in the Kickoff Phase. Both companies should agree to the standards that must be met, and how measurements will be made against those standards. They should also agree on whose responsibility it is to make those measurements and declare when testing requirements have been met.

Important Elements of Phase IV: Delivery

QRPD Commandment #10 calls for us to get "early feedback and nail defects quickly." The development team should be held together long enough to get this feedback. This will ensure that if there are problems that need to be fixed they will be understood and addressed quickly by the people most familiar with the product. Additionally, team members from both partners will benefit from being exposed to the customer feedback, and both companies can learn how to avoid those problems in future projects.

A post-project lessons-learned meeting should be held that includes team members from both partners. This provides feedback that will enable both companies to learn not only how to design a better product next time, but also how to better manage a strategic partnership next time.

Although the contractual obligations may be met, and the development team may be disbanded after the product is in production, communication between the partners must be maintained. Specific individuals should be identified from each partner who will be responsible for on-going support of the product, and their responsibilities should be clearly defined.

While the intense communication required during co-development may no longer be required throughout production life, some form of regular communication should be adopted, like monthly or quarterly update meetings. This will ensure that there is a venue for raising and resolving issues, and they are not ignored.

Project Case Study

A project from my experience illustrates how the above management approaches play out on a real project. The goal of the project was to cost-reduce the small radio transmitter used in high volumes in the company's wireless networks. This project was ranked #1 in priority in the company, and due to the volume of radios being deployed, any delay in the project completion had serious cost impacts to the company.

The only practical way to achieve the necessary cost reduction was to develop an application-specific integrated circuit (ASIC), not a core competency of the company. Therefore the ASIC was developed in concert with an outside IC manufacturer. Since the capabilities of this ASIC were on the leading edge of technology, the team had to be sure to address many technical issues well to successfully develop it on time. The fact that the project was a joint effort by two very different companies created interesting logistical and managerial issues as well. By following the principles of QRPD, the company was able to conquer them successfully. To highlight the QRPD elements used to pull this project off successfully:

- We paid heavy attention to doing a Product Vision. It is easy for this effort to be skipped in setting up an ASIC development effort. Instead of a clear and concise Product Vision document, some firms create only a detailed design specification. Without the Product Vision as a reference, technical decisions are more difficult and time-consuming than necessary.

- We identified staffing problems early by using a team roles and responsibilities matrix to clearly define the job of each team member and identify areas where their skills and abilities might not be a sufficient match. A detailed project schedule was also created, with tasks assigned to explicit team members, to ensure that everyone understood their work. In a strategic partnership this is especially valuable: if any team member has a weakness in experience, the detailed schedule will help ensure that no tasks are left out.

- We put a project structure in place to facilitate exchange of information and resolution of problems. The joint team held regularly-scheduled team meetings via conference call, which included all of the company engineers and consultants as well as the engineers at the IC manufacturer. The team communicated via email mailing lists, and held periodic face-to-face design reviews to help identify problems early and resolve them efficiently. We created and maintained a list of issues and their status, and recorded official action items including owners and due dates. These actions were reviewed at every meeting until they were closed.

- At one critical point in the project, the team "invested" to avoid unwanted project delays and hasten progress toward an upcoming milestone. We brought on two experienced ASIC design consultants, and two other company engineers with experience in these products. We ordered another workstation and associated software. We discussed and agreed upon a game-plan for achieving our goal,

© 1998 Global Brain, Inc.

including definitions of what the team members' roles were.

- The team held a design review where engineers from both companies critiqued the design. We invited to this design review a recognized expert in the field, to provide an unbiased assessment of the quality of our design work and suggest project enhancements.

- After the design review, we discovered an opportunity to reduce ASIC design time and lower the risk in both the ASIC and the radio transmitter. As is usual with early skunk works groups, this ASIC had been specified to support more functions than were necessary. We decided to first focus on only what was required for the initial radio transmitter product, and in parallel develop a second version of the chip to provide other features useful for future products. The first version of the ASIC would allow the company to accelerate the reduced-cost radio ship date. Q*R*PD principles helped this team focus on making the right functionality/cost/time trade-off.

- When this potential trade-off came to light, it was important to make sure that adjusting the schedule would be advantageous to both companies. The solution was to provide the partner with an incentive to do what was right for our company. At the Vice-president level a new development agreement was reached resulting in a win-win situation: the company got the two versions of the ASIC it wanted, and our partner was able to start shipping our ASIC for revenue ahead of schedule.

By adhering to the principles of Q*R*PD, the company successfully identified and addressed many issues and potential problems with this strategic partnership project and delivered the products the company needed for increased profitability.

CONCLUSION

Two independent companies *can* successfully join forces in a strategic partnership to create a product or service that will benefit both companies in the marketplace. But such endeavors face risks and challenges beyond those in a traditional single-company project. The respective Project Leaders can utilize Q*R*PD deliverables and techniques to create a truly synergistic project team, successfully address the unique risks associated with these partnerships, and ultimately deliver a product that neither could have done alone.

© 1998 Global Brain, Inc.

PART IV. FLOW

Q*R*PD 4 Phases and 13 Steps of Product Development Flow

Phase	Objective
I. KICKOFF 1) New Project/Product Proposal (NPP) 2) New Project Evaluation Request (NPER) 3) Select Project Leader, Core team 4) **Product Vision and See-Saw Specifications and Schedules Process** (includes Product Vision, high-level design work, risk assessment, preliminary design reviews, schedule and milestones) 5) New Project Kickoff Announcement, internal	What is the new product (or service or process) idea? Is it worth pursuing? If so, appoint a Project Leader and core cross-functional team to investigate the idea further. Then, create a Vision for this product, and determine the possible alternatives for implementing it: features, schedule, costs. Can we achieve acceptable return on a product development investment? If so, select the alternative, finish planning the project, get the whole team in place and bought-in, and launch the project.
II. DEVELOPMENT 6) Detailed and Critical Design Review meetings(s) 7) Final Design Review meeting(s) 8) Development Pre-Releases	Finish designing the product or service; review it and test it (development). Does it work, and does it meet requirements and its purpose? Release early versions of the product to other cross-functional groups for their work.
III. APPROVAL 9) **Internal Approval** (Alpha testing) 10) Development Release for Pilot 11) **External Approval** (Beta, Regulatory Testing)	Let independent groups, both internal and external to the company, including customers, test the product. Does it work? Does it fulfill its purpose, meet its requirements? Release the product for pilot deliveries.
IV. DELIVERY 12) Pilot Production/Delivery 13) Release to Full Production/Delivery	Do limited production and delivery to customers to test processes and readiness. Then release it, produce it in volume, and deliver it to everyone.

© 1998 Global Brain, Inc.

Description of Each Q/RPD Flow Step

Flow Step	Description

I. KICKOFF: Evaluate the new product idea, negotiate scope and schedules, and plan and approve a project with acceptable ROI for the company.

1.	New Product/Project Proposal	Suggest a new product/project idea.
2.	New Project Evaluation Request	Approve "investing" in a full phase I for this idea, based on a quick investigation of the idea and an estimate of the time required to fully evaluate it.
3.	Select Project Leader and Core team	Select the team for the remaining phase I effort.
4.	Product Vision and See-Saw Specifications and Schedules (SSSS) Process	Identify customer needs. *Iteratively* create a Product Vision, investigate design alternatives and risks, create and refine schedules and milestones, make trade-offs, and recommend how the project should proceed.
5.	New Project Kickoff Announcement, internal	Announce the formal approval of the project.

II. DEVELOPMENT: Create detailed designs and prototypes and test the prototypes within the Development group.

6.	Detailed and Critical Design Review meeting(s)	After creating detailed designs, testing critical innovations, and executing the system chicken test, review the results.
7.	Final Design Review meeting(s)	Confirm that the design and implementation are ready for the approval stage.
8.	Development Pre-Releases	Release the design to groups outside Development.

III. APPROVAL: Test the product independently of the design team and in the real world.

9.	Internal Testing (Alpha)	An internal, independent group tests the product.
10.	Development Release for pilot	Release the product to other groups to prepare for a pilot build and/or deployment.
11.	External Testing (Beta and Regulatory agency)	Let customers test the product in normal environments to make sure it works and meets their requirements.

IV. DELIVERY: Prepare for volume shipments and release the product to customers.

12.	Pilot Production/Delivery	Build and possibly deploy higher quantity of product to test production and delivery processes.
13.	Release to Full Production/Delivery	Release the product for full production and start unrestricted shipments to customers.

© 1998 Global Brain, Inc.

How Quality is "Built In" to Q*R*PD Flow

The QRPD methodology focuses on building in quality throughout the development process. Quality is "value as perceived by the customer." It includes not only freedom from defects, but also the degree to which the product meets the customers' needs. QRPD concentrates on having the team first establish a customer-centric view of the product to be developed. Then while the team creates a product to meet that vision, they work to flush out failures and defects as early as possible in the project. Thus, the steps of Flow are geared to the activities that give us the highest leverage for quality: the Product Vision, design reviews, testing, and releases and change control.

Quality Factor	QRPD Flow Steps
Customer focus	**Flow 4. Product Vision** *Purpose:* • Create an alignment document capturing the high-level customer needs and how the product will satisfy them. Forms the contract for the team. • Adhere to the Vision throughout the project.
Design Reviews	**Flow 4. Preliminary Design Reviews (PDR)** (part of SSSS process) **Flow 6. Detailed Design Reviews (DDR)** **Critical Design Reviews (CDR)** **Flow 7. Final Design Reviews (FDR)** *Purpose:* • Has the Product Vision been met? • Have issues/alternatives been thoroughly investigated? • Will the design work? (PDR, DDR) Does it? (CDR, FDR) • Have all cross-functional and customer concerns been addressed? • Is it OK to proceed?
Approval Testing	**Flow 9. Internal testing: Alpha** **Flow 11. External testing: Regulatory and Beta** *Purpose:* • Was the product tested thoroughly? • Does the product work? Does it meet the Vision and other specifications? • What problems must still be resolved?
Releases and change control	**Flow 8. Development Pre-Releases** **Flow 10. Development Release for Pilot** **Flow 13. Release to Production/Delivery** *Purpose:* • Is the product documentation accurate, complete, and ready for use by other cross-functional groups? • Have all production/delivery/support processes been developed and "tested" adequately? Are they ready for release to cross-functional groups?

© 1998 Global Brain, Inc.

Objectives for Phase I: Kickoff

The purpose of this phase is to determine whether to do a project, and if so, how to best meet the customers needs while maximizing the company's return on investment.

First, the team quickly evaluates the market opportunity (or the extent of the customer need) for a proposed product, and decides whether to proceed further with a project.

If the answer is "yes", the remainder of phase I is focused on defining the right product to develop for the customer, finding the optimal way to manage this project, and getting everyone's buy-in and commitment. By investing some time up-front, the team can find the best overall solution that trades off Performance (P), Time (T), Product cost (C), and project cost or budget (C). The goal is to maximize the company's ROI, and to Do It Right the First Time (DIRFT)—rather than the second or third.

Remember, that 80% of the product's final cost and performance capability are determined in the first 20% of the schedule. So use the time in phase I wisely, to really find the best solution for the customer and the best way to execute the project. The time invested will pay dividends in the later phases.

This is also the time that the team goes through the "storm" stage of development. Work out the disagreements, and learn to gel as a team and to work well together towards completing the mission.

Typical Phase I duration: 15-25% of the overall schedule.

> "The best way to reduce product development cycle time is by management intervention early in the project."
> ~ John Young, retired CEO and President, Hewlett-Packard

© 1998 Global Brain, Inc.

Phase I Flow Steps and Deliverables

FLOW Steps	Deliverables
1. New Project/Product Proposal	**NPP form:** Suggest new product/project idea and justification. Create and attach rough business case.
2. New Project Evaluation Request	**NPER form.** Get approval for conducting a full phase I investigation, based on estimate of time/budget to evaluate.
3. Select Project Leader and core team	**Team roles list and Responsibility Matrix:** Assess and select leader, identify/select core team members and their domains of responsibility. **Action Item matrix, Key Decisions List, Critical Issues and Dependencies List, Meeting Guidelines and Schedules:** Set up team tools.
4. Product Vision and See-Saw Specifications and Schedules Process	*Iterative SSSS process, multiple deliverables:* **Draft Product Vision:** Cross-functional core team creates based on knowledge of Marketing and customer inputs. **Architecture:** Identify and investigate high-level design alternatives. **Innovations Risk List:** Assess technological risks of the design alternatives. **Critical Issues and Dependencies list**: Create and update for risks, open issues, and dependencies for the project, including each design alternative. **Chicken test definitions:** Define early testing of innovations. **Project schedules and Milestones, product and project costs:** Make rough estimates of time, resource, budget for each design alternative. Start identifying milestones. **ROI justification, Late Cost Per Week, and 5-year Road Map:** Evaluate ROI, LCPW, and fit with company's product family and technology road map. **Trade-off tables:** Summarize PTCC, risks, issues for each alternative. **Preliminary Design Reviews:** Hold PDRs to review technical alternatives and make PTCC trade-off decisions. **Product Vision:** Update it for trade-offs made. *Finalize:* **Schedules, Milestone list, Budget, Product cost, Tools and Equipment List, Roles List and Responsibility Matrix, Action Item Matrix, Key Decisions List, Critical Issues and Dependencies List, New Product Introduction Checklist, other deliverables:** Complete planning and documentation.
5. New Project Kick-off Announcement	**NPKA form:** Sign the Vision and milestones, attach them, and publicize the launch of the project. Celebrate!

© 1998 Global Brain, Inc.

Flow Step 1: New Product/Project Proposal

Use this form to suggest a new product or project idea and introduce it into the company's planning process in an orderly manner. Encourage anyone to submit new ideas. Document any business justification understanding in a rough business case to go along with the New Product Proposal. The NPP form and the attached business case provide a sanity check of this product idea. How important is it to the customer and the company?

New Product/Project Proposal (NPP) Form

ORIGINATOR:_____ DATE:_____

PROPOSED NAME OF PRODUCT:_____

1. Brief description of proposed product and targeted selling price.

2. Why should our company do it now?

3. Possible markets and their potential:

4. Technology: What's involved? Risks?

5. Questions/items for further research:

6. Should this product schedule be accelerated (*"Blitzkrieg"*)?
   Why (market window, competition, ROI calculation, etc.)?

© 1998 Global Brain, Inc.

Flow Step 2: New Project Evaluation Request

Use the NPER form to get formal approval to investigate this product idea further. Projects often get launched for no good economic reason. This step formalizes the approval of doing a full phase I, so that development work isn't undertaken without proper due diligence first, at least a sanity check.

On the NPER form, include the "time and effort to evaluate", meaning the time and resources needed to do a good phase I. With quick help from functional managers or representatives from various departments, or from your own past knowledge, roughly estimate the amount of time you would need from various resources to do a thorough phase I for the product. In addition, estimate the resources from each area that might be required for the entire project. (This is just an "order of magnitude" estimate).

New Project Evaluation Request (NPER) Form

PRODUCT NAME:_____ DATE:_____

ORIGINATOR_____

_____ NEW PRODUCT

_____ VARIATION OF OR ENHANCEMENT TO AN EXISTING PRODUCT

PRODUCTS AFFECTED: _____

_____

DESCRIPTION OF NEW PRODUCT:_____

_____

_____

DATE REQUIRED FOR FIRST SHIPMENTS:_____

INITIAL QUANTITY ESTIMATE:_____

MANUFACTURING COST NOT TO EXCEED: _____

TIME, RESOURCES, AND BUDGET TO EVALUATE (time and resources needed for remainder of Phase I work):_____

_____

APPROVALS:

Project Leader: _____ Production Manager: _____

Marketing Manager: _____ VP of Operations: _____

VP OF ENGINEERING_____ VP Sales and Marketing: _____

NEW PRODUCTS ONLY: GENERAL MANAGER _____

© 1998 Global Brain, Inc.

Flow Step 3: Select Project Leader, Core Team

Now you're ready to select the core team members who will do the phase I investigation. Follow the guidelines below. See also Commandments #2 and #3 in the Techniques section.

- **Assess and select Project Leader:** Assess candidates for Project Leader for this project, select an appropriate Project Leader, and formally assign that person to the job. See the earlier Project Leader and Team section and assess your Project Leader candidates against the criteria critical for a QRPD Project Leader.

- **Assign cross-functional core team members:** Then assign the core team members you absolutely need to do a thorough phase I evaluation of design alternatives, schedules, and costs. Core team members include the Project Leader, product champion, and representatives from each cross-functional area. Remember Commandment #3: Early cross-functional involvement and cooperation is crucial for defining your product correctly, planning the project, and gaining full team commitment. See the Project Leader and Team section for a more detailed list of potential team members and their roles.

- **Select outside team members carefully.** Perform special "due diligence" for any remote team members or outside development partners, or contractors/consultants. See the Project Leader section for a checklist that can be used to assess the suitability of these potential team members.

Typical Core Team Members Assigned at Beginning of Phase I

Team member	Role
Project Leader	Leader of the cross-functional project team. Must be fully on board now to get the project off to a quick start.
Product Champion	Executive sponsor of the project who will clear roadblocks and support the team.
Marketing	Product manager to spearhead the efforts to get and understand customer requirements and the business case for the product.
Business users	Key customer and user representatives to participate in early product definition and trade-off decisions.
Manufacturing, customer support, and other cross-functional	Representatives to participate in early design investigations, assess designs for manufacturability and testability and serviceability, review early cost targets; assess project documentation, etc.

Team Roles List and Responsibility Matrix

The team Roles List is a tool that helps ensure everyone knows their function on the team. It also communicates the makeup of the team, and people's general responsibilities, to the outside world.

The Responsibility Matrix clarifies each team member's "domain" of responsibility. Just as the Project Leader is responsible for overall project results, team members will be responsible for results in specific areas: e.g., designing hardware, meeting milestones and cost targets, and ensuring its quality.

Deliverable	Important Guidelines
Roles List	• Create it early in phase I. • Identify the functions that should be represented on the team. • Identify the people who will fill those roles: name, department. • Call out their general responsibilities. • Provide contact information: phone number, location, email address.
Responsibility Matrix	• Create the first version early in phase I. List all core cross-functional team members. Start clarifying who "owns" areas of project work as soon as you get started in Phase I. • List additional names and responsibilities as other project work is identified. • Entries should be clear, specific domains of responsibility. See the example on the next page. • For each domain, indicate who has primary responsibility for the area. • Also identify who has secondary responsibility for supporting and filling in for the primary person if needed. For instance, if the person with primary responsibility is suddenly needed for a critical field problem, becomes sick, or even leaves the company, the person with secondary responsibility would be up-to-speed and able to fill in or take over the area. • For each domain, identify those who will provide input—e.g., review specifications, attend design review meetings. Be sure to include cross-functional team members.

The inclusion of cross-functional team members in the matrix ensures their work is considered early, and they are involved appropriately in Development's work. For instance, the matrix will help clarify who should be present for various meetings and who should be involved in reviews and decisions. The list can be especially helpful in companies where cross-functional team members are not accustomed to full or early participation.

© 1998 Global Brain, Inc.

Sample Team Roles List

The following table shows excerpts from a Team Roles List from a communications product containing hardware, firmware, and mechanical components. The list provides a concise listing of the full cross-functional team. Asterisks (**) indicate leads who are core team representatives for their functional area. See the following page for an excerpt of a Responsibility Matrix for this team.

Project email list alias: network_team

Project web page: //internal/network_team

Team Member	Cross-functional Group	Role	email	Phone
Paul R.	Development	Project Leader; power supply lead designer	progan	X 6603
Rick L.**	Hardware Development	Lead RF Designer	rlord	X 6502
Amy R.	Hardware Development	ASIC and optical designer	araskin	X 6234
Susan K.**	Mechanical Development	Mechanical Design lead	skoch	X 6598
Kamar R.	Mechanical Development	PC Board layout designer	kravijan	X 6322
Wei L.**	Firmware Development	Firmware Lead	weile	X 6744
Raji K.**	Engineering Services	Documentation coordinator	rkumar	X 6899
Harold Y.**	Operations: assembly/test	New product introduction engineer and prototype assembly/test coordinator	hyang	X 6775
Sam G.	Operations: Purchasing	Buyer	sgreenbaum	X 6511
John W.**	Marketing	Product Manager	jwinker	X 6443
Pamela I.**	Customer Support	Field and service representative	piverson	X 6946
Julia K.**	Quality	Software test lead	jkingsley	X 6232

© 1998 Global Brain, Inc.

Sample PSI Responsibility Matrix

The following table is an excerpt from the Responsibility Matrix for a communications product containing hardware, firmware, and mechanical components. You can use a spreadsheet to easily create such a matrix for the entire team, including all cross-functional team members. Create the first version early in phase I, then update it to throughout to clarify who has responsibility for and inputs to the different areas of project work identified during your SSSS process. Get specific enough with the "responsibility" entries to make sure each team member understands the scope of their work.

Responsibility	Paul R.	Rick L.	Amy R.	Susan K.	Kamar S.	Raji K.	Harold Y.	Sam G.	Julia K.	Wei L.
RF Design										
Circuit proof of concept	I	P	S		I					
Vendor arrangement	I	S			I		I	P		
ASIC design/test	I	S	P		I	I	I	I	I	I
Mechanical (chassis)										
Enclosure design	I	S		P	I	I	I	I	I	
Wiring design	I	S		P	I	I	I			
Optical circuit										
Schematic	I	S	P	I	I				I	I
PCB Layout	I	I	S	I	P	I				
Power supply (specification, sourcing)	P	I	I	I	I	I	I	S	I	
Prototypes										
Procurement	I	I	I	S			I	P		
Assembly/test		I		S	I	I	P			
Firmware										
Interface design, code, unit test		I	I		S				I	P
Device drivers design, code, unit test		I	I		S				I	P
System Test	S	I	I				I		P	I
Documentation										
User manuals	P	S								S
Assembly drawings				S	I	I	P			

P= primary responsibility   S=secondary responsibility   I=input

Tools for Managing Phase I and the Project

Phase I is often plagued by analysis paralysis, uncertainty about what path the project should take, and many technical and non-technical questions. This is the "fuzzy front end." Since you don't yet have a detailed project schedule, you need tools to effectively pace the team through phase I work. Here are several suggested tools to set up early in phase I:

- **Use a "phase I timeline":** This timeline, or rough schedule, shows how you intend to pace yourself through phase I, including your goal for the end-date and the date by which you hope to have all Vision issues resolved. Make sure you use the "phase I estimate" recorded on the "time, resources, and budget to evaluate" line on the NPER form in Flow step 2. See the example timeline below. See also the calendar on page 307 that summarizes how the full complement of phase I activities maps out.

- **Track Action Items:** Action items are critical for pacing the team's work during phase I. You will use action items throughout the project to assign and keep track of detailed tasks. See the format on the following page.

- **Track Key Decisions:** Keep a record of the important decisions the team makes. The key decisions list helps ensure that important decisions are not lost, revoked capriciously, or revisited unnecessarily. See the format on the following page.

- **Track Critical Issues and Dependencies:** The Critical Issues and Dependencies List is a deliverable that lives throughout the project. It records each important open project issue, risk, or dependency. This list should be started early in phase I to capture open issues, risks with your design alternatives, dependencies on other projects, etc. For instance, it serves as a place to record all Vision issues that you want to remain open and flexible on until you have more data. It will be an important management tool for keeping these items visible until they are resolved, and it will evolve as issues are dealt with and risks mitigated. See the format on page 278.

- **Create Meeting Schedules and Guidelines:** Your team will use this deliverable throughout the project. We recommend a draft of this early to clarify the meetings that will be held during phase I. See the guidelines on page 279.

- **Prepare the team's environment:** See Commandments #4 and #5. Take time now to set up a synergistic, productive environment for the team and plan for hoopla and rewards.

> Properly run, efficient and effective meetings are a must for a high-performing, happy team.
> Invest the time up front to set yourself up for productive meetings.

Example Phase I Timeline

```
Week 1    Week 2    Week 3    Week 4    Week 5    Week 6    Week 7    Week 8    Week 9
  NPER signed        * |---- Vision Meetings, trade-offs  ---| ←-Final vision issues resolved
                       |----Design work and PDRs-------|
                                  |---planning and scheduling--|--Final scheduling---|
                                            New Project Kickoff Announcement *
```

Action Item Matrix

The team should start action item tracking very early in phase I. Record detailed action items, and review them in each team meeting. Strive to keep your "completion metric" (the percent of actions completed on time during each time period) at 80% or above.

No.	Description	Owner	Due Date	Status	Date Assigned	Date Closed

Key Decisions List

This list records key decisions the team makes during the project: decisions about features, resources, technical issues, team processes, and so forth. Keep the list active throughout the project. It is an invaluable tool for preserving and communicating the team's decisions. It can be referenced as needed to ensure that old decisions are not unnecessarily rehashed or capriciously reversed.

No.	Decision	Date

© 1998 Global Brain, Inc.

Critical Issues and Dependencies List

The Critical Issues and Dependencies List captures all the project issues and risks and provides a tool for managing them throughout the project. Start the list with items that come out of early Vision and team meetings. Your initial list entries will often be open Vision items that must be resolved by the end of phase I. Then, as you assess the technical and non-technical alternatives and their risks, add those items to the list as well.

Your list will ultimately identify risks and dependencies such as long lead time parts, availability of needed software from an outside vendor or other project, unresolved staffing issues, and so forth. The list should be maintained as a living document, kept visible to the team, and updated regularly during the project.

For Each Issue/Risk/Dependency, include:

- Description
- Potential project impact
- Date by which the issue must be resolved to avoid impacting the schedule, costs, or product performance
- Owner of the issue
- Actions to take
- Any back-up plan, and point at which such a plan would be invoked

---

Example Critical Issues and Dependencies List Entries

Item 1: (**Decide before end of phase I) Custom modulator: do we want one custom modulator requiring extra expenditure to develop, or have two sources of standard modulators?

- **Potential Impact and critical need date**: Cost to pay vendor for custom version, plus risk of having it available in time, versus overhead to Sales, Manufacturing, Service of having two product configurations.

- **Owner, actions, backup plans:** Mike to investigate and make a recommendation before end of phase I. (See action item list for specifics).

Item 2: The delivery schedule for the communication software module from the outside vendor is considered risky.

- **Potential Impact and critical need date**: Any slip of the delivery of an alpha-level version past March 31 would delay our project day-for-day.

- **Owner, actions, backup plans:** Stan to monitor status weekly with vendor. Late delivery penalty has been added to their contract. Contract and schedule calls for deliverable of prototype by Jan 31 to demonstrate progress. Backup: if the January 31 prototype date is not met or the software is not functional at that time, we can buy the off-the-shelf package from ABC company and complete our project without the high-speed option. Decision to be made by February 15.

Preparing for Effective Project Meetings

Rapid development requires highly-synergistic communication among team members, and that requires some work done as a group in meetings. Do not underestimate the importance of preparing your team for effective meetings throughout the project! Invest time up front, in the early days of phase I, to get your meeting management tools in place. This is absolutely one of the most important things a Project Leader can do.

- **Meeting Guidelines:** Create a summary of Meeting Guidelines and Schedule for your project (see below).

- **Deliverables before:** Take care of these deliverables prior to every meeting:
  1. Assign roles: facilitator, recorder.
  2. Determine the objective of the meeting.
  3. Identify the decisions and physical deliverables to be produced from the meeting, e.g., email, lists of design changes.
  4. Create an agenda for the meeting and distribute it ahead of time.

- **Deliverables after:** Produce these deliverables after every meeting
  1. An updated Action Item matrix
  2. An updated Key Decisions List
  3. An updated Critical Issues and Dependencies List

Meeting Guidelines and Schedule Document

This deliverable simply helps the team decide and communication what meetings will be held during the project. It also helps ensure that they are planned and conducted as effectively as possible.

> - **Meetings:** List the types of meetings you'll have during phase I and during the rest of the project. See the following page for typical meetings.
>
> - **Attendees**: Identify who should be invited to each type of meeting, including outside experts.
>
> - **Processes:** Identify any desired processes to be followed for meetings such as design reviews, such as how far in advance to publish technical material, how much time to allow, and what deliverables should be produced.
>
> - **Mechanics and Behavioral Guidelines:** Summarize other important meeting mechanics and behavioral guidelines the team will follow. See pages 282 and 286.

See the following page for typical QRPD meetings.

© 1998 Global Brain, Inc.

Q*R*PD Meetings Overview

The team will use a number of meetings during the Flow process to coordinate work, discuss issues, and review designs. This table summarizes the types of meetings the team should plan for, when they are used, and their purpose.

Types	When	Why
Regular team status meetings	Regularly scheduled during entire project: Typically weekly for team, weekly for sub-team leaders. On larger projects, the full team may meet slightly less frequently.	Inform others of things that may affect their work. Identify items to work on and assign responsibility and completion dates. Keep team spirit and synergy alive.
Management status review meetings	At all major milestones, with top management present. May be held at project decision points. Sometimes held periodically, such as once per month project reviews.	Affirm achievement of milestones. Highlight project issues. Make project decisions.
Product Vision meetings and Trade-off meetings	Phase I	Bring the team together to hash out the Product Vision, discuss trade-offs, and ensure team understanding of and agreement with product goals.
Design Review meetings • Technical design reviews • High-level technical reviews	Phases I through III	Find technical flaws, suggest better way to do things. Discuss project impacts of various design alternatives or test results. Eliminate/avoid unnecessary work.
Test Results Review and Change Control meetings	Phases II through IV Frequent, stringent during last 10% of project (phase IV)	Review results of testing activities. Approve changes before allowing Development to implement them
Development Release meetings	Phases II through IV	Perform orderly, complete, responsible hand-off from Development to other groups.
Ad-hoc	Throughout project	Discuss pressing issues, make decisions

© 1998 Global Brain, Inc.

Meetings Throughout Flow

The meetings identified on the previous page occur during various phases of Flow, as shown in the following table.

Phase I	Phase II	Phase III	Phase IV
			Daily "hot-list" meetings (plunging) **Change control meetings, last 10%.**
	Release meetings (Flow Step 8, Development Pre-release)	**Release meetings** (Flow Step 10, Release to Pilot)	**Release meetings** (Flow Step 13, Release to Production/Delivery)
Design review meetings (Flow step 4, PDRs)	**Design review and test review meetings** (Flow steps 6 and 7, DDRs, CDRs, FDRs)	**Test results review meetings** (Flow steps 9 and 11, Alpha, Beta, etc.)	**Pilot build and test results review meetings** (Flow step 12, Pilot production/delivery)
Vision and Trade-off meetings (Flow step 4)			
<----------------------------Team and management status meetings----------------------------> <----------------------------Ad-hoc meetings---------------------------->			

© 1998 Global Brain, Inc.

Meeting Guidelines: Process and Mechanics

The list below is a summary of important meeting guidelines to follow. They can be incorporated into your team's Meeting Guidelines and Schedule Document for the project.

Preparing for the meeting:

1. Send out notice and agenda: When? Where? Why? Who? What about?

2. Distribute technical reading for review *in advance.*

Conducting the meeting:

3. Show up. Be on time!

4. Follow the agenda (see next two pages).

5. Assign a Facilitator and a Recorder.

6. Follow Behavioral Tips.

7. Do not allow interruptions or side-conversations.

8. Take a break about once an hour.

9. Use checklists tailored for each type of meeting.

10. Use process checks: is this what we want to be discussing right now?

Recording the results:

11. Record only major decisions in the minutes (not proceedings).

12. Keep a matrix list of action items: item, person responsible, due date, status, date item was opened, date closed. Track % of items due this period that were actually closed on time. Shoot for 80% or better.

13. Assign action items/responsibilities only to people present in the meeting.

14. In management meetings take technical discussions off-line as assigned action items.

© 1998 Global Brain, Inc.

Meeting Agenda Contents

For each item on your agenda, be sure to define the following:

- **Objective and Deliverables:** What do you want to accomplish during the meeting? What physical deliverables should come out of the meeting? This will help you properly guide the discussion and the level of detail covered in the meeting.

- **Owner:** Identify the owner of the item. They should contribute any preparatory materials before the meeting and come prepared to make sure the item is properly addressed in the meeting.

- **Timeslot:** Assign a timeslot for each item and be sure to stick to it. Keeping each item on track will keep the entire meeting on track. If an item needs more time, you can come back to it at the end of the meeting if enough time remains. Alternately, if you decide to spend more time on the item right then due to its criticality, stop and together adjust your agenda accordingly, to make sure you'll still accomplish all the objectives of your meeting.

Example Agenda, Team Meeting

Item	Objective, Deliverables	Owner	Timeslot
Review current action items, record status	Understand what actions are still open and clarify what work remains on them, including team member responsibilities (NOTE: main emphasis here is to communicate and understand dependencies, not to do detailed status dumps in the meeting)	Irene (Project Leader)	1 – 1:15
Review critical issues and dependencies list	Understand state of critical dependencies; do we need to invoke any backup plans? Specifically review the results of the testing for Issue #2, performance of third party software.	Irene Dave (technical lead)	1:15 – 1:45
Review milestones list	Look ahead to upcoming milestones (next 2 months), discuss any perceived threats to the date; assign actions	Irene (Project Leader)	1:45 to 2:00
Re-cap new action items	Make sure everyone understands what new work they've been given and is committed to making the date	Irene	2:00 – 2:15

© 1998 Global Brain, Inc.

Meeting Guidelines: Agenda

To ensure that your meeting agenda is effective, use this checklist:

Contents
- Background, overall purpose
- Materials distributed, preparation expected
- Sequence of topics
- Objectives, desired outcomes
- Process to be used (for each agenda item)
- Responsible person
- Time allocated for each item

Setting the Order of Activities: Order of agenda items can sometime influence success.
- high energy ---> low energy
- easy ---> complex
- agreeable --> controversial --> agreeable
- if some common info, then for different people, segment
- adequate breaks, strategically placed
- end on positive note

Agenda Screening: Before you have the meeting, sanity check the items on the agenda.
- Are the objectives of each item clear?
- Does this meeting have authority to act?
- Could it be dealt with outside a meeting?
- For a status meeting: is an item a problem that should be addressed in a separate meeting?
- Does it concern at least three members of this meeting? Should it be partitioned into a "sub-meeting"?
- Is/will everyone be properly prepared to discuss it? (adequate materials, in proper state; distributed early enough)
- Given the meeting's time limits, is the item high enough priority?

Publish the Agenda
- BEFORE THE MEETING, with desired outcomes clearly stated.
- For maximum effective participation, people must know what's expected of them to come prepared. Follow up --> make sure they are...

© 1998 Global Brain, Inc.

Meeting Guidelines: Roles

The following table identifies the key meeting roles to be filled, their overall responsibility, and the checklist of their job in each meeting.

Note that sometimes one person will play more than one role in a meeting; and those playing one of the roles below often must function as a participant as well, contributing content to the meeting. In these cases the person must consciously and conspicuously "change roles", indicating to the meeting participants that they have done so. For instance, the leader or facilitator can sit down to make a comment as a group member. They temporarily leave their more powerful position to contribute their ideas to the meeting without being perceived as dictating a decision or outcome.

Role and Responsibility	Checklist
Leader • The person who calls the meeting. • Owns the content. • Will often need to participate in the discussions. • Makes decisions. *The leader invests time in planning the meeting*	• Establish content and desired outcomes. • Work with facilitator to determine meeting processes. • Determine correct attendees, assign roles. • Prepare/gather/distribute materials. • Handle logistics. • Issue agenda.
Facilitator • Makes sure the group is using the most efficient methods for accomplishing their goals in the shortest period of time. • Responsible for all meeting procedures, to allow meeting leader to concentrate on content: discussion, issues, and decisions.	• Control the process but not content. Master of harnessing the power of the group to control itself. • Make sure success conditions are there…buy-in, communication… • Maintain direction, move the group toward conclusion. • Maintain time limits on agenda items, take minority discussions off-line. • Solicit input from quiet people; watch for suggestion squashing. • Acknowledge competence, keep emotional level low; maintain the tone...respect always. • Suggest adjournment if not enough information to continue, or serious disruptions or conflict. • Ensure proper breaks are taken. • Summarize points, get consensus, have minutes taken.
Recorder • Documents: Action items, Key Decisions, Critical Issues, attendees. • Provides data to leader for publishing.	• Capture necessary information without disrupting or slowing down the meeting. • Capture information neutrally, objectively. • Capture information with "fidelity" to preserve intent, details and clarity, ultimate buy-in....

© 1998 Global Brain, Inc.

Meeting Guidelines: Behavioral Tips

1. Focus on the situation, issue, or behavior; not on the person.

2. Speak and act assertively, not aggressively.

3. Maintain the self-confidence and self-esteem of others.

4. Maintain constructive relationships with employees, peers, and managers.

5. Take initiative to make things better.

6. Lead by example.

Meeting Guidelines: 7 Steps to Brainstorming

1. Decide if spontaneous or round-robin

2. Ask open-ended questions

3. Forbid evaluation/critiquing

4. Post all new ideas

5. Seek to build on others' ideas

6. Seek maximum number of ideas

7. Begin prioritizing the ideas and selecting the most appealing ones

---

A meeting is either a three star vital,
a two star question,
or a one star trivial.
~ Sydney F. Love

© 1998 Global Brain, Inc.

Flow Step 4: Product Vision and See-Saw Specifications And Schedules (SSSS) Process

This Flow step puts the creation of the Product Vision and the Mission of the project into the hands of the team. On every project, Marketing typically wants the maximum functionality ready to ship as quickly as possible. On the other hand, Development knows just how long it will really take to develop those features, and wants as much time as possible to do so. The power of the Q*R*PD SSSS process is that it turns typically contentious arguments between Marketing and Development into a true win-win negotiation process.

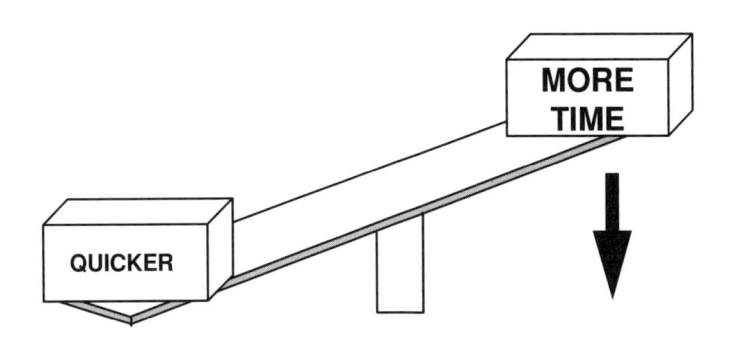

MARKETING & MANAGEMENT

"We need it within X months or else!"

1. Window closes
2. Can't predict market
3. Competition kills
4. Can't pay salaries anymore

TECHNICAL TEAM

"What's the earliest date by which we can't prove we won't be finished?" (Kidder, p. 113)

1. Evaluate design alternatives, risks, iterations
2. Each member commits to own schedule by subsystem

Goal of Negotiation Process

Find an optimal balance that everyone can live with and sign-up to: a Product Vision (P), one Schedule with a set of Key Milestones (T), product costs (C), and project costs (C).

© 1998 Global Brain, Inc.

Concurrent SSSS Activities to Create the Vision

In sequential methodologies, the requirements are handed down, the team makes a schedule, and then does the design. In QRPD, phase I requirements, design, and planning activities happen in parallel. This allows the team to iteratively create a Vision based on their evaluation of multiple design alternatives and the PTCC balance and ROI of each one.

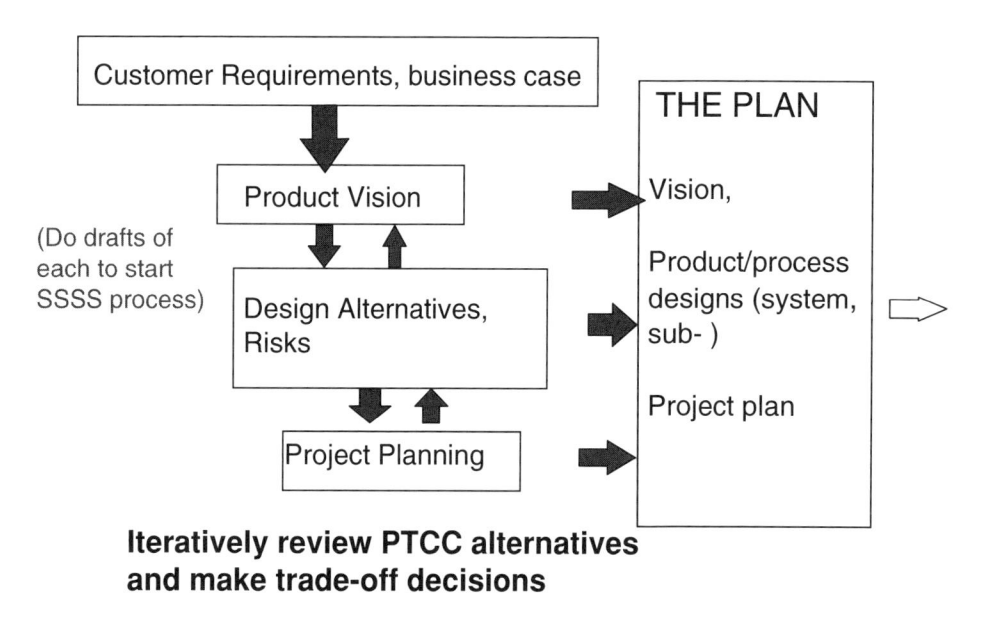

```
Customer Requirements, business case
            ↓
(Do drafts of      Product Vision ──→ THE PLAN
each to start         ↓ ↑              Vision,
SSSS process)    Design Alternatives,
                 Risks           ──→   Product/process
                    ↓ ↑                designs (system,
                 Project Planning ──→  sub-)
                                       Project plan
```

**Iteratively review PTCC alternatives
and make trade-off decisions**

Iterative See-Saw Specifications and Scheduling

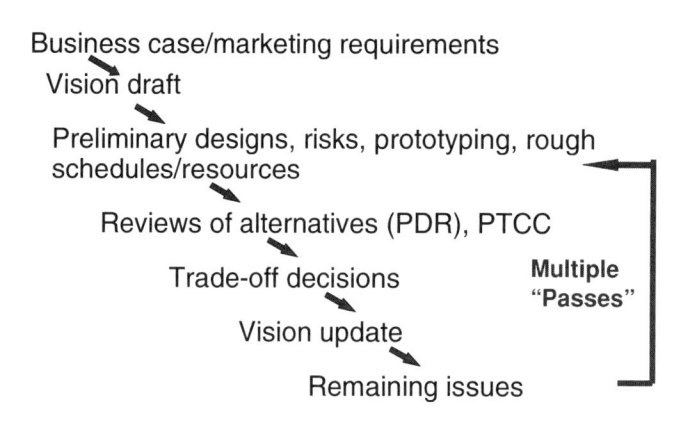

Business case/marketing requirements
  ↘ Vision draft
      ↘ Preliminary designs, risks, prototyping, rough
         schedules/resources
          ↘ Reviews of alternatives (PDR), PTCC
              ↘ Trade-off decisions   **Multiple
                  ↘ Vision update   "Passes"**
                      ↘ Remaining issues

Pass 1 Goal	Passes 2 to n Goal	Final Pass Goal
Quickly identify and assess major design alternatives, make big trade-off decisions.	Refine design(s), identify and assess more subtle, complex PTCC trade-offs, narrow down alternatives, refine schedules and other deliverables.	All trade-off decisions made, Vision final. Finish detailed schedule with resources, finish accompanying management tools. (milestones, critical issues and dependencies list, etc.).

© 1998 Global Brain, Inc.

Deliverables Evolution, Phase I SSSS Iterations

The deliverables are developed iteratively throughout phase I:

Vision:
- Product Vision
- ROI, LCPW, 5-year Roadmap Documents

Goal at the end of phase I:
- Signed-off Product Vision that reflects the PTCC balance chosen
- Solid High-Level Design with all risks understood
- Committed, accurate schedule with cross functional resources assigned

Design and Risk assessment:
- High-level Design Documents
- Product Innovations Risk Assessment List
- Critical Issues and Dependencies List
- PDR Meeting Minutes with PTCC Trade-off tables

Planning:
- Project Budget
- Product Cost
- Preliminary test plans
- Milestone List, Schedule with Resources
- Team Roles List and Responsibility Matrix
- Tools and Equipment List
- New Product Introduction Checklist

	Pass 1	**Passes 2 to n**	**Final**
Vision	Draft	Updated	Signed off
Design and Risk Assessment	Block diagrams, subsystems. Assess risks of alternatives. Categorize risky-ness of innovations. Run initial chicken tests	Best alternatives refined. More risk analysis, tests on remaining alternatives.	High level designs. Critical Issues and Dependencies List. Remaining chicken tests defined.
Planning and Scheduling	Rough timelines or schedules, work dependencies, resources, first cut milestones	Refine remaining alternatives, schedule estimates and detail	Final, most detailed schedules, signed off milestones list and budgets, etc.; other planning and management documents
Trade-offs	Review alternatives, identify PTCC trade-offs, make "big ticket" or "no brainer" decisions.	Make more trade-offs	

© 1998 Global Brain, Inc.

Guidelines for the Vision and SSSS Process

1. **FOCUS ON AND INVOLVE CUSTOMERS:**
    - Interview lead/innovative <u>users</u> and typical customers
    - Be solution-oriented. How are you solving their problem?
    - Warning however: don't rule out internal innovation
    - Establish market window and size
    - Know your competition

2. **IDENTIFY MULTIPLE FEASIBLE DESIGN ALTERNATIVES (but stay flexible)**

3. **IDENTIFY AND DEAL WITH CRUCIAL PRODUCT FACTORS**
   (create company checklist based on past project problems)

4. **INNOVATE INCREMENTALLY:**
    - Strive for an adequate solution (Performance, Time, Cost)
    - Restrict to a manageable number of (typically three) major innovations
    - Avoid the "It can do it all" product
    - See Commandment #1

5. **COMPARE TO COMPANY BUSINESS PLAN AND OVERALL STRATEGY**

6. **INVOLVE ALL FUNCTIONS IN TRADE-OFFS** (create ownership)

7. **VISION EDITOR: PROJECT LEADER**

8. **WRITTEN VISION SIGN-OFF BY TEAM AND TOP MANAGEMENT**

9. **READ VISION REGULARLY—AVOID CHANGING IT AFTER PHASE I**
   (Can the change wait for the next incremental generation?)

© 1998 Global Brain, Inc.

Quality: How the Vision Process Ensures Customer-Perceived Value (Satisfaction)

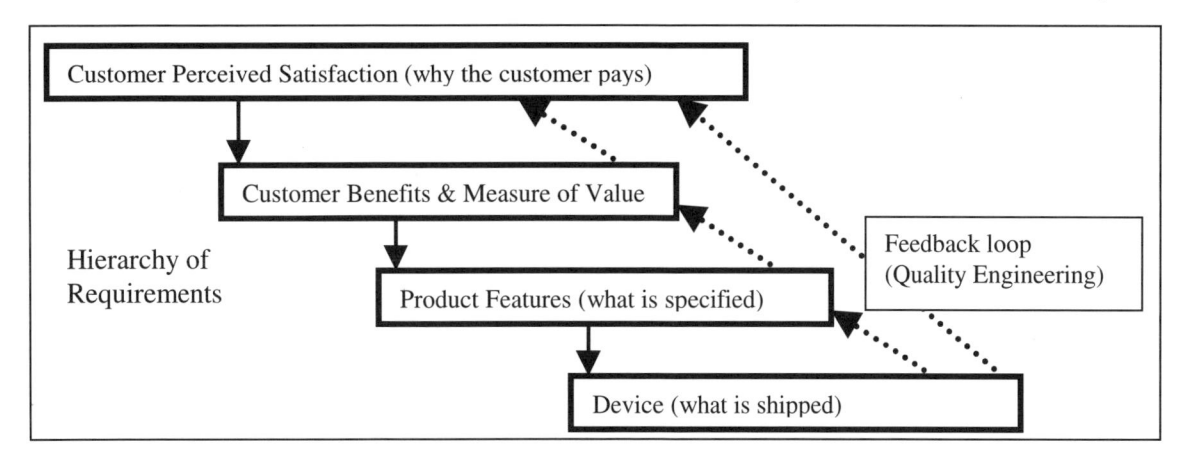

```
Hierarchy of Requirements:
  Customer Perceived Satisfaction (why the customer pays)
    → Customer Benefits & Measure of Value
        → Product Features (what is specified)
            → Device (what is shipped)

  Feedback loop (Quality Engineering)
```

Our product development goal is to deliver value to our customers. They will pay for our products based on their satisfaction with the value we deliver. We must make sure that our projects actually result in products that ultimately satisfy—even delight—our customers.

Benefits: It would be great if we could bottle "satisfaction" and sell it to our customers directly, but we can't. This is why we use the Vision process in phase I to identify the benefits we must deliver to truly satisfy the customer. For example, depending on the customer, satisfaction with a refrigerator may be dependent on keeping a week's worth of groceries fresh or keeping soda cold in a small space. You might define a different product depending upon which benefit you focused. A lack of connection between the requirements defined versus the benefits required for true customer satisfaction is your project's first opportunity to get off on the wrong track.

Features: Unfortunately, you can't ship a benefit either. It is still too abstract. To make a benefit real you first need to turn it into features. For instance, if the benefit is to keep soda cold in a small space, the features would include the necessary size dimensions and the temperature target. Moving to this level can also be fraught with danger. Project teams need to make a concerted effort to ensure that feature decisions are mapped back to benefits. That is the only way to be sure that your end product will really result in a satisfied customer

Device or Product: You can't ship features either. In the end, you must ship a physical device, be it computer hardware, software, a fifty-pound refrigerator or a chemical vapor deposition silicon wafer processing chamber. Most product development teams are already very concerned with ensuring that the hardware and software meets specification. But as was just discussed, the feedback must extend back through the hierarchy above and ensure that what ships will lead to a satisfied customer.

This is Quality Engineering in its truest sense: the process of defining the components and measures of true customer satisfaction; mapping all feature definition, specification, and design activities back to the true measures of customer perceived satisfaction; and ensuring that what is built meets those standards. In Q*R*PD quality begins with the Vision, shown on the following page. It is created during the SSSS process. Its first two sections require that the team struggle with who the customer is, what benefits will result in value to them—and thus their perceived satisfaction—and what measures will drive their perception of value. These sections must be addressed first; then the team can go further to define the specific features and requirements for the device or product in sections 3, 4, and 5 of the Vision. Carefully establish the connections between customer value, benefits, features, and the device design as you descend the requirements hierarchy, to ensure that the finished product satisfies your customers.

© 1998 Global Brain, Inc.

Product Vision Contents

Typically One to Two Pages

PROJECT/MISSION DESCRIPTION and CASE FOR ACTION: One or two sentence summary of this project and why we are doing it.

1. **TARGET CUSTOMERS AND HOW THE PRODUCT WILL MEET THEIR NEEDS. (Problems, solutions, benefits)** Who are your customers, both leading edge and typical; What benefits will this product provide? What problems do your customers have and how will this product solve them?

2. **KEY ISSUES CUSTOMER WILL USE TO JUDGE QUALITY (Measurable).** Clarifies which capabilities of this product (as quantified as possible) will be most important to the customers' perception of its overall value.

3. **KEY TECHNOLOGY AND KEY FEATURES.** Key technology to be employed in the product; specific features required to meet customers' needs.

4. **CRUCIAL PRODUCT FACTORS *AS APPLICABLE* (USE OWN LIST).** Elements that are not a primary part of the product functionality, but are key attributes that must be present. May include:

    - Interaction with associated products
    - Potential for design growth or modification
    - Physical environment product will be used in
    - Patent infringement/protection
    - Manufacturability
    - Safety and liability
    - Quality and reliability
    - Ergonomics
    - Users' abilities
    - Sourcing and assembly
    - Distribution
    - Documentation, training, servicing and maintenance
    - Unusual equipment or facilities needed

5. **RELEVANT FINANCIAL NUMBERS: Sales units, price cost, market window, delivery day, Late Cost Per Week (LCPW), budget (development cost).** The economic factors driving this project.

Without vision, people perish.

~ Proverbs 29:18

Consumer Audio Product Vision

NILES: 1995 Product Vision: IR Keypad With Speaker Relay Revision: Rev 8 June 16/95

Model Number: IntelliPadTarget Intro. Date:January 1, 1996
Target Cost (Landed in Miami): A*Dealer Cost: C*Retail $350
Projected Unit Sales: B*Product Life (years):3
Effect on sales of existing Products: Will have a positive effect on the entire IR category.
*The actual numbers are confidential to Niles Audio.

Target Markets:
Primary: A consumer with a multiple room audio system with infrared remote control desires strategically located, wall mounted keypads. The consumer requires that the keypad be fun to use, inexpensive and aesthetically pleasing.

Secondary: The installer/specifier demands that the keypad be as fast and easy to program and install as the Soundstream Touch One or the Xantech 730. He/she will recommend the Niles keypad to the consumer because of its power status indicator, the local speaker mute, its ability to up and download to a pc for program storage, and the Niles look, feel and reliability (less than 1% defective in the first year).

Key Technology:
PC Interface (Transfer and Storage Only) will only allow a complete keypad program to be down and uploaded via an adapter cable and permanently archived on the PC (program which will run under Windows).

Power Status of the main amplifier is communicated to the keypad and displayed or indicated to the user. The status signal is provided by new versions of the IRP-2, IRP-6A, and IRZ-6A. A new version of the RVL-6 will provide room on/off status to the keypad. A 12vDC (200 - 800 mA) control-in will provide an additional status input. Turn-off must be virtually instantaneous.

A Speaker Relay will completely mute the local room when the Mute button is pressed. The status of the relay will be displayed or indicated to the user. The relay and its status indicator can be defeated by the installer.

Source Macro IR Commands allow the source buttons to power up the main amplifier (if it is off), select input, and issue play and mode commands. Link between the source button and the Power command can be defeated by installer.

Preprinted Replaceable Source Labels allow the installer to correctly label each source button. The source button which was last pressed is displayed or indicated to the user.

Universal Transport Buttons map to the source selected, allowing the same transport buttons to control all of the components in the system.

All Buttons are Programmable with an IR command.

Compatible with virtually all IR remote controls (except old Phillips and those with carrier frequencies above 100kHZ) and installed Xantech and Niles IR remote repeater systems.

Stand-Alone Installation- A variable flasher output allows up to four Niles Flashers to be used without an IRP.

Easy Program Duplication - Can dump only complete contents of memory to another keypad over a 6' cable.

Consumer controls should have a positive tactile feel and should be shaped and/or colored to differentiate function.

Installer controls, indicators, connectors should be hidden from view, and protected from accidental activation by the consumer.

1. Must meet FCC *Part B* regulations
2. Must not be deeper than 2 7/8".
3. Must match the look of Leviton "Decora" styled switches and be compatible with Leviton "screwless" cover plates.
4. Program memory is protected from accidental loss for a minimum of 5 years, preferably more.
5. Should be packed with both White and Bone decora DSI inserts (no Decora cover plate).

© 1998 Global Brain, Inc.

PC Software Product Vision

Project Mission: Produce a fun, engaging flight-simulator game that will appeal to families—in time for Christmas sales. We have the opportunity to be the first to market in this category, and the first to market a realistic 3D flying experience with 6 degrees of motion freedom, all available on a standard PC. Success will also attract other major publishers to engage us to develop their products.

1. **Customers and benefits**
   - Primary: Those who like action games with some story and/or role play and would probably enjoy flight simulators, but don't want to spend time on learning complex flying controls.
   - Secondary: an alternative for normal flight simulator aficionados.
   - Families looking for relatively non-violent but fun, engaging computer entertainment
   - Ages 12 to adult.

2. **Key factors used to judge quality**
   - Game must be interesting and complex enough for more mature gamers but not overwhelming to flight simulator novices or younger users. But not via lots of puzzles. Want at least 6 rooms and 6 different types of flight simulator missions (bombing mission, avoid the enemy, rescue mission...).
   - The act of flying must be so fun and realistic in itself that it attracts novice users to play the game and learn the skills to complete the flight missions.

3. **Key features and technology**
   - 3-D look with 6 degrees of freedom motion
   - Must have at least 6 "levels" or rooms of activities
   - Flying character is a bug instead of an airplane
   - No flight control setup required
   - Custom rendering engine written in-house
   - Use DirectX for desired compatibility
   - Minimum platform: Pentium 90 with 8M and a 2M video card
   - Custom joy-stick available but not mandatory that looks like the main bug character
   - Must support analog and digital joysticks
   - Music in background, different in each room.
   - Movie setup prior to each room, but movies should not slow down players' momentum.

4. **Crucial product factors**
   - Has to fit on one CD ROM
   - Must be extensible such that a later release can add rooms to the game
   - Designed such that localization for Japan and Germany can be accomplished by changing out only small parts of dialog, art, and movie shots, not having to recreate each fully
   - Win95 logo certification desired
   - Box contains CD ROM, joystick, and 1 inch thick user manual produced by publisher

5. **Financials**
   - Must ship from game developer to publisher by September 15 to allow publisher to get it mastered and onto store shelves by Mid-October, to ensure significant Q4 sales. (Distribution channel is standard retail outlets: CompUSA, Fry's.)
   - Window is expected to be minimum 10,000 copies over the first 4 months (Christmas season); 30,000 copies rest of first year.
   - Selling price $50; profit margin (excluding development costs) 80%, profit per unit $40.
   - Development cost must be under $ 1 million.

© 1998 Global Brain, Inc.

High Level Design Iterations in Phase I SSSS

The goal of this activity is to get an accurate understanding of what it will take to develop this product. What design alternatives are there? How much technical work is involved in each? How many technical innovations will be involved? How risky is the work? How long might it take? The purpose is to get an accurate PTCC decision in phase I. Unlike other methodologies where schedules are created based on requirements only, here we will do enough design work to truly understand the development effort required for this project, and make intelligent trade-off decisions.

High-Level Design Iterations

Early iterations of system design: Identify design alternatives and look for "big-ticket" items:
- What are different system designs we might use to accomplish the product objectives?
- How do these fit with our company's technology road map?
- What are riskiest areas of those proposed alternatives?
- What features or other requirements add significant time or resource to the schedule and might be candidates for negotiating out of the PTCC balance *immediately*?

Mid iterations of system design: Once narrowed down to fewer alternatives, identify the remaining issues and decisions.
- Are there any attributes that are more important than others? E.g., is manufacturability more important than cost? Is usability of the software more important than performance of the design? Consult section 2 of the Vision, "Key Issues Used to Judge Quality" for guidance.
- Check "crucial product factors" in the Vision for implications.
- Look for understanding of the customer that will help you make remaining trade-off decisions.

Late iterations of system design: Refine the one or two high-level designs enough to have an accurate understanding of the project schedule.
- Are all the modules identified?
- Are all the interfaces well-enough defined that we understand the work?
- Are data and their sources defined?
- Have we broken up the sub-systems cleanly to allow parallel work? (see commandment #6).

© 1998 Global Brain, Inc.

Typical High-Level Design Deliverables

- **Block diagrams, data/process flows:** Break down quickly to major components.

- **Innovations list, risk assessed:** Identify high-risk areas quickly, look for "easy-to-make" trade-offs. See following page for risk categories.

- **Architecture and interface specs, data definitions:** Flesh out some detail to ensure high-level design will work, find hidden issues.

- **Preliminary Functional Requirements specifications:** Early draft versions can help adequately understand the detailed requirements and the work. Warning, however: Be careful to *not* waste time on specification details for an alternative that will be traded off before the end of phase I! And remember, this document is not to be put in concrete. It will continually evolve—and be distributed—throughout the project as more becomes known.

Technological Risk Assessment

As high-level design alternatives for satisfying the Product Vision are formulated, they are analyzed:

- **Innovations:** What innovations are involved in each design alternatives?

- **Risk level:** What is the level of risk of each one? See the table on the following page.

- **Chicken tests:** Do they need to be chicken tested? The QRPD rule of thumb is to chicken test any innovation of "major" risk or above. (See the table on the following page.)

- **How many innovations?** If we select a particular design alternative and desired "feature performance" from the Vision, will we be taking on too many innovations? The QRPD rule of thumb in Commandment #1 is to take on no more than 3 major or above innovations in one project.

Always Ask: Is this alternative too risky?

****Identify and get rid of risk early wherever possible****

© 1998 Global Brain, Inc.

Product Innovations Risk List

Use a ranking scheme to categorize a <u>list</u> of innovations by risk level. Whatever ranking scheme you use, it is critical that you create an explicit list of all technical innovations.

QRPD uses the categories below because they are not subjective like a "low, medium, or high" rating system. The amount of risk is related to whether an innovation has been tackled before, in-house, or anywhere.

RISK LEVEL	AMOUNT OF UNKNOWN	COST TO RECOVER
1. FLIRTING WITH DISASTER	Believed to have never been done by anyone, anywhere in the world!	INFINITE?
2. VERY MAJOR	Done by somebody, somewhere, once	VERY HIGH
3. MAJOR	Done elsewhere a few times, but never yet in-house	HIGH
4. MEDIUM	Done commonly or by people who now are in-house (but weren't at the time)	MEDIUM
5. MINOR	Done often, including in-house	LOW

Chicken Test Definition Document

This document is created in phase I to define the chicken tests to be run on each identified innovation with a risk of "major" or above and the system chicken test.

For each innovation/ Risk to be tested, and for the system chicken test:

1. Test definition: Brief summary of what is to be tested and the test steps necessary to prove out the innovation or design concept.
2. The date by when the test needs to happen, including the last date for switch to back-up plan if the chicken test failed.
3. Pass/fail criteria.
4. Equipment, facilities, supporting documentation, etc. needed for test
5. Who is responsible?
6. Who is involved in judging success?

© 1998 Global Brain, Inc.

Risk Assessment and Management

Q*R*PD guidelines for assessing and managing risk, both technical and non-technical:

- **Technical and Market risk:** Work concurrently on assessing technical and market risk. But test your product's performance and technical completeness separately from testing issues such as usability and the market's response to your feature set. See also technique 8H in the Part II reading "Q*R*PD Techniques Detailed Explanations and Examples."

- **Financial justification of technical risks:** Justify each innovation financially by benefit versus cost. Factor in risk level, too.

- **Non-technical risks:** Assess non-technical risks such as schedule uncertainty.

- **Critical Issues and Dependencies List:** Generate and maintain a separate Critical Issues and Dependencies List of potential show stoppers such as single source vendors, resources required, etc. See the content guidelines for this list earlier in this section. Keep this list highly visible to the team and management.

- **Backup Plans:** Identify fall-back plans; e.g., what will the project do if the risky technology doesn't work, or if that critical software resource does not become available on time?

- **Visibility:** Promote high visibility for the issues on these lists and review them frequently. For instance, attach them to team meeting minutes; review them each team meeting; report on them to executives.

- **Innovative, early testing:** Find innovative ways to test risky areas early: Use prototypes, simulations, models, CAD, and other tests early on.

© 1998 Global Brain, Inc.

Assessing Other PTCC Elements

As design alternatives are investigated to implement the different features and performance desired, assess the following to help determine the other elements of PTCC. This information can be built into a trade-off table to help the team decide among alternatives.

A note on rough versus detailed estimates: In early SSSS iterations, do rough estimates: we don't want to spend time doing detailed scheduling of design elements that might be traded off to get the best PTCC balance! In later iterations, further analyze a particular sub-systems, to clarify the resources needed, for example. As you hone in on the best system design, you'll estimate other related activities, like testing, to make sure you understand all the aspects of the schedule well enough to forecast the end-date (T).

- **Rough work and schedule estimates for the design sub-systems:** Make rough estimates of the work and schedule timeline for each subsystem, and use the rules of thumb such as the typical project timeline below to estimate the overall project schedule.

- **Rough work and schedule estimates for other cross-functional aspects:** Make rough estimates of the work and timeline for activities such as system testing, alpha and beta testing, technical publications creation, manufacturing planning and processes, etc. For instance, the complexity or risky-ness of your technical design may impact the amount of testing required. The features decided upon may impact the type and amount of regulatory approval required.

- **Rough product cost estimates:** Assess the potential unit costs and other life-cycle costs associated with each design/feature set alternative.

- **Rough project cost estimates:** Make rough assessment of the project budget for the various alternatives to understand the investment the company will be making to develop the product.

- **Late Cost Per Week:** Understand the LCPW for this project (see p. 301).

- **Potential trade-offs:** Use this information to construct trade-off tables that will help you decide between alternatives to arrive at the best PTCC balance for the project. Look especially for schedule and cost drivers: Which sub-systems are the riskiest? Which ones will require the most resources? What features, when implemented in the design, will end up adding the most to the product cost?

- **Potential impacts of other projects:** No project is executed in a vacuum. Unfortunately, your trade-off decisions may be impacted by constraints related to other projects. For instance, a higher priority project may get the software resources you need to implement a particular feature set. This information must be considered during your analysis and factored into your trade-off decisions.

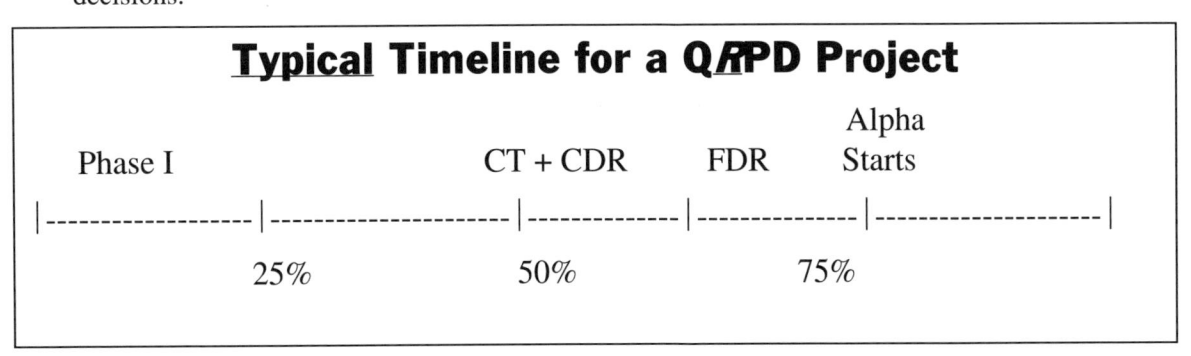

Typical Timeline for a QRPD Project

```
                                                        Alpha
   Phase I                      CT + CDR      FDR       Starts
|------------------|---------------------|--------------|--------------|--------------------|
                   25%                   50%            75%
```

CT = Chicken Test, CDR = Critical Design Review, FDR = Final Design Review

© 1998 Global Brain, Inc.

Preliminary Test Plans and Testing Timelines

You can write very preliminary test plans during phase I that will help the team understand the scope of testing required for different alternatives. It's really important to understand how high the bar is before you get ready to jump over it. This analysis may greatly influence your trade-off decisions. A preliminary test plan can include a paragraph or two briefly specifying the rough scope, timelines, and resources as applicable for each alternative. Consider the following types of tests:

- **Integration testing**
- **System functional testing (alpha)**
- **Beta testing**
- **Regulatory testing**
- **Compatibility testing**
- **Usability testing**

See also Part V DIRFT for more information on these types of tests.

Product Costs

Include the following in estimates of the ultimate product cost:

- **Unit cost:** The cost to manufacture, including parts and labor.
- **Life-cycle costs:** Other costs such as installation, operation, maintenance, and repair.

Project Costs (Budget)

Include the following items in your projections of budget for the project:

- **Salary for all resources.** Quite often this is "guestimated" using a standard such as $10,000 per person-month, which includes pay, taxes, overhead, etc.
- **Capital equipment: The cost of equipment you need to purchase for the project.**
- **Non-recurring engineering charges:** Charges such as those to an outside developer to customize a power-supply.
- **Training:** What new tools should the team be trained on? What skills might you need to bring in training for, such as meeting management or testing techniques?
- **Other equipment or service expenses:** Do you need to rent additional equipment? Engage particular consultants? Pay a regulatory testing laboratory?

© 1998 Global Brain, Inc.

Late Cost Per Week (LCPW)

To keep the importance of time foremost in the team's minds throughout the project, use the LCPW metric. If we're late, how much will our profit be impacted? LCPW keeps the team focused on the importance of time and thus making their project milestones. Further, it gives them a tool for making fast and wise decisions during the project: where should they invest money to save time? What should they trade off to get to market more quickly?

The metric has two components:

- **Lost profit:** For every week we slip past our scheduled delivery date, how much product profit will we lose, by not being out in the market earning revenue?

- **Extra costs or "burn rate":** For every week past that delivery date, how much money is the project team still "burning" in salary and support costs?

$$\text{LCPW} = \text{Lost profit/week} + \text{team burn rate/week}$$

ROI Analysis and 5-Year Road Map

With our PTCC estimates in-hand, we must analyze the project for its potential benefit to the company. The ROI and Road Map deliverables are focused on ensuring that the alternatives we're considering are actually worth doing, from the company's perspective.

- **Profitability and ROI:** Based on the possible PTCC alternatives, will this product be profitable to the company? Is one alternative more profitable than another? What is the potential ROI, the profit or savings from the product or service, compared to the development investment required?

$$\text{ROI} = \frac{\text{Profit (or cost savings) to be gained}}{\text{Development cost}}$$

- **Fit with Product Strategy:** How do the various alternatives fit within the company's overall product strategy: its grouping of products into a product line; its migration to higher-performance systems over time, its plans to move into different market segments, etc.?

- **Fit with Technology Roadmap:** How do the various technical alternatives fit within the company's overall technology roadmap? Does the company have a planned progression through successively more advanced technology, or a master plan for the development of this system over time, that should influence how much gets taken on in this particular project?

- **Fit and priority relative to other company product development efforts:** No project occurs in a vacuum. Companies must decide where to use their precious product development resources. Sometimes a choice must be made between two projects, based on resource availability and the projects' relative ROI. (See also the reading titled "Q*R*PD Phase I Project Evaluations and Project Portfolio Management" later in this section.)

© 1998 Global Brain, Inc.

PTCC Trade-off Table

The trade-off table helps the team capture the PTCC factors associated with each design alternative under consideration. The table can then be used in PDR and Vision meetings to compare alternatives and make trade-off decisions in a more efficient manner.

PTCC Factor	Alternative 1	Alternative 2	Alternative 3
Critical features/specs			
Technical Risks			
Other Risks			
Time-to-customer			
Product Cost			
Resources needed; Project Cost			
Notes and Recommendations			

© 1998 Global Brain, Inc.

Sample PTCC Trade-off Table

This example trade-off table shows the PTCC ramifications of several design alternatives under consideration for a custom micro-computer system for real-time data collection in a variety of applications. It must be small and light enough to be installed in a variety of locations and must be able to operate in the field on battery power for up to 12 hours. The critical trade-offs being discussed include the work to miniaturize the system to maximize mounting options; the desire for long battery life vs. the size and weight impacts of larger batteries; the work to increase performance for the future. Related issues center around impacts on manufacturability of smaller systems; the time required to get smaller systems to market; and software options for implementing smarter battery management.

PTCC Factor	Alternative 1	Alternative 2	Alternative 3
Critical features/specs	Current processor board Battery life = 8 hours HxWxD = 30 x 15 x 12; Weight 30 lbs. Limits customer base for first release.	Current processor board Battery life = 10 hours HxWxD = 15 x 15 x 12; weight 20-25 lbs.	New processor: double data logging throughput of system Battery life 14 hours, all weather conditions HxWxD 12 x 12 x 9; weight 20 lbs.
Technical innovations/risks	Battery early warning system to help manage fact that battery life is lower than desired—major innovation.	New switching power supply—draws less current and is smaller—major risk for FCC compliance and mechanical design will be tricky, affect manufacturability.	New power supply—major Porting code to new-to-market processor—very major New power management software—major innovation Communications interface packaged into ASIC to reduce size—major innovation.
Other Risks	Getting field supports' buy-in to approach.	Power supply vendor is new	No ASIC designer in house yet; no Mfg test capability.
Time-to-customer	12 months	17 months	24 months
Product Cost	$1500	$1700	$1800
Resources needed/ Project Cost	1 hw, 1 sw, 1 mech. Heavy need for field support involvement.	$80K NRE for power supply. 1 PS engr. 2 mech, 2 SW.	2 hardware, 1 ASIC designer, 5 software, 2 mechanical. Special mfg test attention.
Notes and Recommendations	Gets to market most quickly to satisfy most important current customers. Will require follow-on project to increase battery life and processor power and reduce size. Need to understand future upgrade costs.	Satisfies broader range of desired features/specs but cost is a problem and power supply is big question. Tight vendor control and lots of chicken testing required.	We don't have time to wait for this full-blown solution. Too many major innovations. This might be a follow-on project or projects.

© 1998 Global Brain, Inc.

Preliminary Design Reviews (PDR)

- **When it is held:** When enough high-level design work and investigations have been done that the Project Leader and team can suggest PTCC alternatives. Design should only have occurred at the subsystem and block diagram level at this point. More than one PDR will be held as part of the iterative SSSS process.

- **Purpose:** To consider the various design alternatives and the corresponding PTCC balance; to reach a consensus of the best way to proceed with the overall system design; to identify potential project pitfalls; and to make trade-off decisions. See PDR Checklist on the next page. Note: when complex trade-off decisions are required, those the PDRs may focus on reviewing the designs and possible trade-offs, then a separate trade-off meeting may be held to discuss the options and reach a decision.

Materials needed for PDR

- Current draft of Product Vision
- List of open Vision issues--any features the team has not yet decided to support, etc.
- Summary of each design alternative, salient points; architecture, high-level design documents
- Technological risk assessments
- Trade-off tables
- Any cost-benefit analyses done to decide among different features
- Any recommendations the team has about how to proceed

Typical PDR agenda:

- Briefly remind team of key Vision elements.
- Review the elements of the design or designs. Identify areas where the design might not work.
- Step the team through the current trade-off table. Present each alternative, answering the questions in the PDR checklist. Discuss any detail about the design alternatives necessary to understand the trade-off table elements.
- Create action items.

PDR Minutes and other outputs:

- List of agreed-upon changes to the Vision, based on trade-off decisions made in this meeting; and list of remaining key Vision items to resolve
- Revised design document
- Action items with names and due-dates assigned
- Updated Critical Issues and Dependencies List, including open items to keep iterating on
- Target date for next PDR, and if necessary, revised target for exiting phase I

© 1998 Global Brain, Inc.

Preliminary Design Review (PDR) Checklist

CHECKLIST ITEMS (customize with your own items and details)

0. Has everybody done their preparation work?

1. Why are we doing this project? What is the desired result? Reference the Product Vision.

2. What is the LCPW?

3. What are the possible approaches and associated risks?
   a) What are the technical alternatives?
   b) What are the resource considerations? (people, equipment, etc.)
   c) How do different approaches affect the schedule?
   d) What are the performance trade-offs?
   e) What are the cost and manufacturability trade-offs?
      Usability, portability, serviceability, reliability, etc.?

4. What is the Project Leader's recommended approach, and why?

5. What are the **critical issues** to be resolved? How might they be resolved, and/or the risks minimized? (Update the Critical Issues and Dependencies list.)

6. What is the proposed project schedule? When do we ship?

7. What is the impact of the proposed design to the existing product line?

8. What is the impact to the existing customer base?

9. Are any of the designs potentially patentable? (if so, begin processing)

10. Will the designs require regulatory approval? If so, get scheduled in with the agencies.

PDR FOLLOW-UP:

1. Publish meeting minutes. (See list of contents on previous page).

2. Reconvene if more research is necessary to finalize the design approach and/or to follow up on assigned action items.

3. Generate/revise the project schedule.

4. Meet the schedule.

© 1998 Global Brain, Inc.

A Summary of the See-Saw Process and How to Get Started Correctly

The previous pages have explained and gone step by step through the activities in the Vision and SSSS process. Now we can pull them together into an overview of how phase I should unfold on your project.

It is important to start the Vision and SSSS process with vigor and purpose. Now that you have selected your Project Leader and core cross-functional team, it is time to get them to work. Phase I is a collection of concurrent and iterative activities where you raise issues, address them, commit to decisions, and move on to the remaining issues.

This process begins with the first Vision meeting, which is often scheduled as a half-day or full day off-site meeting. The meeting should be well attended by the cross-functional team. Each section of the Vision should have its own space on a white board or flip chart.

The conversation begins with addressing sections 1 and 2 of the Vision: Who are the customers for this product, and how will they measure success?

As the conversation progresses, relevant information should be recorded under all the Vision sections. However, your first Vision meeting may not get past those first two sections. If this is the case, the team should consider itself lucky to have had this discussion early in the project: There were clearly fundamental issues about the purpose of this project and product that needed to be resolved. Without the Vision process, they might not have been discussed until a much later—and more expensive—part of the project.

The key deliverables from this first meeting are the first draft of the Vision, a list of open critical issues, and a list of action items. These deliverables set the agenda for the rest of phase I, including team meetings, design work, planning and scheduling, and Vision, reviews, and trade-off meetings. The team should mobilize to quickly assess and address the open issues and risks that are identified in the Vision meetings. It is critical that the off-line work proceed with as much vigor, commitment, and sense of urgency as the work in the Vision meetings. The Project Leader is responsible for driving this activity forward; the technical and cross-functional leads will drive their sub-teams' contributions.

The table on the next page is a sample calendar of typical meetings and activities in the phase I SSSS process. Detailed analysis and discussion occurs off-line and during design and scheduling sessions. Experiments and prototyping are often required. The results are brought into subsequent design review, trade-off, and Vision meetings. The Vision document matures as customer, feature, design, cost, and schedule trade-offs are addressed.

QRPD projects should plan on spending 15-25% of their total schedule in phase I, not leaving until there is a Vision, schedule, and milestones list that the team is committed to achieving. The five-week schedule in the chart below may in fact require 10 or 15 weeks on your project. You should plan on a Vision meeting at least every other week to keep up momentum and record progress. Other meetings and working sessions may involve smaller groups and be focused on specific issues.

Be sure to keep your Vision document, Milestone lists, Action items, Critical Issues and Key Decisions lists accessible (posted on the walls and distributed by email) and up to date.

Typical Phase I Calendar:
The Vision and See-Saw Process

	Monday	Tuesday	Wednesday	Thursday	Friday
Week 1		Vision Meeting 1 (Full Day) Include cross-functional team (10-20 people)	Begin completing action items. Define alternative design and rough schedules; assess costs and risks.	Develop Responsibility Matrix	Review design alternatives, discuss "big-ticket" trade-offs
Week 2	Vision Meeting 2 (1/2 Day) (Review line by line, update for any trade-off decisions)	Continue design alternatives investigation.	Scheduling meetings—make sure cross-functional aspects addressed in rough schedules.	Create drafts of other Phase I deliverables.	Run early chicken test.
Week 3	Refine Responsibility Matrix. Review chicken test results	Make cost estimates for current alternatives.	PDR with trade-off discussions	Refine remaining design alternatives. Refine schedules.	Work on other phase I deliverables.
Week 4	Preliminary Design Review of remaining alternatives, trade-off decisions	Vision Meeting 3 (2-4 hours). Update for trade-off decisions, any new information.	Resolve final Vision issues. Finalize costs and schedule targets.		Vision Meeting 4 (2-4 hours)
Week 5	Finish detailed schedules, other phase I deliverables…				Sign the completed Vision and milestones

© 1998 Global Brain, Inc.

Exercises: Sample Product Visions from Flow Step 4, See-Saw Specifications and Schedules

Sample Product Vision
Macintosh/PC Exchange

I. **Target Customers/Key Issues Customer Use to Judge Quality**

Macintosh users that work in a mixed environment (DOS/Macintosh computers) need an easy way to share files with their colleagues whether they work on Macs or PCs. This is also a problem for the person that may have a PC at work, but a Macintosh at home. The ability to share files will also facilitate the initial and incremental sales of Macintosh into primarily PC environments.

The target customer needs to be able to copy files, primarily data files, to and from a 3.5" floppy disk that can be read on a PC, as well. The customer will judge the effectiveness of the product by its ease of use, i.e., it is just like copying to any other media and the reliability in terms of preserving the data.

2. **Key Technology and Key Features**
   - Perform all Finder and standard file operations on a DOS floppy
   - Emphasis on copying files and saving to the floppy.
   - Should be a dynamically loadable unit/CDEV.
   - No new user interface except for mapping.

3. **Crucial Product Factors**
   - Can be sold as standalone extension.
   - Quality should be focused on user scenarios and not the robustness of the file system.
   - Product should be consistent with "easy open" strategy.

4. **Relevant Financial Numbers**
   - Intangible but of significant value to the company.

What's wrong with, or missing from, this Vision?

© 1998 Global Brain, Inc.

Sample Product Vision:

Chip-placer2

I. **Target Customers/Key Issues Customer Use to Judge Quality**

- The Chip-placer2 product has the same target customers, markets, and applications as the current Chip-placer family. Namely, manufacturers using automated assembly to insert integrated-circuit chips into printed circuit boards. The new model will replace all existing models of the current family.

- Customers will increase their profits with the 15% increase in the rate of chip placement. Furthermore, cost reductions are planned to allow lower pricing: when fully tooled, a 33% lower cost of materials is expected.

- The product will meet all performance specifications of the current Chip-Placer, except in the following areas where it will exceed:

    1. The pick and place mechanism has 50% greater torque capability for faster insertion times, and 30% greater payload capacity for new, bigger IC packs.

    2. Only 1/2 as much acoustical noise (<70dB at 1 meter vs. 79dB)

- It will be more serviceable: MTTR = 30 minutes vs. 1 hour currently.

- Builds upon and even enhances the Chip-placer's high reputation for reliability by improving MTBF to 1000 hours vs. 500 (at best...) currently.

- A bellows on the quill will lower the dust intake of the system in harsh environments.

- The system will look newer, more advanced, and higher tech.

2. **Key Technology and Key Features**

- Will use a new, off-the-shelf 68000-based integrated controller with an upgradable path. The integration will allow vision, force sensing, belt tracking, and other axis motion control to be added within the same system.

- Direct drive of the primary joints and the encoders will bring about a system with fewer moving parts.

- The product will be highly tooled which implies better and fewer parts.

(continued on next page)

© 1998 Global Brain, Inc.

3. **Crucial Product Factors**
    - Same but updated, documentation, manuals, and training as the Chip-placer.
    - Automation techniques will be used during assembly vs. manual means for the Chip-placer.
    - TUV certification.
    - The system utilizes the protection afforded by the Chip-placer patents.

4. **Relevant Financial Numbers**
    - Cost: $6650 materials, about 16 hrs. labor $\Rightarrow$ out-the-door COGS $10,000 vs. about $17,000 currently.
    - 1 hrs. test vs. 3 hrs. currently.
    - Window (product life effectiveness): 5-10 years.
    - Projected number of units: 200 in year 1, 400 in year 2, 2500 lifetime.

What's wrong with, or missing from, this Vision?

Sample Product Vision:

SunShield *

SunShield is an automotive product that allows the user to tint the windows of their auto to 20% transmissivity. The primary use for the product will be for cars parked in the sun during the day. The product objectives for SunShield are ease of use, low cost, reliability, and safety. SunShield must be able to be adapted to existing automobiles.

Market research has shown that in areas with warm climates 44% of auto owners use some sort of material to block the sun from their parked car when outdoors. SunShield is targeting this market. Research has also shown that the other 56% who do not use a window covering would like to have one but do not want to hassle with putting one in place and removing it each time they park.

SunShield is an adhesive film much like industry standard glass tints. The film is clear in its natural state, however when a low voltage, low current power source is passed through the film, it's transmissivity can be reduced to 20%. Car temperatures can be reduced on average by up to 15-30 degrees Fahrenheit when a car is parked for an hour in the sun with outside temperatures above 80 degrees. By comparison, standard sun visors only provide about 10 degrees of relief, although both do keep the steering wheel and the dash comparably cool.

SunShield can be used with new and existing auto windows, and power is drawn from the battery. Calculations show that an average battery will support SunShield in its on state for four weeks without draining the battery below starting levels.

Safety and reliability are insured by two separate circuits. One circuit will monitor battery levels and turn off SunShield if the voltage falls below starting levels for the auto. A separate circuit will allow SunShield to be activated only when the car is in park or the motor is running. SunShield is operated by a simple switch on the dash.

Market research shows that the product needs to be introduced in the next 12 months to beat competitors to the market. A price point of $130 for end-user product cost has been established. SunShield will take eight months to develop, and the maximum cost per unit out-the-door to meet profit objectives must be under $75.

Total development costs including labor, overhead, capital expenses and roll out costs total one million dollars. Projected sales over the next year are 500,000 units at $130. Installation costs are projected at $50 per unit, charged by the dealers and distributors. The long-term objective is to gain acceptance for the product and license it to auto makers directly.

What's wrong with, or missing from, this Vision?

Thanks to University of California Berkeley Extension Q*R*PD student Todd Austin for the data for this vision.

© 1998 Global Brain, Inc.

Sample Product Vision
"RAPIDSOFT" Statement of Purpose and Direction

Develop an "Alpha Centauri 10" engineering workstation standard cell technology product composed of a cell library, accompanying design tools and methodology designed to reduce the design cycle time from final engineering request signoff to first prototype release from 9 to 3.5 months (!).

Conditions of satisfaction:

- Book the primary customer and technology driver.

- Complete tools and method development by   <date> [50%]

    <date> [90%]

- Complete cell databases by   <date>

- Complete documentation by   <date>

- Have an alpha test vehicle prove the product.

- Deliver design system to primary customer by   <date>

What's wrong with, or missing from, this Vision?

(Solution in Appendix A.)

© 1998 Global Brain, Inc.

Sample Product Vision
"QUAKESENSE"

Motionmatic, Inc. will use it's new motion sensing technology to give advance warning for consumer households of the potential occurrence of earthquakes. Engineering has already reported that the new measurement approach is feasible, though with limited accuracy. Marketing is preparing to sell to this new market segment.

The "Quakesense" must weigh less than 10 pounds so it can be easily wall or ceiling mounted, measure no more than 12"x12"x3", must run on a 9 volt battery, and give user friendly warnings with three different levels of alarm.

Projected sales start at 10,000 units a month within the first six months of shipment, and will grow by 20% per year for five years. This assumes a consumer price of $79 or less.

What's wrong with, or missing from, this Vision?

(Solution in Appendix A.)

© 1998 Global Brain, Inc.

Sample Product Vision
"BioComf"

A portable self-contained medical-biofeedback unit intended to be prescribed by physicians and other primary health care providers for in office, at home and in hospital use for reducing pain and stress associated with symptoms such as headaches, migraine, shoulder pain and soreness, insomnia, gastrointestinal problems, and hypertension. The BioComf is used by the patient following doctor-administered guidelines to progressively achieve higher levels of comfort, reduced pain and other targeted health related goals. What differentiates this product from available clinical biofeedback products are the use of automated protocols built into the product targeted to a few very prevalent symptom areas, the ease of use with minimal physician or health care provider assistance, and the ability of the primary health care provider to prescribe protocols on the BioComf for the patient to follow toward measurable clinical progress.

The patient is given a recommended program to practice with using the BioComf and a structured instructional booklet on how to connect the biosensors to either their fingers, forehead, neck, shoulder, or abdominal areas. Programs are selected by pressing a number on the BioComf from 1- 10, and a challenge level from 1 to 3 (learning, practice, and mastery). After 2 - 15 minutes of practice the patient will report experiencing optimism about being able to alleviate their condition through the positive feedback and continued regular use of the BioComf. This optimism is based upon being given feedback about changes in the body related to positive goals such as warming the hands or releasing tension in the shoulders and also from symptomatic relief and feelings of wellness that occur when these goals are achieved in standard Biofeedback practice with such patients.

This microprocessor based product will take one year to develop. It will utilize standard circuits which already exist on other products for monitoring electromyographic signals from muscles, temperature gauging, and skin resistance measures. The unit must give basic visual and audio feedback. Safety concerns may necessitate battery only operation. The product must cost under $250 to manufacture to sell for under $1000. The BioComf will be durable enough so that it may be prescribed to patients on a rental basis or purchase basis. First year sales estimates range from 1000 to 10,000 units per month, and grow rapidly as they address the headache and stress marketplace.

What's wrong with, or missing from, this Vision?

(Solution in Appendix A.)

© 1998 Global Brain, Inc.

Sample Product Vision
Internet-Based Contracting Service

1. **Target Customers/Key Issues Customers Use to Judge Quality**

   The target customers are engineering managers who will be able to tap into a pool of engineering specialists through the Internet, including experienced design engineers and reliability engineers, at the touch of their PC mouse. Managers will no longer need to rely on temporary services and independent contractors to provide the extra personnel they need. The costs, schedules, and tasks are all arranged over the Internet with the help of the service provider. The engineering manager enjoys the flexibility of using the specialist for as little as one week to as long as two years. The specialists have access to more work opportunities and are better able to take advantage of the telecommuting work environment.

2. **Key Technology and Key Features**
   - Easily reachable from Windows PCs, MACs, Unix platforms with Internet access.
   - Database of pre-qualified candidates and portfolios, including visual images of them and samples of their work.
   - Menu-driven interface with powerful search engine.
   - Ability to narrow down to candidates with particular industry and technical experience from the large overall database.
   - Chat room for one-on-one discussions between candidates before hiring and during the job
   - Variety of contract templates available on-line that can be tailored to suit customer's needs.
   - Implementation must not preclude use by international customers using older browser technology.

3. **Crucial Product Factors**
   - Initial roll-out must include at least 10 contractors/consultants for each of 15 most important technical specialties within electronics engineering and software development.
   - Database must be updated at least once per week
   - Attract applicants by registering with popular web search sites. Get link arrangements with professional organizations with career development activities.
   - Resumes and samples must be in a standard format to ensure customers will always have adequate information available to do an initial screen of candidates.

4. **Relevant Financial Numbers**

   Start-up costs, including labor, overhead, capital expenses, and advertising costs total $50k. Membership fee paid by corporations: annual fee from $1000 to $10,000 per company scaled by company size. Service must be on-line with initial database of candidates by Q4'98.

What is wrong with, or missing from, this Vision?

© 1998 Global Brain, Inc.

Sample Product Vision
Electronic Mail Software

The next generation of SuperMail will provide users with the finest User Agent for Windows 95 operating system. The product will allow SuperMail to make a greater penetration into Fortune 1000 companies, and provide existing SuperMail customers with an upgrade to the latest generation operating system. The product will also be the first SuperMail to be standards based.

The SuperMail product will use the messaging application programming interface (MAPI) that is built into the operating system. MAPI provides several features that have not been available in previous SuperMail products, including some of the most requested features by customers, such as delegation, conferencing, and views. MAPI also supports multiple providers, which allows the SuperMail User Agent to be used with Lotus Notes and other mail systems simultaneously. The capacity to use a single User Agent for all mail systems inside a corporation will be a powerful marketing feature for the product.

The distinguishing feature of the SuperMail User Agent is that it will have the highest degree of usability of any mail application. Without ever reading a manual or using on-line help, users will be able to login to the system, read and compose messages. Users will also have the ability to create more powerful messages through the use of OLE technology, which allows objects from other applications to be embedded into their messages, such as spreadsheets or sounds. The use of Rich Text enables users to style the message with fonts, colors, and paragraph formatting.

The SuperMail User Agent is a key component of the company's overall strategy, providing a single application that works with the SuperMail file sharing architecture, and client/server architecture such as Notes. The product will have an open architecture that allows for future extensibility and enhancement. The product will ship within 90 days of the release of Windows 95. Total development costs are estimated to total one million dollars. Projected sales over the next year are 500,000 units at $40.

What is wrong with, or missing from, this Vision?

© 1998 Global Brain, Inc.

Excerpted with permission from:

PROJECTWORLD® Winter 96 Proceedings

Article: Powerful Product Visions for Developing Products in Half the Time

© 1998 Global Brain, Inc.

Powerful Product Visions for Developing Products in Half the Time

Orion Kopelman, President
Cinda Voegtli, Consulting Partner
Global Brain®, Inc.
555 Bryant Street #369   Palo Alto, CA 94301
(650) 327-2012   Fax: (650) 327-2028   email: globlbrain@aol.com

Abstract

Teams aligned to a powerful product vision can jet forward to complete a new product development effort in record time. Teams using the Q*R*PD®: Quality *Rapid* Product Development methodology have finished projects in half the time of previous efforts, slashing schedules from 18 months to as little as 7 months, by *first* having all cross-functional team members hash out a consensus one-page vision. Using examples from real projects, we'll show the correct process for arriving at a Q*R*PD vision and what it must contain to successfully combat the #1 reason for project schedule slips: changing product definitions that give teams a moving target.

Global Brain has helped technology companies world-wide accelerate their projects with Q*R*PD, including Abbott, Shell, CellNet, NASA's Space Station group, and Plantronics. Orion Kopelman previously served as VP of Engineering of Mountain Computer from 1984-1990 as it grew from 50 to 500 people with 32 consecutive profitable quarters. Cinda Voegtli has held director-level engineering and senior project management positions in high-technology companies, and has consulted on the practical implementation of Q*R*PD in a variety of industries. Orion and Cinda teach Q*R*PD at UC Berkeley Extension and have both served as chair of the Silicon Valley Chapter of the IEEE Engineering Management Society.

Introduction

"Vision without action is just a dream. Action without vision is just activity. Vision and action together can change the world." You have great product dreams, but you can't get a real product out the door. Or you know how to get a product out the door, but it's not necessarily the right one.

The Quality *Rapid* Product Development (Q*R*PD) methodology [1] provides the Product Vision as a weapon against incomplete or off-target product definitions and against spurious requirements changes later in a project. It is one of the most important management tools a team can have, particularly for timely and *accelerated* project completion.

Q*R*PD and the Product Vision apply to projects of all sizes and complexity, and to product development in any industry. Whether your product is to be sold to an external customer or delivered to an internal customer, a Vision is key to your project's success and your customers' satisfaction.

In managing projects and developing products, the number one reason for schedule slippages is changing requirements. These delays indicate a lack of critical understanding of the important purpose of a product and a lack of continued focus on the most important goals. Aggressive time-to-market targets first and foremost mandate a crystal-clear understanding of what you're trying to accomplish for your customers, and

© 1998 Global Brain, Inc.

an unwavering commitment to achieving it.

When the target ship date for your product seems most unreasonable or impossible to achieve, the "miracle" of on-time delivery can still happen—but only if you start the project on the right foot, assuring a *proper* vision is firmly in place before action is taken.

The "Miracle" of Niles Audio

The experiences of a manufacturer of high-end audio equipment illustrate the power of the Product Vision. Fresh off the success of a new amplifier product, the company prepared for their next assault on the marketplace. This time they intended to develop a leading-edge control keypad for custom-built luxury homes. Niles had just adopted the QRPD methodology to help them get this product to market in record time.

The technology necessary for this product was new to their engineers, and the feature possibilities were enormous. The Product Vision grew and grew as the entire wish-list was identified as "must-have" features. The seductive allure of the perfect full-featured product almost led the team to disaster.

In the end the Product Vision process saved the day. As a result of using the principles and processes described in this paper, Niles released their new product in 7 months, compared to the 18 months required for their previous comparable product. Their experiences, and those of other companies, are described throughout the paper to illustrate the power of the Product Vision process.

The Power of Phase I Concentration

Typically the early days of projects are spent defining requirements for the product to be developed. And what chaos it can be! Everyone has pet features. Everyone thinks they know what "must" be included for the customer to buy this product or service. Everyone is afraid to leave out any feature ever mentioned in a review of a competitor's offering. Unfortunately, this "perfect" product has about zero chance of ever being completed.

If a company is serious about rapid product development, the first thing they must do is get a grip on the purpose of the product. What customer needs must the product meet? What benefits must it provide? You must avoid the engineering-driven product definition, which focuses solely on technology and features, not customer benefits. You must avoid the Marketing tendency to want to provide all things to all people. You must avoid having your product strategy capriciously reshuffled due to the latest list of offerings from your competitor.

How do you get through this maze with an on-target product definition and team members who are still speaking to each other? The QRPD methodology uses the Product Vision *process* to negotiate this treacherous time of the project.

QRPD calls for four phases of concurrent-engineering-oriented product development:

- Phase I: Kickoff
- Phase II: Design, Implement, Test
- Phase III: Approval
- Phase IV: Production or Deployment

During Phase I of the project, the Product Vision is defined. *This phase may take as much as 25% of the project's schedule.* The team must spend enough time to get the Vision for the product thoroughly hashed out. The length of this critical phase is related to an important fact: 80% of a product's cost and capability is usually determined in the first 20% of the project schedule.

The Vision process is critical to the ongoing focus of the team as well: once the early definition phase is "completed", suggestions for improvements inevitably arise. New information becomes available, someone who didn't speak up before becomes vocal about the need for a feature or attribute, or perhaps the market changes. But if requirements are allowed to change capriciously mid-stream or late in a project, engineering work will have to be redone, and the project will slip. In some cases, it will slip numerous times—when there is no sense of product purpose, there is no

© 1998 Global Brain, Inc.

corresponding fierce control of product requirements, and a knee-jerk change mentality will rule the day. The Product Vision is a mechanism for both achieving and *maintaining* team alignment.

The ability of a team to define and maintain focus on a set of most important product goals is the essence of the leadership that rapid product development requires. Abraham Lincoln said that "leadership is doing the right things". The purpose of the Vision is to define those "right things". Warren Bennis' four competencies of leadership are helpful for understanding the power of a Product Vision both early in and throughout the project.

- *Management of attention* is accomplished by establishing the intentions of the product through the Product Vision.

- *Management of meaning* is achieved by team creation of the vision, effective communication of the vision, and alignment of the team members to this vision.

- *Management of trust* is realized through reliability and constancy of following the Product Vision.

- *Management of self* occurs because the project leader is absolutely clear about the mission of the project and his responsibility for leading the team to its achievement.

Phase I concentration for 25% of a project was certainly new to Niles, as it is for most companies. "Let's get on with it!" is a common refrain. In reality, you must "slow down to speed up," investing the time early to ensure overall rapid development. Even though Niles wanted to finish this product in 7 to 8 months, they spent the time up front—2 months—to understand their goals.

5 Sections of a Q*R*PD Product Vision

A Q*R*PD Product Vision, typically a one or two page document, defines:

1. **Customers and Benefits:** The Vision starts with the definition of the customer(s) for the product. Who are they? Are there both internal and external customers? Who are the end users? Are there specific market segments the product targets? Are there primary and secondary customers? Are there specific customers where a contractual commitment or possibility is driving this development? Who are the "leading edge" customers who will adopt the new product first, and who are the "target" customers who form more of the mass market for the product for the long term?

    Then, what are the benefits this product is to provide those customers and users? What problems do they have, and what *solution* will your product provide them?

2. **Key issues which the customer will use to judge quality:** In Q*R*PD, quality is defined as "value as perceived by the customer". Over and above the definition of customer benefits in section 1, this section clarifies which items are most important to the customer's perception of the product's value. In a mission-critical system, reliability might be the most important factor. In a time-critical system, performance under load might be. These parameters should be expressed in a quantified, measurable way.

3. **Key technology and features:** Here we finally deal with some of the elements that tend to receive the most (or only) attention in traditional product definitions.

    The vision should articulate any assumptions about technology that will be employed. Note that you do not want to specify implementation here, when the details of the implementation are not germane to meeting the customer's needs. Rather, you specify technology aspects if they are known to be critical to meeting the customer's requirements or staying true to a corporate master plan, for instance.

    You must also call out specific features that are key to the product fulfilling the customer's needs.

4. **Crucial product factors:** These are elements that are not a primary part of product functionality, but are key

© 1998 Global Brain, Inc.

attributes that must be present. These include requirements such as safety, environmental operation ranges, ergonomics, serviceability, manufacturability, testability, user documentation, training, installation tools, interaction with associated products, and design constraints to allow future expansion.

5. **Financials:** What are the economic particulars driving this development? What is the perceived market window and the desired product release date? What is the "late cost per week" if this product is not introduced then? How many units do you expect to ship over time? What is the desired cost target for the product and its preferred selling price? What is the budget for developing this product?

Figure 1 on the next page contains the Niles Audio "Intellipad" product vision. Keep in mind that vision details will vary quite a bit based on industry and type of product, but all visions must address these five areas.

7 Steps for Creating a Product Vision

Q*R*PD states three key tenets required for rapid product development, the first of which is : *Total company commitment to a concrete, well-defined product vision.* The elements of this rule point the way to an effective Product Vision process.

- Total company commitment: The process must ensure that the entire company buys into the vision and supports its achievement throughout the development project.

- Concrete, well-defined Product Vision: The process must yield specific, well-thought-out, based-in-reality, easily understood goals for the product to achieve.

The following 7-step process ensures these desired outcomes.

1. **Understand the PTCC Balance, Investigate Alternatives, and Innovate Incrementally.**

The financials section of the vision gives a clue to the overall process of creating the Vision and in fact supports the need for "total company commitment". The proper Vision process does not allow product definition to occur in a vacuum. The emphasis is on (a) benefits to the customer: what gives the customer value; and (b) benefits to the company: how must the development be achieved to ensure the desired return on investment to the company? Any product development effort must balance among four factors:

- **Product performance (P):** including features and functionality of the product and its quality.

- **Time-to-market (T):** the amount of time the project can take to get the product out the door, to deliver the value to the customer as quickly as possible and begin the economic benefits to the company.

- **Product cost (C):** the unit cost of the product, as well as implications for life-cycle costs related to manufacture, installation, and maintenance.

- **Project cost (C):** the amount of money the company will spend to bring the product to market, in salaries, equipment, and other non-recurring investments.

Together these factors are referred to in Q*R*PD as the "PTCC" balance.

Figure 2. Four Product Development Objectives

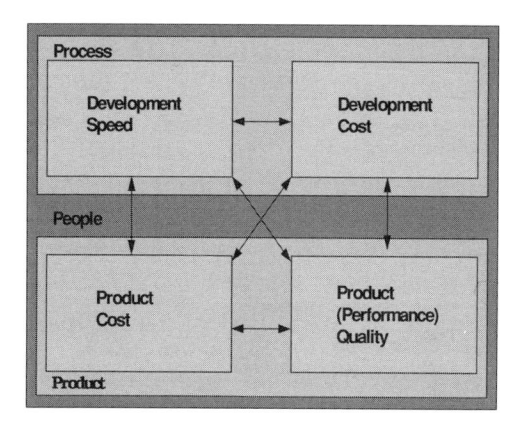

© 1998 Global Brain, Inc.

Figure 1. Niles Audio Intellipad Product Vision

NILES: 1995 Product Vision: <u>IR Keypad With Speaker Relay</u> Revision: Rev 8 June 16/95

Model Number: IntelliPad   Target Intro. Date: January 1, 1996
Target Cost (Landed in Miami): A*   Dealer Cost: C*   Retail $350
Projected Unit Sales: B*   Product Life (years):   3
Effect on sales of existing Products: Will have a positive effect on the entire IR category.
*The actual numbers are confidential to Niles Audio.

Target Markets:
Primary: A consumer with a multiple room audio system with infrared remote control desires strategically located, wall mounted keypads. The consumer requires that the keypad be fun to use, inexpensive and aesthetically pleasing.

Secondary: The installer/specifier demands that the keypad be as fast and easy to program and install as the Soundstream Touch One or the Xantech 730. He/she will recommend the Niles keypad to the consumer because of its power status indicator, the local speaker mute, its ability to up and download to a pc for program storage, and the Niles look, feel and reliability (less than 1% defective in the first year).

Key Technology:
PC Interface (Transfer and Storage Only) will only allow a <u>complete</u> keypad program to be down and uploaded via an adapter cable and permanently archived on the PC (program which will run under Windows).

Power Status of the main amplifier is communicated to the keypad and displayed or indicated to the user. The status signal is provided by new versions of the IRP-2, IRP-6A, and IRZ-6A. A new version of the RVL-6 will provide room on/off status to the keypad. A 12vDC (200 - 800 mA) control-in will provide an additional status input. Turn-off must be virtually instantaneous.

A Speaker Relay will completely mute the local room when the Mute button is pressed. The status of the relay will be displayed or indicated to the user. The relay and its status indicator can be defeated by the installer.

Source Macro IR Commands allow the source buttons to power up the main amplifier (if it is off), select input, and issue play and mode commands. Link between the source button and the Power command can be defeated by installer.

Preprinted Replaceable Source Labels allow the installer to correctly label each source button. The source button which was last pressed is displayed or indicated to the user.

Universal Transport Buttons map to the source selected, allowing the same transport buttons to control all of the components in the system.

All Buttons are Programmable with an IR command.

Compatible with virtually all IR remote controls (except old Phillips and those with carrier frequencies above 100kHZ) and installed Xantech and Niles IR remote repeater systems.

Stand-Alone Installation- A variable flasher output allows up to four Niles Flashers to be used without an IRP.

Easy Program Duplication - Can dump only <u>complete</u> contents of memory to another keypad over a 6' cable.

Consumer controls should have a positive tactile feel and should be shaped and/or colored to differentiate function.

Installer controls, indicators, connectors should be hidden from view, and protected from accidental activation by the consumer.
1. Must meet FCC *Part B* regulations."
2. Must not be deeper than 2 7/8."
3. Must match the look of Leviton "Decora" styled switches and be compatible with Leviton "screwless" cover plates.
4. Program memory is protected from accidental loss for a minimum of 5 years, preferably more.
5. Should be packed with both White and Bone decora DSI inserts (no Decora cover plate).

© 1998 Global Brain, Inc.

The Vision process is designed to help the project team make the trade-offs that result in the best possible balance of these factors when defining the requirements for the product, using "see-saw specifications and schedules" (SSSS) negotiation.

Marketing usually starts by defining the product they want developed. Engineering performs preliminary design work, investigating various technological and architectural approaches to the product. Marketing wants as many features as quickly as possible; Engineering wants as much time as possible to complete the development. These diametrically opposed needs require careful determination of where to balance the see-saw.

During this time the Product Vision is created iteratively by the team to capture agreements on high-level product requirements. The team performs cost-benefit analyses to arrive at the best PTCC balance for both meeting customer needs for solutions and the company's need for economic benefit. In the end, this balance is an optimal solution that the whole team can live with and sign up to.

Using the Vision process has a critical effect on the problem of the "perfect" product. By forcing a PTCC balance with special attention to time-to-market and understanding of the customer's perception of value, the Vision fosters the key concept of "incremental innovation," the identification of a *limited* (and therefore highly achievable!) set of product objectives.

Incremental innovation helps conquer one of the typical pitfalls of product development: long projects geared to producing the "it-can-do-it-all" product. These projects take the "long bomb" strategy [2], where the company lobs a long-range assault toward a distant product objective. If the market changes in the middle of such a long development—which now often happens within a year— you stand a great chance of getting to the target only to discover that the market has moved. Or you try to respond to the shifts along the way by constantly course-correcting, and in the end may never finish a product at all.

In contrast, the QRPD emphasis on incremental innovation forces you to define the most important benefits to the customer, and deliver those as quickly as possible to meet customer needs in the right timeframe. By definition, you try to deliver quickly enough that market shifts during development are minimized, and you are able to produce an on-target beneficial product. Further, you can begin to construct a product strategy and project portfolio that will allow you to continue to satisfy your customers over time through successive product releases.

Niles Audio backed away from their "home run" initial product definition to achieve their market success. Their SSSS negotiation process yielded a clear incremental innovation, a set of critical features that could be delivered rapidly, to the delight of their dealers, who had gotten very excited after seeing a prototype at a trade show.

This process also combats a typical problem with project schedules: lack of team commitment to them! Using the SSSS negotiation process, *based on concrete well-defined preliminary design work*, the project schedule is not considered committed until the product design alternative is selected, resources for the desired schedule understood, and the Product Vision finalized.

Use of the Vision process on a sub-project illustrates this significant benefit. At one information systems development company, a trade show was three weeks away, and the demonstration already promised to the world by Marketing was technically impossible in that timeframe. Tensions on the team were *high*. The team wrote a Vision for the absolute minimum requirements for the show, and used SSSS negotiations to come up with a feasible crash development plan for the next three weeks. The session wasn't concluded until each person indicated that he could live with that plan. The newly-energized team completed the development in the shorter timeframe, and the trade show was a huge corporate success.

© 1998 Global Brain, Inc.

2. Take extreme measures to understand your customers.

To achieve the best PTCC balance you obviously have to have an accurate understanding of your customers and their needs. Who is the customer, or buyer, of your product? Who are the users? The customers and users may be two totally different groups of people, and the product must address the needs of both. To answer those questions for section 1 of the Vision, Customers and Benefits, you can't guess or hope your guts are right. You must find ways to get real data and make decent decisions: by interviewing lead or innovative users as well as later mass-market customers; by getting engineers close to the customer as early as possible; by forming strong ongoing relationships with key customers that provide continual insight into their needs.

3. Get the entire team involved in Vision creation sessions.

The best method for creating a vision is to use group brainstorming and review sessions. Typically the entire project team assembles for a first vision meeting. This first meeting may be an entire day off-site affair. A facilitator uses brainstorming techniques to help the group capture elements for the five vision sections on flipchart paper around the room. Any item with open issues, i.e. one not ready to be approved for the Vision, is parked on an issues list.

This first session captures the big picture: the team leaves with an initial understanding of the proposed customer and the product's purpose, and a clear delineation of what is already agreed upon, and what must be resolved. The project leader takes away the charts from the meeting to create a draft vision document. And herein lies one of the most important team considerations of the vision process: the project leader is the editor of the document, *not the author!* Much of the synergy and alignment benefits of the vision is lost if the vision is "dictated" by any one person.

The importance of the presence of all team members is illustrated by a story from an instrument measurement company. A particular Vision meeting was deadlocked on a feature definition. Finally, an engineer who had never before participated in product definitions, who spoke very broken English, and who culturally was not predisposed to offer his opinions to any assembled group, spoke up, pointed to a competitor's datasheet and said "Why don't we do it like this?" Silence deadened the room, then 15 awestruck people quickly adapted a sentence from the datasheet for inclusion in the vision. The engineer whose input was critical to resolving the vision issue in an appropriate manner didn't say another word for the rest of the meeting: he had made his contribution!

In a company experiencing extreme negative sentiments about the executive staff's ability to direct the company's product development strategy, their first ever Vision meeting included 19 cross-functional team members, the vice-president of Engineering, and the vice-president of Marketing. When the group encountered difficulties in agreeing on the market for the proposed product, the entire team was treated to an in-depth conversation between the two vice-presidents trying to resolve their conflicting ideas for the product. This exchange resulted in an increased respect for the complexity of the problems faced by the company and an improved attitude of the team to working through the definition problems—rather than laying blame and giving up.

This last anecdote points to an important fact about vision meetings: People initially react with horror at the thought of 20 people in a room creating a "product requirements" document. However, these meetings never fail to focus the definition on the customer first; bring critical product definition to light; and provide the chance for those outside Engineering and Marketing to make a significant contribution. In every instance the team leaves with a deeper, more unified understanding of the product to be developed.

4. Use an iterative method of scoping to efficiently home in on the final Vision.

The early Vision brainstorming meeting results in many flipcharts of Vision elements,

© 1998 Global Brain, Inc.

ideas, and issues. Subsequently team members must resolve the issues, such as whether certain features are needed, what the most important items for customer quality are, etc. The team also refines its architectural definition: what are the possible system (high-level) designs that might satisfy the Vision? What are the associated product costs and project duration? These affect items in the Vision as well, especially the Financials section. When design alternatives have been identified, the corresponding resource needs and schedule durations roughly scoped, and issues with meeting certain Vision items understood, the team is ready for a Preliminary Design Review (PDR). At the PDR these issues are discussed, trade-off decisions made, or further investigation identified. Then the team is ready for another (shorter!) vision meeting, where they adjust the vision based on the results of the PDR and agree again upon remaining open issues.

Over time the issues list gets smaller and smaller, and the Vision increasingly well-defined and complete. What started out as many flip chart papers is eventually reduced to a one or two page Vision of the product.

5. Involve the entire team in cost-benefit analysis and trade-off decisions.

During the iterative scoping process, the entire team must be aware of the possible trade-offs for reaching an appropriate PTCC balance, and personally involved in detailed discussions wherever their functions are critically involved. Trade-off decisions are not made in a vacuum by Marketing!

As stated before, the goal of the negotiation process is an optimal balance that everyone can "live with"—as opposed to "be wildly happy about". Pet technology of the lead engineer may be dropped from this increment of the product. A favorite feature of Marketing may be scheduled for the next release. Field Service may choose to live with a "rougher" user interface to get the product sooner. These critical decisions cannot be made without team analysis of their real impacts to the product, and certainly will not be bought off on and supported throughout the project without total team awareness of their origins. Woe to the project leader or marketing manager who attempts to do otherwise!

In the end, a well-run Vision process results in a *team* recommendation on the best way for the company to proceed.

6. Have the whole team and top management sign off the Vision (then celebrate!).

Some product development processes call for legions of signatures on product deliverables that indicate a "checking up" spirit. In contrast, the Vision process uses a signature process in a positive spirit. It calls for formal signing of the Vision document at the end of Phase I to dramatize the "total company commitment" that rapid product development requires. The *entire team* signs the Vision. Company executives sign it as well.

When the team signs the Vision, they also sign the accompanying agreed-upon list of milestones for the rest of the project. These milestones are a vital part of the PTCC balance the team has negotiated. The Vision reflects P, C, and C. The milestone list provides T, the schedule time agreed upon. They are committed to and signed off together.

True to the positive nature of the process, this point marks an important celebratory point for the project. Every team member knows they are developing something the customers want and truly need, they know exactly what it is, and they're committed to achieving it in a way that will provide economic benefit to their company.

7. Read the Vision regularly and avoid changing it.

And then the rest of the project begins....and in a typical project environment, along come those temptations to fiddle with our product definitions, to get distracted from the key customer goals.

The team must leave Phase I not just with the Vision document itself, but with an understanding of the vision and the importance of adhering to it. The vision must

© 1998 Global Brain, Inc.

be kept highly visible. It is a vital management tool throughout the project. At every step the work completed during the project should be reviewed against the Vision: are you still providing what the customer needs?

A project leader at Shell Services Company, a division of Shell Oil, found his team's Vision to be a critical communications tool. This division had to become competitive with outside information technology providers; it used QRPD to deliver a sales force automation product to internal customers in 9 months instead of the usual 15 plus. The Vision was presented in every customer project review meeting to ensure continued understanding and buy-in, and was used as a primary tool for bringing new customer groups up to speed as they became involved in the project. [3]

Here is where the one or two page length of the Vision is key. We purposely keep it short so that we can easily consult it during the project, and better yet, easily remember it! At Hewlett-Packard, the developers of a new CAD software package wrote a great vision and kept it highly visible. Three years after the project, one of the team members was challenged to write their Vision from memory on an overhead for a UC Berkeley QRPD class. He did, word for word. This engineer had no problem understanding his goals during that project!

To achieve a memorable vision, avoid wordiness. Be terse and use bullets where appropriate. Before a team has gone through a vision process for the first time, they are skeptical that it can be kept to one or two pages. When that first Vision is finally in hand, they're amazed at the inverse relationship of its length and its power! When QRPD workshop participants analyze a number of Visions, they always comment that certain examples are too wordy and thus are harder to understand and remember.

7 Most Typical Sins in the Vision Process

Several abuses of the Vision process are typical as teams, managers, and executives work to break old ways of thinking and operating.

1. The Project Leader writes the vision and passes it out.

There is no surer way to negate the buy-in value of the Vision process than to have the project leader "dictate" the product vision. A Vision generated by one person may be a Vision truly believed in and supported by that one person alone!

This sin can also result in an off-target vision. In a perfect world, team members might give feedback and force the vision to change if they believed the project leader had it wrong. However, the world is not perfect, and a wrong vision dictated by the project leader might stay wrong, simply because the team took this process to mean the project leader had the authority to set the vision regardless of their inputs.

2. The whole cross-functional team is not involved.

It is typical for Manufacturing and Field Service to either resist or neglect participation during Phase I of a project. They say they don't have the time... Since these groups are often shared across many projects within a company, and are often not accustomed to being included early on, the hurdles are understandable. However, especially for section 4, crucial product factors, these groups *must* be involved in the Vision process. Visions developed without these inputs result in products that are hard to manufacture, can't be UL approved, are too hard to use by the target customer....the list goes on and on. The inputs of these groups must actually *drive* key elements of the product definition from the beginning.

© 1998 Global Brain, Inc.

In one case a product met customer functional requirements, but not manufacturing's heat testing specifications. Who wasn't involved early in the project? And guess which product had significant, expensive yield problems off the manufacturing line, causing a 3-month delay for re-design! Remember that 80% of the functionality and *cost* of the product is determined in the first 20% of the schedule.

3. The team focuses on features rather than benefits.

Because most traditional requirements specifications concentrate on feature definition, teams must make a profound shift in their thinking. Too often people throw every ounce of their creativity into defining whiz-bang features—but can't articulate what they will do for the customer. Understanding the customer benefits must come *before* the definition of features.

After Hewlett-Packard had successfully delivered an oscilloscope to the market, Marketing brought requests for subsequent enhancements for particular customers, expressed as features and performance: "We now need the sensitivity to be 0.1% instead of 1%." The first several such requests were dutifully honored by Engineering, until the day when Marketing came back with an impossible-to-achieve specification for device sensitivity. The engineers finally said, "Just what is it the customers want to do with this?" They discovered that their users were trying to measure digital signals—and what they *really needed* was a totally new product. Thus was borne the highly-successful HP family of logic analyzers.

4. The team confuses a specification or requirements document with the Vision.

One of the benefits of the vision process is that, properly executed, it eliminates those endless meetings where many highly-detailed specifications are reviewed line by line by large cross-functional teams. In those meetings teams typically argue over details that do not require cross-functional approval, details of the features or implementation that are not critical to whether the product truly delivers value to the customer, and details which often cannot be figured out before some phase II design work takes place. A medical device manufacturer's project post-mortem survey found that only 122 of the over 600 requirements line items were actually critical to the customer. Yet the entire team had spent precious time reviewing and negotiating all 600 of these items.

The vision process puts the full cross-functional reviews and negotiations first and foremost at the highest level of defining the product. Discussions are carried out efficiently to define "what" must be developed, with everyone's eyes fixed on the needs of the customer. The Vision forms a contract among the cross-functional team members that allows the functional groups to then embark upon their individual efforts to work out the details.

5. The Vision lacks adequate definition of or attention to "Crucial Product Factors."

The "Crucial product factors" in the Vision are often omitted or underspecified, or are listed but ignored during the project. Vague or imprecise "motherhood" statements are sometimes included, but the specific implications for the product implementation are not really understood.

For instance, a communications product needed UL approval, and the appropriate specification was dutifully listed in section 4 of the Vision. However, this item was treated as a "no-brainer," a "just like last time" that needed no further specific definition, although the company had not previously received UL approval on this exact type of product. It was not until later in the project, when initial UL review of a prototype was sought, that the team discovered their design was inherently "unapprovable." It included a battery, which invoked new areas of the UL spec, and it would have to be reworked to pass UL tests. Essentially this item of the Vision proved to be useless, because its meaning was not thought through and translated into criteria for ongoing detailed review of the implementation. This illustrates the importance of "concrete, well-defined" statements in the vision, and the importance of maintained alignment to each element of the

© 1998 Global Brain, Inc.

vision, through appropriate more detailed specifications and reviews during the project.

In another example, a company listed "new distribution channel must be developed" as a critical factor for their new product. As the project progressed, the project leader became frustrated because this element was not supported by the same executives who added it to the list. In the end the product itself worked, but the company could not sell it since the channels were never developed. The technology was sold to a competitor.

On the positive side, a software project used section 4 to great advantage. The team was tasked with development of a database management system to be operated by relatively unskilled computer users. Early project work had been plagued by disagreements on what constituted a "good", "usable" graphical user interface. Many screen designs had changed many times. Later on, when a particular feature had been developed and coded, Marketing requested yet another change. The developers (and the project leader) pushed back, not wanting to jeopardize the schedule for this change. The arguments continued until the Product Manager pulled out the Vision line that talked about the skill level of the target user, then described the sequence of menus, buttons, and keyboard entries this user would have to complete to use this supposedly straightforward feature. "Are we really delivering the intended value to the customer with the current design?" Case closed. The team took a few extra days to make sure the target customer would truly be able to use this feature in a reasonable manner.

6. Vision sessions are managed poorly.

Even with the best of intentions and good data, the vision process can still falter due to poor meeting management techniques. Especially in the earliest brainstorming phases of vision creation, many people with diverse backgrounds and perspectives are in a room together making their opinions known for the first time. Agreement on the Vision elements may not come immediately or easily.

Vision sessions must be facilitated by a strong, objective leader, usually the project leader. (However, if he has strong opinions to assert in the vision meeting due to his technical or market knowledge, he might appoint someone else to fill the facilitator role.) Discussions and digressions must be managed. The leader must be able to decide which items need in-depth discussion right then and which should be put on an issues list to be handled off-line. People must feel heard and respected even if their ideas do not end up in the Vision. Tense situations must be diffused. The creative process of obtaining the "right" product definition and team alignment and buy-in must not self-destruct due to poor meeting management!

This often calls for companies to determine the best meeting process for their particular cultures and teams. A fast-growing, entrepreneurial communication systems company, with many outspoken, highly-opinionated technical contributors, modified their Vision process to achieve group synergy without chaos. In any meeting discussing features or technical aspects, the engineers naturally gravitated toward detailed discussions of implementation, tended to nit-pick vision statement wording, and had difficulty making SSSS trade-offs. To counter this, the leader used a more controlled format for vision meetings. The team stepped through their draft vision line by line. For each line item, the group took a "vote" to either accept the item or place it on a list of issues to be resolved. In the course of this review the team spent no more than 2 minutes discussing any disagreed-upon item, leaving the more involved discussions for off-line meetings of smaller groups of people. The vision meeting thus resulted in a list of issues and possible alternatives to be investigated off-line before the next session. The team received all the benefits of hearing each other's opinions, questions, and concerns with the Vision in a highly efficient and productive session.

7. The Vision is changed capriciously (rather than consciously) during the project.

Product definition changes are often made as knee-jerk reactions to external circumstances or new knowledge. In contrast, well-created, well-written Product Visions generally change

© 1998 Global Brain, Inc.

only once or twice during the course of a 6 to 18 month project. This is wonderful for team members: they can't develop products rapidly when the target keeps moving!

A communications company was nearing the end of alpha testing of a new device. In a team meeting, an engineer proposed a number of changes that would make the performance of the device even better, but would delay the project several months. Before the group could get carried away with those "perfect product" thoughts, another team member invoked the Vision process, and the team gave itself action items to analyze the costs of this delay vs. the benefits of the changes. Ultimately the changes were *not* made and the product was completed as planned.

That being said, sometimes we may not be able to avoid changes to our Vision. Despite attention to incremental innovation, some projects may be long enough (due to technology or staffing issues) that market changes will occur. Or we may discover something about our ability to implement certain technologies or features in the desired timeframe or at the desired cost, that cause us to re-evaluate our overall product definition. However, all the difference is made by how we approach the changing of our Vision. If we make changes consciously, being sure that we are adjusting the PTCC balance for valid reasons, we are not subjecting our project to uncontrolled requirements whimsy.

A medical device manufacturer decided mid-stream to change the target market for their initial product release from the U.S., Italy and Spain to the U.S., Germany, and France. Before making the decision, the team analyzed the new requirements and their designs to understand the impact to the schedule. The team was able to make a sound decision and shift the Vision without impacting the schedule, because they knew that their design would support the desired change. They made a conscious, informed decision to allow the change.

Conclusion

The Product Vision process provides a powerful tool for rapid, high-profit development of quality products. It guides a team through the daunting maze of product definition and design decisions in our world of evolving technology and chaotic, competitive markets. It enables us to harness the energy, drive, and creativity of large numbers of diverse individuals, to accomplish aggressive, important goals, and ultimately to delight our customers.

With a proper Vision, you can have the kind of success Niles Audio achieved. After delivering a product in 7 months—less than half the time they had previously spent on this type of project—and "wowing" their customers, they are currently running 50% ahead of forecasted sales. They also won best technical product of 1996 at the audio industry's CEDIA show. Niles even discovered that they didn't need a follow-on project for another incremental innovation: Their vision process had helped them understand the market and the most important customer benefits, and their first incremental innovation was enough. They have moved those precious resources onto other new products, to begin the Vision process anew.

Invest the time and money to arrive at a powerful Product Vision in the first 25% of your schedule, and you too can develop products in half the time!

References

[1] Kopelman, Orion, and Voegtli, Cinda with Josephs, Adam: *Projects at Warp Speed with QRPD: The Definitive Guidebook to Quality Rapid Product Development*, 8th Edition, Global Brain, Inc., Palo Alto, CA, 1998.

[2] Patterson, Marv, *Accelerating Innovation: Improving the Process of Product Development*, Van Nostrand Reinhold, New York, NY 1993, pp. 114-117.

[3] Hockenberry, Jon, "QRPD: A New Way to Deliver Software Applications," *ProjectWorld Summer '96 Proceedings, Volume 2*, Center for Management Research, Wellesley, MA, 1996.

Evolving the Phase I SSSS Deliverables

As the SSSS process homes in on the Vision and PTCC balance for the project, the phase I deliverables are created and refined iteratively as decisions are made. Even as the team nears agreement on the Vision, there is still lots of work to be done before phase I can be officially completed and signed-off. Teams may spend up to one third of phase I refining and finishing their phase I documents. This work will allow them to leave phase I with a detailed, accurate, committed schedule for the rest of the project, as well as other critical planning deliverables and management tools. The team must:

- **Identify other team members:** Select remaining team members so that the entire cross-functional team is in place before starting phase II, and participates in as much of the phase I investigation work as possible. Remember the trapezoidal resource profile under Commandment #2.

- **Complete detailed schedules:** Complete the detailed scheduling of the project, assign all schedule tasks to specific resources, and make sure all dependencies are identified.

- **Finish the Milestones List:** Finish identifying milestones for tracking progress.

- **Update other planning deliverables:** Complete other documentation that will help manage the rest of project, such as the Critical Issues and Dependencies List, Tools and Equipment List, etc.

"*SMART*" Scheduling

"What gets measured gets done!"
— *Bill Hewlett*

S -   Specific
M -   Measurable
A -   Achievable
R -   Risk Assessed
T -   Time table

The "SMART" scheduling acronym came from a former University of California Berkeley Extension QRPD student, Dario Sanchez. Thank you.

© 1998 Global Brain, Inc.

Scheduling Process and Tips

The schedule process occurs throughout phase I. Follow these steps to get a full project plan including tools you can use to management the project. See also the techniques under Commandment #9.

1. **Create the project schedule, team selection, and resource assignments.**
   - Use an iterative process during development of the Product Vision and design alternatives.
   - For high-risk projects, iterative development may be used; early estimates will be less exact.
   - Create SMART schedules (see previous page).
   - Use project management software as a planning tool, but not to replace reason. Don't get bogged down using the tool in an ineffective manner.
   - Break the work down logically: technical areas, tasks, deliverables. Identify the physical deliverables each person has to create rather than stopping at the more abstract task level, in order to get more concrete and accurate work estimates.
   - Write preliminary plans if necessary to help scope the later cross-functional efforts: documentation, manufacturing, testing.
   - Ensure breakdown of design far enough for accurate scoping—have you really identified all the work that needs to be done?
   - Have team members commit to their tasks' durations, broken down to manageable chunks.
   - Have whole team review schedule dependencies for missing links, tasks.
   - Update the team roles list and responsibility matrix.

2. **Check estimates and schedule dependencies.**
   - Project Leader should gauge—sanity check—team members' time estimates.
   - Take into account other commitments, sustaining, holidays and vacations.
   - Be sure you've built in time for design reviews and all necessary testing.
   - Learn from the past (for instance, number of design cycles required), develop simple metrics.
   - Use rules of thumb to sanity check estimates. For instance, refer to the typical QRPD project timeline for rough length of project phases; or factor in two or three design iterations for major innovations.
   - Use industry-standard estimating techniques; use more than one to sanity check your estimates.
   - Estimate best and worst case schedules to get a feel for possible variations.
   - Do both top down and bottom up estimates and sanity check them against each other.
   - Ask multiple experts to estimate the work and compare the estimates.

3. **Assess risks, decide back-up plans, factor into schedule.**

4. **Look for ways to shorten the critical path.**

5. **Update the Milestone list.**

6. **Update the New Product Introduction Checklist.** (See page 340.)

7. **Make sure you've planned to follow as many QRPD techniques as possible.**

Note: Some of the above tips came from a talk by Joseph Berger to the IEEE Engineering Management Society on March 30, 1994.

© 1998 Global Brain, Inc.

Guidelines for Milestones List

- **Frequent:** Milestones should be no further than 3 weeks apart; make them more frequent for short projects.

- **Capture changes:** Use your milestone chart to capture changes in the plan as well as actual finish dates. See the format below.

- **Include cross-functional milestones:** Make sure cross-functional groups have milestones shown in the list, not just Development.

- **Highlight dependencies:** Show critical dependencies from other projects as milestones to heighten visibility.

- **Checklists of deliverables:** Create checklists to define the deliverables that must be done for each milestone to be complete.

Sharp Milestones

"Sharp milestones are in fact a service to the team, and one they can properly expect from a manager. The fuzzy milestone is the harder burden to live with. It is in fact a millstone that grinds down morale, for it deceives one about lost time until it is irremediable. And chronic schedule slippage is a morale-killer."

Frederic Brooks, *The Mythical Man-Month*

Sample Milestone Chart

Milestone	Plan	Current	Variation	Actual	Notes
Funding received	11/24/94	11/24/94	0wd	11/24/94	
Vision off-site Meeting.	01/01/95	01/03/95	2wd	01/03/95	
Software PDR	01/22/95	01/22/95	0wd	01/22/95	
Phase I exit	02/15/95	02/10/95	-3wd	02/10/95	
Innovation 1 CT Passed	03/22/95	03/29/95	5wd		Vendor late
DDR	04/10/95	04/10/95			
Pre-release controller board	05/01/95	05/01/95			
Start system integration	05/10/95	05/10/95			
System CT passed	06/02/95	06/02/95			
FDR	06/25/95	06/25/95			
Release sheet metal	07/10/95	07/10/95			
Alpha Starts	08/07/95	08/07/95			
Beta Starts	09/01/95	09/01/95			
Release to pilot	09/03/05	09/03/95			
Pilot done	09/30/95	09/30/95			
Final Release	10/31/95	10/31/95			

© 1998 Global Brain, Inc.

List of Tools and Equipment

This list provides a simple mechanism for formulating and documenting the equipment that will be needed during the project. It should not only list those items, it should capture the indicated information about need dates and responsibilities to ensure that the equipment is available on schedule.

Equipment or Tool	Date Needed	Owner	Comments

© 1998 Global Brain, Inc.

Flow Step 5. New Project Kickoff Announcement to Exit Phase I

To officially exit phase I, do the following:

- **Checklist:** Use the Phase I deliverables checklist below to ensure that you have completed all work and documentation necessary for a thorough phase I, including the NPI checklist.

- **New Project Kick-off Announcement:** Attach the Vision, milestones, and deliverables checklist to the New Project Kick-off Announcement, and get it signed to indicate company approval for the project to proceed.

- **Celebration:** Celebrate the completion of phase I!

Checklist of 19 Deliverables To Exit Phase I

Key PTCC deliverables
1. Product Vision (P)
2. Project Milestones List and checklists of deliverables for each (T)
3. Project Budget (C)
4. Cost Breakdown for product (C)

5. ROI Justification Document (including LCPW metric)
6. 5 Year Road Map Document

Design and Risk Assessment:
7. High-level design documents
8. PDR (Preliminary Design Review) meeting minutes including PTCC trade-off tables
9. List of Product Innovations (categorized by risk and justified)
10. Chicken Test Definition Document

Planning:
11. Preliminary Test Plan
12. Project Schedule with Resources
13. Team Roles List and Team Responsibility Matrix
14. Meeting Guidelines and Schedule Document
15. Action Item Matrix
16. Key Decisions List
17. Critical Issues and Dependencies List
18. Tools and Equipment List
19. New Product Introduction Checklist

© 1998 Global Brain, Inc.

New Product Introduction Checklist

Fill out the NPI checklist in phase I to make sure you've planned ahead—have you identified and planned for everything that must be in place before the project is complete? Customize the form below for your type of product. Then use it throughout the project to be sure each item is being addressed.

PROJECT: _____ **STATUS DATE:** _____

QUANTITY: _____ **PRE-PRODUCTION BUILD DATE:** _____

PRODUCTION RELEASE DATE: _____

X	**ITEM**	**STATUS**
__	**ENGINEERING RELEASE**	_____
	___ User Software	_____
	___ Firmware	_____
	___ Hardware Design	_____
	___ Mechanical Design	_____
__	**DESIGN VERIFICATION (ALPHA) TESTING**	_____
__	**BETA SITE TESTING**	_____
__	**REGULATORY APPROVALS**	
	___ FCC/FDA	_____
	___ UL	_____
	___ CSA	_____
	___ ESC/ISO	_____
	___ Other	_____
__	**DOCUMENTATION RELEASES**	
	___ Manuals	_____
	___ Structures Defined (?)	_____
	___ Media Database (?)	_____
	___ Assembly BOMS	_____
	___ Assembly Drawings	_____
	___ PCB BOMS	_____
	___ PCB Drawings	_____
	___ Schematics/Wiring	_____
	___ Spec. Sheets	_____
__	**TEST ENGINEERING RELEASE**	
	___ Test Software	_____
	___ Firmware	_____
	___ Hardware	_____
	___ Burn-In	_____
	___ Equipment Purchases	_____
	___ Test Procedures	_____
	___ Quality Control Tests	_____
	___ Customer Service Tests	_____

© 1998 Global Brain, Inc.

New Product Introduction Checklist (cont.)

X	ITEM	STATUS
__	**MATERIAL ISSUES**	
	_____ Vendor Selections	_____
	_____ Long Lead Items	_____
	_____ Multiple Sources	_____
__	**MANUFACTURING ISSUES**	
	_____ Process Flow Chart	_____
	_____ Forecast/Capacity Plan	_____
	_____ Floor Layout	_____
	_____ Workstation Layout	_____
	_____ Anti-Static Protection	_____
	_____ Material Handling	_____
	_____ Jigs/Fixtures	_____
	_____ Small Tools	_____
	_____ Capital Equipment	_____
	_____ Assembly Procedures	_____
	_____ Spare Parts Definition	_____
	_____ Operator Training	_____
	_____ Supervisor Training	_____
	_____ Customer Support Training	_____
__	**PACKAGING DESIGN**	_____
__	**PACKAGING TESTS**	_____
__	**COST ISSUES**	
	_____ Material Standard	_____
	_____ Labor Standard	_____
	_____ Material Cost Reductions	_____
	_____ Labor Cost Reductions	_____
__	**SALES/MARKETING ISSUES**	
	_____ Selling Configuration/ Price Literature	_____
	_____ Brochure	_____
	_____ Export Licenses	_____
	_____ Press Release (?)	_____
	_____ Customer Mailing (Is product new, upgrade or update?)	

© 1998 Global Brain, Inc.

Company Internal
New Project Kickoff Announcement Form

ORIGINATOR:_____ DATE:_____

PROPOSED NAME OF PRODUCT:_____

1. BRIEF DESCRIPTION:

A)   Marketing, including targeted price.

B)   Technical (modules, etc.) and approximate materials cost.

2. IF THIS IS A MODIFICATION OR ADD-ON TO EXISTING PRODUCTS, HOW IS IT DIFFERENT?

3. DATES:
   - A) Scheduled Engineering Release: _____
   - B) Scheduled shipments: _____
   - C) Other department involvement: _____
     - a. Materials/Purchasing, starting: _____
     - b. Manufacturing Engineering, starting: _____
     - c. Production starting: _____
     - d. Sales/Marketing, starting: _____

4. OTHER NOTES:

APPROVALS:

PROJECT LEADER:_____ DATE:_____

(Add other appropriate cross-functional executive and manager approvals here)

© 1998 Global Brain, Inc.

Objectives for Phase II: Development

Phase II is where the heart of the detailed development is performed, including detailed design, prototyping, integration, and other development testing. The Flow steps in phase II focus on the important reviews necessary to build in quality as we go, and ensure the project is still on track.

The cross-functional team will also prepare in the background for the phase III, Approval, by writing alpha and beta test plans, preparing equipment and facilities for testing, creating draft user documentation, etc. The table below shows phase II Flow steps and their key deliverables. The diagram on the following page shows the relationship of phase II activities.

Phase II Flow Steps and Deliverables

Flow Step	Deliverables
6. Detailed Design Reviews, Critical Design Reviews	**Detailed Design Review minutes** **Critical Design Review minutes, including chicken test results:** After innovations testing, review the results and ensure that risks have been mitigated. **CDR sign-off form:** Formal indication that the system chicken test has passed, technical risks have been mitigated, and the project can proceed to completion. *Related deliverables:* • Chicken test definition document from phase I • Specification documents • Design documents
7. Final Design Review	**Final Design Review minutes:** Confirm that the design and implementation are ready for the approval testing stage. *Related deliverables:* • Final specification and design documents • Test plans and test results • Defect tracking database • Plans for testing work, manufacturing work, etc. in next phase
8. Development Pre-releases	**Change control paperwork including applicable signatures:** Release the design to other groups outside Development. *Related deliverables:* • Design and build documentation • Prototype test results

© 1998 Global Brain, Inc.

Phase II Activities

The diagram below shows how the aspects of Q*R*PD that ensure quality—testing, reviews, and releases—occur concurrent with technical development and other cross-functional work during phase II. The team can cycle through this work iteratively as necessary.

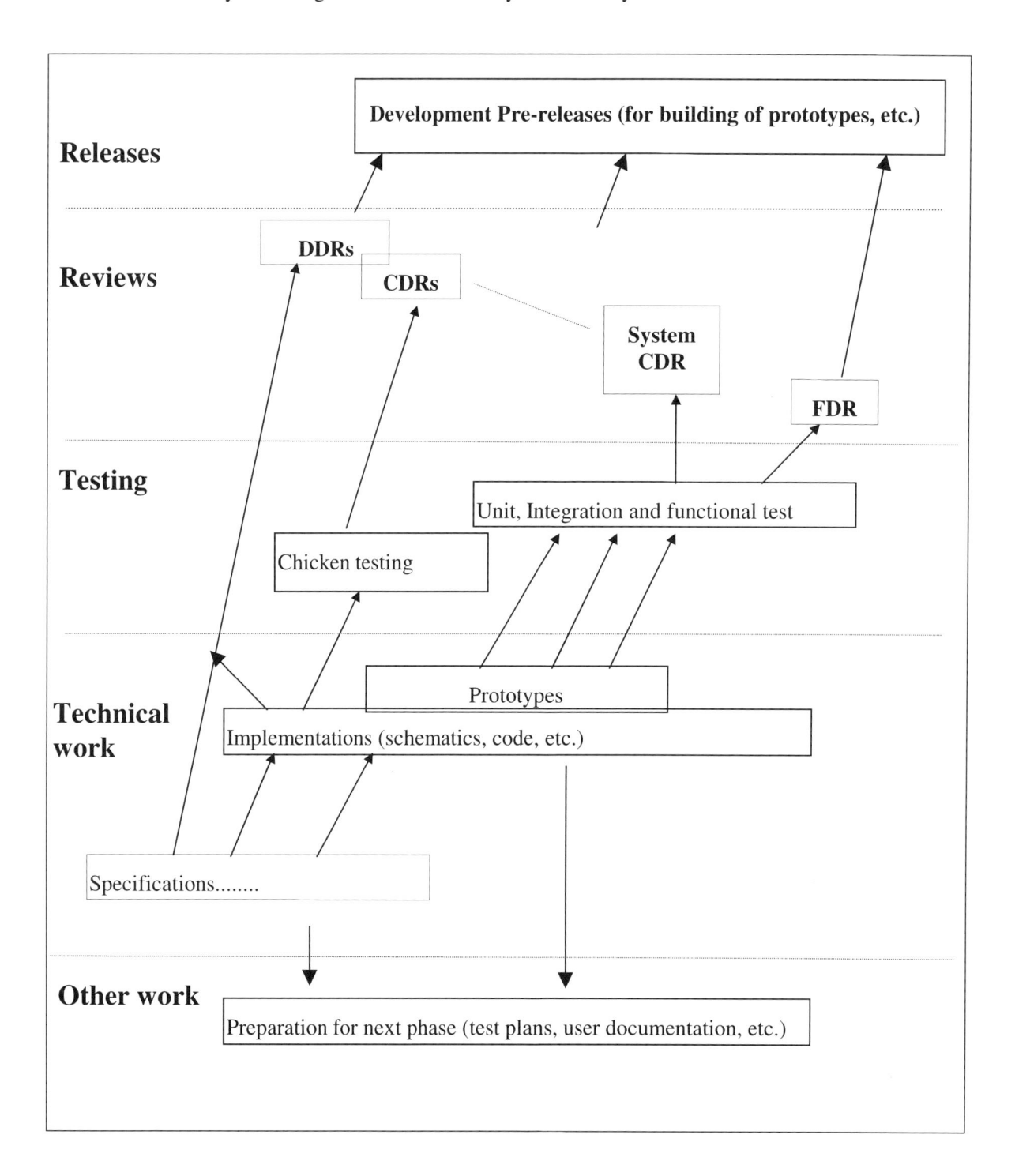

Releases

Development Pre-releases (for building of prototypes, etc.)

Reviews

DDRs
CDRs
System CDR
FDR

Testing

Chicken testing
Unit, Integration and functional test

Technical work

Prototypes
Implementations (schematics, code, etc.)
Specifications........

Other work

Preparation for next phase (test plans, user documentation, etc.)

© 1998 Global Brain, Inc.

QRPD Design Review Meetings

TYPE	WHEN	WHY
PDR PRELIMINARY DESIGN REVIEW(S)	**Phase I Flow step 4**. Enough high-level design work and investigations have been done that the Project Leader and team can suggest PTCC alternatives. Design should only have occurred at the subsystem and block diagram level at this point.	To reach a consensus of the best way to proceed with the overall system design; to consider the various alternatives, their corresponding PTCC balance, and how well they meet requirements such as manufacturability; to make trade-off decisions; and to identify potential project pitfalls. See PDR Checklist.
DDR DETAILED DESIGN REVIEW(S)	**Phase II Flow step 6.** After a preliminary specification has been written, and sufficient detailed design work and/or simulation have occurred.	To ensure that the design meets the Vision and other detailed requirements; to find flaws or suggest improvements in the design at a detail level before proceeding to a prototype. See DDR checklist.
CDR CRITICAL DESIGN REVIEW(S)	**Phase II Flow step 6.** A prototype exists that everyone can huddle around and constructively criticize. At this point a critical innovation has passed the "chicken test." The final CDR reviews the system chicken test results.	To convince everyone that a technical risk has been conquered. Or alternately, that it's "time to go back to the drawing board...." See CDR Checklist. This is a project decision point for management: OK to proceed?
FDR FINAL DESIGN REVIEW(S)	**Phase II Flow step 7.** The majority of the design work has been completed, and Development testing has occurred. One or more prototypes work well enough that pending minor design or implementation corrections, the product is ready for phase III Approval testing, and Development Release to Pilot (Flow step 10) should be able to occur soon.	To give everybody one last chance to review the design and implementation, to make sure it meets the Vision and requirements, and suggest minor changes. Then to discuss what's necessary to reach the Development Release stage. See FDR Checklist.

Note: the corresponding checklist for each design review calls out important items to discuss such as how well the design meets requirements for manufacturability, serviceability, etc.

© 1998 Global Brain, Inc.

Design Review Meetings

1. Must have them   (small price to pay)
2. Can be short (<1 hour)
3. Use checklists ✓
4. Invite the right people
5. Reconvene if missing information

Who Should Attend Design Reviews

- Project Leader (who calls the meetings)
- Core project design team
- Product Engineer (represents all other disciplines)
- Project Leader's boss (or other Executive Management)
- Product Champion
- One respected developer or engineer not involved with the project
- Representatives from other departments

Note: Design reviews can be "segmented" into detailed technical reviews for developers, versus higher–level reviews of the design concept for cross-functional team members. See the suggestions on the following page.

Key Factors for Successful Design Reviews

- **Realize that you must have them.** They are an investment; a small price to pay considering the problems you'll find and nasty surprises you'll avoid later.

- **Have them early enough to change approaches.** Once implementation of a design is well underway, people are reluctant to change the design, even if the basic approach is a bad one. Encourage reviews of draft specifications and designs to catch mistakes before a design is set in concrete.

- **They can be short, sometimes less than an hour.** Pieces of designs can be reviewed. Conversation can be limited to a small set of technical issues. Don't get trapped in the mindset of monolithic review meetings.

- **They can be informal.** The goal is to find mistakes, not to impress management with a slide show. Concentrate on the work!

- **Use checklists.** Don't miss the chance to avoid a mistake someone has made in the past. Use standard and customized checklists to make sure you consider everything in the review.

- **Do reviews iteratively**. The above reviews are seldom held just once.

  - You can break a product down into various parts and review them separately (although you must be sure to do a "system-level" review, too, to make sure the pieces will play together).

  - For review of a given part of a design, often a team will need a second or third get-together if more information or time is required. These additional meetings are generally briefer than the first.

  - You can separate your audience into appropriate subgroups. For instance, Development might have a detailed design review of the electronics and software for a new design. Customer Support doesn't need to be in the review at that level. But they do need to review the design for serviceability, and they need to understand how the pieces will operate enough to help them troubleshoot field problems. You can schedule different DDR meetings to address the different levels of detail your audience needs.

- **Invite the right people.** Make sure all the necessary cross-functional team members will be in attendance, and prepared. See the figure above for a list of typical attendees.

- **Keep the meeting on track, and don't allow design by committee.** Poorly-run design reviews are the cause of many a missed defect. Don't let any design review degenerate into arguments over alternatives, or attempts to design a solution on the fly. Take down action items and work the issues off line.

- **Reconvene if missing information.** Don't be afraid to stop the meeting if you've gone as far as you can. If a developer needs to go look at an issue, or run a test in the lab, to answer a critical question from the review, end the meeting and schedule a follow-up session. Likewise, if you need inputs from an absent cross-functional team member, don't guess! End the meeting and reschedule it for when that person is available.

© 1998 Global Brain, Inc.

Flow Step 6. Detailed Design Review (DDR) Checklist

Detailed Design Reviews are held during Phase II, after a preliminary specification has been written, and sufficient detailed design work and/or simulation have occurred. The purpose it to find flaws or suggest improvements in the design at a detail level before proceeding to a prototype. These reviews will be held at the level of individual system or design modules, and at the product or system level as well, to ensure that the entire design concept "hangs together".

CHECKLIST ITEMS (customize with your own items and details)

0. Has everybody done their preparation work?

1. What areas of the design might be flawed?

2. How could certain parts of the design be improved?
    a) What are the technical alternatives?
    b) What are the resource considerations? (people, equipment, etc.)
    c) How do different approaches affect the schedule?
    d) What are the performance trade-offs?
    e) What are the cost and manufacturability trade-offs?

3. What parts of the design may have proven problematic in previous projects?

4. How could risk be further minimized?

5. Are DFX (design for manufacturability, serviceability, reliability, etc.) guidelines being properly adhered to?

6. Are any of the designs potentially patentable? (if so, begin processing)

DDR FOLLOW-UP:

1. Publish meeting minutes. Should include a revised design document, list of the critical issues identified, and specific action items assigned.

2. Reconvene if more research is necessary to finalize the design approach and/or to follow up on assigned action items.

3. Generate/revise the project schedule.

4. Meet the schedule.

© 1998 Global Brain, Inc.

Flow Step 6. Critical Design Review (CDR) Checklist

This review is held when a prototype exists that everyone can huddle around and constructively criticize. At this point a critical innovation has passed the "chicken test." The final CDR reviews the system chicken test results. The purpose of the review is to convince everyone that a technical risk has been conquered. Or alternately, that it's "time to go back to the drawing board. This is a project decision point for management: is it OK to proceed according to the current design and plan?

CHECKLIST ITEMS (customize with your own items and details)

0. Has everybody done their preparation work?

1. Where do we stand regarding the innovative and risky parts of the design), and the other project risks on the Critical Issues and Dependencies List (Review list.) How much has been done?

2. Can a demonstration of proof be shown? (Do it!)

3. What tests have been performed on these parts? What were the results? Did we pass the "chicken tests"?

4. Do we feel confident that the project can proceed as planned? Why?

    a) If not, what do we need to do to get there? When will that be?

    b) Have we run into "show stoppers" that merit considering aborting the chosen design approaches, commencing other approaches, or even aborting the whole project?

5. Have new critical issues been identified? Discuss them, and add to the Critical Issues and Dependencies List. What will be done about them?

6. What does the progress to date indicate about how realistic the project schedule is? Change it?

CDR FOLLOW-UP:

1. Publish meeting minutes. Include action items assigned.

2. Reconvene if more research or tests are necessary to convince everyone that the risks have been shown to be acceptable for continuing as planned, and/or to follow up on the assigned action items.

3. If this is CDR for the system chicken test results, get the appropriate Development executive to sign off on this critical project decision point. See the next page.

4. Generate/revise the project schedule if necessary.

5. Meet the schedule.

© 1998 Global Brain, Inc.

CDR Signoff Form
(System Chicken Test Passed)

The system chicken test is a critical executive signoff point for the project. This form can be used to obtain the official "ok to proceed," once a Development executive has witnessed the system chicken test.

Project: _____

Date of System Chicken Test: _____

Description of System Chicken Test: _____
_____
_____
_____
_____
_____
_____

System Chicken Test Results Summary: _____
_____
_____

Approvals to Proceed:

Project Leader: _____ Date: _____

VP Development: _____ Date: _____

Product Champion: _____ Date: _____

© 1998 Global Brain, Inc.

Flow Step 7. Final Design Review (FDR) Checklist

This review is held when the majority of the design work has been completed, and Development testing has occurred. One or more prototypes work well enough that pending minor design or implementation corrections, the product is ready for phase III Approval testing, and Development Release to Pilot (Flow step 10) should be able to occur soon. The purpose of the FDR is to give everybody one last chance to review the design and implementation and suggest minor changes, then to discuss what's still left to do before Development Release to Pilot can eventually be accomplished.

CHECKLIST ITEMS (Customize by adding your own items and details)

1. What was done? (Huddle around prototype, demonstrate it.)
2. What features were compromised to save time?
3. Does the product meet the specification and performance requirements?
4. Does the product meet current marketing requirements if now new or different? If not:
    a) What changes need to be made?
    b) Do these impact the schedule, and if so, should they be done anyway?
5. Is the product manufacturable as is? If not:
    a) What changes need to be made?
    b) Do these impact the schedule, and if so, should they be done anyway?
6. Does anyone have suggestions for other minor changes?
7. What testing has been done? What problems were uncovered?
8. What are the remaining technical hurdles that would prevent timely development release?
9. Who will do Alpha, Beta, and Regulatory testing? When? Are the plans for this testing in place?
10. What remains to be done for Flow step 10, Development Release to Pilot?
    a) Documentation.
    b) Manuals.
    c) Testing.
    d) Test Engineering/Manufacturing procedures.

FDR FOLLOW-UP:

1. Publish minutes. Project Leader should include which changes have been accepted and declined, and which action items have been assigned.
2. Reconvene if more research is necessary to agree upon the design changes, and/or to follow up on the assigned action items.
3. Generate/revise the project schedule.
4. Meet the schedule.

© 1998 Global Brain, Inc.

Flow Step 8. Development Pre-Releases

Flow step 8 marks the first use of formal change control during the QRPD Flow process. "Release" refers to delineating that a particular version of the product is ready to be handed off to another group or groups. And once it is handed off, all changes must be handled carefully: to avoid dropped information and to avoid capricious changes late in the game that could derail or slow down the project.

- **When Development Pre-Release occurs:** After sufficient design and Development testing have been done to make it acceptable to take the risk and begin to spend money buying parts for later test and production builds. (In some companies, a development pre-release also occurs to enable other groups to help with the creation of prototypes for development.) The development pre-release may even pre-empt the Final Design Review. These pre-releases may occur several times, as designs become available.

- **Purpose of the Pre-Release:** To allow procurement of long lead-time items, start vendors or Manufacturing on tools, fixtures; or permit other interdisciplinary tasks to occur in parallel with the design effort. See the New Product Introduction (NPI) Checklist created earlier during the phase I planning process.

Typical Development Pre-Release Deliverables

- **Design and product documentation.** The primary deliverable at this release is the documentation for building the product, including any supporting design documentation.

- **Process documentation:** Plans and procedures for building and testing the product in Manufacturing, installing the product, supporting the product. This documentation would usually be only in draft form at this point.

- **Supporting documentation:** Drafts of such items as training programs and user manuals.

Change Control after Development Pre-Releases

- **Further changes:** Change control is handled relatively informally while the product is at a pre-release level. Informal records are kept and minimal signatures are required.

- **Typical hardware revision level and change control:** Development pre-release drawings are used during the design part of the new product development and are given to cross-functional groups to help with hardware builds, including the units that will be used for alpha and beta testing during phase III. History copies of changes are kept, but no formal change orders are written or distributed. Project Leader or designate signs all documents.

- **Typical software revision level and change control:** The software group maintains version control of all code through a configuration management system. Generally individual developers make changes to their code without oversight, but with the configuration tool keeping track of changes, until some point during integration testing.

© 1998 Global Brain, Inc.

Change Control and Development Releases

A number of later Flow steps implement "releases" of the product. This table provides an overview of each release, when it occurs, and its purpose.

TYPE	WHEN	WHY
DPR DEVELOPMENT PRE-RELEASE(s)	**Phase II, Flow step 8.** After sufficient design and testing has been done to make it acceptable to take the risk and begin to spend money buying components. This may even pre-empt the Final Design Review. These pre-releases may occur several times, as designs become available.	To allow procurement of long lead-time items, start vendors or Manufacturing on tools, fixtures; or permit other interdisciplinary tasks to occur in parallel with the design effort. See New Product Introduction (NPI) Checklist. It is paramount that the Project Leader sign-off ALL pre-releases. Depending on the circumstances, not all persons mentioned must attend the meetings.
DR DEVELOPMENT RELEASE For Pilot	**Flow step 10.** After sufficient Alpha and Beta testing has convinced the Project Leader and others that the specifications have been met and pilot production and delivery can commence.	To allow all other departments to play their roles in shipping pilot units as soon as possible after this hand-off of the complete design package. See New Product Introduction (NPI) Checklist. Can also serve as a celebration ritual for reaching this key milestone.
FR FINAL RELEASE to Production	**At Flow step 13.** After sufficient pilot production and approval testing have unearthed the majority of the remaining defects, the Project Leader and team have determined which are necessary; and the design team has implemented them.	To transfer responsibility to the production and delivery organizations, and allow unrestricted customer deliveries (for revenue) to begin.

© 1998 Global Brain, Inc.

Development Release (DR) Meetings

Meetings are used to effectively accomplish the various Development Releases:

- Ensures a responsible hand-off process
- Done in parallel with design to save time
- Makes continuous use of the New Product Introduction (NPI) checklist

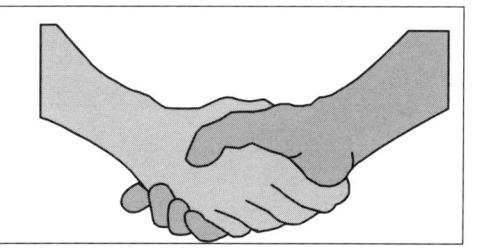

Who Should Attend Release Meetings

- Project Leader (calls the meetings)
- Product Engineer; Technical leads as appropriate
- Project Leader's boss (or other Executive Management)
- Product Champion
- Materials/purchasing representative
- Manufacturing Test Engineering representative
- Manufacturing representative
- Quality representative (including Software Quality Assurance)
- Finance representative
- Marketing/Sales representative
- Customer Support representative
- Director/V.P. of Operations

Key Factors for Successful Release Meetings

- **Realize that you need them.** These handoff meetings are the best way to ensure that a transfer to another group happens smoothly. Don't neglect them due to "lack of time."

- **Don't treat them as just a group signature session.** Plan to discuss changes, ensure everyone understands, and agree that you're ready for release. The "change board" procedures at many companies include a meeting where everyone comes together and signs all the change orders and documentation. Unfortunately, those signing the documents may not really provide any oversight of their quality or content; they just sign it. Your release meetings should be similar to design reviews: participants review the documents ahead of time are ready to discuss and resolve issues and approve the release.

- **Invite the right participants.** The purpose of holding meetings to accomplish these releases is to ensure a smooth and thorough hand-off between groups. Release meetings must include all the appropriate cross-functional team members for your industry.

© 1998 Global Brain, Inc.

Typical Revision Control Levels for Releases
(Hardware Product)

The following table provides an example of how "revision control" systems can be used to implement progressively tighter change control as a hardware-oriented project proceeds. The Flow release steps take the product from one of these revision levels to the next, indicating more stringent change control, requiring more approvals as you get farther along in the project.

Revision (example numbering)	Phase and Flow Step	Signatures Required for Changes
1 - 49	At this level during phase II, Development and phase III, Approval. Released to this level by Flow step 8, Development Pre-releases.	Project Leader
50 - 99	At this level during phase III, Approval and Phase IV, Delivery. Released to this level by Flow step 10, Development Release to Pilot.	Project Leader, Product Engineer, Quality or Operations
A - ZZ	At this level during phase IV, Delivery. Released to this level by Flow step 13, Release to Production/Delivery.	Company-wide per normal documentation control procedures.

REV.   **TYPICAL PROCEDURES:**

1 – 49   Engineering pre-release drawings are used during the design part of the new product development and are given to cross-functional groups to help with builds, including the units that will be used for alpha and beta testing during phase III. History copies of changes are kept, but no formal change orders are written or distributed. Project Leader or designate signs all documents. Note: As an exception, if more than a few hardware modules are needed for alpha or beta before the release to pilot, and/or a large number of functional groups are involved in building the alpha/beta units, formal change orders may be used. The purpose of a bit more formality would be to ensure that the changes are communicated properly.

50 - 99   After sufficient alpha/beta testing have occurred, the product is released to pilot level. During pilot builds, all documents are at Rev. 50 - 99. Engineering and manufacturing jointly red-line a documentation package to make changes. If other departments (e.g., Materials) are affected, formal change orders are written, and signed by the Project Leader and other team members such as a product engineer or a Quality person, and distributed to all affected parties.

A - ZZ   When the product is ready for customer delivery and full production, the documentation package is moved to Rev. A, and normal company-wide change order procedures take effect (usually requiring signatures from all departments).

© 1998 Global Brain, Inc.

Typical Revision Control Levels for Releases (Software)

The following table provides an example of how "revision control" systems can be used to implement progressively tighter change control as a software-oriented project proceeds. The Flow release steps take the product from one revision level to the next, indicating more stringent change control, requiring more approvals as you get farther along in the project.

Revision	Phase and Flow Step	Signatures Required for Changes
Dev	At this level during Phase II Development. Released to this level by Flow step 8, Development Pre-releases.	None until software enters integration testing. Thereafter, Project Leader or integration manager.
Alpha-Beta through Pilot	At this level during Phase III, Approval and Phase IV Delivery. First released to this level during phase II by Flow step 8, Development Pre-release. Then during phase III, Flow step 10, Development release to Pilot occurs.	Once alpha and beta testing start, the Software Quality Assurance manager and Project Leader approve changes.
Master	At this level during phase IV, Delivery. Released to this level by Flow step 13, Release to Production/Delivery.	Company-wide per normal documentation control procedures.

REV.   **TYPICAL PROCEDURES:**

Dev. The software group maintains version control of all code through a configuration management system. Generally individual developers make changes to their code without oversight, but with the configuration tool keeping track of changes, until some point during integration testing.

Alpha/beta and pilot Once alpha and beta testing start, the software has been "promoted" to a new level of control. The configuration management tool still accomplishes the mechanics of controlling and documenting code changes. If developers need to fix "bugs", issues meetings are usually used to determine which bugs should be fixed and developers are allowed to correct only those bugs. The software version number is updated as new "builds" are made each day.

When the software is ready for Flow step 10, Development Release to Pilot, the same configuration management mechanisms are used, but changes are controlled even more tightly by the Project Leader. Limited releases, such as developer's kits or shipments to critical customers, may occur.

Master When the product is ready for unrestricted customer delivery, the software is released, master media turned over to Operations, and normal company-wide change order procedures control any changes to the media or database used to supply the "production-level" software to customers.

© 1998 Global Brain, Inc.

Objectives for Phase III: Approval

The objective of phase III is to perform independent (of the Development group) testing of the product to ensure that it is ready to go to customers.

During this time cross-functional groups will also prepare for delivery to customers: training, deployment, documentation, etc. Phase III includes several types of testing as shown on the following page, as well as a release for pilot builds and/or delivery.

Phase III Flow Steps and Deliverables

Flow Steps	Deliverables
9. Internal Testing (Alpha)	**Alpha Test results:** Have an internal, but independent group test the product, document the results, and review the results with Development. *Related documentation:* • Alpha test plan, usually created during phase II to ensure all test equipment and personnel are ready. • Updated problem tracking database: problems uncovered are usually tracked in a database to facilitate correction.
10. Development Release for Pilot	**Change control documentation and Release meeting minutes:** Release the product to other groups to allow them to prepare for a pilot build and/or deployment. *Related documentation:* • Updated design and product documentation
11. External testing (beta, regulatory)	**Beta and regulatory test results:** Let customers test the product in normal environments to make sure it works and meets their requirements. Perform any required formal agency certification. *Related documentation:* • Updated problem tracking database. • Updated product documentation.

© 1998 Global Brain, Inc.

Flow Step 9. Internal Testing (Alpha)

Alpha testing is performed to allow a group independent of the development team to test the product and uncover issues. These testers are still internal to the company, but they take a "customer perspective" when testing the product. They not only want to find defects, they want to make sure that the product meets its Vision. This testing gives the team critical feedback and a chance to correct issues and defects before letting a customer perform later beta tests. Here are several guidelines for successful alpha testing:

- **Good mix of tester skills:** Use testers at various levels of proficiency with the product to simulate your leading edge and typical customers.

- **Independent and pro-active:** Make sure the testers are truly independent of the design team and will pro-actively try to "break" the product.

- **Significant, thorough test plan and detailed specification of test cases:** Make sure the testing will cover all the functions and other specifications of the product. It must be a significant test of the product.

- **Measurable and verifiable**: Make sure everyone understands the success criteria and can measure and verify that the product meets its requirements, including its Vision.

- **Plan ahead:** Plan the tests ahead of time to ensure you have committed testers, a thorough test plan, the right equipment, etc. Many an alpha test has been less than thorough or efficient because the team did not plan far enough ahead to obtain adequate quantities of test equipment and product prototypes.

- **Identify other types of approval testing that may apply to your products:** Other types of common "external testing" include compatibility testing to ensure that your product meets particular interface standards; and formal acceptance testing by a particular customer.

- **Proven to top management**: Make sure Management agrees that the tests have passed, and don't just rely on the leader's verbal assurances. This is a critical time for "checks and balances".

© 1998 Global Brain, Inc.

Alpha Test Plan Contents

Typical contents of a thorough alpha test plan include:

- **Test objectives:** What is the scope of the testing?

- **Testers:** What groups and people will do the testing? Who else will be involved as support?

- **Responsible person:** Who will manage the testing process?

- **Equipment/facilities required:** Where will the tests take place? Will any external facilities be required? How many test beds will be needed? What other equipment will be needed?

- **Management strategy and mechanisms:** How will test results be reviewed, issues recorded, and decisions about correcting defects made? Weekly meetings? Track issues in database? Approve changes once a day in "bug" meetings?

- **Success criteria:** How will you know the testing is done? What are the criteria for being ready to transition to beta testing?

- **Test sequences and cases:** What specific test sequences and operations will be done? (Detailed cases may be put in a separate document.)

Alpha Test Results Reviews

- **When to hold the reviews:** When internal testing has started and results are available. Often accomplished by weekly "issues" meetings during testing, with final review at end of testing.

- **Purpose:** Review test results and errors found so far. Ensure that the product is still meeting its Vision and detailed requirements. Determine what problems need to be corrected and prioritize them for the developers.

Change Control during Alpha Testing

- **Typical hardware revision level and control**: 1-49. Hardware used for alpha testing will usually have been built at a Development Pre-release level (1-49 in the example QRPD scheme). If changes are made during alpha testing before Flow Step 10 Release to Pilot, change control mechanisms will be somewhat informal. History copies of changes will be kept, but formal change orders might not be written or distributed. The Project Leader or designate will sign all documents.

- **Typical software revision level and control:** Alpha-level. For alpha testing, the software has been "promoted" to a new level of control via a Development Pre-release. A configuration management tool accomplishes the mechanics of controlling and documenting code changes. If developers need to fix "bugs", issues meetings are usually used to determine which ones should be fixed and developers are allowed to make only those bugs. The software version number is updated as new builds are made each day or week.

© 1998 Global Brain, Inc.

Flow Step 10. Development Release to Pilot

- **Held when:** After sufficient Alpha, Beta, and/or regulatory testing have convinced the Project Leader and others that the specifications have been met and pilot production and delivery can commence.

- **Purpose:** To allow all other departments to play their roles in shipping pilot units as soon as possible after this hand-off of the complete design package. See the New Product Introduction (NPI) Checklist. Can also serve as a celebration ritual for reaching this key milestone.

Typical Deliverables at Release to Pilot

- **Design and product documentation.** The documentation for building the product, including any supporting design documentation.

- **Process documentation:** Plans and procedures for building and testing the product in Manufacturing, installing the product, supporting the product. This documentation should now be nearing its final state. It will get tested out during the pilot build and delivery.

- **Supporting documentation:** Near-completed items such as training programs and user manuals.

Change Control after Release to Pilot

- **Further changes:** After this point, any changes will be handled using formal control procedures, but with limited signatures required.

- **Typical hardware revision level and control:** During pilot builds, all documents are at Rev. 50 - 99. Engineering and manufacturing jointly red-line a documentation package to make changes. If other departments (e.g., Materials) are affected, formal change orders are written, and signed by the Project Leader and other team members such as a product engineer or a Quality person, and distributed to all affected parties.

- **Typical software revision level and control:** After release to pilot, the configuration management tool accomplishes the mechanics of controlling and documenting code changes as before, but changes are controlled even more tightly by the Project Leader and Software Quality Assurance manager. If developers need to fix "bugs", issues meetings are usually used to determine which bugs should be fixed and developers are allowed to correct only those bugs. The software version number is updated as new "builds" are made each day or week.

© 1998 Global Brain, Inc.

Flow Step 11. External Testing (Beta, Regulatory)

Beta testing is performed to allow customers to use the product in a normal operational environment prior to its release. This testing helps uncover remaining issues, especially since many real-world conditions cannot be simulated in the testing lab. Regulatory testing refers to mandatory certification that agencies such as the FCC, FDA, and Underwriters Laboratory must perform to gauge product emissions and safety. Here are several guidelines for successful beta and regulatory testing:

- **Good customer mix.** Use both leading edge and typical customers for beta testing.

- **Full communication.** Get the straight story from the customer or testing agency, not just from a sales person or agency liason.

- **Be pro-active.** Ask lots of questions to make sure you understand how the product is being used and tested and what the real issues are.

- **Plan ahead.** Plan the tests ahead of time to ensure you have committed testers, a thorough test plan, the right equipment, etc. Regulatory agencies often have very busy schedules, requiring you to schedule your test slot far in advance.

- **Get an early look at regulatory tests.** For regulatory testing, make sure you've taken "early looks" during earlier phases of the project. Waiting until phase III for a regulatory agency to get its first look at your product is a recipe for disaster!

- **Identify other types of approval testing that may apply to your products.** Other types of common "external testing" include compatibility testing to ensure that your product meets particular interface standards; and formal acceptance testing by a particular customer.

External Test Plan Contents

Typical contents of a thorough test plan include:

- **Test objectives:** What is the scope of the testing?
- **External testers:** What companies, groups, and people will do the testing? Who else will be involved as support?
- **Responsible person:** Who will manage the testing process? Who in the external organization will be responsible for their activities?
- **Equipment/facilities required:** Where will the tests take place? Will any external facilities be required? How many test beds will be needed? What other equipment will be needed?
- **Management strategy and mechanisms:** How will test results be reviewed, issues recorded, and decisions about correcting defects made? If the testing is happening at a customer, how will they record and report the issues they encounter? E.g., weekly review meetings? Track issues in database? Approve changes once a day in "bug" meetings?
- **Test sequences and cases:** Are there specific test sequences and cases to be performed? NOTE: When beta testing is done at a customer, you may not want to provide detailed cases—the object is to see how the customer will use it day-to-day.
- **Success criteria:** How will you know the testing is done? What are the criteria for being ready to transition to phase IV?

© 1998 Global Brain, Inc.

Beta and Regulatory Test Results Reviews

Test review meetings are highly recommended.

- **When to hold the reviews:** When external approval testing has started and results are available. Includes final beta, regulatory, compatibility, customer acceptance testing. These reviews are usually accomplished via weekly or daily "issues" meetings during testing. A final wrap-up review should be held at the end of testing.

- **Purpose:** Review test results including errors found. Ensure that the product is still meeting its Vision and specifications. Ensure customer is using it as expected. Determine what problems need to be corrected.

Change Control during External Testing

- **Typical hardware revision level and control**: 1-49. Hardware used for beta testing will usually have been built at a Development Pre-release level (1-49 in the example Q*R*PD scheme). After sufficient alpha/beta testing have occurred, the product will be released to pilot level for pilot builds. During pilot builds, all documents are at Rev. 50 - 99. Engineering and manufacturing jointly red-line a documentation package to make changes. If other departments (e.g., Materials) are affected, formal change orders are written, and signed by the Project Leader and other team members such as a product engineer or a Quality person, and distributed to all affected parties.

- **Typical software revision level and control:** Beta-level. For beta testing, the software has been "promoted" to a new level of control via a Development Pre-Release. The configuration management tool still accomplishes the mechanics of controlling and documenting code changes. If developers need to fix "bugs", issues meetings are usually used to determine which bugs should be fixed and developers are allowed to make only those bugs. The software version number is updated as new "builds" are made each day or week.

Objectives for Phase IV: Delivery

The objectives of the Delivery phase are to begin to build and deploy the product in volume. The team's responsibility is to ensure a smooth transition from Development to Operations and Support.

Many projects sail through the earlier phases only to flounder in this late "end-game". Attention to detail, and plunging through the product development funnel (see Commandment #9, technique Z) is key to wrapping up your project successfully. The team must still be involved in phase IV, and the Project Leader still fully "obsessed" with results.

Phase IV Flow Steps and Deliverables

Flow Step	Deliverables
12) Pilot production/delivery	**Larger build of units:** Accomplished according to normal production processes. **Review of results of pilot builds:** Make sure the pilot results indicate you're ready to ramp toward volume production and delivery. **Updated product and process documentation:** Incorporate any changes from pilot into the documentation. This includes not only the documentation to build the product, but also supporting production test plans and procedures, manuals, and training. **First Customer Ship approval form and New Product Introduction Checklist:** First customer shipments—restricted delivery to critical customers, for instance—often happens using pilot units. Review the NPI checklist to ensure that any work needed prior to customer shipment has been completed. Summarize the rationale for approving these first customer shipments, and have the team and executives sign off the FCS approval form.
13) Release to Full production/delivery	**New Product Introduction Checklist:** Before releasing for production and delivery, have the team make sure all necessary work has been done. **Official Release to Production/Delivery:** Make the final release of documentation and the product to production level. **Unrestricted delivery to customers:** Start standard shipments to customers, using normal production and delivery processes.

© 1998 Global Brain, Inc.

Flow Step 12. Pilot Builds/Deliveries

The purpose of this step is to produce and possibly deploy the product in limited quantities, to test out internal build and testing processes, installation and configuration procedures, etc.

- **Prepare:** Make sure all functional groups understand their responsibilities. Other planning, including quantities to build for pilot, should have occurred during phase II or III work, so that parts procurement and facilities setup could be done ahead of time. Make sure goals of the pilot build and testing are spelled out—at the end of pilot the team should be able to judge whether the product, and all of the related documentation and processes, are truly ready for release to production.

- **Build the product:** Execute the pilot builds. Build a large enough quantity to test the normal production processes and issues, including varying vendor parts, production testing procedures, etc.

- **Make limited deliveries:** For some products, the pilot may involve making limited deliveries to customers, primarily to test out all associated processes (including installation, configuration, and customer support) in more volume than Beta, in a real-world environment. Have the team fill out the First Customer Ship (FCS) Approval form shown on the next page. It is critical that everyone agree: is the product really ready to be shipped, even to just one customer? Can we support it properly? The entire team makes the call, and executives are asked to sign off on the decision as well. Use the New Product Introduction checklist to make sure everything needed prior to a customer shipment has been completed.

- **Review and evaluate the pilot results:** Verify that the draft processes for building and deploying the product are correct. Verify cost targets for materials and labor involved in manufacturing and deployment.

- **Plunge:** Plunge through this last part of the project. During the process, record process and product issues, hold daily issues meetings, and assign action items to get problems resolved quickly.

- **Update:** As issues are resolved, update appropriate documentation in preparation for final Development Release.

© 1998 Global Brain, Inc.

First Customer Ship (FCS) Approval Form

Product: _____ **Date:** _____

Team Notes, Recommendations, and Approval:

- **Pilot Run Status/Completion Date:** _____
- **Documentation Status** (User Manual, Release Notes, Product Configuration Guidelines, etc.):
  _____
- **Beta or Acceptance Test Results Summary:** _____
- **Recommendation to approve FCS:** _____

Cross-Functional Team Signatures

Project Leader: _____	Date: _____
New Product Introduction Engineer: _____	Date: _____
Product Manager: _____	Date: _____
SQA Manager: _____	Date: _____
Quality Manager: _____	Date: _____
Field Engineering Services: _____	Date: _____

Additional Team Signatures (as needed)

_____	Date: _____
_____	Date: _____
_____	Date: _____
_____	Date: _____
_____	Date: _____

Executive Signatures

VP Development: _____	Date: _____
VP Data Services: _____	Date: _____
VP Operations: _____	Date: _____
VP Sales/Marketing: _____	Date: _____
VP Finance: _____	Date: _____

© 1998 Global Brain, Inc.

Flow Step 13. Release to Production/Delivery

This is the final step in Flow, the point at which the product is officially released for unrestricted delivery to the customer. The job of the team is to make absolutely certain that the product is ready for release, and that a smooth handoff of remaining documentation from Development to Operations and Support are accomplished.

- **Review test and build results.** Review the results of the phase III testing and phase IV pilot builds/deployment with the team. Make sure all issues have been resolved.

- **Update and check NPI checklist.** Make sure all applicable items on the New Product Introduction Checklist have been addressed to the team's satisfaction.

- **Hold a release meeting.** Use a release meeting to review the documentation in preparation for final release and responsibly transfer the product to Operations.

- **Make the official Release to Production**. Make the final Development Release to Production/Delivery. Use your company's formal document control process to approve the transition to production level and unrestricted builds and deliveries.

- **Start the ramp to production volumes.** At this point the quantity of product builds and delivery can be ramped higher based on successful outcome of the pilot build and release of all the documentation for normal use in Operations.

- **Celebrate!** Take this opportunity for the team to celebrate the completion of the project.

- **Capture lessons learned.** Hold a "lessons learned" meeting and distribute the results to other Project Leaders.

- **Support the product.** During ongoing delivery, record and address installation and maintenance issues and solicit customer feedback.

- **Prepare for the next time.** Feed information into the next incremental innovation cycle.

© 1998 Global Brain, Inc.

Final Release Meeting for Flow Step 13

- **Held when:** After sufficient pilot production and approval testing have unearthed the majority of the remaining defects, the Project Leader and team have determined which are necessary; and the design team has implemented them.

- **Purpose:** To transfer responsibility to the production and delivery organizations, and allow unrestricted customer deliveries (for revenue) to begin.

- **Tools:** Use the New Product Introduction checklist to ensure that all necessary items have been completed.

Change Control after Final Release

- **Further changes:** After this point, any changes will be handled via company-wide per normal documentation control procedures.

- **Typical hardware revision level and control:** A – ZZ. When the product is ready for customer delivery and full production, the documentation package is moved to Rev. A, and normal company-wide change order procedures take effect (usually requiring signatures from all departments).

- **Typical software revision level and control:** Master. When the product is ready for customer delivery, the software is released, master media turned over to Operations, and normal company-wide change order procedures control any changes to the media or database used to supply the "production-level" software to customers.

© 1998 Global Brain, Inc.

Excerpted with permission from:

PROJECTWORLD® Summer 96 Proceedings

Article: QRPD® — A New Way to Quickly Deliver Enabling IT Solutions

© 1998 Global Brain, Inc.

Q*R*PD®—A New Way to Quickly Deliver Enabling IT Solutions

Jon T. Hockenberry
Shell Services, Inc.
Houston, Texas

Abstract and Speaker Biography

Today's IT customers are looking for rapidly developed, enabling IT applications. Year-long waits for delivery are no longer acceptable. In the IT world at Shell, almost every new enabling solution represents a super-urgent demand. If you cannot quickly deliver quality solutions to your customers, somebody else will. This presentation will review a unique approach, Q*R*PD, for ensuring successful, quick delivery of software applications. Q*R*PD is a project management best practices methodology that increases the probability of successful quick application delivery. This presentation examines the real-life use of Q*R*PD principles by project teams at Shell. We will also review how the project team was indoctrinated into the Q*R*PD approach and the resulting customer reaction to the entire process.

Jon Hockenberry holds degrees in Computer Science from North Carolina State University and a MBA from the University of Houston. He is an Information Systems Manager working on special assignment for Shell Oil Product's Company in the Lubricant's division.. Recently he worked as a Senior Project Manager for Shell Services Company managing enabling IT client/server applications in the business performance analysis systems area.

Background

January 1, 1995 began a new era for Shell Oil Company. Shell split into four separate companies: Shell Chemical Company, Shell Oil Products Company, Shell Exploration and Production Company and Shell Services Company. This presentation explores a different approach Shell Services Company (SSC) utilized while developing some of its IT projects for customers in several divisions of the Shell Oil Products Company. Prior to this period, Shell Services Company was a cost center, building enterprise wide systems for all divisions of the Shell conglomerate. The IT development mentality at that time was one of multi-year projects, lots of staff, controls and, therefore, lots of cost. With the split up of Shell, each separate operating company was given complete control over its IT decisions. Shell Services Company, as a separate enterprise, has to compete for IT, business processing and other service related activities within the other Shell Companies, as well as in the external market. This requires a whole different paradigm on the approach to IT development projects. The Services Company can no longer dictate Information Technology. This new company has to respond to the demands of its customers. These demands are to quickly deliver systems that work with limited funding. If Shell Service Company could not figure out how to do this, these customers would find someone who could. That was the dilemma faced when a group of Shell Services Company staff was chartered to deliver client/server systems for several parts of the Shell Oil Products Company.

In December 1994, I attended Orion Kopelman's Q*R*PD training as a part of a Project World conference. That seminar left me with a lot of thoughts of how I could incorporate these concepts into the management of IT software projects. I made a personal commitment to take advantage of the opportunity to introduce these concepts into Shell Services Company. Our group already had several client/server projects underway and was on the verge of starting up several more within the next year. The approach I

© 1998 Global Brain, Inc.   Reprinted with permission from ProjectWorld Summer 96 Proceedings took was to organize these projects around the series of "best practices" learned at the class. I also introduced several project teams to the concepts I picked up from the class. The results were so successful they have since been spread to several other areas within the Services Company. Following are examples of some practices that were incorporated.

Types of Projects

The type of projects this particular group delivers center around using client/server technology for decision support and analysis purposes. These applications include sales force automation, head office analysis tools, division budget and financial reporting, Internet home pages, customer non-conformance, and plant planning systems. The customers include field sales staff, head office staff and plant personal. The technologies include NT and UNIX servers, relational data base technology, OLAP multidimensional data base technology, Visual Basic front end development, HTML, and Lotus Notes for collaborative computing.

Project Vision Statement

One of the refreshing concepts taught at the QRPD class was the idea of doing your homework first. In order to speed up delivery you must first slow down and think through what you are going to be doing. Fully one fourth of the project should be spent in the requirements and early logical design. This is where all the key decisions that dictate the success of a project are made. One of the cornerstones to establishing this foundation taught in QRPD is to develop a "Project Vision Statement". A project vision statement identifies several things:

- Key customers, and how they will use the system.

- Case for action (why we are doing this project in the first place).

- Key features. These are features, that when the project is complete, you will look back on and say that is what made this such a good system.

- Project benefits, including lost opportunity costs for every month the project is late.

- Project scope, including specifics on what is not in scope. It is sometimes more definitive to identify what is not in scope of a project than to list what is in scope.

- Technologies that must be incorporated in order to deliver the system.

- Assumptions and risks.

- Constraints including time and budget constraints. Sometimes the constraints are so important that they, in fact, define the scope.

All of our project vision statements are concise (two-three pages), in bullet form and we keep them visible throughout the project. The whole project team, including the key customers and project sponsors, participated in the creation of the vision statement. We don't create strawman vision statements. In the very first project meeting the vision statement is created. The only things carried into the meeting are the category titles listed above. In the second project meeting we review the vision statement and make changes. Everybody on the project then has the responsibility to make sure the project is on track with the vision statement. At any time during the project, any person associated with the project can challenge or question anything that might violate the vision statement. This doesn't mean that the item that violated the vision statement is wrong. We may have to modify the vision statement. It becomes a living, breathing, evergreen guidepost for the project.

In one of the projects, we presented the vision statement in virtually every customer project review meeting we held, up to the first implementation. This project had two difficult items that the vision statement helped overcome. First, the specifics of what we were doing were a little difficult to identify from the project name. Second, as the project progressed, more and more customer groups needed to be included. The project vision statement was used to bring them up to speed on the purpose of the project and why their participation was important. In practically every one of these meetings, some alteration was made to the project vision statement. The project vision statement clearly guided the development of this project.

Other Important Project Start up Steps

At the time of the development of the project vision statement, several other important tasks need to be done. Most of us know we should be practicing these techniques but for whatever reason we fail to follow through. Q*R*PD reminds us of the importance of these techniques. It is just as important to go through the effort to create the deliverable as it is to create the actual deliverable itself. These items include:

- Develop a project Plan. Most feel this is the job of the project manager. A project plan belongs to the members of the project team. They need to be involved in the creation of the plan. They have to feel ownership of the plan.

- Identify risks early. The value of a risk assessment is not in identifying the risks but in identifying ways the risks can be mitigated and avoided early in the project.

- Identify key players and get them on board early. Include not only the project stakeholders and advocates but also folks who might play a small part on any aspect of the project. It is also important to identify those who might resist the project in some way and address that resistance early. The goal is to turn these adversaries into advocates.

My approach to starting projects is to spend the first meeting fully dedicated to the project vision statement. This can take as little as a couple of hours to a full day's exercise. The second meeting we spend an hour or two reviewing and revising the vision statement. At this second meeting we start our project planning. The first thing we do is to develop a work breakdown structure (WBS). We try to keep this no more than four levels deep. We then identify the staff resources responsible for every major item on the WBS. We find at this early point in the project we rarely need to go down past level three of the WBS. The person assigned to the task at this level is later given the responsibility to develop his own project plan of this part of the project. We also assign rough approximations of development time and elapsed calendar time to deliver these level three tasks. We make a quick approximation of dependencies and then throw everything on a timeline in Gantt form. The last thing we do is associate risks with every level three task in the WBS and develop a mitigation strategy to minimize the risk. Using this approach we find we can quickly develop a cost, resource, timeline and risk mitigation strategy for a project in as little as two hours. The longest I have seen for this effort is two days for a really big project. The key is to get the right players in the room when you do this. The right players include members of the development team, key customers and any management who have budgetary control over the project.

Managing Change—one of the keys to project success:

Usually in the risk mitigation strategy one of the key risks is getting resources outside the project involved. We have found that during the first 25 percent of the project it is key to identify these individuals and get them involved. It is also key to keep their involvement throughout the project. All the reading material always talks about making sure you have the proper and committed project sponsor. That is very important, but I have found that the people who can really make or break the acceptance of your application are those who will be using the application on a daily basis. One factor that will determine their acceptance of the system is how well they go through change at their personal level. Whenever change is introduced people go through a period of internal turmoil before they accept something new. Understanding how people go through change and dealing with the emotions directly leads to very successful acceptance of new systems. People go through change cycles, called the emotional roller coaster in phases similar to these:

1. Denial (emotions starting to rise) - it will not affect me, I can ignore it or it is so far away from happening I am not going to worry about it right now.

2. Anger, apprehension, stress (emotions are at their peek) - it is starting to affect me and I don't like it because it is taking me away from what I am used to.

3. Acceptance (coming down off the emotional high) - it is here to stay. I see my peers starting to accept this, so I guess I better get used to the idea and get on board.

4. Excitement and enthusiasm (starting a new, positive emotional upswing) - This thing is really good and is making a difference. I am really going to like this.

The key to project success is to move the target user community to the fourth step as quickly as possible. The idea is to move the organization to this fourth step while the project is under development and don't wait until it is fully developed. We have used a couple of concepts in our projects quite successfully. One is to expose the intended user community to prototypes, screen mock ups and other communication devices early in the development. We look for opportunities where the business has called our target customers together and then ask for an hour to demonstrate what we are thinking about for the new application. This exposes individuals early and starts them on their emotional roller coaster path. It is not unusual to get some of the denial and anger reactions in these first meetings. We make sure we have several members of the project team around during this time. The key is to find the most vocal individual during the presentation and catch them off-line for private discussions. Catching the intended target community, exposing them and getting feedback early is key to our success.

The second thing we do is to develop a project focus group of key individuals who get with the project team every four to six weeks. We try to put together a mixture of the more progress oriented computer literate individuals and folks from the other end of the spectrum. This group is responsible for making all key design decisions on the project. They decide the project priorities, collaborate and approve screen designs and make decisions regarding training and delivery. They are also our guinea pigs for beta versions of the software. They will actually go through the training and delivery of the application about a month before actual full delivery. One of the side benefits we have found is that members of our focus groups move quickly to stage four of the emotional roller coaster and become advocates of the new system. They develop a lot of ownership. They also communicate with their peers and lend a lot of credibility to the impact the new system will have. We find their peers move pretty quickly to level three of the emotional roller coaster which sets them up to move to level four shortly thereafter. By understanding the emotional impacts of change and doing things to address these emotions early in the project we have found ways to increase the chance of high acceptance of the new application.

Chicken Test—A Reality Test on a Prototype

One very important item to do in the early period of a project is to develop a working prototype. With just about all of our projects we develop a working prototype of the intended final solution. We develop and demonstrate this prototype within the first three months of the project at a gathering of as much of the user community we can get together. We also test key technical internal components such as data load times, query response times and technology interfaces during the early part of the project. With technology advancing so rapidly the projects are faced with a new, continually changing dilemmas about which technology to use. In order to cope with this dilemma we have adopted a few technology guidelines:

- Don't be afraid to try a new technology.

- If there are several options test more than one.

© 1998 Global Brain, Inc   Reprinted with permission from ProjectWorld Summer 96 Proceedings

- Try to simulate as much as possible how the new technology will be used inside the final application.
- Stay with what works today and plan on delivering the system using that technology. Don't get caught with the promises of better versions tomorrow.
- Don't box yourself into a corner with technology. Plan your application so it can migrate to new technologies once they become proven.

With these strategies we find we can deliver something that works and meets the business objective using state of the art technologies. Yet we still have applications that are migratable to the new technologies of tomorrow.

Innovate—Don't Invent

Another important concept to consider early in a project is find ways to innovate using existing technologies and to avoid inventing new ways to do things. In our projects we often find we are not the first to develop an idea. One of our innovations is to borrow good ideas from other organizations and improve on them. We talk with the developers of other applications and ask them such things as "what worked well" and "if you had to do this over again what would you do differently?" We then proceeded to incorporate into our projects everything that worked well and avoided all the things that didn't work as well. We are now finding other organizations coming to us seeking the same advice and we freely give it.

We have found we can leverage our projects by utilizing existing technologies. Today's technology environment is rich in enabling tools. One such tool is Lotus Notes. One particular problem was getting data to a remote sales force group so they could utilize it in a stand alone mode on their laptops. Instead of writing technology to replicate data to remote users, we looked around and asked what technologies were doing this today. We discovered that Lotus Notes already had data replication built in as a part of the package. We decided to utilize Lotus Notes as the backbone of our system and replicate data packets of the salesmen's daily sales to their laptops. In the end, it worked beautifully. Since that time we have found at least three other ways to use this same Lotus notes backbone to solve other problems.

Another innovation we have found is to reuse as many existing software assets as possible. In one application we were combining decision support data into a central client/server database. Instead of writing all new interfaces to populate the data, we utilized existing interfaces that were already moving this data between old mainframe systems. We just pointed the data feeds to the C/S environment. As all developers of IT systems know, interfaces can sometimes be as big an effort as the rest of the project. In this way we made this part of the project a relatively minor component of the overall effort.

Another type of innovation is to utilize existing proven technologies on the desktop. We utilized a Visual Basic tool for GUI presentation development. The major innovation was rather than writing a lot of code we bought already existing code (OCX's) wherever we could. I have one rule of thumb with the developers. If it costs more to develop than buy than go ahead and buy the code. By purchasing the code the amount of time in developing the front end GUI's was cut tremendously.

These types of innovations help in several aspects. We are able to keep the project teams rather small. We utilize existing proven technologies to minimize coding. We also reduce our risk on new ideas. These benefits enable us to deliver systems with limited budgets. This also enables the project team to successfully deliver quality, highly functional and reliable systems on very aggressive time schedules.

10 Commandments

In Ori's Q*R*PD class, he teaches a list of ten commandments that contain 118 techniques which are nothing more than a series of "best practices." The rule of thumb to use this list is that if you know you are abiding by a technique, you increase your chance of success in the project. If you know you are violating a technique, it doesn't mean you are wrong; you only have to be aware you are increasing your risk of not succeeding. Following is a sampling of some of the techniques our projects utilized.

1) **Focus**—Focus on a clear and limited vision.

   - *Innovate incrementally*—The GUI's are developed over time and actually evolved to their final form with the help of the focus group.

   - *Satisfy the Customer*—The formation of focus groups which meet on regular basis guide the project team.

   - *Limit major innovations to no more than three*—Innovations include leveraging technologies such as Lotus Notes. Other innovations include the reuse of code and borrowing others ideas.

2) **Team**—Assemble the right team and leaders

   - *Full time team members*—The development teams have a core of full time members with clear lines of responsibilities.

   - *Enlist experts as adjunct members*—The team is assisted part time by staff experts in the data analysis, database and technology areas.

   - *Find a champion with clout and authority*—All projects have the full backing and sponsorship of the management of the customer organization.

3) **Cross Functional**—Initiate early cross functional cooperation

   - *All committed from day 1 and kept up to date*—With the continual introduction of new technologies we are constantly faced with those who advocate a competing technology such as our introduction of Lotus Notes into the customer organization. This particular customer had a CIO team that approved all new technologies. This project team worked closely with that team and presented white paper arguments on the different technologies. We ultimately gained their acceptance and endorsement.

   - *No substitute for face-to-face communications*—All opportunities are sought to keep the project highly visible through demonstrations in order to keep the enthusiasm and excitement high in the customer organization.

4) **Synergy**—Create a Synergistic, mission oriented environment

   - *Shared sense of mission/purpose, product vision and milestones*—Project teams are enlisted to help develop the project vision and plan. They were given the business milestones and asked to develop a course of action around those.

   - *Ensure team members "feel" cost of delay*—The delivery schedules are based on real customer milestones. The project teams understand those milestones and the repercussions to the business of delay. They are then asked to personally commit to the customer they will meet those milestones. This creates a personal commitment for each member of the project team.

   - *"Hoopla", have fun*—We developed a catchy name for the projects and bought coffee mugs and note pads to give out with each delivery. This increased awareness and acceptance of the system with the customer.

5) **Reward**—Reward all participants

   - *Recognition at major milestones or other significant events*—The development teams are publicly recognized via internal department announcements at major milestone dates. Team lunches, dinners, special outings and other incentives are used. Several teams have received the ultimate recognition by receiving a nomination for prestigious awards within the customer's own organization.

6) **Innovate**—Use innovative, parallel design strategies

- *Beg, borrow, steal or buy subsystems or expertise, and avoid the "not invented here" syndrome*—We are not afraid to utilize best practices or ideas from other systems and organizations. In one case we based our entire concept on another proven system.

- *Use spiral, not waterfall approach*—We developed the GUI's first, then developed the infrastructure. We then go back and redeveloped the GUI's. We continually readjust the infrastructure as needed.

7) **Invest**—Invest money to buy time and tools, and to minimize risk

- *Invest early and speculatively in long lead time tooling*—When there are many technology options to solve a problem we don't hesitate to buy and test several early in a project.

- *Invest early and excessively in equipment, support, and training*—Our project teams are given the latest in tools and equipment. For example, if they are developing a laptop system for a sales force they are given laptops to develop with. If they are developing Lotus Notes business related collaborative applications they are trained and set up to use Lotus Notes for their own internal project collaboration.

8) **Prototype**—Prototype, and test key design concepts early

- *Do a reality check with real prototypes within the first 25% of the timeline (a "chicken test")*—We strive to develop working prototypes and deliver them to the customers within the first three months of the project.

- *Prove out individual subsystems and interfaces early*—We developed the GUI front-end prototypes first and then prototype the internal infrastructure components before developing the final system.

- *Know when to kill a feature and do it* - We have concepts in and out of scope continuously throughout the projects. The project team utilizes the focus group to make project change decisions. The focus group is made aware of the effort to deliver a feature, and the focus group makes an informed decision based on business need and value.

9) **Flow** - Follow a Flow process to meet milestones

- *Post the milestones & track them*—Business milestones with real impacts of delay are identified. The project team commits personally to understanding and meeting the milestones. The major milestones were posted and reviewed at regular project team meetings.

- *Use project management computer software to plan tasks*—One of the side benefits of using Lotus Notes is that we discovered one of the standard databases in Notes is a task planning database. The project team members started using this to plan out their individual tasks. It became an ideal tool to monitor the overall

© 1998 Global Brain, Inc.   Reprinted with permission from ProjectWorld Summer 96 Proceedings project task plan. Others are using MS Project to plan projects at a higher level.

- *Technically respected outside observers review key designs*—We proactively seek out technology reviews of our infrastructure and technology decisions.

10) **Feedback**—Get early feedback after delivery and nail defects quickly.

- *Close feedback between development team and customers on first delivery*—On one project the project team enlisted the help of the customer help desk during testing and implementation and included this person in regular team meetings. The project team also participates in the training of the customers. This leads to an intimacy on a personal level between the customer and the development team. This working relationship enabled the development team to quickly identify and resolve problems after implementation.

- *Use beta sites to weed out defects before release*—We strive to deliver a working copy of the entire system to the focus group more than a month prior to final delivery. We also do early implementation of components of the systems where possible. This includes training. These events allowed us time to make adjustments before the final delivery.

Conclusion

With the help of QRPD techniques, we can successfully deliver enabling business performance applications on time and on budget. The projects are delivered in months from inception to final delivery utilizing smaller working teams. The customers are extremely satisfied with the products and have continued to fund additional efforts. These techniques are currently being utilized by dozens of projects and have truly allowed us to deliver technology in half the time with half the cost.

Reading: QRPD® Phase I Project Evaluation and Project Portfolio Management

QRPD® Phase I Project Evaluation and Project Portfolio Management

Cinda Voegtli, Global Brain, Inc.
Orion Kopelman, Global Brain Inc.
Contributing Author: Konrad Knell, Strategic Decisions Group

Introduction

No project is executed in a vacuum. Unfortunately, one of the biggest impediments to realizing the potential of QRPD is that companies take on too many projects at once. They don't have a clear idea of the relative value of the various projects on their lists. They feel that everything is critical to the company's success, even survival. So they split development teams across 3 projects, 5 projects, or more. A consumer audio company had 12 engineers working on 15 different projects at once. Needless to say, until they pared down the number of projects and performed the "miracle" described in detail starting on page 324, lots got done, but nothing got finished.

A key principle of QRPD is to "Do Less Sooner." Commandment #2, "Right Team and Leader," calls for full-time team members whenever possible. The more time and uninterrupted attention team members can devote to the project, the faster the project will get done, and the greater return on investment the company should be able to realize.

So which projects should get the precious resources of your company? What tools can you use to figure this out? The process of evaluating and making decisions on the set of projects your company should undertake is what we refer to here as project portfolio management.

The QRPD methodology focuses on how to execute a particular project most effectively, so portfolio management is not the main subject of this book. However, how well a company makes its portfolio decisions will affect how many and what resources are made available for any given project. Therefore, a company's skill at portfolio and resource management has a critical influence on whether QRPD can be fully put to use for maximum gain on any given project. Will you get that full-time team? Will you get the resources your project really needs?

It is also critical for teams to understand that the information they create during phase I of their QRPD projects is key to sound company project portfolio decisions. In phase I a team identifies technical risks, the resources required for their project, and the anticipated return on investment to help make PTCC trade-off decisions. This data is not only needed for the project's decisions; the company needs it too, in order to make conscious, wise overall decisions about which projects should get the organization's precious resources.

This reading provides a brief overview of project evaluation methods, project portfolio management, and their relationship to each other and to QRPD Phase I activities. References for further reading are included.

Project Evaluation Methods

As covered in the Part I, Blitzkrieg, the aim of QRPD is to make decisions that maximize return on investment (ROI) to the company for a particular project, with the importance of time-to-market fully accounted for. According to Robert Cooper, the father of phase gate development processes, there are four main approaches to such "project evaluation:"

- **Market research models**, which include focus groups and interviews, and are most appropriate for relatively simple consumer products. They assume simply that if the

© 1998 Global Brain, Inc.

market wants a product, the project to create it should proceed.

- **Benefit measurement models**, which include checklists and scoring models, and concentrate on subjective assessment of variables rather than traditional economic data. Such variables include competitive advantage, fit with corporate objectives or business strategy, and fit with the company's longer-term technology plan.

- **Economic justification models**, which include quantitative approaches such as payback period, break-even analysis, and ROI to judge the worth of a project as an investment. Q*R*PD ROI and cost-benefit analysis and the late cost per week metric (LCPW) fall into this category.

- **Portfolio selection models**, which help a company identify a group of projects to maximize a particular company objective.

The following sections provide touch briefly on benefit measurement and economic justification models, then provide a look at one decision analysis model for project portfolio management.

Q*R*PD Phase I: Project Evaluation and Resource Analysis

Benefit Measurements: Scoring Projects

Companies often employ different types of qualitative ranking systems to assess the value of different projects. A phase I New Product Proposal will often be issued with some or all of these factors already assessed, at least roughly, by Marketing as part of the business case. Typical checklist or scorecard parameters include:

- **Strategic Fit:** How well does the product serve the company's core business strategy?

- **Contractual requirement:** Is there a direct contractual requirement that this product be developed by a certain time?

- **Needed by Sales:** Is the product needed to get into a customer or market?

- **Needed by Customer Service:** Does the project provide a financial benefit related to installation, serviceability, or maintainability of the product?

- **Technology roadmap:** Is this project needed to add capability to the product's "system infrastructure," for example, for future performance requirements? Is it required for a technology needed in future products?

    A technology roadmap depicts the progression over time of the company's own technology development, and/or the timeline on which they will adopt new technologies from outside. Roadmaps are especially important when large systems are involved that must evolve over time to support additional functionality, performance, and customers. Examples of such systems include: large networking systems where basic platforms are developed and protocols and management services are added over time; corporate IT infrastructures that will evolve and migrate as new technology and applications become available and necessary; and evolving desktop productivity software.

- **ROI or Net Present Value (NPV):** What is the financial justification for the project, based on any economic analysis methods employed?

Your company can create a list of its own critical assessment factors.

Note that projects scored this way during phase I can then be ranked against each other, by weighting the factors, calculating an overall score for each project, and comparing the scores. Such a list can then be used as a reference for staffing projects in order of their importance and clarifying priorities when resource conflicts arise.

Economic Justifications

During phase I a Q*R*PD team assesses the various possible PTCC alternatives for their project and the resulting economic justification for doing it, and strives to make the best financial decision for the company. The team determines, for each alternative being considered:

1. Rough manpower needed.
2. Rough completion timeline.
3. Associated risks.
4. The full complement of resources needed.
5. The complete schedule.
6. The potential ROI and LCPW for the project.

The following techniques are used for the economic justification during phase I. See step 4 of Flow earlier in this section for more detail on how such analysis fits into the team's phase I work.

- **ROI analysis:** What is the potential profit compared to the development "investment" required to create the product? NPV can be calculated also, taking into account the time value of money and the project's cash flow impact on the company.

- **Cost-Benefit Analysis and LCPW:** What are the incremental costs and benefits of developing a particular product feature, compared to the costs and benefits to company profits if we ship without it and get to market earlier? For every week we delay shipping the product, what profit will we give up and what extra development dollars will we spend?

As individual projects use these techniques during phase I to assess their resource requirements and the project's value, the company should be busy "one level up" assessing their portfolio of projects. Organizations typically use a standard planning process to continually look at the mix of projects being proposed; compare their resource requirements and values to each other; and make decisions on which ones to fund.

Some ranking of projects can be done based simply on an early benefits assessment such as strategic fit, competitive advantage, etc. But there are often too many "important" projects, and the decisions will come down to riskyness, resources required, and other parameters of individual projects. Management must take the data from each project's phase I analysis, and use it along with other ranking data to decide what projects the company will invest in at that point.

This analysis will thus have a direct bearing on whether a project gets kicked-off at the end of phase I. Is it important enough to get the company's resources, and make the list of current projects?

Resource Analysis (Manpower Loading)

For instance, the resource and schedule snapshots from each project's phase I planning can be folded together to get an overall resource plan for the company. A spreadsheet or project management software can be used to consolidate the manpower estimates from multiple projects. With the projects listed in priority order based on benefits scoring, ROI, NPV, etc., management can easily see where a department "runs out of people" to staff the suggested projects.

Note that it's important to do this analysis not just in Development. Even if you have enough software resources, what about the technical publications resources? The manufacturing test engineers? These support groups are all too often left out of project portfolio-wide manpower planning; but all too often these are the people stretched too thin across multiple projects. The result is a significant violation of QRPD commandment #3, early cross-functional cooperation. Cross-functional team members will end up with no time to participate in the fuzzy front end and the high-level definition of the product—where 80% of the cost is determined.

In short, employing benefits scoring, economic justification and manpower planning can help a company understand each project's value and needs and make some decisions among projects. But a more quantitative and detailed approach may be required to make all the project portfolio decisions you face.

© 1998 Global Brain, Inc.

Quantitative Project Evaluation and Project Portfolio Analysis

Contributing Author: Konrad Knell, Strategic Decisions Group, Menlo Park, California

A number of comparative and mathematical methods exist that give a more in-depth analysis for comparing the value of projects—and making decisions among them—than the simpler ranking system above. These methods involve quantitative understandings of both the potential risks and rewards of your projects. Real success in product development requires both obtaining the desired technical and functional results from your development efforts, and ultimately capturing high commercial value from the product—achieving a high return to the company on the development investment. To achieve this success requires an understanding of both the probability of technical success and the probability of its commercial value given technical success.

The quantitative aspect of these evaluations is important. Companies typically talk about uncertainty using phrases like "high risk," "low risk," "very likely," "probably," etc., which mean very little. Strategic Decision Analysis is a process that explicitly quantifies uncertainty and integrates it into useful measures like the overall value of a project and the value of the "portfolio" of all the company's projects. Quantifying risk forces people to think very clearly about outcomes and their implications. They can then make explicit trade-offs between risk and profit on projects as they perform their Q*R*PD phase I trade-off analysis. They can design project strategies that reduce risk while maintaining or increasing profit.

Quantitative analysis also allows for meaningful comparisons across projects, even when they are in different business sectors. Companies often want to understand the answers to questions such as:

- Which projects should be funded and which not?
- How can we improve the value of a project—the ROI we'll achieve?
- If there are limited resources (funds, researcher's time, equipment, etc.), which projects should be given priority?
- How can we get the right mix of long-term vs. short-term, high-risk vs. low-risk, and revolutionary vs. evolutionary projects?

Strategic Decision Analysis helps a company see how they can strike a balance between highly innovative, risky, high-potential projects and evolutionary, low-risk, incremental projects in the portfolio. It also helps them determine which projects to fund when there are not enough resources to fund all desirable projects. The next two sections introduce the Portfolio Grid and the Productivity Curve for these two situations. See the reference list at the end of the reading for sources of further information.

Portfolio Grid

Analyzing your projects for technical difficulty and commercial potential can help you reach an appropriate balance of risk and return. If you create a chart with technical difficulty (measured as probability of technical success) on the x-axis and commercial potential (measured as the expected commercial value given technical success) on the y-axis, you have a portfolio grid. See the chart on the following page.

Technical risks include all the risks of successfully getting a product to market. These may include uncertainties in research, development, regulatory, freedom to operate, and public acceptance (in the case of controversial technologies). All technical hurdles must be defined and evaluated. The probabilities of making it through each hurdle are then multiplied together to arrive at the probability of successfully reaching the market.

Using this success measure and the economic value figure, all projects in an organization's portfolio can then be plotted on this grid, and it can be used to help balance the portfolio on the dimensions of low-risk vs. high-risk and revolutionary vs. evolutionary. The grid on the following page is divided into four regions to aid in diagnosing a portfolio. The four regions are as follows:

Bread and Butter — These are projects with a high probability of technical success but low commercial value. They are typically product or process improvements that apply to existing commercial activities. They are "evolutionary" technologies. They must be done to maintain or improve the organization's short-term performance.

Oysters — These are projects with a low probability of technical success but high commercial value, the opposite of the bread-and-butter projects. These are typically new products or processes, and often require new commercial activities. They are "revolutionary" technologies. They must be cultivated to obtain new products or processes in the long term to ensure the future of the organization.

Pearls — These are projects with high probability of technical success and high commercial value. These "pearls" are the result of cultivation of oysters. These projects lead to sustaining the long-term growth of the organization through technological leadership.

White Elephants — These are projects with a low probability of success and a low commercial value. These projects require much care and expense and yield little profit. They are called "white elephants" because the King of Siam supposedly would give disagreeable courtiers white elephants, the upkeep of which would cause financial ruin.

Once we have plotted an organization's projects on this grid, we get a good picture of the balance of the portfolio. We can use this information to adjust the portfolio, and to manage projects more effectively. Projects in different categories should be managed differently:

- Bread and Butter Project — "Deliver It"
  ◊ Manage budget.
  ◊ Manage specifications.
  ◊ Manage schedule.
- Oyster Project — "Prove It"
  ◊ Resolve hardest hurdles first.
  ◊ Screen rapidly for missing technology.
  ◊ Verify and monitor potential applications.
- Pearl Project — "Exploit It"
  ◊ Make time the top priority.
  ◊ Target the best markets.
  ◊ Strategize full range of commercial applications and future generations.
- White Elephant Project — "Move It"
  ◊ Up: simplify technical approach.
  ◊ Over: expand commercial scope and time horizon.
  ◊ Out: replace with more promising opportunity.

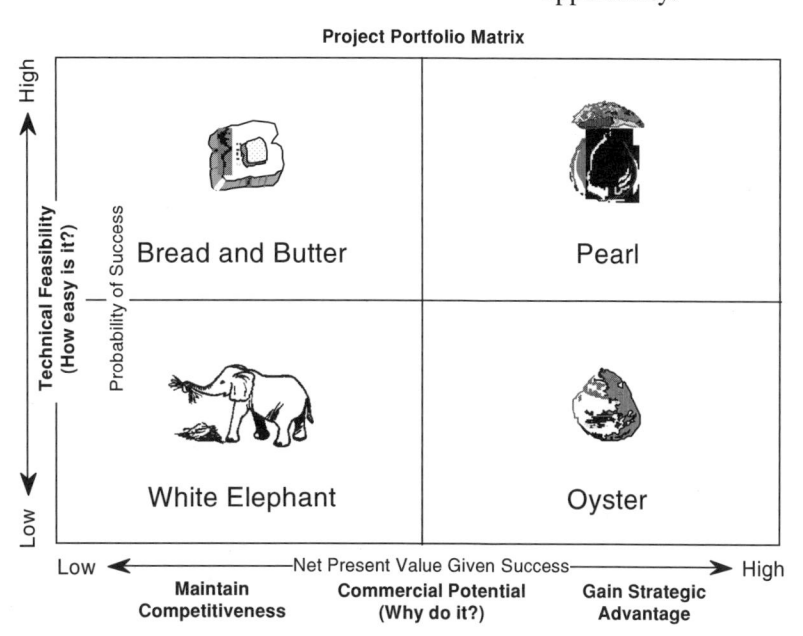

Project Portfolio Matrix

© 1998 Global Brain, Inc.

Other Decision Analysis Tools

Decision Analysis also makes use of quantitative tools such as a productivity curve to help decide which projects to fund in a situation where there are not enough resources to fund all desirable projects. Using three primary measures of each project—probability of technical success, development cost, and expected commercial value—a productivity measure is calculated. The most useful productivity measure is "bang for the buck." It is simply the expected value of a project (including technical uncertainty) divided by the development cost. Think of it as simple ROI with technical risk explicitly and quantitatively factored in. The projects with the highest productivity by this measure will deliver the most commercial value per R&D dollar invested. Given a hard budget constraint, the optimal portfolio is always obtained by funding the highest productivity projects first, working down the list until the budget is used up.

Decision Analysis also includes a measure called Segment Productivity. In a large R&D organization, there are usually many areas or segments of the project portfolio that address different markets or types of technologies, and often support distinct business units within the corporation. One or more of these segments address the core business of the corporation, and others address expansion opportunities. It is usually useful to diagnose the productivity of each segment individually, to answer questions about the balance of the portfolio across its segments and to understand how the R&D organization is supporting the future of the businesses the corporation is in.

In addition, Decision Analysis includes many other tools for helping you quantify and assess your projects, portfolios, and business strategies. For more information, see the Further Reading list.

Conclusion

To ensure the success of Q*R*PD techniques on any one project, your organization has to invest time and attention toward wisely managing its total collection of projects. No one project can succeed if the organization is stretched too thin across projects. Phase I data from each project is critical for making sound overall project portfolio decisions. The potential market benefits, development and product costs, technical risks, and manpower requirements are analyzed for various development alternatives during phase I and used to understand that project's potential value to the company. The same data can then be used in analysis and decision-making techniques such as those discussed in this reading, to ensure that the company chooses to fund the most beneficial portfolio of projects.

About the Contributing Author

Konrad Knell is a Senior Consultant at Strategic Decisions Group and has specialized in R&D and technology decision-making for the past 7 years. He has helped R&D-intensive organizations develop strategies for projects, portfolios, business units, and corporations, and has helped organizations build their own decision analytical capability. Strategic Decisions Group (SDG) is a recognized leader in assisting corporations in the development and implementation of successful long-term strategies and sustainable competitive performance. Their unique decision-focused approach, developed over the past three decades, helps clients surface and analyze creative business strategies and manage and profit from risk and uncertainty. Konrad can be reached at (650) 233-6252.

References and Further Reading

Cooper, Robert G., *Winning at New Products: Accelerating the Process from Idea to Launch,* 2nd Ed., Addison Wesley, 1993

Howard, Ronald A., and James E. Matheson, ed. *Readings on the Principles and Applications of Decision Analysis.* Menlo Park, CA: Strategic Decisions Group, 1983.

Matheson, James E., Michael M. Menke, and Stephen L. Derby. "Managing R&D Portfolios for Improved Profitability and Productivity," *The Journal of Science Policy and Research Management,* Vol. 4, No. 4.

Matheson, James E., and David Matheson. *Smart R&D.* Harvard Business Press, 1997.

Menke, Mike M., J. Gelzer, and J. Peizer. "Evaluating Basic Research Strategies," *Long Range Planning,* Vol. 14, June 1981.

© 1998 Global Brain, Inc.

PART V. DIRFT

5 Keys to DIRFT:
Doing **I**t **R**ight The **F**irst **T**ime

1) **COMMITTED:** Everyone is consistently committed, whole-heartedly and knowingly, to a limited, worthwhile Vision.
   a) Phase I concentration: Vision, customer involvement, clear objectives
   b) Project justified for Return on Investment (ROI) based on Performance, Time, Cost (PTCC)
   c) Innovations limited and agreed upon
   d) Vision and milestones signed at end of phase I by team
   e) Real commitments of specifications and schedules
   f) Commitments re-examined throughout project

2) **SENSE OF MISSION:** Everyone feels the sense of purpose and works urgently on a "put a man on the moon" Mission.
   a) Milestone charts
   b) Action items
   c) Management by Objectives (MBO)
   d) Management by walking around (MBWA) and team synergy
   e) Team meetings

3) **FOLLOW FLOW:** Everyone follows and continuously improves a FLOW process
   a) Written product development process, with steps of Q*R*PD FLOW
   b) Project assessed against the Q*R*PD checklist of techniques
   c) Step-by-step procedures and templates to execute steps with high quality
   d) Interim lessons learned meetings

4) **TEST ENOUGH:** Test! Test! Test! Early, throughout, thoroughly
   a) Early design testing: concepts, simulations, chicken testing of prototypes
   b) Customer feedback throughout
   c) Design verification, integration, and system tests
   d) Real Alpha and Beta approval tests
   e) Reliability and life testing

5) **PLUNGE:** Plunge through the product development funnel and micromanage the last 10% to get it out!
   a) Daily team-wide "Hot-list" meetings to manage details of the end-game
   b) Testing metrics and bug meetings to decide what to fix and priorities
   c) Agreement on definition of DONE from all parties

© 1998 Global Brain, Inc.

Quality Definitions

#1

"QUALITY MUST BE JUDGED AS THE <u>CUSTOMER PERCEIVES IT</u>"

—Tom Peters, *Thriving on Chaos*, p. 100

DR. DEMING

- Improvement of the customers' experience
- Not a lack of things wrong, but the sense of overall presentation and design

TQM

TOTAL QUALITY MANAGEMENT

- A continuous improvement process where every employee participates, including the management
- Find failures and defects as early as possible

Quality is <u>profitable</u> in the long run

DO YOU WANT IT GOOD OR FAST?

=

We don't have enough time to do it now, but we have enough time to do it over again!

"**When quality goes up, costs go down.** *Quality improvement is the primary source of cost reduction.*" (usually due to simplification).
— Tom Peters, *Thriving on Chaos*, p. 97.

"On average, those firms whose products score in the top third on relative perceived product quality out-earn those in the bottom third by a two-to-one margin."
—Tom Peters, *Thriving on Chaos*, p. 82

Savings are brought about by saving rework, reject items; repeat business generated from satisfied customers.
—*Quality is Free*, by Phillip Crosby, 1975.

DIRFT #1:
How NOT to Write a Specification

We, the	UNWILLING,
Led by the	UNQUALIFIED,
Are doing the	IMPOSSIBLE
For the	UNGRATEFUL

DIRFT #2: Management By Objectives (MBO)

ADVANTAGES

- Minimizes need for top management supervision

- Allows engineers to self-motivate, monitor their own progress

- Allows engineers to participate in goal setting toward common project aims: they know what's expected individually and collectively

- Implements *rapid* product development (RPD), and more general goals, through top management directives
    - Include milestones and other RPD objectives
    - Link to personnel review process
    - Track/review quarterly (perhaps on a percentage basis)

WARNING

- EMPHASIZE GRADING THE WHOLE TEAM!
- CREATE "COMPETITIVE COOPERATION," WITH OVERALL COHESION
- REWARD INDIVIDUAL AND TEAM

NOTE: For more information, see *Managing by Results.*, Peter Drucker, 1964. Also "New Product Development Game" article, Ouchi, on Theory Z and how people like to work for self-fulfillment, a similar concept.

© 1998 Global Brain, Inc.

DIRFT #4: Q*R*PD Testing

Testing Types	When	Why
Early Design Testing		
Concept Testing	Really early: early Phase I.	Mock-ups to test key design concepts before investing time and money to build them.
Simulation	During Phases I and II.	Test concepts more thoroughly using computer tools, to explore concepts without building things. See Commandment #8.
Chicken Testing:	Phase II, before 50% point. Early chicken testing possible in phase I.	Early testing will prove if the essential technology is actually functioning as it should, and will indicate if it's necessary to take a different approach to the over-all plan.
Customer Feedback		
Usability testing	Test throughout project. Approval testing in phase III.	Ensures that customers will be able to easily and effectively learn and use the product.
Compatibility testing	"Early look" testing in phase II. Final approval testing in phase III.	Ensures that product will be compatible with customers' real-world environment and their related equipment.
Development Testing		
Unit Testing	Phase II	Developers ensure that the components of the product work.
Integration Testing, Functional Testing	Phase II	Developers ensure that the components of the product work together and function properly.
Approval Testing		
Alpha testing	Phase III	Internal but independent, verifiable tests that show the product works.
Beta/acceptance testing	Phase III	External customer tests to ensure the product works in the real world.
Regulatory testing	Final approval testing in phase III. "Early look" testing in phases I and II.	Regulatory agencies certify that the product meets their specifications.
Other Testing		
Life, Reliability testing	Phases III and IV	Ensure that the product works over time under all real-world conditions.

© 1998 Global Brain, Inc.

Testing Ideas

> Knowledge-based innovation is the super star of entrepreneurship.
> ~ Peter F. Drucker

- Use company resources creatively to test throughout

- Use problem solving tools

- Invest time and money on tools

- "See" the elusive once in a while problems (attempt "a stab in the dark" only once or twice)

- Beware of "shot-gunning"

- Expect 5 stages of (hopefully) decreasing problems
    1. During subsystem design.
    2. System integration (2 prototypes, perhaps).
    3. First 10 pilot production units.
    4. First 100 manufacturing units.
    5. 10 power X regular production units.

- Alpha should be:
    - Independent (of design team)!
    - Significant
    - Measurable and verifiable
    - Proven to top management not just by leader's verbal assurances

- Beta:
    - Get the straight story from the customer
    - Ask lots of questions
    - Use leading edge and typical ones

Using DIRFT Daily

Using DIRFT #1: Committed

1. Did you concentrate on the Vision process in phase I (25%); involve customers and suppliers; fully understand and clearly document the objectives? Did the entire team participate?

2. Have you justified the project for ROI (Return On Investment) based on Performance, Time, and Costs (PTCC), and made sure everyone understands the reasons for doing the project this way?

3. Have you done an innovations risk assessment to make sure you haven't bitten off too much? Have you cost-justified those innovations?

4. Did everyone sign the Vision and milestones at end of phase I?

5. Did the team make real commitments of specifications and schedules?

6. Are you re-examining these commitments at each QRPD design review? Is the Vision being held constant, or allowed to change?

Using DIRFT #2: Sense of Mission

1. Are you using visible milestone charts to chart progress and clearly show delays? Is the team staying on track?

2. Are you tracking the team's action items? Do you see low completion rates that indicate the mission is faltering?

3. Are you using MBO to set clear personal objectives for each team member based on their project responsibilities? Are team members making these objectives?

4. Are you doing management by walking around and using hoopla to create a continued sense of mission and team synergy? Does your team act like it's getting ready to "put a man on the moon?"

5. Are you holding effective team meetings that continually reinforce the team's mission and ensure that real progress is being made? Is everyone attending these meetings?

© 1998 Global Brain, Inc.

Using DIRFT #3: Follow Flow

1. Do you have a written product development process, with at least major steps defined according to QRPD Flow? Does your project milestone list show where the 13 steps of Flow happen in your project?

2. Have you assessed your project against the QRPD checklist of techniques? Are you taking advantage of as many of these tools as possible?

3. Do you have procedures, templates, and company examples of key deliverables, to help execute the Flow steps with high quality? Are team members really using these tools?

4. Are you holding interim "lessons learned" meetings to find areas for improvement? Are you acting on the results?

Using DIRFT #4: Test Enough

1. Did you do concept testing, simulations, chicken testing of prototypes as early as possible in the project? Have all innovations been chicken tested? Did you perform a system chicken test before the half-way point?

2. Are you planning and really doing thorough customer feedback testing throughout? (usability, compatibility, etc.)

3. Are you planning and really doing thorough design verification, integration, and system tests? Did you write test plans and cases for these and identify expected results?

4. Are you planning and really doing thorough, real Alpha and Beta approval tests? Did you write plans for these tests to ensure they accomplished what you needed?

5. Are you planning and really doing thorough reliability and life testing?

Using DIRFT #5: Plunge

1. Are you using daily team-wide "Hot-list" meetings to manage details of the end-game?

2. Are you recording and reviewing testing metrics, and using "bug meetings" to decide which problems to fix, and their priorities?

3. Do you have agreement on definition of DONE from all parties? Do you have a tool such as a sign-off form that will give everyone a chance to give their official blessing to shipping the product?

The 7 Deadly Sins that Prevent Q*R*PD, and their Remedies

	SIN	REMEDY
1.	Trying to do too much in one project, and the NIH—Not Invented Here—Syndrome	Use incremental innovation; innovate rather than invent (re-package).
2.	Not everybody buys-in to a common product vision.	Re-do "SSSS" negotiation
3.	Functional organizations refuse to relinquish control to project teams.	Get top management to buy in to Q*R*PD.
4.	Weak project team leader(s), or one that lacks authority.	Select carefully, and anoint with responsibility
5.	A poor product development process, or none at all.	Work on the process and product simultaneously
6.	No "chicken test" on a working prototype early in the schedule.	DO IT!
7.	A disintegrating, endless endgame	Micro-manage the last 10%: The whole team works together closely to handle details and get it out the door.

© 1998 Global Brain, Inc.

Salvaging A Project In Trouble
(Didn't DIRFT)

> I am not discouraged,
> because every wrong attempt discarded
> is another step forward.
> ~ Thomas Edison

1. **ADMIT HONESTLY WHERE THE PROJECT'S AT!**
   Missed a major milestone
   And >20% behind schedule --> trouble

2. **IDENTIFY THE REAL PROBLEM(S), MAGNITUDE, AND IMPACT:**
   - Schedule (time, resources, personnel)?
   - Technical?
   - Market change?

3. **RE-ASSESS THE BUSINESS CASE**
   (Use the economic calculation approach from "Blitzkrieg" to make trade-offs)

4. **EXAMINE EXECUTION AGAINST METHODOLOGY --**
   Which QRPD techniques were followed/violated?

5. **INVESTIGATE SOLUTIONS**
   - Change Product Vision
   - Delay schedule
   - Add resources
     (inside and outside, including technical and management consultants)
   - Better management
   - Other

6. **DECIDE QUICKLY/DECISIVELY ON NEW, ATTAINABLE OBJECTIVES**
   (including the schedule)

7. **COMMUNICATE THE PLAN OPENLY AND HONESTLY TO EVERYONE**
   => Gain new commitment

"Emebo Opportunity #2"
An Enhanced QRPD Benefit-Cost Trade-Off Case Study

A company is developing a next generation version of its Emebo product line that uses molecular beam epitaxy (MBE) to deposit gallium arsenide on certain kinds of semiconductor wafers. This piece of equipment carries a price tag of about $500,000 each and the company expects to sell 50 over the next 4 years, at an average profit of 20% before tax. Since the product's market window of opportunity is about 4 years, every month delay may cost the company about 1/50th of the life time sales of the product, i.e. one machine. The project leader estimates it will take 12 months to complete the development using QRPD, at a burn rate of $50k per month of R&D investment. (so far this is all the same as the first "Emebo" in the "Blitzkrieg" chapter).

However, the new VP of Sales/Marketing has requested that the design also include a software feature to graph the wafer deposition depth. S/He claims that adding a color monitor to the product with the additional software will add 10% additional sales. The Project Leader protests that this will delay the project a month, occupy the whole team for that month, and raise product cost by $6,000 per machine.

Who's right? Should the graph be done?
Why or why not?

(Solution in Appendix A.)

© 1998 Global Brain, Inc.

"Solar444"
A Complete QRPD Case Study

FAFCO, a Silicon Valley diversified solar energy equipment manufacturer with about $10 million in annual sales, branched out into a new market by developing a domestic (household) solar water heating system. The project took almost two years, and ran 40% over budget, at a total cost of about $2.5 million. Fortunately, the company had raised $10 million in a recent public offering, and could afford the investment.

10,000 units were sold over the lifespan of the product, at an approximate price of $1200 each (to the distributors). End users paid about $2500, that included the installation fee from the distributors. The product came with a five-year warranty which is customary for the water heater industry. Upon its release, several newspapers, including *The San Jose Mercury News*, applauded it as a wonderful new product.

Unfortunately, the Solar444 experienced a 5% return rate in the first year because they leaked water, and greater than 40% cumulatively over the next 4 years. Sales had been expected to be much higher, but the expiration of the solar energy tax credit in the 1980s all but killed sales of solar energy products (not cost effective). The leaking didn't help either. Some customers, who disconnected these heaters from their house's plumbing system and reverted to gas or electric ones, still proudly display the units on their roofs as "art objects;" but didn't exactly refer friends to go buy more of them....

Technologically, the water heaters employed a revolutionary idea: the team had come up with a way to use thin-gauge stainless steel for the water tank/absorber. Competing products used heavy copper. This was a leapfrog innovation over the rest of the industry, because of the lower installed cost of stainless steel. A lot of time was spent concurrently engineering a manufacturing process to weld the stainless steel tanks properly. R&D people cooperated in an inter-disciplinary team approach with manufacturing people. Everyone exuded an excitement of "we're going to take the world by storm."

The project also included three other major innovations including: no electronics, no pump, and solar collectors with shrink-formed fluoropolymer films and a roll-formed pre-painted steel housing which cut the weight of the assembly by 50% while improving thermal performance for this high performance, low-cost product.

The team leader, Rich, was a very competent, gung-ho engineering manager, with excellent educational background in Mechanical Engineering. This was his first attempt at project leadership. In his words, "we did about 70% right the first time. Corrosion never occurred in the alphas, because we used Hetch Hetchy (very pure) water in them. We didn't do failure mode analysis/ brainstorm that might have led us to test with well water, Arizona water. (Also), accelerated fatigue (pressure-cycle) testing did not accurately mimic field conditions which were often much worse."

Rich goes on to say, with QRPD "80% of the reliability problems could have been avoided ... and about half the development cost overrun could have been avoided. We certainly could have kept from having to spend another year and a half after the initial shipments trying to solve the corrosion problem. We finally replaced the stainless steel with a 'copper heart,' after even a number of metallurgists failed to solve the leakage problem."

(Many years after first shipments FAFCO settled a lawsuit out of court with the stainless steel vendor for false representations made during the design phase).

(continued on next page)

© 1998 Global Brain, Inc.

QUESTIONS:

1. What are 3 things that were done right on Solar444 according to Q*R*PD?

2. What are 3 things that violated the Q*R*PD methodology?

3. Speculate on a different, more successful, possible outcome.

(Solutions in Appendix A.)

"SysTD": A Complete Q/RPD Case Study

Not long ago, Sysgen, Inc. decided to have better control of its own destiny and to improve its profits by developing its own tape drive. As a leading and reputable company supplying tape backup *systems* for IBM PC computers, it had successfully relied on outside suppliers like Archive for the drive itself, and simply packaged it in a box with hardware and software. Now it seemed like the right time to squeeze out the external suppliers, and to insert their own tape drive.

Bob Russell was given the assignment of managing the "SysTD" as its Project Leader, in addition to his other duties as VP of Operations. He assembled a team of insiders and consultants, limited at first to engineering specialists in tape and disk drive expertise, and later added specialists for head design, packaging and technicians. Ultimately the team size was about 10: 3 engineers, 1 CAD designer, 2 technicians, 1 clerk, a couple of outside consultants as needed, and Bob of course.

The team started out working from 5 to 10 PM after already working their regular positions. The initial task of this unofficial "skunkworks" group was to determine what the tape drive should be, and if in fact to fund a full-blown project; or to fall back on just continuing to buy from the existing suppliers.

Since the initial customer was internal only, the team had excellent input about what the market requirement was. The target customer's needs and wants were easily definable, and good rapport could be established with the "user"—the manufacturing group— from the beginning of the project. The president even sat in on many of the initial sessions to play the role of customer. Furthermore, since at the time Sysgen had to buy the various tape drives used in its core business from outside manufacturers, it was in a position to know what the various suppliers (its future competitors) were offering and planning to offer.

Despite such clear inputs, the team took its time in Phase I. Only after much debate and a review of existing drives on the market, they finally settled on a 3-1/2" form-factor using the DC2000 cartridge with an initial target capacity of 100 MB and a fully burdened cost of less than $125. The argument revolved around the risk factor, given that existing drives using the DC2000 were only offering 20 MB at the most at that time, and were priced in the $300 range in volume. Nonetheless, once this major decision had been thoroughly investigated and made, the rest of the objectives fell in line, and resulted in a clearly defined vision. In fact, the specification was so clear that it fit on a single page, enabling the team to focus on a goal that was understood by all participants, and fully bought into.

Once the upper management had a vision to sign-off on, Bob started searching for money to fund the project. Fortunately, he convinced Sysgen to relocate to a new facility in a deal with Prudential where Sysgen occupied a new 55,000 square foot facility, which it got for free for one year—Prudential even paid for relocation. The President personally approved this arrangement, and it increased cash flow for the year of the project in excess of $600,000, which they applied toward the development and tooling costs of the SysTD.

Bob's team then proceeded to determine the project plan and setup parallel design segments such as head design, firmware, mechanical design, and vendor selection. Each of these major subsystems were well understood by the experienced engineers that were assigned to them. The risk was restricted to the tape positioning/head subsystem where the team had to break new ground.

Knowing the risk involved, they rushed to get actual samples of new heads from their supplier in Hong Kong within three months. They almost worked—close but no cigars.... However, what they learned from these first

© 1998 Global Brain, Inc.

samples enabled them to make a few critical adjustments to the tape positioning subsystem. As a result, the next round of prototypes worked acceptably well, requiring only *some* firmware "tweaking."

The team set up a schedule to enable testing a full SysTD prototype of the main concepts within six months, and to be ready for a pre-production run by 12 months. Since all of the interfaces were clearly defined, and the risk was managed, the subsystems went together quite well, and the prototypes worked almost immediately.

The team was very motivated, and felt like it had a real mission. They used milestone charts, handmade PERT charts, and offered special stock options that increased in number significantly depending on the results of the project's team's performance against the goals.

Bob can't under-emphasize the importance of the product development flow process they followed. He says, "we never could have accomplished what we did without one. We had the proposal, did the business case study, developed the mission (vision) statement, selected a project leader and a core team, negotiated a schedule with the team and management, announced the project to the company, and went into high gear—we prepared our plans and executed them:

"designing, prototyping, testing, testing again and again, more prototyping, more testing, progress reviews and analysis conducted weekly and eventually daily, alpha testing, beta testing, FCC/safety testing, environmental testing. etc. It worked."

The end result was a 3-1/2" form factor drive with 120+ MB at a cost of $118 using the DC2000, that was ready for pre-production in 11 months. What a success! Sysgen created a new subsidiary, Stream Technology, to focus on tape drive products and OEM backup systems. The only unhappy team in this SysTD, DIRFT win were the previous suppliers, now competitors behind the eight-ball on cost.

To summarize this blitzkrieg success, Bob says, "I believe the use of Q*R*PD types of techniques such as setting a CLEAR objective, selecting and assembling the right team, developing a plan to facilitate a modular (subsystem) approach to the design, investing money to buy time and tools, prototyping as early as possible and then rewarding the participants, actually caused this project to get done in close to **40% quicker** than normal expectations for a product of this complexity —11 months vs. 18 months. Does Q*R*PD work? Damn right it does."

Which Q*R*PD techniques were adhered to and violated?

(Solution in Appendix A.)

Implementing QRPD Into An Organization

The following steps are those recommended for implementing QRPD in an organization. See also the Reading *"Executive Overview of QRPD Principles and Practices"* in the Introduction.

1. Use **consultants/experts** for <u>more rapid</u> absorption with less mistakes. Cost-justify it:
    - Buy actual QRPD experience.
    - Buy access to a broad range of options known in the industry.
    - Avoid potential pitfalls (mistakes others have made).
    - Use as a tool for neutral, "objective", independent selling of the changes into the organization.
    - Tap expertise for analyzing a QRPD project that's in trouble.

2. Define an **implementation project** and follow the QRPD methodology for it.

3. **Educate** top management, project leaders, and key personnel to affect a paradigm shift.

4. **Top management facilitates** and supports a first attempt:
    - Plenty of resources.
    - Contributes time and attention (not control).
    - Makes major decisions only (example: modifying product vision).
    - MBO linked to review process.
    - "Let the team run the team" (Reinertsen, p. 262)

5. Select the **right pilot project** (use QRPD from day 1 of this project).

6. Select the **right** ("Obsessed") **Project Leader.**

7. **Train team on QRPD** approach and teach new skills.

8. Learn from first attempts and **improve, repeat** process on other projects.

9. Create a company guidebook/**cookbook** to practice QRPD consistently.

© 1998 Global Brain, Inc.

Time to Adopt QRPD

The adoption of any new methodology will take time. The following graph shows the stages companies progress through on their way to "unconscious maturity," the state where QRPD principles and practices are second nature, the normal accepted way of doing business. Reaching this state usually requires 12 to 36 months depending on the size and current maturity of the company.

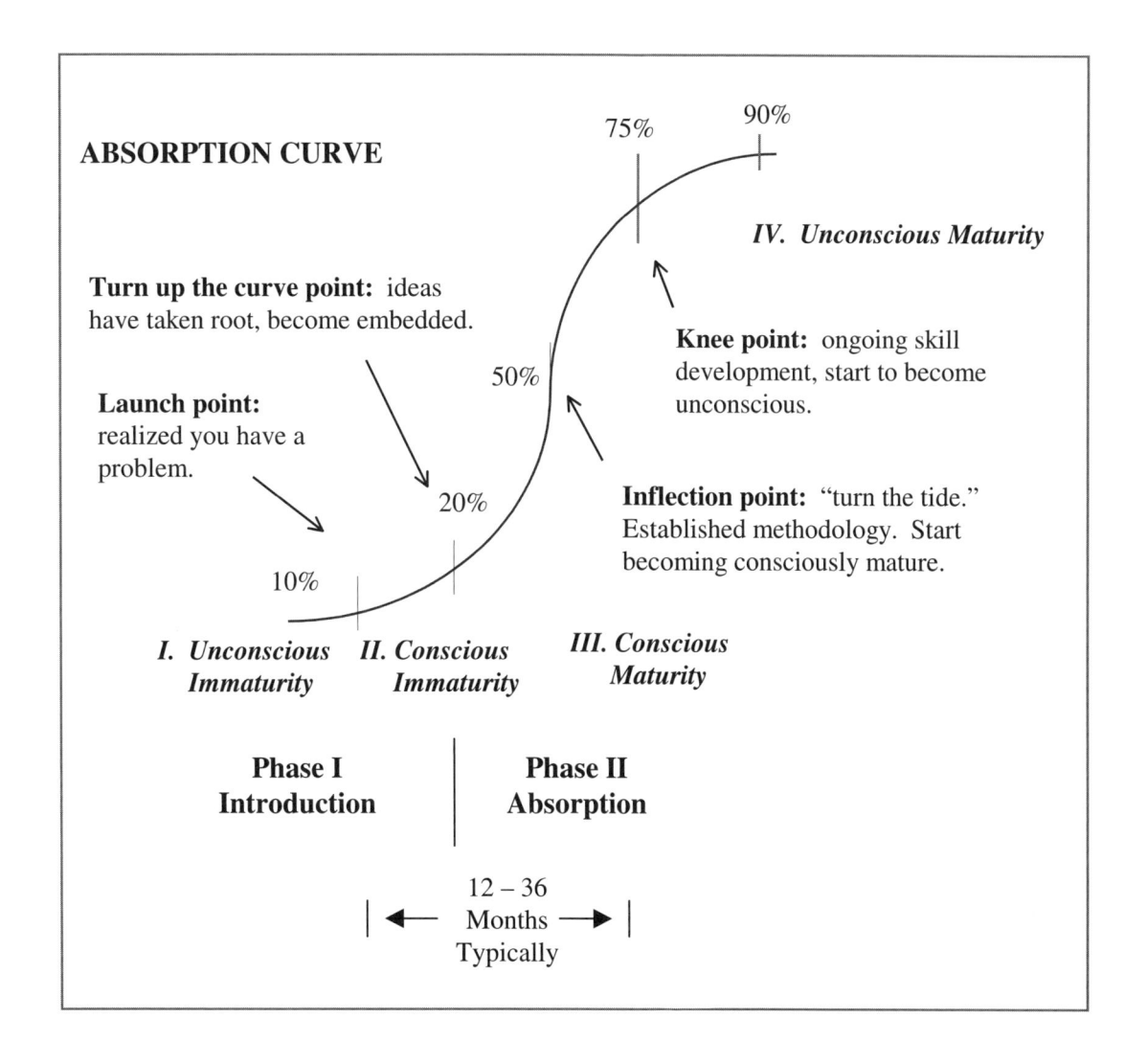

ABSORPTION CURVE

Turn up the curve point: ideas have taken root, become embedded.

Launch point: realized you have a problem.

Knee point: ongoing skill development, start to become unconscious.

Inflection point: "turn the tide." Established methodology. Start becoming consciously mature.

- 10%
- 20%
- 50%
- 75%
- 90%

I. *Unconscious Immaturity*
II. *Conscious Immaturity*
III. *Conscious Maturity*
IV. *Unconscious Maturity*

Phase I Introduction | **Phase II Absorption**

12 – 36 Months Typically

© 1998 Global Brain, Inc.

Characterization of Adopters

Different companies will vary in how soon they adopt new practices such as those found in QRPD. This figure shows a typical distribution of companies according to their tendency to adopt a methodology "early" with respect to the availability of the new practices and with respect to other companies. However, remember that it's never too late for any company to start adopting QRPD and implementing the changes it requires.

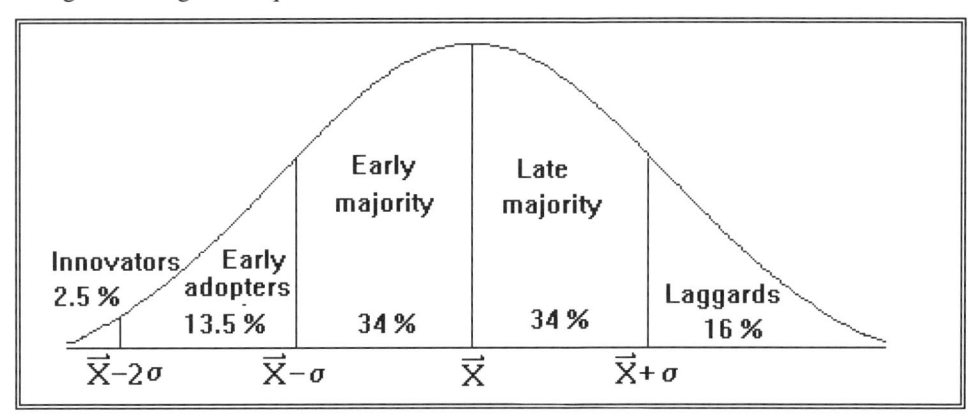

Time to Adopt Innovation/Idea ➜

Changes Required for QRPD Absorption

Effective product development is primarily a people problem, not a technical one. Adopting QRPD in an organization generally requires four types of change aimed at bringing people's work, expectations, and environment in line with the goals of QRPD.

- **Logistical**: Individuals and departments must adopt new practices, new methodologies and techniques for people's day to day work.

- **Individual**: Each individual must buy in to the need to adopt the new practices, and commit to participating appropriately on QRPD teams. Some will come on board right away; others will take time.

- **Organizational**: The company must align itself properly to these new practices via project-friendly reporting structures, project-influenced performance reviews and incentives, and job descriptions that emphasize full cross-functional participation on project teams.

- **Cultural**: The culture must evolve such that use of the best practices becomes expected, unquestioned.

See the article "Overcoming Obstacles to Rapid Product Development: Implementing QRPD" later in this section for further discussion of the changes that are encountered along the road to full QRPD absorption.

Excerpted with permission from:
PROJECTWORLD® Summer 96 Proceedings

Article: Do It Right the First Time and Develop Products in Half the Time!
The 5 Keys to DIRFT

Do It Right the *First* Time and Develop Products in *Half* the Time! The 5 Keys to DIRFT

Orion Kopelman, President
Global Brain®, Inc.
555 Bryant Street, #369, Palo Alto, California, 94301-1704
Tel# (650) 327-2012   Fax# (650) 327-2028
E-Mail: missioncontrol@globalbrain.com

Abstract & Speaker Biography

Today's unprecedented speed of technological growth is creating an equally pressurized environment. As competition expands to a global scale our time-to-market window is shrinking. Not only do you have to focus on superior quality, you've got to hit a target that is being carried away by rapid change. Timely product development is becoming a do or die situation. In today's market, there are few second chances—so how do you ensure success? You Do It Right The *First* Time, of course.

The following simple yet immensely effective individual and team management techniques are helping many high-tech companies to bring successful products to market on time, the *first* time.

The 5 Keys To DIRFT

1. **COMMITTED:** Everybody commits whole-heartedly and knowingly to a worthwhile vision.

2. **SENSE OF MISSION:** Create a 'Put A Man On The Moon' mission.

3. **FOLLOW FLOW:** Follow and continuously improve flow processes.

4. **TEST ENOUGH:** Test! Test! Test!

5. **PLUNGE:** Plunge through the product development funnel.

ORION KOPELMAN is President of Global Brain, Inc., a company which provides technology acceleration consulting and products. He was VP of Engineering and co-founder of the Media Equipment Division at Mountain Computer, a company which grew from 50 to 500 people between 1984-1990, with 32 consecutively profitable quarters.

Kopelman's enthusiasm for quality and solid command of the product development cycle have made him a much sought after lecturer. He served for three years as Chairman of IEEE's Engineering Management Society in Silicon Valley. He teaches Q*R*PD at UC Berkeley Extension and to technology-driven companies world-wide such as NASA's Simulator Technology and Operations Division, Abbott Labs, CellNet Data Systems, and Meyer Sound. He plans to make Q*R*PD an industry-wide standard by the year 2000. Orion makes his home in Santa Cruz, California and Maui, Hawaii.

Presentation

The plane is hovering at 20,000 feet. With each deep breath the parachute straps tighten around your chest. Sharks are circling the small island far below—the bull's-eye. Timing is critical—if you don't jump in three seconds, you'll miss the mark. One. "Has someone dropped down a survival kit?" Two. "Which way is the wind blowing?" Three. "Did I test my parachute before take off?" (The sharks are smiling.) Three and a half... You're shark meat.

© 1998 Global Brain, Inc.

By eliminating unscheduled rework time resulting from "surprise gotch-ya's," more and more companies are actually meeting their original, aggressive schedules. Without the unexpected delays of past projects, this often means delivering products in up to *half* the time, and Doing It Right the *First* not the *Second* Time.

Philip Crosby, author of the legendary *Quality Is Free*, reminds us that: "when it is clear that management policy is to DIRFT, then everyone will DIRFT." [1]

The 5 keys to **DIRFT** are part of a powerful management methodology called Q*R*PD: Quality *Rapid* Product Development.[2] Although Q*R*PD is focused on technology-driven product development—hardware, software, system, mechanical, medical equipment or any other type of high-tech product—DIRFT could just as easily be applied to a home gardening project, repairing your kitchen cabinets, or any other project where we invest our time and resources with great expectations for a return.

Plantronics, a leading supplier of telecommunications headsets, recently reaped the rewards of DIRFTing a project. Competing in a hot new market, they delivered a miniature audio input/output device for personal computers to a major manufacturer, on time. Fortunately, Q*R*PD techniques enabled them to complete the project in 12 months instead of 18 months (which is the amount of time a project comparable in size and done in parallel had taken). Gordon Simmons, the Project Leader says, "At times we ran counter to the accepted norms of doing things, but we met all expected customer deliverables. We could easily do this again and again, if management continues to clear the runway, and says 'go.'"

Doing it right as Plantronics did is defined by the quality of the final product. Quality is the value of the product as judged and perceived by the customer. Customers base their purchases on both practicality and pleasure, and the range of needs and wants between the two is extremely varied. The renowned management expert on quality, Edward Deming Jr., showed us that customers aren't just satisfied with a minimum number of defects with the products that they buy, rather, their evaluation is based on their overall experience from the product, including its presentation and design.

This is a distinction that remains clearly ingrained in the minds of many Detroit automobile executives. Regrettably, the 1980s was a time for the U.S. auto makers to play catch up while they worked to eliminate an average of 13 manufacturing defects per vehicle. As American cars rolled off the assembly line, Japanese cars were capturing the U.S. consumer. By the time U.S. manufacturers remedied the defect issue, there was a new obstacle to surmount: winning back the market from foreign contenders.

Tom Peters and Nancy Austin in their management classic *Thriving On Chaos*, find that on average, those companies whose products score in the top third on a 'relative perceived product quality' test, out-earn those in the bottom third by a 2-1 margin. Those are the rewards of DIRFT: Doing It Right the First Time!

The global corporate community has recognized this bounty for Quality. In response, the International Standards Organization (ISO) has issued guidelines for continuous improvement geared toward achieving higher quality products, called ISO-9000. Many high technology companies are now seeking to conform to ISO-9000. Q*R*PD and the 5 keys to DIRFT discussed below in no way conflict with ISO-9000, but rather augment it.

KEY #1: COMMITTED

Everybody commits whole-heartedly and knowingly to a worthwhile vision.

a) Make real commitments of specifications and schedules.
b) Involve customers and suppliers.
c) Justify project for ROI based on Performance, Time, Costs (PTCC).
d) Fully understand and be clear about the objectives.

Management studies repeatedly cite lack of common understanding of project objectives as the number one most common reason why a

© 1998 Global Brain, Inc.

project fails. You may have heard this in the office hallways: "How can we meet the schedule when we keep working on a moving target?" This is typical chaos with predictable results: nebulous corporate objectives evoking minimal commitment on the part of team members to actually accomplish the goals.

Crosby tells us that "the key to DIRFT is getting requirements clearly understood and then not putting things in people's way." [3]

Even if some members of the team do fully understand the project goals, often other players on the team, usually in other departments, will have a completely different set of ideas about manufacturability or marketability or other issues critical to the project. This becomes the classic right hand – left-hand scenario. Although many time-critical projects kick-off with a genuine sense of urgency to get it done, often times the team isn't allowed the necessary time to investigate what is really required to accomplish the task. Consequently, projects get under-staffed, resource requirements over-looked, or the workers are over-committed for the amount of work to be delivered.

Q*R*PD attempts to harmonize corporate objectives with those of the new product development teams. This happens by creating a synergistic environment, one where the whole is greater than the sum of its parts. Jim Barbera, a Project Leader for the Vitacom Corporation is an enthusiastic advocate of Q*R*PD: "With the synergy it creates 10 people could do the work of 20 people. We met our demanding schedule and successfully deployed a complex satellite transceiver system in Brazil right on time. This experience will make the next project go even faster!"

Equip your team with a vision. Create a synergistic environment by communicating all of the required information to the team, enabling them to feel fully committed to the project objectives.

Q*R*PD uses a very powerful process called the Product Vision to facilitate the buy-in process. Over a period of weeks or months the product vision writing process results in a one or two page document incorporating not only the most important specifications for the product, but also its costs, objectives, and key milestones. At the end of this process, team members and executives declare their commitment by literally signing-off on a package of documents that completely describes a well-planned out project.

Avoiding the pool-syndrome

Obviously, no team member would buy-in without having had an opportunity to fully realize what their individual commitment will accomplish for the over-all project. It's similar to diving head-first into a swimming pool. We usually dip our toes in to check out the temperature and depth (and if there's any water in it at all). This is how we can 'avoid the pool-syndrome', meaning jumping into something without knowing what you're getting into.

A couple years ago, an anti-drug campaign commercial showed a teenage girl on a diving board high above a pool. The commentator stated, "You better think about it before you get high." The pool far below had no water in it at all. Let's look before we leap! Examine the market, evaluate your current resources and compare your ideal time line with the true costs of lateness.

How NOT to Write a Specification:

We, the	UNWILLING,
Led by the	UNQUALIFIED,
Are doing the	IMPOSSIBLE
For the	UNGRATEFUL.

I must humbly recount that in the mid 1980s as Vice President of Engineering at Mountain Computer, Inc., I found this lovely note on my desk when I arrived to work at 7 o'clock in the morning. I reached the ingenious conclusion that we had a morale problem. I immediately called a staff meeting and our management team proceeded to address the problems, which we discovered stemmed from a lack of buy-in and commitment to what, in retrospect, were unrealistic and unachievable objectives that we had mandated.

Finally, once the team has agreed to realistic, achievable goals, will you maintain one or two schedules in the company? Quite often the product development and managing and

© 1998 Global Brain, Inc.

marketing groups can become adversaries, and they end up working on two different schedules for the same project. For example, engineering might commit to delivering the product in nine months; but sales, being previously "burnt," will tell customers twelve to fifteen months. Or of course, the opposite can occur where sales appeases the customer with an earlier delivery time than engineering has committed to. Either way it costs the company money: the former in lost sales if the customers choose another supplier instead of waiting, and the latter as a result of an upset customer waiting for product to arrive.

Neither approach works, because due to internal informal lines of communication everybody finds out what the defacto schedule is anyway. This again creates a fractured, non-harmonious environment. Establish a Product Vision, and one schedule that everyone can commit to whole-heartedly and knowingly.

Phase I Concentration

QRPD prescribes a relatively prolonged and concentrated time and financial investment in the first, kick-off phase of the project. This beginning process is a most critical time in which the foundation is laid. Quite simply, take your time in the first phase and accelerate the pace in the following stages. Although this is elemental to Doing It Right The First Time, it is where most companies fall short; rocketing through the initial stage only to be hung up down the road by mistakes and changes that could have been caught early on.

Phase One should usually take about 25% of the overall timeline. This extra time allotted allows for the thorough research and strategizing that is crucial to the smooth progression of the project. Investigate. Educate. Communicate. Interview your customers and spend time learning what their needs are. Connect with your key suppliers and establish realistic delivery times. This steadied pace also offers the time needed by the team to soundly resolve who's going to do what, and when and how.

Typically, 80% of the final cost of a product is determined in the first 20% of the production schedule. That, combined with the exponentially rising cost of making changes to the product in subsequent stages (see chart), highlights the importance of Phase I.

Skyrocketing Cost of Changes
(Major Electronics Companies) [4]

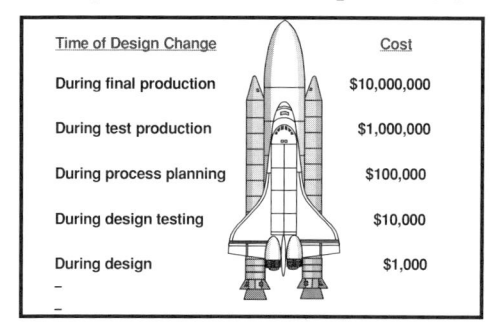

Time of Design Change	Cost
During final production	$10,000,000
During test production	$1,000,000
During process planning	$100,000
During design testing	$10,000
During design	$1,000

John Young, retired CEO and President of Hewlett Packard promotes the value of emphasizing Phase I. He agreed with me on the phone that, "Improved new product development cycle time is not only free, it's profitable. It doesn't cost you anything, it's more fun for everybody, and you do it right the first time by investing up front!"

KEY #2: SENSE OF MISSION

Create a 'Put a man on the moon' mission.

a) Use milestone charts, MBO, MBWA

b) Motivate the project team, create synergy

In 1960, President John F. Kennedy motivated an entire generation of scientists and engineers toward pursuing technological projects. He did this by declaring to America, "We will put a man on the moon by the end of the decade." His dramatic statement was prompted by a fearful reaction to the competition—the Russians had recently raced into space with Sputnik. Arguably, the entire aerospace industry and semiconductor boom was a result of that nation-wide mission. Many doubted that the goal was realistically achievable, but nonetheless, it was a powerfully inspirational mission that pulled the technological community together to make it happen. As we now know, the mission was in fact fulfilled in less than a decade.

In September 1993, the Clinton Administration made a joint announcement with the 'Big Three' auto makers: they would produce a "clean car" within a decade (2003) that would get 80 miles per gallon—greatly reducing the toxic emissions of even today's most fuel efficient automobiles. This would compare to 1992's average of 29 mpg and only 14 mpg in 1970. Clearly this will require a great number of new technologies that are not in existence in today. Does this sound like a familiar mission? Again, trying to make the seemingly un-doable happen. If it is done right the first time, both individuals and the nation will be getting great economic mileage (and perhaps keeping pace with the foreign auto-makers, this time).

> *Steve Jobs, the founder of Apple, used to walk throughout the office and declare about the Macintosh Computer, "It's going to be insanely great!"*

It's this kind of 'bigger than life' vision that a project leader must impart to the team. Emphasize the extensive importance of the project to your people: what is it giving the customer?, where will it take the company?, how will it advance their career?

Consider this dramatic example.... A team of engineers was designing a very important piece of medical equipment. How did they know it was of such great importance? The project leader calculated the number of intensive care patients who were dying throughout the world for each day that this new piece of equipment was not yet ready for use. How's that for a motivating sense of purpose?!

As team members are shown the range of valuables, enthusiasm and a deeper sense of meaning is cultivated, which is intrinsic to commitment. In the classic, *Soul of A Machine*, Tom West, the project leader at Data General for a very successful mini-computer once said, "There's thirty guys out in that lab who think it's *their* machine. That's very useful to me right now."

The project leader responds to achievement with rewards, more than just financial compensation but also the implicit promise that team members who succeed on a project will be assigned to future 'hot' and exciting projects.

> *Two medieval stone cutters were asked what they were working on. The first answered, "I'm blocking off a piece of stone out of this corner." The second stone cutter, who was doing identical work, replied, "I'm building a cathedral." [5]*

A highly charged team of professionals who embark on a project that they all believe in, will do whatever it takes to engineer a giant leap for their companies' profitability. Once you have provided them with the information and the inspiration, you need only to put a measurement system into place to monitor results.

Create a calendar of 'do or die' tasks and dates that will serve as milestones; or more accurately, 'footstones', to chart progress in frequent intervals. Make it clearly known that even one missed footstone could possibly result in cancellation of the entire project. The project leader should break the project down and ask his team members to come up with schedules that they are comfortable committing to for their portion of the work. A strong leader will be the primary gage for achievement and will consistently appraise individual and team progress, because, "the same work can be estimated differently by ten different estimators, or estimated by one estimator at ten different times."

A final recommendation about footstones. Post footstone charts in two columns: one for projected completion date, and one for the actual date the goal was met. Use a color-coding scheme to distinguish the rate of progress. Use green for dates met or beaten, yellow for a few days late, and red for more than a week behind. Staying in the green zone will also keep the green coming in for the company.

> *"You can bamboozle an engineer into committing to an unreasonable deadline, but you can't con him into meeting the deadline."*

Two additional commonly practiced management methodologies also encourage the creation of a mission oriented

© 1998 Global Brain, Inc.

environment: MBO (Management By Objectives) and MBWA (Management By Walking Around).

MBO came into existence twenty years ago and since then has gone out of vogue and come back in again. Basically, MBO provides a pyramid-like structure to set in motion all corporate objectives. Usually used for salaried professionals, each person independently sets their goals for the coming quarter and has them approved and mutually agreed upon by their manager. The manager does the same and so on, until the final management layer reaches the president of the company. This process fosters self-motivation and allows team members to monitor their own progress toward previously agreed upon objectives.

Problems can arise with MBO if it becomes a competition for individual achievement. However if the achievables are also graded according to the whole team's performance, then competition evolves into *cooperation*, combining together to form *co-petition*. By correlating the goals of the project, to the goals of the individual, management can empower the team and take a more hands-off approach. Performance reviews are based on these easily identifiable requirements.

Many companies will use a scale for MBO of 0 to 100% with an expected minimum of 80%. Imagine how well the company president sleeps at night knowing that everyone in the company is meeting at least 80% of their objectives, thereby fulfilling at least 80% of his goals for the whole company.

A large CAD software company in Silicon Valley uses MBO and typically has 30 to 40% of it's objectives be team-oriented. Furthermore, they write up their objectives each quarter as a group activity and use 80 to 100% of the goals as their overall objectives. At the end of the quarter, they grade them and go on to use the average results for yearly reviews.

MBWA (Management By Walking Around) in it's simplest practice, requires the project leader and other managers to get out of the office and survey their territory frequently. By doing this they can offer both constructive criticism and positive reinforcement, as well as uncover potentially problematic issues. It also allows the project leader to reinforce his or her sense of mission and convey it to the rest of the team, in a genuine and personal way.

By creating such a meaningful atmosphere, you are providing the synergy that energizes people to go the extra mile, improve quality, and meet and/or beat schedules. Edward Deming Jr. also knew that "environment is the over riding factor... what management perceives as the performance of people is actually the efforts of people in the presence of the environment they work in. Management has to fix the environment, make it cooperative". Create a mission atmosphere, and you too can take a giant leap for your company and mankind.

KEY #3: FOLLOW FLOW

Follow and continuously improve flow processes.

a)   Follow Quality *Rapid* Product Development (Q*R*PD), and checklist of techniques for new product development

b)   Step by step procedures

Most successful product developers have found the value of mapping the flow of a project step by step. For the most part, manufacturing divisions mastered this quite a while ago. They track all incoming raw materials, inspection checklists are applied, further labor and quality tests are conducted and timed each step of the way, return rates after shipment are surveyed, and so on. Engineering involves an even greater number of variables, yet too often this becomes an excuse for not following a production process. Venturing into the unknown is no excuse for poor navigation.

When we don't adhere to a process, oversights and errors are inevitable—it becomes impossible to do it right the first time. Like in a manufacturing assembly line, the earlier we catch mistakes, the less they cost us. So often, when we have completed 90% of a project, we find a major error and wonder, "How could

© 1998 Global Brain, Inc.

we have missed this?" Unfortunately, many times we realize that had we used a detailed checklist of design questions, someone could have recognized the critical issue and prevented the oversight. Perhaps someone was out sick that ill-fated day, or collectively, the team decided that they "didn't have time for a meeting."

To DIRFT make sure to have a process, and while you will spend a varying amount of time on each step, don't skip any steps.

KEY #4: TEST ENOUGH

Test! Test! Test!

a) Start early: subsystems and working prototype

b) Test throughout

c) Real Alpha and Beta tests

d) Reliability and life testing

The Carpenter's Law:

"Measure twice, cut once."

The later in the project we unearth mistakes, the more it costs to remedy them. As technological complexity increases and the amount of time we have to deliver it decreases, we need to make frequent tests to ensure that we're still on the right track. If we test and find mistakes we can adjust our course early on. Most successful products have gone through numerous micro or mini adjustments before running to completion. This is okay. Going on faith alone can be disastrous —an unpredictable crap shoot—so start testing early and keep on testing until the product's ready to ship.

The Chicken Test [6]

A thorough reality check on a working prototype should be conducted in the first 25% of the project schedule. Early testing will prove if the essential technology is actually functioning as it should, and will indicate if it's necessary to take a different approach to the over-all plan. Neglecting to test early on can result in late-breaking bad news.

For example, a major mainframe computer manufacturer decided to re-package its systems into a new market application, telecommunications switching. The project was scheduled to run one year. Like many companies hoping for everything to work out perfectly, they waited until the ninth month to attempt system integration for the first time. Unfortunately, many of the mechanical subsystems didn't fit together. Over 180 drawings had to be redone, causing a three month delay in a highly contested market. A *chicken test* on an early, albeit primitive working prototype may deflect future disasters such as this one.

The chicken test gets its name from tests performed on airplane jet engines in the 1950s. Manufacturers designed what they believed was a highly capable engine, but found that when airborne, the planes were being halted by birds flying into the engine. They came up with a most basic and effective test: while the jet engines were running, a barrel gun several feet in diameter fired chickens directly into them in a wind tunnel. Even today this serves as an early warning system to uncover a possible fundamental flaw in a design, before spending the whole $250 million necessary to develop a new engine.

One last remark about the chicken test: the war archives of many companies reveal that on average, after you pass your assessment point, you still have about half the project left to complete. So don't kid yourself. Plan well, and allow plenty of time for system integration, testing, and debugging.

What we really meant

"Preliminary operational tests were inconclusive." What we really meant.: "The poor thing blew up when we first tested it."

"Test results were extremely gratifying." What we really meant: "It works! Boy, are we surprised."

© 1998 Global Brain, Inc.

The Alpha and Beta Tests

Alpha and *beta* testing goes beyond the testing done by the product design team, and provides additional levels of verification. Alpha testing is performed by a group that's independent of the design team and still within the company. These may be members of the team at large or perhaps another organization in the company such as a quality assurance or product test lab, etc. We can trust the results of the alpha testing only if significant, measurable, and verifiable procedures are run.

Beta testing calls in the customer. Two major types of customers can be identified: *leading edge* and *typical*. You want to have a representation of both types of customers to get feedback on your products. Leading edge beta customers are technologically sophisticated and knowledgeable. They can provide invaluable guidance and input to your design from the very beginning of the project. Typical beta customers offer a different type of feedback. They may simply want a "plug and play" product, but undoubtedly, they will find problems that we or the leading edge customers would not have thought of looking for. A beta test recently run with typical customers identified an elementary problem with a particular product's design: customers couldn't find the power switch because of it's awkward location....

Once we have delivered the product to several of these two types of beta sites, it is paramount that we evoke their sincere opinions about our product. Too often we rely on the sales person to get in touch with the customer and tell us what they think. They may say, "We're pretty sure the customer is satisfied," which really means, "we were so far behind schedule that the customer was happy to get anything from us." Have you been there before?

As painful as critical, honest and specific feedback might be at this point, we need to hear it. At this time of the project, there is no substitute for frequent and if possible, face-to-face communication with the beta customers. The project leader and team members will find invaluable information and motivation from personally visiting the beta sites. Your time out of the office and a flight to meet with your customers will save money in the long run. When you do talk with the beta customers, ask a lot of open-ended questions and be receptive to direct feedback. Most importantly, listen. Afterwards, take what you've learned back to the project and fix the problem before hundreds or even thousands of units have been shipped.

One area of problems that alpha and beta testing may fail to uncover is long-term reliability of the product. We should specifically design tests that accelerate usage and attempt to simulate operation of the product over its whole lifetime.

Testing early on, including chicken testing working prototypes, testing throughout the project, doing alpha and beta tests, and finally reliability and life-cycling substantially increases your odds to Do It Right The First Time.

KEY #5: PLUNGE

Plunge through the product development funnel.

a) Micro-manage the last 10%

b) Project Leader, Product Engineer and core team work with all departments to get the product out the door right, and on time

---
The last 10% of the project can seem like 90% of the work.

In the final stretch of the project, and only in the final stretch of the project, the project leader needs to use a style of *micro-management* that keeps the chaos moving in a positive direction. It's a balancing act of leaning on the team to follow through with the critical details while creating the space and support for them to plow through and get the work done. The team is most susceptible to burn out at this stage. Like Tom West says, "It's a long term tiredness. Going home won't solve it anymore."

It's time to rally—the Project Leader, product engineer and the core team must pull together to get the product out the door right, and on

© 1998 Global Brain, Inc.

time. Meet everyday first thing in the morning to create a hit list, and review it at the next day's meeting. The face-to-face contact helps everyone to focus on the details, so frequent contact is critical. Refer to the Product Vision and specifications and drive home that sense of purpose so that you can focus on shipping the product sooner rather than later.

You've committed whole-heartedly, you've created a mission, you've tested, tested, tested and now you have plunged through the long and sometime arduous product development funnel. The future is waiting for you, and you'll be getting there first; just on time, and have done it right the first time. Don't let the future happen without you!

References

[1] Philip B. Crosby, *Quality Without Tears*, Plume, 1992, p. 58.

[2] Kopelman, Orion, and Voegtli, Cinda, with Josephs, Adam, *Projects at Warp Speed with QRPD: The Definitive Guidebook to Quality Rapid Product Development,* 8th Ed., 1998, Global Brain, Inc.

[3] Crosby, *Quality Without Tears*, p. 58.

[4] "A Smarter Way to Manufacture: How Concurrent Engineering Can Reinvigorate American Industry," page 110, *Business Week*, April 20, 1990.

[5] Willis Harman, *Global Mind Change*, Warner Books, 1988, p. 144.

[6] Peters, Tom and Austin, Nancy. 1985. *A Passion for Excellence, The Leadership Difference*. Random House, p. 130.

© 1998 Global Brain, Inc.

Adapted from article originally published in

Electronic Design Magazine

Article: The Seven Sins that Prevent Quality *Rapid* Product Development, and Their Remedies

© 1998 Global Brain, Inc.

The Seven Sins that Prevent Quality *Rapid* Product Development, And Their Remedies

Orion Kopelman, President
Cinda Voegtli, Consulting Partner
Global Brain®, Inc.
555 Bryant St. #369
Palo Alto, CA 94301

Introduction

Many companies have used Q*R*PD® techniques to realize dramatic improvements in their product development efforts. And yet, many companies have not found the will power and determination to consistently implement the fairly well known techniques advocated by Q*R*PD. Habitual ways of doing things have kept them chained to their past modes of operation.

This article presents

- The most common malignant practices we've observed in the technology-driven industry—we call them seven deadly sins that prevent Quality *Rapid* Product Development.

- The Q*R*PD secret that was violated, and an example of how to use the DIRFT keys from the previous chapter to monitor and avoid the sin.

- The remedies, straight out of the Q*R*PD arsenal of tools.

The Seven Deadly Sins that Slow Product Development

To break the chains that have kept companies from realizing all the benefits of the common sense best practices we call Q*R*PD, they must overcome the seven deadly sins shown in Table 1. These sins are the seven most common ways companies fail to achieve the benefits of Quality *Rapid* Product Development.

Using DIRFT to Recognize the Sin and Implement the Remedy

Table 2 illustrates how the DIRFT keys from the previous chapter can provide you with early warning of trouble and help you avoid or remedy the 7 sins.

Sin 1. Trying to do too much in one project, including the NIH — Not Invented Here — syndrome.

Technical people usually underestimate the number of unknowns that arise during the development process. Consequently, many projects are packed with risky development efforts. Some of these risks directly result from NIH: the tendency of many technical people to think that they can come up with a better design themselves, even at the expense of not having a justified return on investment for their company for spending the time and money to do it. By not using technology available from previous projects or from outside the company, one creates a monster size endeavor. These "megatrap" projects rarely complete on schedule.

Recall the story on page 48, in which Mountain Computer scored a big market "win" by repackaging existing disk drive technology to create hard drive capability for the original diskless personal computers. More recently, NASA and McDonnell actually developed a prototype of a reusable rocket, the Delta Clipper, on schedule and within budget—18 months, and $60 million.

© 1998 Global Brain, Inc.

Table 1. The Seven Deadly Sins that Prevent Q*R*PD

SIN	REMEDY
1. Trying to do too much in one project, including the NIH — Not Invented Here— syndrome.	USE INCREMENTAL INNOVATION—identify the limited number of innovations that really matter. INNOVATE RATHER THAN INVENT (re-package).
2. Not everybody buys-in to a common product vision.	RE-DO "SSSS" NEGOTIATION to get a Vision everyone can live with and sign up to. Sign it!
3. Functional organizations refuse to relinquish control to cross-functional project teams.	GET TOP MANAGEMENT TO BUY INTO Q*R*PD, and allow project teams to have the authority they need.
4. A weak project team leader, or one that lacks authority.	SELECT PROJECT LEADER CAREFULLY, AND ANNOINT RESPONSIBILITY.
5. A poor product development process, or none at all.	WORK ON THE PROCESS AND PRODUCT SIMULTANEOUSLY to improve the project without stopping it.
6. No test on working prototypes early in the schedule.	DO A CHICKEN TEST IN THE FIRST 25% OF THE PROJECT.
7. A disintegrating, endless end-game.	MICRO-MANAGE THE LAST 10%—the whole team works together closely to handle details and get it out the door.

(By comparison, a re-design of the space shuttle toilet cost the taxpayers $23 million.) The Clipper team achieved this by using "hand-me-downs" — a guidance system from an F-15 jet fighter and some leftover fuel tanks from another program. The rocket flew successfully in the summer of 1993, and restored hope to the US for a viable commercial space launching program that competes with the French *Ariane* and the Russian *Proton*.

The Q*R*PD remedy exemplified by these successes? We must become *incremental innovators*, rather than inventors. Innovation can be defined as introducing novelty (new know-how) into practical use (technology) to increase the customer's value and satisfaction obtained from the seller's or manufacturer's resources. By packaging available inventions as part of your product, you can get to the market faster with competitive products, and become adept at quickly completing multiple development cycles that each result in a salable, desirable product. By introducing successive generations regularly, you can lower overall risk while learning more about the market and the technology and continuously refining your products.

Best of all, with this approach, everybody wins: You rarely strike out completely, and always get paid by the customers along the way. They win, too, since you presumably provide them with value and a better way to do something. Engineers, product managers, and other project team members win in the long run as their companies prosper. But management must steer technical people clear of their natural propensity to want to invent everything by themselves, and restrict Marketing from demanding that everything be ready for the product that must ship next month.

© 1998 Global Brain, Inc.

Table 2. Recognizing and Avoiding the 7 Sins

Sin	DIRFT Key	Early Warning
1. Trying to do too much in one project, including the NIH — Not Invented Here— syndrome.	DIRFT #1: Is everyone committed wholeheartedly and knowingly to the worthwhile and limited vision?	Use the innovations risk assessment list: how many innovations is the project taking on? Quantitatively justify them: are they really needed?
2. Not everybody buys-in to a common product vision.	DIRFT #1: Is everyone committed wholeheartedly and knowingly to the worthwhile and limited vision?	Write a Product Vision, then watch for signs of disagreement—arguments, grumbling, changing requirements, or changing designs—during the rest of the project.
3. Functional organizations refuse to relinquish control to cross-functional project teams.	DIRFT #2: Does everyone feel the sense of purpose and work urgently on a "put the man on the moon" mission?	Watch for disruption to the Mission: contention on project decisions; resources not making their action item dates or milestones due to conflicting priorities, etc.
4. A weak project team leader, or one that lacks authority.	DIRFT #2: Does everyone feel the sense of purpose and work urgently on a "put the man on the moon" mission?	Watch for disruption to the mission: an aimless team without an effective leader; multiple people acting as leader; contention on project decisions, holes in responsibilities, etc.
5. A poor product development process, or none at all.	DIRFT #3: Are you following and continually improving a written Flow process?	Watch for mistakes slipping through; low-quality deliverables; team members who don't know what to do.
6. No test of working prototypes early in the schedule.	DIRFT #4: Is everyone testing early, throughout, thoroughly?	Use the innovations risk assessment list; plan chicken tests for all major and above innovations, and the system.
7. A disintegrating, endless, end-game	DIRFT #5: Are you plunging through the funnel together to finish the last 10% and get it out?	Watch for endless "gotchas" at the end; slipping ship dates due to last-minute problems, team members who don't know what tasks are most important.

How do we avoid committing sin #1? We remember, and monitor, DIRFT key #1: Is everyone committed wholeheartedly and knowingly to the worthwhile and limited vision? First, make sure that your team has developed a product vision. Then strictly enforce the concept of incremental innovation, using the innovations risk assessment list created in Phase I. (See Flow.) Categorize each innovation as minor, medium, or major risk, and carefully justify its benefits and return on investment. By combining minimal invention, taking advantage of existing technology, and introducing a limited number of innovations, everyone comes out ahead on an ongoing basis.

© 1998 Global Brain, Inc.

Sin 2. Not everybody buys-in to a common product vision.

To successfully innovate incrementally, the *entire company* must agree on a clearly defined, limited set of product objectives. Too often not everyone buys into the emerging vision of the product. This results in either technical failures or delays. For example, in one company where Marketing and Engineering were at odds with one another, a specification called for a quick two-week redesign of a door on an armored vehicle to make it "airtight". Unfortunately, the specification also stated a maximum allowed rate of air leakage. Engineering decided to meet the numerical specification, and of course the customer had expected "airtight" to mean zero leakage (required for chemical warfare, especially). The company eventually sent a team halfway across the world to retrofit a totally new design at the customer's site. A simple "slam-dunk" project turned into an eleven-week fiasco, due to the lack of a common understanding of the product.

The obvious remedy involves getting the whole project team together to hash-out a written one-page Vision. (See Flow, the Seesaw Specifications and Scheduling process). Everyone must participate in the negotiation process of trading-off product features, benefits, and costs for the resulting amount of time and budget required for design and production. The goal is to have all team members commit whole-heartedly and knowingly to a Vision that delivers a valuable product to the customers and makes financial sense for everyone: DIRFT Key #1.

How do you get early warning on this sin so that we can avoid its ill effects? Monitor the signs of true commitment to a common Vision, by watching for signs of disagreement or lack of understanding of the Vision—arguments, grumbling, changing requirements, or changing designs—during the rest of the project. Such problems indicate that evidently everyone really didn't fully understand the Vision or sign up to it. Review the Vision with the team; work out misunderstandings; and if necessary, do the SSSS negotiations again.

© 1998 Global Brain, Inc.

Sin 3. Functional organizations refuse to relinquish control to project teams

Management experts have touted the concept of organizing companies along the lines of project teams since the beginning of the Space Age. In 1959 Paul O. Gaddis warned in one of the first articles on "*The Project Manager*" that, "The United States today faces the enormous problem of how to regain undisputed technological leadership.... Advancement ... will shape our future and determine our survival or extinction.... The role of project management will be challenging, exciting, and crucial." This rings as true today as then. And yet many functional managers refuse to give up control over their domain of influence and fail to provide adequate, timely cross-functional support to project teams. The result is often late, costly product changes.

Managers must recognize that their workers' loyalty must lie first and foremost with small interdisciplinary project teams, chartered with rapidly developing a product. Association with a department like marketing or quality should become secondary. Fostering this kind of spirit of commitment to a project yields remarkable results. The Project Leader for a supplier of phone equipment, a graduate of the Q*R*PD training program, used Q*R*PD to complete a project in half the time of previous projects, 9 months instead of 18. In his words, "At times we ran counter to the accepted norms of doing things, but we met all expected customer deliverables. We could easily do this again and again, if management continues to clear the runway *by giving us dedicated people from all departments*, and says 'go!'"

How do you tell if you're successfully avoiding this sin? Answer DIRFT Key #2: Does *everyone* feel the sense of purpose and work urgently on a "put the man on the moon" mission? Watch for disruption to the mission: multiple team members trying to act as leader to carry out particular department agendas; cross-functional contention on project decisions; and team members' schedule priorities being changed by their functional managers, results in missed action item due dates or milestone dates. If you see these signs, you've still got work to do; you must sell your company's management on the critical need for full cross-functional participation on project teams.

Fortunately, re-organizing lines of responsibility into these kinds of project teams doesn't degrade product quality, but even improves it. On average the cost of a change in the design increases tenfold at each later stage in a project. Early cross-functional involvement helps minimize unforeseen risks and thus prevent tardy changes that cause quality problems, astronomical costs, and time delays. Top management should be able to understand these benefits and encourage functional managers to release their workers to the project teams early on in the development.

Sin 4. A weak project team leader, or one that lacks authority.

Another consequence of the layers of entrenched functional middle managers is that often the wrong project leaders get selected. A functional management mentality often leads to the assumption that a particular technical person is by default the best person for the Project Leader job. For example, a company making a linear accelerator for cancer therapy, an instrument with digital control and a computer interface, chose by default the Engineering Manager as the team leader. Unfortunately, he did not have the best background for this job: his lack of experience in linear accelerator technology caused the end product to not meet its specifications, take four years to develop instead of three, and come in 50% over budget.

A primary functional orientation also can lead to situations in which no single Project Leader truly has responsibility or authority for completing the overall mission. For example, a company making a laser to correct far-sightedness had three people assume the role of leader on the project: the lead hardware designer, mechanical designer, and laser designer. None agreed on an overall approach or schedule. Worse yet, none of them perceived that they had overall responsibility. Consequently, no one identified a pitfall in one of the easiest areas of the project— insufficient software resources—the area of least innovation on this project, but still highly time consuming. The project was shipped in 12 months instead of 9, ironically two months after a competitor introduced a comparable product.

How do you tell if you're successfully avoiding this sin? Again, the answer lies with DIRFT Key #2: Does *everyone* feel the sense of purpose and work urgently on the same "put the man on the moon" mission? Watch for disruption to the mission: an aimless team without an effective leader as evidenced by missed milestones or action items; multiple people effectively acting as leader, making conflicting or inconsistent project decisions; and issues "falling through the cracks" and causing rework and project delays.

Top management must take the initiative to force a matrix, project-oriented organization chart; assume the burden of choosing the right team leader; and give them all the authority they need to meet their huge responsibility. This includes assigning at least dashed-line reporting of the team members to the Project Leader. The leader should have heavy influence on the individuals' performance reviews, emphasizing the importance of everyone pulling together to pull the project on time. See the Project Leader and Team section for example performance appraisal forms.

Sin 5. A poor product development process, or none at all.

As discussed in the Introduction, the Carnegie Mellon Software Engineering Institute has observed five maturity levels in the software development process. Unfortunately, an educated guess predicts that over half of development projects operate at levels one or two, about a quarter at level three, and maybe 10% at levels four and five. That last 10% are usually highly successful companies.

© 1998 Global Brain, Inc.

Recall the Blown Balloon story in the Techniques section, where a "level two" company with a repeatable but not yet defined new product development process stumbled into trouble. The lack of a fully-defined process resulted in a three month delay that cost the company about $5.6 million in lost profit.

How do you avoid this sin? Use DIRFT Key #3: Are you following and continually improving a Flow process? Here are sure signs that you aren't: You don't have a written process. Team members express uncertainty about their roles and responsibilities. Project "deliverables" are of low quality, and design mistakes slip through to cause later rework. Worst of all, past mistakes get repeated.

Make sure you document your process and educate team members on the critical parts they play. Many companies at levels three and above create and use a guidebook. Much like cookbooks, these books help teams to more predictably follow a "recipe" for successful product development every time. (Even master chefs use basic recipes, then improvise on the fly.) Guidebooks don't assure success, but they definitely increase the odds of developing quality new products quickly, and repeatedly.

Your guidebook doesn't' have to be big, long, or fancy. Start with a basic process framework based on the QRPD phases, basic descriptions of your Flow steps and important deliverables, and clear concise directions for cross-functional team members' most important contributions.

One admonition: while many companies are eager for the benefits of an improving development process, too many fall short due to a standard problem: they don't have the time to stop and "sharpen the axe," when so much wood needs to get chopped so soon. Rapidly expanding, successful companies have learned to emphasize equally, and work simultaneously on, both improving the development process and executing individual product projects. Use DIRFT key #3 tools such as "lessons learned" meetings during your projects and capture critical new knowledge as you go. Encourage team members to add their suggestions to the guidebook on the fly. See Commandment 11 for more ideas.

Sin 6. No "chicken test" on a working prototype early in the schedule.

Every project should undergo a critical "chicken test" before the 50% point in the project, to tell you if the essential technology actually functions as it should. The chicken test gets its name from the "early warning" tests performed on new jet engines, to uncover any fundamental flaws in the design before the company spends the entire $250 million necessary to fully develop the new engine. Unfortunately, old habits all too often prevail, and teams still wait to test until late in the project, when all the features of the product are complete.

To avoid this sin, use DIRFT Key #4: Is everyone testing early, throughout the project, and thoroughly? Use your phase I innovations risk assessment list, plan chicken tests for all major innovations and above, and execute them as early as possible in the project. Plan a system chicken test to prove the overall design, and complete it before the 50% point. The time and money for this testing are well worth the investment. See Commandment #8.

Sin 7. A disintegrating, endless endgame.

When teams get near the end of a project, it often seems like 90% of the work occurs in the last 10%. There are many details to closely coordinate to get the product out the door. This is also the time when other projects are clamoring for engineers to be let loose from the project, when cross-functional groups have more and more of the daily work, and many tedious "unexciting" tasks such as documentation must be done well to ensure successful delivery. All too often, even if the team has performed well until now, this complex "end-game" can disintegrate and wipe out the rapid development efforts. Sometimes products never successfully make

© 1998 Global Brain, Inc.

it out the door in volume due to these late issues.

How do you know if you're experiencing, or on the verge of, an endless end-game? Use DIRFT Key #5: Are you plunging through the funnel together to finish the last 10% and get the product out? Watch for repeated "gotchas": rework on documentation, failed tests in manufacturing, slipping ship dates due to last minute design bugs or missing parts? Look for delays resulting from information overload, confusion in priorities, and team members not working on the most important tasks.

B*efore* you get to the last 10%, make sure your team members understand their upcoming roles, responsibilities, and detailed tasks. Then use the DIRFT key #5 tools such as daily hot-list meetings to manage the end-game and avoid this sin.

Conclusion

Sluggish product development can cost companies thousands of dollars in lost profit per day, due to late entry into the market. These seven sins are the most-often-seen violations that prevent quality rapid product development. Use the five keys to DIRFT to avoid or recognize these sins, and use your Q*R*PD toolkit to remedy them and complete your projects successfully.

© 1998 Global Brain, Inc.

Excerpted with permission from:
PROJECTWORLD® Winter 96 Proceedings

Article: Rescuing and Revitalizing the Off-Course Project

© 1998 Global Brain, Inc.

Rescuing and Revitalizing the Off-Course Project

Cinda Voegtli, Consulting Partner
Global Brain®, Inc.
555 Bryant Street #369   Palo Alto, CA 94301
(650) 327-2012   Fax: (650) 327-2028   email: missioncontrol@globalbrain.com

Abstract

There's no worse "super-urgent demand" than the looming end-date of a critical project that's behind schedule—a schedule that was probably highly aggressive to start with. Time-to-market demands can't be ignored, so how do you course-correct, get back your momentum, and succeed in spite of the setbacks?

This presentation describes how to use the guidelines and techniques of Quality *Rapid* Product Development (Q*R*PD®) to pinpoint and fully understand the project's past problems, revitalize your plan and your team, and get that product out the door. Typical scenarios from actual projects will be used to illustrate how these approaches come into play in the real world. The paper will also discuss how the same guidelines and techniques could have been used to avoid the problems in the first place.

Global Brain, Inc. is a management consulting firm specializing in the practical implementation of the Q*R*PD methodology in high-tech companies. Ms. Voegtli has extensive experience in product development, engineering management, project management, and consulting. She has worked in a wide variety of industries including data communications, medical devices, software and information technology, and virtual reality and game products. She serves on the international board of governors of the IEEE Engineering Management Society and was chair of the Silicon Valley chapter for two years.

Introduction

It's no fun when a project falls behind schedule. The demands on an already pressured team get worse, but the recovery plan may be unrealistic or non-existent. The natural tendency toward denial kicks in: "We'll catch up somehow" (method undefined). Often the sheer magnitude of the actual slip is not realized until the situation is grave.

Once the project's predicament is obvious, all too often the energy that's needed for finding a solution goes instead to recriminations, "spin control", and attempts to place blame elsewhere. The fact is that time-to-market still matters, so the company and the project team must go beyond those natural reactions to constructive action: a real plan for getting the product out the door. Unfortunately, since people may experience weighty feelings of failure and burn-out from efforts to-date, the enthusiasm, energy, and momentum the team needs for a recovery can be extremely hard to come by.

So how do we get there from here? By accomplishing the following steps:

- **Step 1. Assess current status:**

Step 1a. What were the project's problems, at a nuts-and-bolts level? What other problems might still be lurking?

Step 1b. Based on those problems, where are we with respect to our technical design, our schedule, and the marketplace?

© 1998 Global Brain, Inc.

Step 2. Analyze alternatives: What can we do now to best meet the company's goals?

- **Step 3. Decide new course**: Pick the best alternative and finalize the plan.

- **Step 4. Re-launch:** Get the team's energy up, everyone recommitted to a realistic plan, and get going!

These activities sound standard, but the way in which they are carried out has significant impact on whether the project can be recovered. The techniques of Quality *Rapid* Product Development (Q*R*PD) can be put to good use in recovering the problem project. Q*R*PD [1] is a set of management principles and best practices geared to fast-paced development by high-performance teams in chaotic market environments. Q*R*PD emphasizes the ultimate return on investment of the project, to put the "time-to-market" part of the equation in its proper perspective. The importance of individual team member contributions and responsibility is paramount. Q*R*PD emphasizes honest, realistic, thorough assessment of a problem project: to have the best chance of revitalizing the plan and the team, you must look back at root causes of project problems, and look ahead for opportunities for synergy and ultimate overall success. This practical, personal, honest, realistic focus helps diffuse the negativity of the "impossible" project situation and get the project on the road to recovery.

Step 1. Assess the situation

The Importance of an Accurate Assessment

When a project is in trouble, the normal response is to simply start re-planning the rest of the project, possibly adding resources in an attempt to finish the same amount of work in less time. That method deals only with the symptoms (the lateness) and not necessarily the root causes of the lateness, and therefore may not actually be able to improve the outcome significantly. We must first accept the importance of understanding the real root causes of the project's problems.

Before deciding how to fix our project, we must also be honest about where we really are with respect *to meeting the corporate goals of this project.* We can't correctly decide our plan for recovering if we don't know *with accuracy* where we are, with respect to the end-date we originally planned, and with respect to being successful at that end-date with the right product. The corporation's definition of success is "return on investment" from a project. For the dollars invested in product development (the development cost), what is the return in revenue from the product? The other factors that contribute to a products return are its "performance" (its feature set and attributes: does it provide what the customers want? is it manufacturable and serviceable?), its time to market (did we get to market fast enough?), and its cost (are customers willing to pay for it?). To achieve maximum return on investment on any project, the development team must choose the right balance of these factors: performance (P), time-to-market (T), product cost (C), and development cost (C). This balance is referred to in Q*R*PD as the "PTCC" balance. We likewise need to pay attention to the PTCC balance in our decisions of how to recover from a floundering project.

Step 1a. Assessing the Project Against Q*R*PD

The most thorough and revealing way to assess a project is to look for violations of the 10 Q*R*PD management "commandments". Q*R*PD recommends numerous day-to-day techniques for carrying out each of the commandments; project problems can often be traced to violations of those techniques. If we methodically examine our execution against the recommendations of Q*R*PD, we can get a realistic assessment of what has gone wrong, the magnitude of our underlying problems and their potential impact to the project, and opportunities for getting back on track.

The following sections provides questions for recognizing the cause of your project's problems based on the Q*R*PD commandments, and the Q*R*PD-recommended actions for correcting those problems to help recover the project. QRPD provides over 100 detailed techniques for carrying out the 10 commandments; this section highlights one or more typical technique violations for each commandment.

1. Focus on a clear and limited vision.

The number one reason for not getting done on time is to take on too much, of too risky a nature, at once, and to lose sight of that limited set of objectives. To hold our time-to-market we have to carefully choose the features most important for maximizing return on investment, and maintain our focus on those goals. Which of these characterized your project?

"The requirements are still changing, changing..." "So what is this thing we're developing?" "Here's the feature list of the week." These all mean that the definition of the product is not stable and changes are not controlled.

If your requirements are unstable, it is imperative that you stop and create a Product Vision. The Product Vision is a short, high-level document, created by the team, that captures non-negotiable product requirements. It focuses on the benefits provided to the customer and an understanding of what the customer will use to judge quality, key technologies and mandatory features, crucial product factors, and financial goals and constraints. No matter where you are in the project schedule, you may not have the right product definition, and changes may still happen to lengthen your schedule further. The fastest and most profitable way to finish the project may be to redefine the product! The Vision will bring team understanding and agreement upon what the product must be to meet the company's goals.

"This product isn't what we want." This suggests that the vision was incorrect, because customers weren't adequately involved in defining the product. Or the vision may have been defined correctly, but the team strayed from the vision during development. When you defined this product, did you talk to customers? Did you ensure that everyone on the team participated early in defining the product vision? Did you control changes to the Vision and other product specifications?

In writing the Product Vision, make sure you have real data from the market. If that hasn't happened to-date on your project, do it now. Interview both leading edge and target customers. Leading edge customers will help you understand where visionary users think the market is going. Target customers will give you the perspective of how to make your product succeed for the masses, for a sustained period of time. If the market soul-searching and high level of cross-functional inputs necessary to write this document has not been performed, you may have missed a critical aspect of the product definition, and it is still worth doing, no matter how far along you are in the project. Then the team MUST keep the Vision accessible and review it periodically.

"This is a complex do-it-all product; we can't predict when we'll be done". This is symptomatic of a team that didn't pick its battles or identify which features and technologies were absolutely necessary in the light of balancing PTCC.

Were you trying to do too much technologically in one project? Analyze the technological risks. Have you undertaken more than three innovations which no one currently in-house has ever tried? A QRPD rule of thumb is to limit these "major" innovations to 3. Because of the unknowns involved, the probability of disruptions to the schedule is high.

After the full assessment, this understanding of technical risks will be used to help decide whether the first release should contain everything you are attempting, to get the project done with the best balance of PTCC.

© 1998 Global Brain, Inc.

2. Assemble the right team and leader

The first QRPD commandment dealt with the appropriateness of the product definition and the team's focus on it; the second commandment deals with the appropriateness of the team itself. Look for the following problems:

Is the leader viewed as powerless or not worthy of respect? The team leader is of paramount importance in rapid product development. This factor is often underestimated, especially by companies new to the discipline of project management. Project management for intense product development efforts is far more than developing and tracking a schedule. The leader also has responsibility for ensuring the PTCC balance is defined during project planning; maintaining a thriving team in the face of all obstacles; and constantly judging real results and working actively to keep the project homed in on its PTCC goals.

QRPD describes the right leader as "an obsessed leader that is confident, honest, technical, a model worker, a people person, and has high standards and management ability."

It is important to note that often a "wrong" leader is not replaced because of the negative "demotion" connotations. Overcome that barrier! In tough situations, the individuals usually realize they're wrong for the job and welcome a graceful reassignment; and your project will not be able to recover without a strong, obsessed project leader.

Are people moving on and off the team? Since urgency tends to permeate everything we undertake, we often unrealistically expect our team members to "do it all", not just on one project but on several. However, if time to market is really important, we MUST stabilize our project team. It only looks like it costs less to have people split among projects. In reality, the project end-dates will suffer and the company will lose revenue because the projects will not ship on time. In QRPD we calculate a "late cost per week" based on this lost revenue, to clarify the dollars associated with time and ensure proper resource decisions. The proper PTCC balance may involve more development cost to achieve shorter development times.

Have there been major technical snafus? Determine whether experts have been used to lower the risk of your technological innovations. To finish your project, find the right experts, even if they're out of house, and make sure the path is clear for the rest of project. Combat any "not invented here" syndrome that may exist. Everyone's lives will be easier.

3. Initiate early cross-functional cooperation

Common causes of project delays: usability, testability, manufacturability, and maintainability issues that are not discovered until late in the project and are serious enough to necessitate re-design. Did cross-functional groups either not participate in earlier product definition and design reviews, or did they participate but not understand what they were supposed to contribute? Signs:

You're supposed to be shipping in volume and the technicians can't test the boards.

It's almost time for release and the beta customers are complaining about the user interface.

No one thought to plan for deployment so you have to stop at the end and write a database conversion tool.

The only remedy for people not being involved is to get them involved. No matter how far down the road you are in the project, STOP and get every functional group involved. Review the designs or prototypes in their current state. Have your cross-functional team members look for areas where they will have to spend "extra" money if they don't

© 1998 Global Brain, Inc.

get what they want. Have them think about past problems they've encountered once products have been released. DON'T assume that you're close to the end of your project and the product is good enough as is. Although it might not seem like the fastest way to finish a super-urgent project, a redesign now may be quicker than trying to limp through volume manufacture, and will definitely be less expensive than rejection of your product by the customer.

4. Create a synergistic, mission-oriented environment

It isn't enough to have a good team in place; the team has to operate within an environment that promotes their sense of mission, supports that mission, and allows them to achieve phenomenal results. Assess the following:

Is there a lack of urgency on your super-urgent project? It will carry over to the super-urgent completion schedule!. Are individual team members in the dark about the overall goals of the project? Involve them in creating a Product Vision. Do they understand and buy into the PTCC balance? Do they know the cost of delay? Calculate the late cost per week number and make sure everyone understands it.

Is the team mired in unproductive work, slowing them down and probably affecting morale as well? Endless management meetings (especially prevalent for "problem" projects); excessive status reporting; lack of proper communication tools? Have the team members analyze individually where their time is going and rate the usefulness of that time to the project's goals. Then make sure the project leader follows through and removes the obstacles to productivity.

5. Reward participants commensurably

The lack of proper rewards is usually not directly related to huge schedule hit until things get so bad that members of the team leave—and then it's too late to correct the reward issues! Lack of rewards can also have insidious effects on the team's productivity. Assess the following:

Are some people not dedicated? Not paying attention to milestones? Are their bad attitudes rubbing off on the team? Look for large and small ways to appreciate people. Include milestone celebrations, "going the extra mile" awards, plans for a big party at the end, both team and individual recognition, financial rewards commensurate with the culture of your company, industry, and geographical area.

NOTE: Attention to rewards can be very important to getting your team's momentum back. When you are late and must depend on your team to work hard to recover, an out-of-whack reward system will keep people from buying in and fully supporting the recovery effort

6. Use innovative parallel design strategies

Here the emphasis is on what the team can do technically to ensure success. System design problems unfortunately usually show up late in the project. By the time you figure out that integration is a nightmare because the code is "spaghetti", or not modularly designed, the code is already a mess. Unfortunately, the concept of "system engineering" is often relegated to the aerospace or defense industry; fast-paced commercial projects may throw that thoughtful high-return time out the window. Commandment 6 is meant to get those ideas firmly rooted (and scheduled) in our project strategies. Look for these problems:

Did a number of beautifully-optimized subsystems or modules come together to produce a system with sub-par performance? Was integration testing a nightmare? Did the correction of every problem discovered in system test yield bugs somewhere else? Were several modules highly risky in technology or design, such that contingency planning for all the risks was prohibitive or not done?

© 1998 Global Brain, Inc.

Did the first 100 units out of manufacturing work, but the next lot fail due to poor design margins and varying parts tolerances? All of these problems point to poor systems analysis, design partitioning, and margin definitions.

If you're late in the project, it might seem that this commandment can't help you. There's no time to redesign. Or maybe there is. When system failures are caused by system design problems, the tendency is to try to patch the problem. But poorly designed systems do not usually lend themselves to predictable correction. The resulting frustrating, potentially non-converging test and debug cycle may end up taking longer than doing some re-design. For behind-the-eightball projects, the best lesson is to look for the underlying system design causes of your problems, and identify where the investment of real correction time will pay off in the long run.

7. Invest money to buy tools and time, and to minimize risk

This commandment focuses on understanding the true cost of being late and the benefits of spending money to buy time. Considering our PTCC balance, have we done all we could to use development cost to achieve time to market?

Has time been wasted doing things in an inefficient manner because "we can't afford the tools"? Such assumptions must be reexamined in the light of "late cost per week". How much revenue are you losing because doing things inefficiently will delay your completion date? If a $10,000 tool could save 3 weeks of time (after learning curve time) on a project with a $50,000 late cost per week, the tool is well worth the investment.

Have you used outside services for fast turnaround, then had your time savings disappear because of mistakes or delays at the outside group? A common mistake is to treat outside services as a risk-free panacea to internal resource shortages. The project leader MUST manage outside resources closely to be sure to achieve the desired time benefits.

Now that the project is late and recovery is super-urgent, what options for such time/money trade-offs still exist? Identify options and compare them to late cost per week. Then build the appropriate investments into your plan for the rest of the project.

8. Prototype, and test key design concepts early

We don't really know how well we've done until we start testing our product. The later the testing starts, the less time we have to recover if something is wrong. Assess your project for the following:

Did an area of the design "blow up" and cause the team to go back to the drawing board? "Chicken testing" is the technique of testing your major innovations at the earliest opportunity, as airline manufacturers do to test new engine designs—by shooting chickens into engine prototypes to ensure that they will not stall. It is crucial to not wait for a full product prototype because of the length of schedule time it may take to get to a first prototype. Instead, define the pieces of the design that are risky, and identify and perform small tests within the first 25% of your schedule if possible and no later than the first half of the schedule. Then there will still be time to work out the problems with the first design, or go to a backup plan. If your project is well down the road, you should still stop and identify your major innovations, determine if any are unproved, then design and perform chicken tests on them immediately.

If you haven't had a blow-up yet, ask the following: *Have you explicitly identified remaining technical risks, as well as a means of testing them and a schedule for testing them?* If you haven't done this, the amount of technical risk on your project is unknown, and yet again, you could end up being later than you think. Do the risk analysis and chicken testing.

© 1998 Global Brain, Inc.

9. Follow a "flow" process to meet milestones

This commandment focuses on the need to follow a defined product development process geared to helping the team plan and achieve a series of periodic milestones that will smoothly pace the project to the end. Q*R*PD calls for a general four-phase concurrent-engineering type process that can be tailored to different environments and development models. The first phase, Kickoff, focuses on defining the PTCC balance for the project by means of team negotiations for the product features and product cost versus delivery date and development cost, and making an accurate schedule (with milestones) based on the product definition and preliminary design work. All four phases, Kickoff; Development; Approval; and Delivery emphasize review points to ensure that progress is measured and the product is on target as it moves through development. Assess your project's performance:

> *Did this project use any development model at all?* Did you break down your project into identifiable groups of activities, with "gates" (review points) that help pace you through the complex interrelated tasks that make up the project and ensure that proper reviews are done? Can you identify what development model you are using, such as evolutionary prototyping? (Certain models are best suited to particular types of products or those with technology or market risks. [2]).

If the project is not proceeding according to some sort of pacing, gated development model, you have lost a major advantage in assuring early attention to risky areas. You may have missed the chance for early cross-functional contributions to product cost issues. Incorrect product definition or design decisions may have been made, and major risk could still be lurking. Define where you are in the general Q*R*PD model, determine what technical review points have not been carried out, and do them.

Is the project late because resource assessments were drastically inaccurate? Look for the absence of these good scheduling practices: Were schedule tasks all shorter than 4 weeks in duration? Did individuals create their own schedules? Did the project manager sanity-check these schedules? Did the team sanity check dependencies? If these aren't true, you may be even later than you think, because the whole schedule could be a dream. Did schedules have all resources identified and take into account all the real hits on people's time? Time must be incorporated for design reviews (including involvement of peers in each other's reviews), vacations, maintenance work, conferences, interviewing, etc. This sounds obvious, but even teams conscious of these other time-sinks tend to underestimate their magnitude and leave insufficient schedule time for their main project tasks.

This step is crucial for being honest about the true remaining schedule time for your project. Re-do your estimates from the bottom up, keeping in mind all the real demands on team members' time and the other guidelines above for accurate schedules.

Did the project slip because one or more people "suddenly" discovered that they were 4 weeks late? Milestones should be every several weeks, and their completion criteria must be clear. It's typical to "fudge" milestone completion: "Oh, let's call that one done....we've met the spirit...there isn't much left to do; it pretty much works...." As Frederick Brooks said in *The Mythical Man Month* [3], "Sharp milestones are in fact a service to the team...the fuzzy milestone is the harder burden to live with. It is in fact a millstone that grinds down morale, for it deceives one about lost time until is irremediable. And chronic schedule slippage is a morale-killer." To have any chance of getting your project back on track and staying there, the Project Leader must help the team members define solid, frequent milestones, keep them visible;

keep the team serious about them, actively track the team's true progress; be up front about recognizing and admitting slips; and attack slips vigorously.

10. Get early feedback and nail defects quickly

Beyond the testing by engineering, what testing can prevent problems such as off-target or hard-to-use features? The best approach is to get feedback from customers as early as possible. (Sounds like a no-brainer, but read on: the reality of execution often doesn't live up to the intent.) Sometimes projects don't become seriously late until the product goes into beta testing and horrible disconnects with customer desires are uncovered. In the worst case, real feedback is not gotten until the product goes to market, and then it might as well have been late, because customers don't want it or can't use it. Check your project:

Have you identified ways you could test the product in-house with "customer-equivalent" employees or informally at a "friendly" customer? Or did you wait until late in the project for an outside beta? As with commandment 8, the earlier you find a way to test the product, the more time you have to address the issues raised. Stop and define how you can test the product as early as possible in the remaining schedule.

Did you, or will you, do a beta test? Everyone who puts Beta testing in their schedules of course signs up to the concept that early feedback is good. However, the execution determines whether the spirit of this commandment is truly met. *Did you, or how will you, make sure you get real results?* Many beta tests are poorly planned and managed: the customer didn't use the product because they got unexpectedly busy; or the right customer mix, lead and target, wasn't chosen to ensure broad feedback. Or the beta delivery turned into a means of satisfying a waiting customer, rather than providing the testing you really needed. *Did the, or will the, beta results get acted on?* Did you or will you get to improve the product based on the feedback? Have you left time to act on them and do you have a plan for quickly deciding what to act on and how to get to the end?

Step 1b. Assess Current Status

The assessment against the 10 commandments gives us data about where we really are with respect to our technical state, the market we're trying to satisfy, and the schedule on which we can really get there. To help decide what the 'recovery plan' should be, use your knowledge from the assessment to answer the following questions.

- **Regarding your technical challenges:** Based on identification of technical problems and an honest assessment of their level of risk and state of resolution, is this project still technically viable? Are there contingency plans for your remaining innovations or will the project be really dead in the water if they don't work? How predictable can your remaining schedule be considering those risks?

- **Regarding that schedule:** After understanding where you are with regard to your technical design, where are you relative to the original schedule? Have you missed one or more major milestones? What tasks do you need to add? What remaining tasks need to be re-estimated? When could you realistically deliver the product as currently defined?

- **Regarding your market:** Based on any new understanding about customers, what features are still on track? Is the market window still the same? Does your business case hold? What options might you have for feature reductions, or steps of incremental innovation, by delaying some things to the next release?

© 1998 Global Brain, Inc.

Step 2. Analyze Alternatives

The assessment helps us know accurately what it will take to finish. This includes what we'll have to fix in our execution to get there, how serious an impact each problem is to the project, and how serious a task fixing each underlying problem might be. Then we weigh the PTCC elements based on that accurate data from the assessment about our product and our ability to perform the rest of the project. We must consciously make a new, revised PTCC trade-off analysis to ensure that a "return on investment" understanding will lead to the best decision for how to carry out the rest of the project.

The team should participate in these trade-off discussions and decisions. Note that a major benefit here is that we will help the team go beyond "re-planning" to "re-vitalizing the plan." The team's ability to go forward with high energy and positive attitude is crucial. This is possible when management pays attention to the underlying problems rather than just patching the surface, emphasizes the full PTCC negotiation rather than blindly sticking to an end-date or a feature set, and involves team members in the decision process.

The following options should be considered:

1. Should the product vision be changed, to omit or scale back certain features, to finish as soon as possible with a minimum acceptable feature set?

2. Should we keep the vision the same and delay the schedule to finish? Sometimes this is not even considered as an option, but it might be the right thing to do for the market! It's important to push away political pressures for holding an original end-date if that date is outside the realm of possibility.

3. Should we add resources to still try to finish on time, or as close as possible? Use the late cost per week metric, and consider various kinds of technical resources and management help, from both inside and outside the company.

4. Do we simply need better or tighter or more experienced management for the rest of the project? Do we have the right leader to go forward?

5. Based on our situation, what other options might there be?

Step 3. Decide New Course

The above exercise leads to a decision on PTCC balance and an accompanying new set of product and schedule goals developed by the team. The detailed assessment and PTCC analysis process, and a management commitment to setting only *attainable* goals, are the best insurance the project can have against further trouble. There is nothing more powerful and more revitalizing in tense schedule situations than a plan the team believes in, with PTCC-based goals they can understand.

Step 4. Re-launch: Go for it!

Then all that's left is to go for it, and do so quickly and decisively. Management, and the team, can't afford to waffle or linger in failure mode. A clear-cut "re-launch" sends a powerful message, puts the old trouble behind, and sets the team's eyes ahead to remaining challenges. The launch should communicate the plan openly and honestly to everyone, and gain a fresh new commitment.

Examples from Actual Projects

These vignettes from actual projects illustrate how the types of everyday Q*R*PD "violations" above lead to schedule slips, and how the techniques can be applied to recover projects in trouble.

Case 1: The under-specified, over-promised project: A database development project was outsourced by an inexperienced, first-time, project leader to a small company. The schedule was based on the outside company's fixed-price bid on an incomplete product specification. The resulting schedule was totally unrealistic. The product requirements changed almost daily—(everyone had a

© 1998 Global Brain, Inc.

vehement opinion about the user interface. The main project wake-up call was the non-existence of an operational prototype 3 weeks before the supposed alpha release date, and 6 weeks before the supposed project completion date.

A consultant was brought in to perform an assessment. As a result, the following actions were taken: A new experienced project leader took charge (commandment #2). The product feature requirements were reviewed and prioritized and certain ones eliminated (commandment #1). The project leader defended against feature creep and user interface polishing for the rest of the project. The schedule was re-planned; calling for short development cycles of specifying, developing and testing features one group at a time, based on feature priorities and the need for early deliveries to trade shows and particular evaluation customers (commandment #9). Technical risks were analyzed and testing of these areas planned, to be carried out by the sponsoring company since the outsource group was not strong at software quality assurance (commandment #8).

The PTCC bottom line: From the day of the first assessment, it was clear that the original schedule could not be held. But the resulting longer schedule, with interim deliveries to key "leading edge" customers, was sufficient to meet market requirements. The additional development cost was deemed worth it to develop the features that the leading edge customers with deep pockets would require.

Case 2: Loss of vision "It's not what we wanted!"

A multimedia company undertook development of a new game. Periodic milestones had been defined to pace the project. Early milestones had been passed. The project wake-up call came when the delivery of a video of early artwork along with a game description document was considered grossly incomplete by Marketing, and totally at odds with their understanding of what the product needed to look like for the envisioned customer base. The situation was assessed and the following actions taken:

A vision statement was written, including a one-line memorable, quotable summary, and a one-page bullet list defining customers and key non-negotiable guidelines and requirements. Marketing did some more homework to get much more specific about the main customers and less important customers (commandment #1). A game design consultant was hired to help guide the team in defining the details of a game to satisfy the vision (commandment #2). Marketing and Engineering defined checkpoints for trading more "visibles" to ensure frequent feedback on the artwork and music's alignment with the vision (commandment #8, #9). The project milestones were re-cast to be honest about the effect of the vision-related schedule slips (commandment #9). A new project leader was appointed who was more savvy about the game market, more able to take initiative to combat feature creep, and able to provide more people-oriented leadership for the somewhat chaotic creative environment of game development (commandment #2, #4). A closer interaction with Marketing was cultivated, and the leader took special pains to periodically communicate the vision and mission to the team and step them through the entire game design as it was refined (commandment #1, #4).

The PTCC bottom line: The impact from the vision problem was determined to be 3 months of lost development work. To recover, Marketing defined their drop-dead time for hitting the market as 5 months later than the original due date; engineering defined a game that could be developed in that timeframe with the staff that the company budget deemed was acceptable for this project, and a game that would meet in complexity, content and look the requirements of the intended audience. The team has had to be careful to keep the vision in view at all times; there have been a few instances of straying from the vision, and of Marketing changing its mind about elements of the vision, and some resulting throw-away work; but the project completed within 2 weeks of the worst-case schedule that was set last November.

© 1998 Global Brain, Inc.

Case 3. The case of the disappearing resources:

The main problem of a major network management software development project was constant resource poaching: key engineers were pulled off for weeks at a time to fire-fight problems in the field. This project was already abiding by many elements of Q*R*PD; the project leader kept his critical resource issues visible to management, but the company had across-the-board staffing shortages that were difficult to resolve. The financial reward systems were not necessarily competitive in the area, for the people they were trying to attract. To make matters worse, several key resources left the company for those reasons (commandment #5).

The PTCC bottom line: The company has already used the "late cost per week" metric to help decide to staff up with consultants to help hold the schedule as close as possible (commandment #2). However, in cases of severe resource shortages, sometimes more drastic action is required. Rather than hoping for the best and letting the project slip out further until more resources are found, the project leader is projecting worst case schedules and impact to the company's financial return. The company will determine whether they should "do less sooner" and divert resources from other efforts to hold this software project's schedule.

Avoiding Problems

Projects have a much better chance of never earning the *problem project* label if they adhere to Q*R*PD principles from the beginning. All of the 10 commandments apply. To reiterate several key points:

- Pay attention to balancing PTCC, assessing technical risks, and attempting only incremental innovation wherever possible to help keep the team from taking on the impossible project. The Product Vision will help make sure requirements are developed with customer input, are understood by the team, and are kept visible during the project, and are not allowed to change capriciously.

- Make a conscious selection of the right leader and team, with full-time members, the necessary number of members, and proper expert participation. Understand the cost of delay to make appropriate trade-off decisions. Get cross-functional members involved from the beginning and make sure their participation is meaningful and their inputs are used. Reward the members for their contributions and the team for their accomplishments.

- Use a defined development process to pace the team through an aggressive schedule. The concurrent engineering phase gate approach, with liberal design reviews, and early and continuous testing, will ensure that you don't get too far down the road without uncovering problems. Detailed scheduling in phase I, based on solid preliminary design work and good scheduling practices, will ensure that the plan is based in reality. Tracking by frequent milestones will ensure progress is accurately measured.

Conclusion

It's a fact of life that if problems are discovered too late in a project, it may be hard to hold an original schedule. In even that worst case, however, the end of the world is not necessarily at hand. The project can still be successful. The proper work must be put into an honest assessment of the past problems and an analysis of the best way to proceed, keeping the company's financial goals in mind. The project must be re-launched with precise and on-target action plans and a revitalized, committed team.

The commandments and techniques of Q*R*PD provide the tools for that successful recovery effort, and the framework for planning future projects such that the dreaded super-urgent recovery effort will never be required.

© 1998 Global Brain, Inc.

[1] Kopelman, Orion, and Voegtli, Cinda with Josephs, Adam, *Projects at Warp Speed with QRPD: The Definitive Guidebook to Quality Rapid Product Development*, 8th Edition, Global Brain, Inc., Palo Alto, CA, 1998.

[2] Boehm, Barry W., "A Spiral Model of Software Development and Enhancement", *IEEE Computer Magazine*, IEEE Computer Society Press, May 1988.

[3] Brooks Jr., Frederick P., *The Mythical Man-Month*, Addison-Wesley Publishing Company, Philippines, 1975.

Excerpted with permission from:
PROJECTWORLD® Summer 96 Proceedings

Article: Overcoming Obstacles to Rapid Product Development: Implementing QRPD®

Overcoming Obstacles to Rapid Product Development: Implementing Q*R*PD®

Cinda Voegtli, Consulting Partner, Global Brain, Inc.
555 Bryant Street, #369 Palo Alto, CA 94301-1704   (650) 327-2012

Abstract

Attempts to incorporate changes into an organization to accelerate its product development efforts inevitably encounter real-world, sometimes fatal obstacles. Some of these include cultural resistance, staff inexperience, or lack of real upper management support. This presentation discusses typical obstacles and gives detailed examples of the techniques used to overcome these impediments, implement the Quality *Rapid* Product Development methodology (Q*R*PD), and cut development cycle times by up to 50%. It highlights areas of Q*R*PD which have produced near-term and highly-visible results for client companies, thereby building long-term buy-in for product development process improvement.

Global Brain®, Inc. is a management consulting firm specializing in the practical implementation of the Q*R*PD methodology in high-tech companies. Ms. Voegtli has extensive experience in product development, engineering management, project management, and consulting. She has worked in a wide variety of industries including data communications, medical devices, software and information technology, virtual reality, and game products. She serves on the international board of governors of the IEEE Engineering Management Society and was chair of the Silicon Valley chapter for two years.

Introduction

Organizations often attempt to use industry-, company-, and product-influenced development processes, along with sound project management techniques, to improve their development efforts and achieve accelerated time-to-market.. The goal is to maximize return on product development investment.

The focus of this paper: techniques for getting a development process into *effective use*. Defining an effective company-specific development model involves time, money, and a commitment to unearthing "best-practices." It also requires highly-cooperative work of those who are attempting to synthesize the process from a scattered store of industry and corporate wisdom. However, the ultimate challenge is in getting that wisdom used: by everyone, consistently, and every day.

Background for This Paper

The implementation of process improvements to achieve rapid product development should be treated as a process itself. It is a long term effort. It requires initiative, discipline, learning of new skills, and sustained behavior change. The problems generally encountered in these efforts are predictable and may not all seem significant at first glance. However, together they can seriously impact the success of attempts to accelerate product development. It is therefore instructive to examine the day-to-day ways in which companies work to overcome these problems.

Q*R*PD is a product development methodology focused on delivering quality products to market in significantly reduced timeframes. "Quality" here means *value as perceived by the customer*. The Q*R*PD methodology calls for a phased development process with

© 1998 Global Brain, Inc.

emphasis on a focused, on-target product definition and a high-performance project leader and team following concurrent engineering practices. It refers to these as "Vision, Mission, and Flow".

This paper includes specific examples from several companies' recent efforts, including a 150-person software and database products provider; two 400-person divisions of large medical device manufacturers; two 250-person data communications companies, and a 100-person manufacturer of consumer audio equipment. Several of these companies have completed their first QRPD project, successfully accelerating their typical development cycle. The others are nearing the successful conclusion of their first QRPD project.

Typical QRPD Implementation Sequence

A typical sequence of events for QRPD implementation is as follows:

- Someone recognizes a need for improvement of a company's product development efforts.

- Someone champions QRPD and initiates in-house adoption.

- The company's QRPD-based process is documented, usually as a process flow diagram or a table of project phases and deliverables. Some companies also create a guidebook based on QRPD.

- A pilot project is selected for implementation, and a project leader is selected

- The project is launched.

- The project is executed.

- At some point during or after this first project, additional projects are launched using QRPD.

Phases of Change

Companies who successfully follow the above recommended QRPD implementation sequence go through the following underlying phases of *change*:

- *Recognizing and selling the need for improvements.* Someone takes the initiative to get the effort underway.

- *Adjusting to a new process framework and tenets.* When the first (QRPD pilot) project starts, the team has to make a potentially significant mindshift from past methods and habits and translate the new QRPD framework into a plan for their project.

- *Developing the supporting corporate, team and individual attitudes and skills:* As the pilot project progresses, everyone encounters areas in which they need to develop new capabilities or new perspectives.

- *Ensuring Long-Term Change.* As QRPD is implemented on more projects, companies take measures to ensure that the above behavior and skill changes are lasting.

The remainder of this paper discusses typical issues encountered during each of these four phases of change and specific techniques for addressing them.

Recognizing and Selling the Need for Improvement

Taking the first step. In each of the six example companies, *one person* took the initiative to suggest a new look at the current way of doing product development. In two cases this person was a Vice-President, in one case a Director, and in the three others a project manager or functional manager. It has been our experience that most QRPD efforts are initiated by the managers most closely responsible for the daily running of a project. They tend to be the most likely to be exposed to various project management methodologies through their own continuing education, and have great personal incentive to help effect changes that will make their projects run more smoothly.

© 1998 Global Brain, Inc.

Overcoming Inattention, Myopia, and Inertia
Decision-makers in an organization have to also see a need for change in order for a QRPD effort to even get off the ground, and people throughout the organization have to come on board for there to be a chance of long-term success. The following techniques were used in the example companies:

- The initial champion in each company actively sold the need for development process improvements to their executives, at least to the degree necessary to obtain approval for QRPD guidebooks and/or an internal training class. Where the need for change wasn't readily accepted, they presented examples of past project problems and QRPD techniques for preventing or overcoming them. The credibility of these individuals and the passion with which they championed the need for change were both crucial to getting approval for a QRPD effort.

- Interviews were held before each in-house QRPD workshop, to obtain first-hand the perspectives of executives, managers, and individual contributors, and to "pre-sell" the benefits of a good development process.

NOTE: the most effective technique for getting the interest of the individual contributors was discussing *specifically* how the process would help prevent problems that caused them extreme difficulties, such as design changes and excessive overtime, on past projects.

- Post-mortems were performed on past or current company projects, either during the QRPD workshop or in separate sessions, using QRPD techniques checklists. Within an hour, project teams can usually agree upon changes which should provide significant improvement in their future projects. A first level of "buy-in" for the new process is thus achieved.

Overcoming Skepticism, Distrust, and the Victim Syndrome In many companies there is inherent skepticism about a new process, often caused by some past "failed" improvement effort. "This is just the process du jour" has been cited in more than one interview as a justification for not taking the QRPD effort seriously. The extreme manifestation of this attitude is what I sometimes call the "victim syndrome," illustrated by quotes such as "It's not worth the trouble; no matter what I do, the executives will mess it up anyway." The milder forms of this attitude were encountered in all six of the companies to some degree; the extreme form was encountered in only one. A more positive attitude is encouraged using the following techniques:

- In the pre-workshop interviews, in-house classes, and continuing coaching, there is a pervasive emphasis on ***personal responsibility***. In the class, participants are asked to decide how many of the 10 "commandments" of QRPD they can personally *influence*; the correct answer, which most arrive at after only slight hesitation, is "all of them". Managers are asked to envision the improvements possible if they together take responsibility for managing according to the new process, thereby helping establish it in the culture.

The QRPD methodology and team structure heavily emphasize the project leader and team's *full* responsibility for the project, in *partnership* with each other and with the executives. This perspective helps shift the team from laying blame to planning action.

- Emphasis is placed on demonstration of executive commitment. The more visible executives are at any QRPD-related sessions, the more likely the rest of the company will be to believe that the change efforts will be supported. We encourage the vice-presidents to attend the main QRPD training and follow-on sessions of project planning.

- A by-product of executive involvement is giving the engineering team a chance to directly gain understanding and trust of the executives. In one communications company, negative attitudes toward the process efforts were rooted partly in a

© 1998 Global Brain, Inc.

lack of understanding of, and resulting distrust of, where the executives were taking the company. After the Q*R*PD class, a follow-on session concentrated on defining the next major product. The engineers participated in a discussion with the Marketing and Engineering vice-presidents about the goals of the company, and their impact on product decisions. They heard firsthand the two executives discuss the difficulties with predicting the market. The session didn't produce all the answers but increased the level of trust and cooperation. Both sides left with action items for fleshing out the product definition. And the marketing vice-president instituted regular lunch briefing sessions with the engineering team.

Overcoming Cultural Resistance In some companies there is also an initial negative attitude towards process born of a cultural resistance to "bureaucracy", especially in the engineering ranks. One effective way to deal with this issue is to immediately show the usefulness of the process by applying it to a pressing problem that is affecting the morale of the anti-process contingent. At one client, a trade show was three weeks away, and the demonstration promised to the world by Marketing was technically impossible in that timeframe. Tensions were high and patience for taking time out to attend a two-day Q*R*PD development process workshop was *low*. Using Q*R*PD tenets for feature/schedule negotiations, in a facilitated session, the team identified the absolute minimum requirements for the show and came up with a feasible crash development plan for the next three weeks. The session wasn't concluded until each person indicated that he could live with the plan. The process gained some instant credibility. And the trade show was ultimately a huge corporate success.

Adjusting to a New Process Framework and Tenets

Once a Q*R*PD pilot project is selected, the team must make a mental shift to the new process, and translate that framework into specific actions on their project.

Overcoming Interpretation Problems A common issue with implementing a process is deciding how to apply it on a given project. Within a company or a division or department, various projects can look very different, based on the particular product, the type of project, e.g. totally new development vs. feature enhancement to an existing product, or the technical nature of the product, e.g. hardware- vs. software-intensive. In our experience all teams initially struggle with this interpretation. The best initial tool is the company Q*R*PD-based process guidebook. It should clearly document the phases of the development cycle and the key deliverables and decision points of each phase.

Project managers must then be able to help the team create a specific project plan. A medical company's major stumbling block was its project managers' inability to make judgment calls about what tasks in the general process definition applied to their particular projects. They assumed they had to perform every task, write every document, even if it didn't seem appropriate. They felt hemmed in and hamstrung, and began blaming the process for actually *decelerating* their project cycles. These problems were addressed in the following manner:

- The company held an off-site meeting of all project managers to discuss the process-related issues. Teams were formed to suggest the minimum mandatory requirements for different types of projects. A short document was created to reflect those interpretations and was added to the process guidebook.

- As part of the project planning process, each team marked up a copy of the general process map to show the applicable items for their project. This kept the project plans and the process in sync but clearly showed what would and would not be done.

The initial Q*R*PD -based process for a particular communications company seemed to not apply directly to software-only projects. Software project teams initially struggled with creating their project plans. These teams are currently working out their issues with the

© 1998 Global Brain, Inc.

process definition as they go, documenting the suggested changes, and submitting them for a company guidebook update at the end of the year.

Overcoming Product Definition Problems It is common for projects to take serious time-to-market hits due to product definition problems, such as lack of customer input up front, lack of consideration of serviceability and reliability issues, unrealistic goals for a single project, or spurious requirements changes during the project. Two key Q*R*PD techniques were used by all of the example companies:

- The *product vision* is a one or two page document which defines the highest level requirements of the product. It forms the contract among the cross-functional team members. Creation of the vision by the team is a key activity, done regularly with clients in the follow-on day after a workshop. The intent is to immediately apply Q*R*PD techniques to get the project off to the right start, or back on track if it was already in progress. The entire team is identified and assembled in a room. On flipchart paper around the room, we interactively capture the essence of the product under development in five categories: key customers and benefits, key issues customers will use to judge quality, key features and technologies, crucial product factors, and financials. People initially react in horror at the thought of 20 people in a room creating a "product requirements" document. However, these meetings never fail to focus the definition on the customer first; bring critical product definition issues to light; and provide the chance for those outside of engineering and marketing to make a significant contribution. In every instance the team leaves with a deeper, more unified understanding of the product to be developed.

- *"See-saw schedules and specifications"* refers to the negotiation that occurs after the initial Product Vision is composed, and the team evaluates the schedule required to implement that vision. Features and schedules are negotiated together to ultimately achieve the optimal balance of product cost, development cost, product performance, and time to market. Cost-benefit analyses are used to decide if certain features are worth the time they add to the schedule. The product vision and the schedule are not considered committed until that negotiation has been completed and signed off by the entire team. If changes to the vision are later suggested, this negotiation process is again employed by the team to reach formal agreement before the changes are approved.

Developing the Supporting Attitudes and Skills

As the pilot Q*R*PD project progresses past the kick-off point, the organization and its individuals may struggle with development issues in their new roles.

Overcoming Resistance to Synergy This is a cultural issue, manifested as cross-functional team members who are not used to closely working together or technical contributors who are used to working alone and somewhat technically unconstrained. The Q*R*PD emphasis on teamwork can meet with some resistance.

- Meeting management skills are paramount. The unaccustomed group activity must go as smoothly as possible. To this end, team meetings are often facilitated and the project leader coached separately on setting agendas, pre-selling before meetings, and following up to smooth interpersonal conflicts. In a communications company with mostly inexperienced project leaders, the most important help in early projects involved weekly coaching and facilitation of both project meetings and critical technical sessions.

- Project leaders must also be coached on determining what activities and issues should take place in a team meeting vs.

© 1998 Global Brain, Inc.

off-line. Some new leaders have responded to the increased emphasis on teamwork by conducting project business only in the meetings, which can grossly slow down the resolution of issues. Conversely, if team interactions are too cursory, people will not become enough of a cohesive team to effectively manage the project. Design by committee must also be avoided, for the sake of both the project timeline and the engineers' buy-in.

- Generally the resistance to teamwork eases with time, once the team makes it through the product vision and scheduling phase, where the benefits of the team process have become more evident.

Overcoming Chaotic Resource Management
A new development process will not compensate for insufficient people needed to do the job. Inefficient management of available resources can sabotage efforts to speed development as well. And if people switch back and forth between projects daily due to simultaneous project assignments, or because of corporate priority changes, or wait on each other because they're spread across multiple unsynchronized projects, the opportunity for significant speed improvements can easily be lost.

- To help with resource issues within a project, each team calculates the "late cost per week" of the project, which includes two components: the revenue lost each week the project slips past the planned end date; and the money lost as additional development cost, due to the team staying on the project longer than planned. This number puts resource decisions in context for the project leader: an expensive tool or fast turnaround charge may actually be much less significant in cost than the money lost per week due to lateness.

- A key Q*R*PD technique for managing multiple projects is the calculation of return on investment and/or net present value for projects, to provide tools for making resource trade-off decisions. At the communications company with 30 projects, each project is assigned a priority, based on net present value calculations, strategic importance, and contractual requirements; the priority number is shown on a Marketing project priority list; and team members who are spread across projects know the relative importance of each project.

- For companies with multiple simultaneous projects, major planning sessions are held to assess the effectiveness of the project portfolio. Based on manpower requirements and relative project "value" in terms of return, decisions are sometimes made to drop or delay certain projects to free resources for more lucrative ventures. This exercise was especially important for the audio company, which initially had 15 people in engineering working on 12 different projects. Only six projects survived the assessment; the others were canceled or delayed. A communications company with 80 engineers went from 50 projects to 30.

- The larger companies with multiple projects also hold regular project review meetings where all departments consider current resource issues and priorities. In some cases it has been necessary to educate new product managers that they must continue to fight for their projects.

- Engineering is encouraged to account for the time spent in maintaining other products, so that estimates of resources available for new projects are accurate. Based on such an assessment, one communications company decided to form a sustaining group to keep their other engineers focused on new development.

- Individual project leaders at a communications company started regular informal meetings with the engineering vice-president to confirm priorities and lobby for changes. Resource issues were discussed at a detailed level to ferret out inconsistencies, e.g. "Do you want Bill on project A or project B?" These meetings were especially important since

© 1998 Global Brain, Inc.

this VP had a tendency to suddenly give people special projects, and some team members had a habit of working on pet "unassigned" projects.

- At the personal level, people's ability to manage their own time will obviously affect their project performance. In companies where engineers are moving into project leader and technical lead positions, training and coaching on time management and delegation has sometimes been required.

Overcoming the Lack of Corporate Project Management Culture The most fertile ground for implementing product development process improvements is a company where one or more influential executives and managers have prior experience with project management. They will naturally help create the new culture and reinforce the QRPD process as it is being implemented. If that experience is lacking, executives must be taught how to champion QRPD and operate within its tenets. Otherwise inconsistent and conflicting actions at the executive level can derail improvements made at the team level.

- The first recommendation is always to select an executive QRPD /project management champion. One company appointed an informal champion with the authority to schedule classes and obtain consulting help. A medical company implemented a guidance council of all development directors to guide the definition and refinement of their process.

Product Vision sessions often point out areas where executives might operate outside the rules. For example, marketing executives at a networking company were outwardly supportive of QRPD, mostly because they hoped it would "fix Engineering", but in a product vision session it became clear that the initial product definition had been created without corroboration by actual customer input, in violation of a key QRPD principle. This problem came to light naturally in the meeting, and action items were assigned to get customer input.

- Project teams must be encouraged to push back on executives who violate the process. In one company a founder continued to make unilateral product funding decisions, cutting short the team's business case and feasibility analyses. The project teams in this case were confident enough of the process to raise the issue and receive the executive's blessing for finishing their analysis work.

- At several companies informal executive briefings were held periodically to discuss key QRPD principles and how they applied to projects in progress. The executives were told if any of their actions were disrupting the new process and given suggestions for future behavior.

- In larger companies with many simultaneous projects, regular high-level project reviews for the executives are especially helpful. They provide a continuing forum for educating the executives, as well as a chance for the executives to show their support for QRPD. An executive who consistently asks questions in these meetings, using the terminology of the process, is reinforcing its importance and helping build it into the culture.

- In the more complex project environments, marketing planning meetings and process sessions with product managers can be beneficial. At the company with the most simultaneous projects and a rapidly-growing product management staff, regular sessions allow these product managers to ask questions about the process, how it applies to their projects, and how they should work with the project leaders.

Building Project Leader Skills Team leaders must have credibility, influence skills, sound judgment, and incredibly high levels of initiative. These traits are especially critical if a peer is promoted to be a new team leader, which is a common occurrence. Organizations implementing QRPD do not necessarily have experienced project management personnel, and realistically may not be able to hire them immediately. Conversely, someone who does have project management experience may not necessarily be effective at the QRPD process. For example, a person from a more bureaucratic project management environment, characterized by more emphasis on paperwork and coordination and less emphasis on leadership and development speed, must make significant adjustments to be an effective QRPD project leader. These types of issues have been successfully dealt with in the following manner:

- The QRPD guidebook contains numerous templates for important project deliverables to give the new project leader proven tools. Those companies who have implemented company-specific process guidebooks have tailored those forms further and included detailed examples from actual company projects.

- Inexperienced leaders should receive heavy off-line coaching early in the project. This can be provided in-house by more experienced managers or by outside consultants. This coaching should help the project leader do a good job of running meetings and delegating and managing work, to help quickly build credibility for his/her leadership skills. Attention must also be paid to traditional project management skills such as estimating. Coaching was provided weekly for over a year to a fast-growing wireless technology company. The audio company chose to have three follow-on sessions with a consultant at critical project junctures.

- Technical credibility of the project leader is critical. Before important technical brainstorming sessions and design reviews, a project leader on a particularly complex software project with a challenging team received extensive coaching. This coaching focused on the need to discuss controversial issues and pre-sell solutions one-on-one before the meetings, maintain clear separation between the project leader role and any personal technical opinions during the meeting, and follow up individually with team members to confirm closure and support for team decisions. Dramatic improvements in the tenor and outcomes of the technical meetings, and support for the new leader, were seen over time.

- In one organization with many new project leaders and very little project management background, regular discussions are held with the engineering vice-president to discuss the progress of the new leaders in his department, providing him with the opportunity to reward their work and encourage them in their challenges. It also reminds him of good leader characteristics to guide future hiring.

- In a medical company with heavy emphasis on software quality assurance as the keeper of the process, a process guru was added to the SQA group to assist the new project leaders.

- Growing companies with little project management experience are encouraged to hire at least one experienced project manager from outside the company for new project leader positions.

Building Risk Management Skills One sign of inexperience is a lack of first-hand understanding of real project risks and how to plan for and manage them. Inexperienced project leaders need to be reminded of the most important QRPD project leader trait: "obsession" with getting the project done on time, making sure at every opportunity that days and weeks are not lost due to poor risk management.

- QRPD provides a framework for classifying technological risks and rules of thumb for determining whether a dangerous number of technical risks are being undertaken. This assessment exercise is always performed early in the project. The scope of the project is often scaled back or divided into two releases.

- Critical issues lists are encouraged to keep important dependencies in front of the team.

- Schedules undergo review by the team and people outside the team to identify areas of risk. Recent examples of problems caught in schedule reviews: a beta plan was scheduled so close to the beta test period that customer readiness could not be guaranteed; a software integration period was cut unreasonably short to pull in a schedule.

Ensuring Long-Term Change

To achieve a lasting capability for rapid product development, the organization must strive for constant, consistent process awareness. This calls for a continuation of earlier efforts:

- A process champion must be in place. This person "owns" the process of Q*R*PD implementation and ongoing development process improvement. This champion must work to ensure that upper management comprehends both Q*R*PD and the company-specific development process, and that employees are brought on board. He coordinates process issue resolution and process evolution.

- Executives must reinforce the importance of key elements of the process in project status reviews and in daily personal behavior. For example, they should ask high-level questions relative to Q*R*PD: not "Why did you miss this date by two days?" but "What are the risks and what are the contingency plans?" At every chance executives and project managers reinforce the importance of key decisions points in the process: "Have you had the kickoff phase review yet?" "We can't quote a schedule date to sales yet because we aren't through with the planning phase."

- A company-specific product development process should be developed and documented in a guidebook. The level of detail may depend upon the size of the company and the complexity of its projects and products. Material from the Q*R*PD guidebook can be used as the basis.

- Periodic training in the Q*R*PD methodology and the company-specific development process should be held for new employees. The fastest-growing company in our examples holds Q*R*PD training every three months and internal process training every month.

- Inevitably incorrect decisions will still be made and a project will deviate from Q*R*PD principles. The team must watch for these instances, analyze the cause and results, and refine their actions accordingly.

- And finally, all of these efforts to change must be rewarded and the successes celebrated.

Conclusion

Companies who successfully implement the Quality *Rapid* Product Development methodology for product development go through several phases of change. Along the way they deal with typical problems such as cultural resistance, lack of project management experience and skills, product definition issues, and chaotic resource management. The Q*R*PD methodology provides specific tools for dealing with these challenges; the recommended implementation approach provides tools such as training and coaching to reinforce it.

Given the normal challenges associated with implementing any new development process and the length of time it can take to establish real change, it is important to create immediate or near-term "successes" that demonstrate the benefits of the process, boost morale, and build buy-in for long term improvements. Fortunately, several aspects of the Q*R*PD methodology have proven valuable in that regard: performing project lessons-learned meetings to identify areas for future change; holding Product Vision sessions to align the development team; using cost-benefit analyses for feature and cost trade-off

© 1998 Global Brain, Inc.

decisions and enforcing the sanctity of the "see-saw scheduling and specification" process; and using late cost per week to prioritize the company's projects and alleviate any resource management problems.

During ongoing product development process improvements, there will always be problems to solve, issues to negotiate. Those who are serious about making the QRPD process work for the long term will find a way through these challenges. "The only place where success comes before work is in the dictionary." The rewards of rapid product development are high and worth that work.

APPENDICES

Appendix A. Exercise Solutions

Simple Benefit-Cost Solution

COST		**BENEFIT**	
2 MONTH DELAY ($.5M/month x 2 months)	$1,000,000	ADDITIONAL PROFIT ($100m X 1% X 15%)	$150,000
	--------------		-------------
	$1,000,000		$150,000

**COST OUTWEIGHS BENEFIT.
DON'T DO IT!**

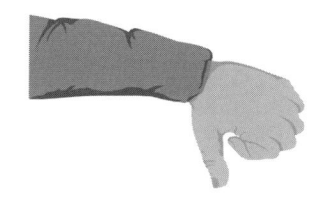

"EMEBO" Solution

COST

ENGINEERING LABOR: $20,000

1 MONTH DELAY $100,000
(1 machine less sold
 at $500,000 x 20% profit)

R&D burn rate, 1 month $50,000

$170,000

BENEFIT

SAVINGS IN PRODUCT COST: $245,000
$5000/machine x 49 machines
(lose sale of one)

$245,000

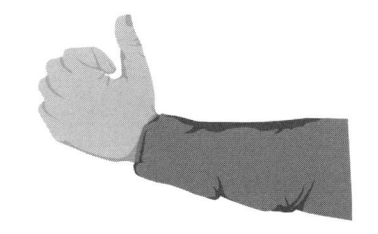

Benefit outweighs cost for a 1-month delay.
DO IT!

ENGINEERING LABOR: $20,000

3 MONTH DELAY $300,000
(3 machines less sold =
 3 x $500,000 x 20% profit)

R&D burn rate, 3 months $150,000

$470,000

SAVINGS IN PRODUCT COST: $235,000
$5000/machine x 47 machines
(lose sale of three)

$235,000

Cost outweighs benefit. Not worth a 3-month delay.
DON'T DO IT!

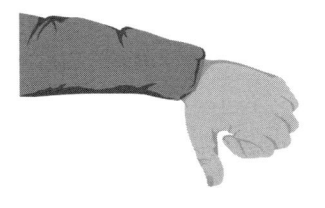

© 1998 Global Brain, Inc.

"*FAXIT*" Solution

1)

COST		BENEFIT	
Non-recurring engineering	$100,000	Total boards sold: (10,000/month x 10 months)	100,000
		Savings in product cost: $5/board x 100,000 boards	
	------------		------------
	$100,000		$500,000

1. Benefit outweighs cost. DO IT!

2)

COST		BENEFIT	
Non-recurring engineering	$100,000	Total boards sold: (10,000/month x 9 months)	90,000
Additional engineering cost (7 months x $5000/month)	$35,000		
Engineering burn rate (1 month)	$50,000	Savings in product cost: $5/board x 90,000 boards	$450,000
1 month profit (10,000 boards x $10 each)	$100,000		
	------------		------------
	$285,000		$450,000

2. Benefit still outweighs cost. DO IT!

© 1998 Global Brain, Inc.

Verichina Solution

Q*R*PD techniques followed:

⊃1A) INNOVATE INCREMENTALLY (BASE HITS NOT HOMERUNS)

⊃1B) RESTRICT EACH PRODUCT TO A MANAGEABLE NUMBER OF MAJOR INNOVATIONS, TYPICALLY THREE

1C) AVOID BREAKING NEW GROUND SIMULTANEOUSLY IN (ALL 3): TECHNOLOGY, APPLICATIONS, MARKETS/CUSTOMERS

⊃2A) SELECT THE LEADER(S) VERY JUDICIOUSLY

⊃2B) HAVE ONLY *ONE* OVERALL TEAM LEADER

2C) ANNOUNCE LEADERS' AND TEAM'S RESPONSIBILITIES FORMALLY AND CLEARLY

⊃2E) USE EXPERIENCED, TALENTED VOLUNTEERS: COMMITTED, FLEXIBLE, ENTHUSIASTIC, EAGER TO RESPONSIBLY COMPLETE THE MISSION

⊃2F) STRIVE FOR ONLY FULL-TIME MEMBERS ON THE TEAM

2H) STRIVE FOR TEAMS AND SUB-TEAMS OF UP TO 8 TO 10 PEOPLE (4-5 IDEAL)

2K) ENLIST "EXPERTS" AS ADJUNCT MEMBERS OF THE TEAM

⊃3A) ALL COMMITTED AND INVOLVED FROM DAY 1, AND KEPT UP TO DATE

⊃4A) CREATE A SHARED SENSE OF MISSION/PURPOSE, *PRODUCT VISION*, AND MILESTONES

⊃4E) INSULATE THE TEAM FROM THE PARENT ORGANIZATION'S CULTURE ("SKUNKWORKS") ONLY IF THE COMPANY IS NOT Q*R*PD-LIKE; OR FOR A HIGHLY RESEARCH-ORIENTED PROJECT

⊃4F) PROTECT THE TEAM'S AUTONOMY

⊃4H) MINIMIZE AND STREAMLINE ADMINISTRATION AND REPORTING REQUIREMENTS

4K) DO NOT ALLOW MANAGEMENT REVIEWS OR DECISIONS TO DELAY WORK, INCLUDING SEPARATING FORMAL STATUS REVIEWS FROM TECHNICAL MEETINGS

4V) HAVE FUN!

⊃5E) USE RITUALS AND CELEBRATIONS

⊃6D) CONCENTRATE TECHNICAL RISK IN AS FEW SUBSYSTEMS AS POSSIBLE

⊃6H) "BEG, BORROW, STEAL" OR BUY SUBSYSTEMS OR EXPERTISE, AND AVOID "NIH": THE *NOT INVENTED HERE* SYNDROME

⊃8A) DO A REALITY CHECK WITH REAL PROTOTYPES WITHIN ABOUT FIRST 25% OF THE TIMELINE: A "CHICKEN TEST."

8B) BUILD A TALL JUNK PILE, REAL AND ABSTRACT, OF EXPERIMENTATION, ANALYSIS, AND SIMULATION TESTS THROUGHOUT THE PROJECT, ESPECIALLY AT KEY MILESTONES.

10D) USE BETA SITES TO WEED OUT DEFECTS *BEFORE* RELEASE

© 1998 Global Brain, Inc.

Product Vision Solutions

"RAPID SOFT"

- no customers, market data
- no financial #'s (price, market size)
- no market window
- no product features
- no WHY

"QUAKESENSE"

- No measurement accuracy (crucial factor!) - open-ended....
- Benefit unclear (amount of warning time)
- no mention of how to judge quality
- quality image of company and product liability not addressed
- no product and development cost, only price
- weak technical justification
- new market and new technology (violates technique 1C)
- no ROI analysis (how reliable are the marketing projections?)
- too many "musts" - inflexible
- no mention of how to judge quality
- marketing and engineering at odds with each other

"BIO COMF"

- too detailed, wordy (organize better)
- second paragraph too detailed
- no development cost
- regulatory approvals?

"Emebo" Opportunity #2 Solution

COSTS		**BENEFIT**	
ENGINEERING LABOR:	$50,000	ADDITIONAL PROFIT BASED ON 10% MORE SALES	$470,000
1 MONTH DELAY (1 machine less sold at $500,000 x 20% profit)	$100,000	(5 more machines, @ 20% profit, less $6000 additional cost per machine) = 5 X ($500,000 x 20% - $6000)	
ADDITIONAL PRODUCT COST ($6,000/machine x 49 machines)	$294,000		
	------------		------------
	$444,000		$470,000

Both and neither are right (Small difference)!

--> Compare risk to market advantage

Also, how about doing an incremental innovation, or charging for the graph feature?

© 1998 Global Brain, Inc.

Solar444 Solution

1. FOLLOWED Q*R*PD	2. VIOLATED Q*R*PD
Right team and Project Leader (2A, E, I), and team building (4G)	Lack of Project Leader experience (2A,E)
Concurrent Engineering (manufacturing involved early) (3A, B)	Benefits not cost justified for market and risks associated (1D)
Did test early (8B)	Wrong chicken test (8A,C)
Committed to a vision, and synergistic (4A, C), and knew the competition (1J)	Tried to do the mega-project (sin #1): 4 major innovations (1B), broke new ground in technology and markets (1C), and didn't innovate incrementally (1A)
"Lessons learned" review (C#11A)	Crucial factors missing from product vision (water purity!)
Kept key engineers on project to work on <u>major</u> defects (10C)	Solve <u>major</u> defects quickly once discovered (10 A,E)
DIRFT #1 (whole-hearted)	DIRFT #1 (commit knowingly)
DIRFT #2 (mission environment)	DIRFT #4 (no Beta sites)
Hoopla, fun (4O, V)	No backup plan (6F)
	Design reviews (Flow steps 6, 7)
	Know when to kill a feature (8J)
	20% slip rule
	NIH (sin #1)

3. The "Second Chance"

a.	Introduce the new product with copper first, then upgrade it to steel later (incremental innovation).
b.	Have an experienced senior manager/angel.
c.	Do beta site testing with various customers, including leading edge and target ones.

© 1998 Global Brain, Inc.

Appendix B.
QRPD: Quality *Rapid* Product Development Most Recommended Reading List

1. Kopelman, Orion and Voegtli, Cinda with Josephs, Adam, 1998. *Projects at Warp Speed with QRPD: The Definitive Guidebook to Quality Rapid Product Development.* Global Brain, Inc., Palo Alto, CA, USA, 1998. A very practical handbook of checklists and bullet-style guidelines that can be followed in a cookbook-like manner. When followed rigorously, result in significantly improved time to market and return on R&D investment!

2. Reinertsen, Donald and Smith. 1991. *Developing Products in Half the Time.* Van Nostrand Reinhold. An excellent book, very closely related predecessor to QRPD. Lays down the theory superbly.

3. Russell, Peter and Evans, Roger. 1992. *The Creative Manager: Finding Inner Vision and Wisdom in Uncertain Times.* Jossey-Bass. Excellent reading for furthering the paradigm shifts that QRPD leaders must go through. John Sculley, CEO and chairman of Apple Computer, Inc. calls this, "A sensational book on personal empowerment... and the ability to use our minds differently."

4. Kmetovicz, Ron. 1992. *New Product Development: Design and Analysis.* Wiley Press. Terrific quantification and numerical analysis of projects as an in-out "black box" function of resources (money and time) to produce products, resulting in new tools for accelerated project management. Particularly applicable to larger projects.

5. Covey, Stephen R. 1990. *The 7 Habits of Highly Effective People.* Fireside, Simon & Schuster. Best book I've ever read on managing one's personal life and career, getting along with people, and becoming an influential leader.

6. Raheja, Dev G. 1992. *Assurance Technologies.* McGraw-Hill, Inc. Fantastic updated primer on a TQM (Total Quality Management) approach that emphasizes using your head instead of only numerical and statistical process control.

7. Kidder, Tracy. 1981. *The Soul of a New Machine.* Avon Books, a division of The Hearst Corp. Enjoyable reading about how one remarkable project leader, Tom West, made it happen at Data General, a minicomputer company. Slightly outdated.

8. Geneen, Harold with Moscow, Alvin. 1984. *Managing.* Avon Books, a division of the Hearst Corp. Written by the legendary man who built ITT into a $20 billion a year company. One of my favorite books on the basics of down to earth, solid management.

© 1998 Global Brain, Inc.

9. Badiru, Adedeji. 1991. *Project Management Tools for Engineering and Management Professionals*. Industrial Engineering and Management Press. Good practical information; fairly up to date.

10. Patterson, Marvin. November 1992. *Accelerating Innovation*. Van Nostrand Reinhold. In a book endorsed by John Young, CEO of Hewlett Packard and several other major CEO's, the author explains the innovation cycle time process. Particularly interesting use of metaphors between manufacturing and new product development processes.

11. Anderson, Dr. David M. 1990. *Design for Manufacturability: Optimizing Cost, Quality, and Time-to-Market*. CIM Press, PO Box 1082, Lafayette, CA 94549-1082, (510) 283-1330. Gives practical advice for how to consider manufacturing issues early on, which results in built-in quality, lower costs, and fewer product introduction delays.

12. Watts S. Humphrey,. 1990. *Managing the Software Process*. Addison-Wesley. An excellent summary of the work done at the Carnegie Mellon Software Engineering Institute.

13. Christopher Meyer, *Fast Cycle Time: How to Align Purpose, Strategy, and Structure, for Speed*. Free Press, 1993. Teacher of the time-based competition class at Caltech.

14. McConnell, Steve, 1996. *Rapid Development,* Microsoft Press. Incredibly comprehensive treatment of the factors influencing the rapid development of software. Good reference book.

15. Crosby, Philip B. *Quality is Free: The Art of Making Quality Certain*. New York: Mentor, 1980.

16. Rushkoff, Douglas. *Cyberia: Life in the Trenches of Hyperspace*. San Francisco: Harper Collins, 1994.

17. Thompson, Charles. *What a Great Idea: Key Steps Creative People Take*. New York: Harper Collins, 1992.

18. Phillips, Donald T. *Lincoln on Leadership: Executive Strategies for Tough Times*. New York: Warner Books, Inc., 1992.

19. Love, Sidney F. *Planning and Creating Successful Engineered Designs: Managing the Design Process*. Los Angeles: Advance Professional Development, Inc., 1986.

20. Moody, Fred. *I Sing the Body Electronic: A Year With Microsoft on the Multimedia Frontier*. New York: Viking, 1995.

QRPD: Quality *Rapid* Product Development
Further Reading List

1. Adams, James L. 1974, 1986. *Conceptual Blockbusting*: A *Guide to Better Ideas*. Addison-Wesley. The classic on creativity, now in its third edition. Look for Adams' new book, too.

2. Augustine, Norman. 1989. *Managing Projects and Programs*. Harvard Business School Press. A collection of articles written by a cross-section of people from industry, the financial community, and the academic world.

3. Drucker, Peter, 1985. *Innovation and Entrepreneurship*. Harper and Row. Particularly applicable for start-ups or R&D-intensive projects.

4. Meredith, Jack R. and Mantel, Samuel J. Jr. 1989. *Project Management. A Managerial Approach*. John Wiley & Sons. A textbook that's OK for use as a reference guide.

5. Peters, Tom. 1987. *Thriving on Chaos*. Handbook for a Management Revolution. Perennial Library, Harper and Row, Publishers. A classic on management for the '90s, written by the author of the well-known *In Search of Excellence*. Be sure to use the table of contents to select chapters to read first in this 700 page monster!

6. Peters, Tom and Austin, Nancy. 1985. *A Passion for Excellence, The Leadership Difference*. Random House. Very insightful information on innovation and particularly "Skunkworks."

7. Ed. Ray, Michael and Rinzler, Alan for the World Business Academy. 1993. *The New Paradigm in Business: Emerging Strategies for Leadership and Organizational Changed*. Tarcher Perigee. An anthology of excellent articles from Stanford Business School professors and other experts.

8. DeMarco, Tom. 1982. *Controlling Software Projects*. Yourdon Press. Detailed treatment of qualitative and quantitative tools for managing software projects: schedule planning, estimating, progress tracking, etc.

9. Jones, Capers. 1994. *Assessment and Control of Software Risks.* Yourdon Press. Reference style book that provides hard data on the problems common to software development projects, their impacts, what industries suffer from them the worst, and where to go for help.

10. Kerzner, Harold, 1995. *Project Management, A Systems Approach to Planning, Scheduling, and Controlling, 5th Edition.* Van Nostrand Reinhold. Comprehensive project management reference book. Excellent exercises and case studies.

11. Maguire, Steve. 1994. *Debugging the Development Process.* Microsoft Press. Readable, practical discussion of what's wrong with software development processes and how to correct them.

12. McCarthy, Jim. 1995. *Dynamics of Software Development.* Microsoft Press. Practical treatment of the day-to-day issues encountered in software development and how to handle them.

13. Remenyi, Dan, Money, Arthur, and Twite, Alan. 1991. *Effective Measurement and Management of IT Costs and Benefits.* Butterworth-Heinnemann. Terrific coverage of how to measure the costs and benefits of Information Technology projects.

Appendix C.
Personal Development, The Global Brain, and Evolution of Consciousness
<u>Most</u> Recommended Reading List

1. Peter Russell, *The Global Brain Awakens: Our Next Evolutionary Leap*; Global Brain, Inc., 1995. Ted Turner says: A fascinating vision of how the information revolution is shifting consciousness. A much needed, optimistic perspective of humanity's future." Foundation for the paradigm used for many of this authors' ideas. Top notch, scientifically-oriented approach to consciousness.

2. Orion Kopelman, *The 2nd Ten Commandments: The Guide to Success in the Age of Consciousness*; Global Brain, Inc., 1995. A must on understanding the evolutionary laws of human nature that each person must adapt to as s/he becomes a cell in the currently forming global brain. Explains succinctly how technology brought us to this important point in evolution, in which a whole generation can choose to make an exodus that transforms humans into a new species called Motofs -- Members Of the Tribe Of the Future.

3. Peter Russell, *The White Hole in Time, Our Future Evolution and the Meaning of Now*; Harper San Francisco, 1992. A dazzling and innovative picture of humanity, that integrates evolutionary perspective and a startling vision of what the future means to the living in today's eternal present.

4. Ken Keyes, Jr., *Your Life Is A Gift, So Make the Most of It*, Love Line Books, 1987. A very short, cartoon book which serves as an excellent primer on personal growth. Written by the founder of the "Science of Happiness" who has over 4 million books in print internationally. Who says we have to suffer?

5. Stephen R. Covey, *The 7 Habits of Highly Effective People, Powerful Lessons in Personal Change;* Fireside, 1990,. Perhaps the best book to date for successfully managing one's personal life and career; while also getting along with people, and living with fairness, integrity, honesty, and human dignity.

6. Key Keyes, Jr., *Handbook to Higher Consciousness*; Love Line Books, 1975. Excellent tools and methods for understanding our individual evolution from cave person days to now. Million copy bestseller.

© 1998 Global Brain, Inc.

7. Harville Hendrix, Ph.D., *Getting the Love You Want: The Guide for Couples*; First Perennial Library, 1990. Great book on romantic relationships, and how they are meant to help us grow and develop.

8. M. Scott Peck, *The Road Less Traveled: A New Psychology of Love, Traditional Values and Spiritual Growth*; Touchstone, 1978. The classic (over 5 million sold!) on how to get on to the path of no return toward self-actualization.

9. Ken Keyes, Jr., *The Power of Unconditional Love: 21 Guidelines for Beginning, Improving, and Changing Your Most Meaningful relationships*. They can <u>all</u> work. This shows how.

10. John K. Pollard, III, *Self-Parenting: The Complete Guide to Your Inner Conversations*; Generic Human Studies Publishing, 1987. A practical guide to integrating the different parts of your personality.

11. Louise Hay, *You Can Heal Your Life*; Hay House, 1987. Find out how you can cure almost any persisting physical problem by linking it with an emotional cause!

Personal Development, The Global Brain, and Evolution of Consciousness
Further Recommended Reading List

1. John Bradshaw, *Bradshaw On: The Family: A Revolutionary Way of Self-Discovery;* Health Communications, Inc., 1988. How to understand and remedy our dysfunctional "baggage."

2. John Bradshaw, *Bradshaw On: Healing the Shame That Binds You;* Health Communications, Inc., 1988.

3. Mihaly Csikszentmihalyi, *Flow: The Psychology of Optimal Experience*; Harper Perennial, 1990. Living a balanced life, by showing what state of mind to be in to experience maximum enjoyment. Why bother living otherwise? You can read half the book and still get the point.

4. Willis Harman, Ph.D., *Global Mind Change, The New Age Revolution In The Way We Think*; Warner Books, 1988. Solid analysis of consciousness and science merging to synergize a new science.

5. Robert A. Heinlein, *Stranger in a Strange Land*, Berkley Books, 1961. Dubbed as "the most famous science fiction novel ever written." Amazingly close to an emerging reality.

6. Gerald G. Jampolsky, MD., *Love Is Letting Go of Fear*; Bantam Books, 1981. Simple, yet true. A powerfully transforming book.

7. Abraham Maslow, *Toward a Psychology of Being*; D. Van Nostrand Inc., 1962. The original on self-actualization theory and satisfying physical and psychological needs at ever higher levels.

8. Melvin Morse, MD., *Closer to the Light, Learning from the Near-Death Experiences of Children*; Ballantine Books, 1990. Amazing. Provides insight into the bigger picture of life.

9. Ayn Rand, *The Virtue of Selfishness*; Signet New American Library, 1961. Often misunderstood, nonetheless one of the originals on individual wholeness, consciousness and goals as prerequisites for synergy with societal goals.

10. Marsha Sinetar, *Do What You Love the Money Will Follow: Discovering Your Right Livelihood*; Paulist Press, 1987. Shows how to self-actualize through a spiritual yet practical approach to following your heart and making a living.

© 1998 Global Brain, Inc.

11. Adin Steinsaltz, *The Thirteen Petalled Rose*, translated by Yehuda Hanegbi; Basic Books, 1980. A discourse on the essence of mystic Jewish existence and belief. A great summary of the spiritual world and humans place in it.

12. Alvin Tofler, *Future Shock*; Bantam Books, 1970. Classic reading on the hypnotic society and the racing pace of evolution. Far ahead of its time, now appears to be a reality of the day to day..

13. Connie Zweig and Jeremiah Abrams, *Meeting the Shadow, The Hidden Power of the Dark Side of Human Nature*; Jeremy P. Tarcher, Inc., 1991. Read and understand this about your self before taking on social causes like saving the world. Save yourself first!

© 1998 Global Brain, Inc.

Appendix D. Glossary

Alpha Site
A location usually within the company but independent of the design team that performs significant, measurable, and verifiable tests on a new product.

Architect
Usually a single engineer who masterminds the overall design at the highest level. This might include choice of technologies, and implementation schemes.

Beta Site
A friendly customer willing to give a lot of input to product design and perform early testing before the product becomes available to the general market. They can be one of two types: "target" or "lead" (see definitions listed below). Their feedback provides vital information both early in the design process and once the product is functional, both in terms of bugs, and direction and enhancements.

Blitzkrieg
A time-based paradigm for "lightning-fast" product development. The financial benefit of emphasizing time-to-market is brought into all product development decisions.

CAD
Computer Aided Design. Software tools on personal computers or workstations that allow designing hardware and sometimes software. Often times includes simulation testing. May take as long to input as doing manually on initial entry, but saves tremendous amount of time for modifications, fixes, and using modules of the design for future products.

Check List
An aid for executing each step of your process or creating a particular deliverable. Checklists should be used to make sure no details are forgotten and past lessons learned are not ignored.

CE - Concurrent Engineering (or concurrent development)
A management method introduced in the 1980s which calls for engineering design to occur in parallel with activities by other functions in the company. For example, manufacturing may begin inventing test procedures and buying parts, and sales may begin to promote and market the product during some of the design phases. Previously companies had always used the serial approach where first marketing would specify the product then engineering would design it, then manufacturing would build it, and finally sales would begin to sell it. By performing many of these functions in parallel significant time reductions can be realized, and improvements in quality due to tighter communication between groups.

Customers

Lead: Customers on the cutting edge of technology and or specific use of a product. They will use it in sophisticated ways, possibly using every last feature available and even requesting more.

Typical: More representative of the typical customers who comprise the majority of purchases. Often times they use products in a simpler way and just need them to "work" in the broadest sense.

Design Reviews

A meeting held with key people required to critically assess designs at various stages of the project. These can be broken down in four types: preliminary, detailed, critical and final. For typical attendees and definitions see *Flow* section.

DR

Development release. In the guide book 3 types are discussed: preliminary, release for pilot, and final (see *Flow* chapter). All of these involve transfer from the design group to the operations department of the instructions for how to procure parts for and manufacture and/or deliver the product.

DIRFT

Do It Right the First Time. QRPD suggests five keys to follow to accomplish this. Many, many projects have a schedule that stretches double its original length. If we could do it right the first time and stick to original schedule we could deliver products to market in "half the time," thereby delivering the promise of QRPD. Right means it meets the quality as perceived by the customer.

Cost-Benefit Analysis

A financial tool to assess both individual features based on innovations, and whole products, for their return on investment potential and consequent financial viability. Cost means amount spent by the company and benefit means additional profit taken in.

DFX

Design for X. X could be quality, reliability, testability, manufacturability and others. As we have attempted to speed up product development with methodologies such as concurrent engineering, people have recognized the benefit of taking into account early in the project design issues that will affect the product's completion later in the process. For example, DFM or "design for manufacturability" dictates that hardware design engineers place components on a board during layout in such a way that will ease automated in-circuit-test in production.

FCS

First Customer Ship. The point in phase IV when the product can be shipped to a customer. FCS is often done with pilot units during step 12 of Flow, Pilot build/delivery. Note that if FCS is done with pilot units, unrestricted shipments to customers are not yet allowed. The team and executives should sign off on this very important point in the project.

Flow

The name for QRPD's product development process. It is the sequentially and ongoing part in an otherwise parallel and chaotic effort. QRPD uses four phases and 13 steps. These serve only as guidelines, and any process with decision check points is acceptable.

© 1998 Global Brain, Inc.

Funnel
A metaphorical symbol to represent the sum total of a company's product development efforts. Lots of information, ideas, and specifications for products get thrown into the top but only a limited number of products can get formed from these and come out through the bottom and narrower part of the funnel. Often-times at the entrance to the tube midway in the funnel bottlenecks develop.

Guidebook
Something every company should have for its new product development process that *each* member of any product development team owns. The Guidebook to Q*R*PD is meant to serve as a template for a company specific cookbook.

Innovative
Introducing novelty (new know-how) into practical use (technology) to increase the customer's value and satisfaction obtained from the seller's or manufacturer's resources. Differs from inventive which typically requires much greater amounts of time and risk to come up with completely new ideas, such as the light bulb. Usually has a much greater chance of having a good return on investment.

Iteration
A valuable concept in both engineering discipline for designs and for product development management. It is better to do something, evaluate, learn from it and repeat it than to hope for everything to just work out at the end.

JITPD
Just-in-Time Product Development. An analogy for product development similar to just-in-time-manufacturing. Teams start with inputs from the market, formulate product ideas, then proceed to add value to those ideas they craft them into fully-defined products. To achieve JITPD, team must improve the quality and timeliness of input materials at each step; eliminate variation and waste in the outputs of each step; and shorten the overall response time.

LCPW
Late Cost Per Week. A measure of how much profit will be lost for each week a product is delayed in getting to market, plus the extra development money that will be spent during each of those weeks. Calculated during phase I and used as a metric to help the team focus on the financial advantage of minimizing time-to-market.

Lists
Q*R*PD recommends making use of the following lists:
1) Innovations - categorized by risk level and justified benefit to cost ratio.
2) Critical Issues - other than the risks listed that may prevent project objectives from being realized. Examples would include: resource availability, including money, supplier issues such as single sources, etc.
3) Crucial Factors - those issues that have historically been important in a project's specifications. These are listed in a product vision document and can include things such as UL approval, "no louder than 90dB," etc.
4) Bug/Failures - generally a log book, which can be kept in a computerized version such as a bug tracking program, of all the failures that have occurred on a project and a record of fixing them.
5) Checklists for Q*R*PD techniques, design reviews and DR's.

MBO - Management By Objectives
A system of setting and grading objectives on a quarterly period that allows self evaluation and supervision. (See *DIRFT* chapter). Discovered in the 1960s, it has gone out of vogue and come back in again, now with part of an individual's score being dependent on the team's total performance.

MBWA - Management By Walking Around
A technique whereby managers get out of their office and walk around and chat with their employees, including asking questions that may lead to new discoveries and providing positive and constructive critical feedback on the spot.

Methodology
A System of "how to " do things which will result in a more predictable outcome. Q*R*PD is a methodology for product development to occur with a quality quickly developed product.

Milestones
Critical "do or die" dates that represent time on a project where major accomplishments can be measured to ascertain progress against the overall schedule.

Mission
A project that has a greater purpose behind it and thus creates a greater endeavor for its participants. A classic example is putting a man on the moon within a decade, as declared by John F. Kennedy in 1960.

Phase
Stages of a development project defined in the flow process which usually involves a transition from one company function to the next, such as from planning or marketing to engineering. Q*R*PD uses 4 phases but some companies use up to 7.

Pool Syndrome
A disease encountered by many projects which were not fully understood before undertaken. The pool syndrome gets it name from not looking before one leaps into a project or pool: Is there water in the pool at all? How deep is it? What are we really getting ourselves into here?

Product Engineer
An engineer who live with a product from "cradle to grave," and functions as a company liaison or doctor. Takes responsibility for any technical problems or issues related to the product other than those designed by engineering.

PL
Abbreviation for Project Leader, the individual who leads a cross-functional Q*R*PD project team.

Project Leader
The individual chartered to lead the project team's effort. Requires a very particular set of skills and experience, and is a very important selection decision made by upper management. (See chapter on *Project Leader*).

© 1998 Global Brain, Inc.

Project Manager
A title often used in matrix managed organizations where people report to both a functional group manager and a project team managed by a project manager. QRPD does not recommend the use of the term because it espouses having all the team members report to one "leader", at least for the duration of the project. Furthermore, QRPD prefers the term leader to manager: "managers do things right. Leaders do the right things".

Product Manager
Usually a person in marketing assigned to a product or product line responsible for its pricing, promotion, sales literature, forecasting, and future planning.

Product Champion
Usually an executive or other type of top manager with clout and authority, who supports a particular project and will help to push it through the company.

Revision Level
Documentation numbering scheme for parts of a project to denote how complete their design is (see the *Flow* chapter).

Risk
Something always present in every project. QRPD recommends intelligently managing it by careful assessment and taking-on of technical and marketing risk. (See *Flow* section)

ROI
Return on Investment: A measure of the financial benefit a company will receive from the money it spends on product development: a ration of the profit to be realized compared to the development expenditure. Calculated for different alternatives during phase I of QRPD to ensure that a project will truly result in a financial benefit to the company, and to help choose the best alternative.

QRPD
Quality *Rapid* Product Development. A management methodology for product development projects that always delivers quality first but emphasizes doing it in a timely manner. First formalized in the early 1990s it synthesizes a set of best practices discovered through many theories, studies and practice in the 1980s, that deliver products in up to half the time.

Shotgunning
Attempting to fix a problem with an educated guess, having not seen the actual problem when it occurs. Somewhat like killing a fly with a shotgun, which while it may accomplish its purpose may also have harmful and detrimental side-effects on the environment—"other parts of the design."

Stab in the Dark
Similar to Shotgunning, it involves making a minor fix based on an educational guess, but again having not seen the problem or bug actually as it occurs.

SSSS - See Saw Specifications and Schedules
The QRPD trade-off process by which objectives are optimally found for performance time and cost of the project and product. (See *Flow* chapter).

© 1998 Global Brain, Inc.

Synergy
Synchronous energy. Commonly defined as the whole is greater that the sum of its parts, or one plus one equals three or more. In Q*R*PD the goal is to achieve a team with high synergy amongst the members to achieve almost miraculous results.

Technique
A management practice. Those listed in Q*R*PD (150) when followed greatly increase the odds of a successful *"Blitzkrieg"* project, and when violated can often result in egg on our face. Q*R*PD at a minimum asks that if you plan to violate a technique that you do so consciously, by deciding ahead of time that you have no other choice in this situation.

TQM - Total Quality Management
A management methodology popular in the late 1980s whereby it is recognized that every employee in the company must participate in creating quality in the company, including the management.

TTM - Time To Market
A measure of the amount of time it takes a company to get the product to market. Used as a benchmark to grade the performance of various project teams, and a company's effectiveness.

TTV - Time To Volume
Similar to TTM but emphasizes the importance of the last part of the project, namely ramping up completely to volume production capabilities. Particularly on high volume products this serves as a better measure of a project team's performance than TTM which may consider the project complete when one or several units have shipped.

Tools
Something that helps us be more efficient in designing and production processes. Often these include computer based equipment such a simulation, etc.

Vision
A document, usually one or two pages long, that aligns the whole project team towards a common set of goals. The process followed to arrive at the vision looms critical to really getting everybody to buy-in to not only the feasibility but also the probability of accomplishing the mission. (See *Flow* chapter).

© 1998 Global Brain, Inc.

GLOBAL BRAIN®, INC.
ORDER FORM

Ordering information: Call 1-800-U$_8$-G$_4$O$_6$-G$_4$L$_5$O$_6$B$_2$AL

Other ways to order:	**CALL** Global Brain at 1-650-327-2012	**FAX** form below to: 1-650-327-2028	**MAIL** form below to: Global Brain Inc. 555 Bryant St. #369 Palo Alto, CA 94301-1704 USA

Please send us the following (indicate quantities and total prices):

Product Selection	Price	Quantity	Total
Q*R*PD Products:			
*Projects at Warp-Speed with Q*R*PD:* The Definitive Guidebook to Quality *Rapid* Product Development	$69.95		
The 1-hour *QRPD* video	$49.00		
The 5-hour *QRPD* video	$395.00		
Subtotal			
Shipping and Handling @ $5.00 (per item)			
Total authorized by P.O. #_____			
Total		**Total**	

Check Method of Payment

[ ] Money Order
[ ] Visa
[ ] Amex
[ ] Master Card
[ ] Purchase Order (P.O.)
[ ] Check*

*Make Check payable to
Global Brain, Inc.

Card Number:

Expiration Date:

Name on Card:

Ship To:_____
Attention:_____
Address:_____
City:_____
State:_____ Zip:_____ Country:_____
Telephone:_____
Fax:_____
Authorized Signature:_____
Purchase Order #:_____
Date:_____

Global Brain Inc. 555 Bryant Street #369, Palo Alto, CA
94301-1704 USA 1-800-U-GO-GLOBAL